THE GOOD WAR

THE
GOOD WAR

Why We Couldn't Win the War
or the Peace in Afghanistan

Jack Fairweather

BASIC BOOKS

A MEMBER OF THE PERSEUS BOOKS GROUP

New York

UK MOD review of this work has been undertaken for security purposes only and
should not be construed as an endorsement.

Designed by Pauline Brown

Library of Congress Cataloging-in-Publication Data
Fairweather, Jack.
  The good war : why we couldn't win the war or the peace in Afghanistan / Jack
Fairweather.
    pages cm
  Includes bibliographical references and index.
  ISBN 978-0-465-04495-5 (hardcover)—ISBN 978-0-465-04091-9 (e-book) 1.
Afghan War, 2001– 2. Afghan War, 2001—United States. I. Title.
  DS371.412.F35 2014
  958.104'7—dc23
                                    2014021456

10 9 8 7 6 5 4 3 2 1

For my girls,
Chrissy, Amelie, and Marianna

"UNLIKE OTHER WARS, AFGHAN WARS
BECOME SERIOUS ONLY WHEN THEY
ARE OVER."

—Olaf Caroe

CONTENTS

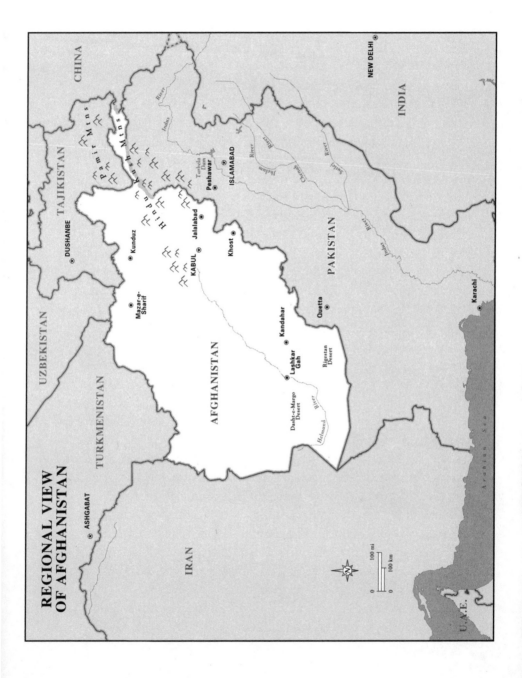

REGIONAL VIEW
OF AFGHANISTAN

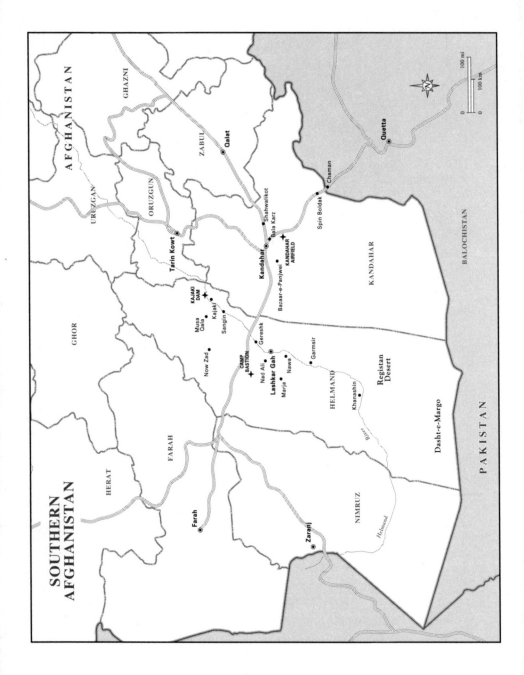

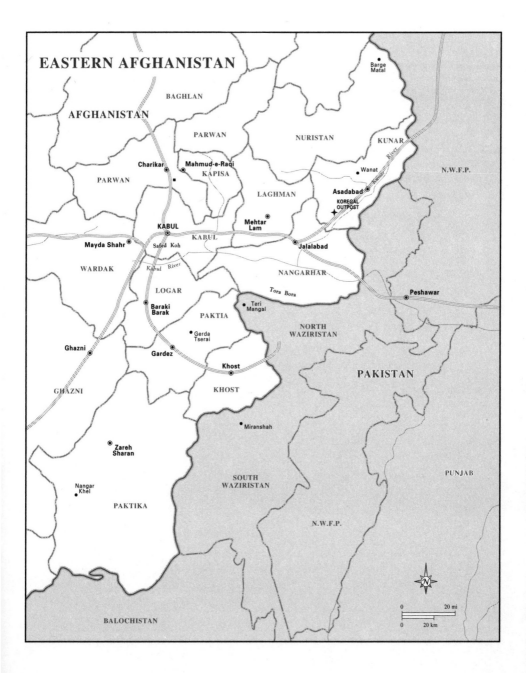

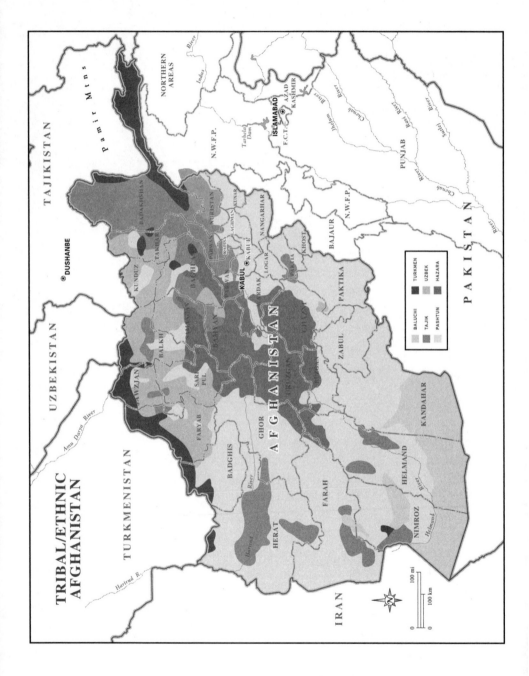

TRIBAL/ETHNIC
AFGHANISTAN

NOTE ON TEXT

Quotations attributed to individuals are from their own recollections, except where endnotes indicate another source. Subsequent quotations from the same individual without notes indicate that the same source is being used.

I have sought to protect the identities of special forces personnel and intelligence officials except when their names are already in the public domain or they are no longer serving.

For Pashtu and Dari names and places I have sought to use the most common transliterations.

The Mask of Anarchy

Hamid Karzai often walked around the circle of his small garden in the palace grounds. Most evenings he could be found, head down, his hands clasped behind his back, striding in measured paces. He liked to keep fit, to ease the tension of a hundred meetings, to dwell on the past. This evening in early 2014 was no different.

The palace itself was a sweeping complex of hulking stone structures, round houses, and even a quaint Victorian mansion set in eighty acres of grounds guarded by high walls and barbed wire. Karzai had opted for a humbler concrete building, constructed by one of Afghanistan's former princes in the 1960s, that contained its own courtyard. His guards usually stood to one side under the foliage of a cypress tree, trying not to intrude on these private moments as Karzai paced the worn earth. In the final years of his presidency his walks had gotten longer than usual as he worked through a particular source of angst.

As he paced, he could see an American surveillance blimp overhead, one of the helium-filled balloons with an array of cameras that had proliferated across the city, and which provided the US contractors operating them with the remarkable ability to peer into nooks and crannies. Some Afghans ascribed near-magical powers to the balloons. One rumor in the south was that the Americans had trained mice to run up the cable connecting the balloon to the surveillance station, make notes on what they saw, then run back down to tell their US overlords.[1] Others feared the blimps were emitting harmful rays that filled their heads with western fantasies while they slept, and that women were particularly susceptible.

Karzai knew the balloons were in the sky in part to protect him, and there was a time when he would have been reassured by their presence. It was he who had brought the Americans to the country, knowing that they alone possessed the wealth and power to rebuild Afghanistan. He had always seen himself as the father of the nation, a bold reformer who could transform his shattered country. Indeed, Karzai's most frequent complaint throughout the thirteen-year war was that the West wasn't doing enough to fulfill their shared vision.

The war, Karzai had freely professed to the world in the early days, was a righteous struggle against the forces of chaos and disintegration. The same evil that had perpetrated the attacks in New York and Washington was responsible for tearing apart his own country in the preceding years. He wanted more troops, more aid experts and development consultants, and more defense contractors and NGO workers. Poor and benighted countries like his, he had publicly argued, needed this paraphernalia of nation-building to join the modern world. Karzai's call to drag Afghanistan into the light, establish a democracy, and uphold the rule of law had captured the mood in Washington after 9/11.

Yet when the money had flowed and the soldiers surged, they had not quelled the deadly violence gripping the country. American forces battled a resurgent Taliban, and the Afghan civilians Karzai believed he was helping were caught in the crossfire. Over the course of 2007 there were at least 1,633 casualties, a threefold increase on the year before.[2] By 2013 two hundred Afghan civilians were dying each month in the fighting, and thousands more had fled their homes or had their livelihoods destroyed.[3] The refugee camps outside the Afghan capital of Kabul were overflowing.[4]

At first Karzai had been sure he was somehow to blame for not doing enough to temper American firepower or steer the reconstruction process.[5] In the long, grinding middle stretch of the war he fell into what appeared to be a fog of depression. US diplomats who worked alongside him noticed a change in his countenance, mood swings, and erratic behavior. Rumors spread in the western press that he was addicted to heroin or was on serious medication. According to those who knew him, he became susceptible to real and imagined maladies and increasingly locked himself away in the palace.[6] He appeared to be waging an inner battle to prove to himself and his countrymen that he wasn't to blame for the past thirteen years of bloodshed and mayhem.[7]

Only in the long perambulations at the end of his presidency did Karzai recognize what he saw as an incontrovertible truth: The blame for the mounting pile of war dead lay with the outsiders. Karzai hadn't wrecked the country; rather, the westerners had betrayed the ideals of the Good War to which they had subscribed together. The West had never seen him as a genuine partner, he now understood. How else to explain their high-handed treatment of him? When he demanded that the US stop its aerial bombing, he was defied. When he asked to be informed of all American military operations, generals sometimes briefed him, but frequently he was ignored. Washington continued to side with Pakistan—even though that country appeared to support the insurgency—and President Barack Obama presumed to conduct negotiations with the Taliban without involving Karzai. The Afghan president came to believe that he was no more than a tool to service the real aims of the West: permanent instability in his country, so that Afghanistan's natural resources could be plundered.[8]

The thought of being a puppet of the US and its British allies seemed to gnaw at him.[9] At times, he wished he could smile and dismiss their obsequious blue-eyed ambassadors and generals with their proud talk of the war dead.[10] In darker moments, he told advisers, he dwelled upon his predecessors' success at driving out invaders at the tips of their soldiers' spears. A favorite poem of his was Shelley's "Mask of Anarchy," a cry for freedom against the bonds of tyrannous overlords, which he cited to one visiting journalist.[11]

But if this narrative frustrated him it also leant him a new sense of purpose. He told his confidants that he should have stood up to the West sooner.[12] He began to see himself not as the leader who had allowed the foreigners in, but as the man who had extracted from them what he could and was now pushing them out. At the end of his presidency, Karzai was a man reborn. He seemed to bound into meetings with visiting dignitaries, tribal chiefs, even American diplomats. They might accuse his government of corruption or his family of controlling the opium trade and stealing almost a billion dollars from Kabul's national bank, but he told colleagues he no longer cared.[13]

Instead, at every opportunity he took delight in denouncing the West's betrayal of Afghanistan. The Americans hadn't come to fight al-Qa'eda, he would intone. They had sought to wage war against the country and its people. "The West wanted to use Afghanistan," Karzai told the *New York Times* in November 2013, "to have bases here, to create a situation whereby in the end Afghanistan would be so weak that it would agree to a deal in which Afghanistan's interests will not even be secondary, but tertiary and worse."[14]

Now that he could see—and speak—clearly, Karzai appeared intent on redeeming himself in the eyes of his people by ridding Afghanistan of these foreign powers. He had refused to sign an agreement with the US military that would let them stay beyond 2014. It would be one of the final acts of his presidency. Yet even this gesture of independence had a hollow ring.

The Americans were already scaling back their presence and dismantling their vast war machine. The flow of money was ebbing, and the troops were going home. Beyond the palace walls, Kabul was emptying of westerners; their mansions, once the scenes of lavish parties, were shuttered and quiet. Outside the city, soldiers were packing up their patrol bases for the last time. Karzai would not get to oust the Americans and their allies; they were doing that themselves.

T he West has reached its own conclusions about the nature of its intervention in Afghanistan. By 2014 the war was already one of the most costly in American history.[15] While there had been significant improvements in Afghans' lives, including greater access to basic health care and a sevenfold increase in the number of children attending school, the costs in blood, money, and political capital far outpaced these gains: $100 billion had been spent on American aid. Yet only an estimated 15 percent of this money had reached its intended recipients.[16] The rest was siphoned off by western agencies, warlords, local contractors, petty criminals, and at times even the Taliban. Thousands of projects from power plants to turbines to refrigerated food depots had been abandoned, left half finished, or destroyed as western forces withdrew.

The Afghan people had suffered greatly: 32,000 had perished in suicide bombings, missile strikes, mortar attacks, and shootings with more dying each week. The United Nations estimated that the fighting had forced at least 600,000 from their homes, many to end up in refugee camps and shanty-towns outside Kabul and other major cities.[17] In southern Afghanistan, a third of all children were acutely malnourished, with famine-like conditions affecting much of the area.[18] Hanging over the country was the prospect that the Taliban would return and reignite the country's civil war. Then there were the western casualties: 3,400—mostly soldiers—had died in Afghanistan by the beginning of 2014.[19]

The Good War had gone badly. The question was what, if anything, could be salvaged of the shattered ideal that western military intervention had promised to deliver to Afghanistan and other dark corners of the world. When US soldiers had arrived in October 2001, their mission in President George W. Bush's War on Terrorism was simple: Punish those responsible for the worst attack on American shores since Pearl Harbor and ensure that they couldn't harm the nation again. The enemy, in their eyes, was clearly defined: al-Qa'eda and the Taliban government, which had refused to hand over Osama bin Laden and dismantle the shadowy terrorist group's training camps in southern Afghanistan. As Bush famously divided the world in his speech to Congress on September 20, 2001, justifying the war: "Either you are with us, or you are with the terrorists."

The US quickly routed al-Qaʾeda and threw the Taliban from power in December 2001. With the war seemingly over, US special forces mopped up the remnants of al-Qaʾeda and the Taliban in the mountains. Washington then turned its attention to Iraq. The United Nations was left to assemble an interim government in Kabul and lead a cohort of aid agencies that wanted to spend billions on rebuilding the country. Many in the international community saw the Taliban not just as a security threat but as an affront to those closely held ideals of human rights, democracy, and the free market. Images of Afghan women clad in full-body veils became symbols of the past that the aid world was sure the country was leaving behind. Afghanistan's status as one of the poorest nations on earth was frequently cited as further evidence of the need to act. The Good War, in the soaring rhetoric of this idealism, was more than a necessary act of retaliation; it was a test case for humanitarian intervention, and aid workers' ability to transform the lives of oppressed people in the developing world.

These aims were little more than rhetoric at first, but they contained the seeds of almost certain failure. To begin with, the Americans—from their political leaders down to their soldiers—had dangerously conflated al-Qaʾeda and the Taliban. The two groups had similarities, of course, but they differed in vital ways. Al-Qaʾeda was primarily made up of Arab nationals who believed in global jihad to advance their fundamentalist interpretation of Islam. By contrast, the Taliban's ambitions were strictly limited to controlling their communities. They drew their values from the conservative mores of the Pashtun tribes of southern Afghanistan, and thus they could not be defeated by force of arms alone. A long and subtle process of education would be needed to change the mind-sets of those who supported them.

In addition, America and its allies, who until that point had played a limited role in the international reconstruction effort, came to believe that to eliminate the terrorist threat and alleviate Afghans' suffering, the West needed to play a more activist role in creating a strong, democratic state. At the same time this nation-building agenda needed to be backed by more forces to combat the returning Taliban. This approach at once sidelined Afghanistan's post-Taliban political leaders and threatened to overwhelm their fragile government with aid projects the country could not support or realize.

The warriors and liberals responsible for managing the war and its aftermath were critically out of touch with the political reality of the country they were attempting to pacify and the nature of the people they were attempting to help. Only as the conflict smoldered and slowly began to reignite did it become clear to the Americans and their chief allies, the British, that they had misconceived of their intervention in this complex and unforgiving country.

The result of America's failures in Afghanistan, following the debacle in Iraq, has been to fundamentally shift how Washington and allied nations view their relationship to the developing world, thus completing a cycle that began with defeat in Vietnam in the 1970s. The lesson from that bloody war in Southeast Asia—to steer clear of military action overseas—was largely observed. During the first Gulf War, the US was prepared to drive Iraqi forces out of Kuwait but not to seek Saddam Hussein's removal. Washington also avoided intervention in the Balkans and Rwanda until public outcry over the slaughter in those countries prompted a rethink.

Yet after the Kosovo conflict in 1999 and particularly after 9/11, politicians and the military showed a growing readiness to intervene in the name of values rather than national interest, an urge that became overwhelming when the two strands ran together. Both the Left and the Right united in the first decade of the twenty-first century to rid the world of bin Laden's aberrant strain of Islam and save Afghanistan from its own fundamentalist adversaries.

This is the story of how the world's most powerful leaders plotted to build a new kind of nation in Afghanistan that was pure fantasy. It is the story of how those leaders pinned their hopes on a marginal tribal leader and failed to heed his prescient advice, and how he in turn outplayed them. It is the story of why the long-suffering Afghan people rejected salvation from a global army of would-be rescuers. And finally it is the story of how the promise of a new military doctrine was ended by the Good War in Afghanistan and what it means for the future of western military action in the developing world.

PART I

THE
MISSING
PEACE
2001–2003

CHAPTER I

The Wrong Kind of War

The gaping hole in the Pentagon was still smoldering when Air Force One landed in Washington, DC, late on the afternoon of September 11, 2001. Businesses throughout the capital were shuttered and the streets were deserted. The few people who ventured outside had a hurried, feral look.

Hours earlier, two airplanes had crashed into the Twin Towers in New York and a third had slammed into the Department of Defense headquarters, just across the Potomac River from the National Mall. A fourth had plowed into a field near Shanksville, Pennsylvania, killing everyone aboard but sparing its target, which was presumed to be either the White House or the US Capitol. By the time President George W. Bush returned to the capital from an appearance in Sarasota, Florida, the immediate threat of another attack seemed to have passed, but fear and shock lingered throughout the country.

For an hour, after landing, Bush locked himself away in a small study with his chief speechwriter, Michael Gerson, to prepare for a televised address that evening. Bush knew that what he said before the cameras would define his presidency.

As soon as Bush had heard about the second plane that morning in a Sarasota kindergarten classroom, he had reached a conclusion that was to have profound consequences: He must declare war to unite a grieving nation and to give the administration the broadest possible mandate to respond to this act of terrorism.[1]

Speaking from the Oval Office that evening, Bush explained to his fellow Americans that the country was now at war against both "terrorists who committed these acts and those who harbor them." The pronouncement would lead quickly and inexorably to the war in Afghanistan. And the result of Bush's finding, though seemingly reasonable to many on the evening of September

11, would be a far more sweeping and bloody war than he and his supporters expected.

At the time, critics noted that no one in Bush's inner circle had vetted this crucial speech except National Security Advisor Condoleezza Rice. As Matthew Waxman, Rice's special assistant, later reflected, "What was incredible was how momentous a decision this is, to say we're in a state of war with al-Qa'eda, because it set us on a course not only for your international response, but also in our domestic constitutional relations. You'd expect that the cabinet would have met, and that different options would have been developed, and they would have debated the pros and cons, and that allies would have been consulted."[2] An alternative approach would have been to regard the attack as a crime, just like Omar Abdel-Rahman's bombing of the World Trade Center in 1993 or Timothy McVeigh's bombing of the Oklahoma City federal building in 1995.

Bush didn't hold with such legalistic thinking, which he considered to be part of the problem with his predecessor's long-winded approach to the terrorist threat.[3] As president, Bill Clinton hadn't gone all out to kill Osama bin Laden; instead his administration had spent years trying to get the Taliban regime in Afghanistan to hand over bin Laden. America had been sending the wrong message, Bush felt, and it was time for drastic action. He was not alone in this opinion. After his television address, Bush met with his principal advisers in the oak-paneled situation room beneath the White House's West Wing, where they expressed broad agreement with his views.[4] Far less clear was how to prosecute a war against a shadowy terrorist organization like al-Qa'eda.

Bush naturally turned to US Secretary of Defense Donald Rumsfeld, who had prepared a shotgun list of questions that he rattled off with his usual crispness: Who are the targets? How much evidence do we need before going after al-Qa'eda? How soon do we act? Rumsfeld then explained that the US military would not be ready for at least sixty days. After a moment of awkward silence, Rumsfeld promised to pressure the military, and the meeting broke.[5]

In fact, the time it would take to deploy the military was hardly a surprise to those in the room, least of all Rumsfeld's counterpart in foreign affairs, Secretary of State Colin Powell. As former chairman of the Joint Chiefs of Staff, the nation's top military job, Powell had spent much of his time ensuring that America could not rush into war. Like most officers of his generation, Powell had witnessed defeat in Vietnam and had concluded that the US military should avoid being drawn into another quagmire at all costs.

In the 1980s, Caspar Weinberger, a US defense secretary to whom Powell served as a special assistant, introduced conditions that must be met before sending troops to war: Vital national interests had to be identified, clear political and military objectives formulated, and force used only after all diplomatic options had been exhausted. Weinberger's preconditions removed the decision to go to war from the whims of politicians and placed the determination back in the hands of the military. His goal was to protect the military from another fiasco like Vietnam and to ensure that America entered only those fights it couldn't avoid. In the context of the Cold War, the one conflict that could meet these conditions was a doomsday battle against the Soviet Union in Europe, the prospect of which, though terrifying, was receding.

The Weinberger Doctrine rapidly dominated how the military viewed its role by placing an emphasis on large mechanized forces and firepower. When Powell became chairman of the Joint Chiefs of Staff in 1989, he added further stipulations: US forces would fight only when they could be assured of having overwhelming force. Furthermore, before even launching an attack, the military must also plan its exit from the conflict.

The trouble with Weinberger and Powell's approach was that while shielding the military from politicians' whims, it also made the military impervious to the changing world around it. As the military confronted the breakup of the Soviet Union, its instinct was to do nothing, to the exasperation of even Madeleine Albright, Clinton's former secretary of state, who complained to Powell in 1993: "What's the point of having this superb military that you're always talking about if we can't use it?"[6]

In 2001, Rumsfeld had taken the top job at the Pentagon for the second time in his career, vowing to rid the US military of its inertia. He wasn't a neoconservative like some in the Bush administration but he shared with them a belief that America needed to project power to ensure its preeminent status. During his first stint as defense secretary—in Gerald Ford's administration of the mid-1970s—he had developed a distrust of the generals, whom he regarded as obsessed with building their own empires within each branch. To change the military, Rumsfeld knew he would have to shake up some of these fiefdoms—and sure enough, the generals opposed his efforts.

Like Robert McNamara, another defense secretary who had promised to radically change the military, upon his second appointment Rumsfeld surrounded himself with a cadre of civilians. McNamara had his "Whiz Kids"; disgruntled military brass dubbed Rumsfeld's advisers—most of them as old as the sixty-nine-year-old defense secretary—the "Wheeze Kids."[7]

One of these advisers was seventy-three-year-old Andrew Marshall, head of the Pentagon's obscure Office of Net Assessment. In the 1990s, Marshall had pondered how advances in smart missiles, spy satellites, and drones could be used to develop new and deadly weapons systems better suited to the post–Cold War world. The result would be a streamlined military, capable of deploying rapidly and with devastating force. The generals hated Marshall's ideas, which he had dubbed the "Revolution in Military Affairs." The top brass correctly saw them as a threat to the status quo, which threatened to make the generals' formations of tanks and planes obsolete. They went public with their discontent in the summer of 2001, and Rumsfeld backed down.

Rumsfeld had been thwarted but he didn't drop his reform agenda, the need for which was underscored by the two options the military developed to attack al-Qa'eda and its allies. One was for a cruise missile strike at al-Qa'eda training camps in Afghanistan, a suggestion Rumsfeld dubbed the "Clinton option" in mockery of the previous administration's attempts to destroy the organization in 1998; a US cruise missile strike that year had blown up a few deserted training camps in the country, missing the terrorist leader.[8] The other option was to mount a major assault that would take months to organize, and seemed to evoke the Soviet Union's ill-fated invasion of Afghanistan in the 1980s that resulted in its defeat at the hands of Afghan rebels.

Rumsfeld told his staff to go back to the drawing board. There had to be a better plan for Afghanistan. And to Rumsfeld's intense frustration, it belonged not to him but to the Central Intelligence Agency.

On September 13, 2001, CIA Director George Tenet and Cofer Black, the CIA's coordinator for counterterrorism, briefed President Bush on their plan to attack al-Qa'eda—both in Afghanistan and anywhere else its members might be lurking.

The CIA had been badly shaken by the attacks, not least because the agency had missed the opportunity to prevent them. Since becoming director of the agency in 1996 under Clinton, Tenet had been warning of the dangers al-Qa'eda posed. A former staff director on the Senate Select Committee on Intelligence, Tenet had spent much of his career putting a polish on the grimy world of espionage for his political masters. He was a natural people pleaser—warm, blunt, and deferential. But those qualities had not always served him or his country well in fighting terrorism.

In 1999 Tenet had presented Clinton with an opportunity to kill bin Laden—what turned out to be the best chance to eliminate the al-Qa'eda leader before he started plotting the 9/11 attacks. Afghan informants had spotted the terrorist leader at a hunting camp in the barren hills of Helmand, a large province in southern Afghanistan. Mike Scheuer, the CIA station chief tracking bin Laden, urged his superiors to launch a missile strike. The Saudi had been in America's sights since the early 1990s, when he'd first started preaching global jihad; in

1997 Clinton had issued an executive order authorizing the CIA to capture bin Laden and use lethal force if necessary. Now the administration had its chance to eliminate the terrorist leader with an air strike that would avoid the complexities of trying to capture him.

In the White House situation room, Clinton, Tenet, and the president's counterterrorism adviser, Richard Clarke, stalled. Satellite imagery and cell phone intercepts confirmed the presence of bin Laden's entourage at the Helmand camp but, in an era before drones, there was no way of knowing for certain that the al-Qa'eda leader was there. The reasons against attacking were also considerable. The 1998 strike had been an embarassing failure after what were thought to be al-Qa'eda facilities in Sudan and Afghanistan turned out to be a pharmaceutical factory with no links to the terrorist group; the training camp in Afghanistan had been largely deserted following a possible tip-off from Pakistan. The fear of another high-profile mistake was exacerbated by the fact that bin Laden's hunting companions turned out to be wealthy princes from the United Arab Emirates, the Gulf state with which Clarke had negotiated an $8 billion arms contract the year before. The moment passed.[9]

Clarke later blamed the CIA for failing to eliminate bin Laden before 9/11. From Clarke's point of view, the president's executive order gave the CIA clear authorization to take action against bin Laden. And Clarke felt there was much more the agency could have done to take him down.[10]

There was some truth to Clarke's accusation. The CIA had become excessively hidebound, more interested in covering its own ass than in killing terrorists, according to Scheuer and other agents.[11] However, the CIA's meekness also stemmed from the Clinton administration's outright skepticism toward the spy agency. The White House acted as if the end of the Cold War had made the CIA obsolete. Its budget had been slashed, its stations closed, its agents and their prized assets quietly mothballed. At one point in 1994, Congress had even debated whether the agency should be disbanded. In this climate of suspicion, many in the CIA felt Clinton's directive for bin Laden to be deliberately soft: The president had backed away from ordering them to simply assassinate bin Laden, and had instead given the agency the nearly impossible task of capturing him. "If Clinton wanted them to kill him, then he should have just said so," said Scheuer.[12]

After the missed opportunity in Helmand in 1999, and with growing awareness of the danger al-Qa'eda posed, the CIA tried a more aggressive approach. As one part of this new strategy, Tenet brought in Cofer Black—a former CIA station chief in Sudan with firsthand experience tracking al-Qa'eda—to run the National Counterterrorism Center. For years the organization had been a bureaucratic backwater, rife with infighting and petty squabbles with the FBI, with which it shared the job of tracking al-Qa'eda operatives. Black tried to change the center's office culture. In his late forties, Black looked like an overeager scoutmaster, with flabby jowls, an owlish squint, and an aggressive buzz cut that suggested a military career (though he'd never been more than a volunteer in the air force reserves). He liked to exhort his staff with rallying cries like "Be tough! This is no time to go introspective!"[13]

His results were mixed, but he did develop an outlandish new plan to eliminate bin Laden that involved supporting the Northern Alliance, a loose confederation of Afghan warlords and tribes. Assembled by the national leadership that had been unseated in 1996 by the Taliban, the Northern Alliance had since been fighting a rearguard action against the Islamist movement, which now controlled the Afghan capital of Kabul and vast swathes of the country, including the mountainous region where al-Qa'eda had its training camps. If Taliban control over Afghanistan were loosened, Black thought, the CIA might be able to get close enough to al-Qa'eda to strike at it with something other than long-range missiles.

This new approach amounted to taking sides in Afghanistan's long-running civil war, and the Clinton administration had balked at such a radical shift in policy toward the country. The Alliance's warlords were a less than savory bunch, the State Department pointed out, with several accused of human rights abuses and drug trafficking. There was no way the US could overtly support such men. The incoming Bush team had fewer qualms about Black's plan. Deputy Secretary of State Richard Armitage approved the scheme and its $125 million budget on September 4, 2001—too late to stop 9/11, but just in time to provide a blueprint for a limited war in Afghanistan.

Tenet now presented this plan to Bush, starting with a list of fearful provisos. The CIA estimated that the Northern Alliance had 20,000 irregular fighters to the Taliban's 45,000. The Alliance was poorly equipped and lacked supplies, electricity, and running water. Just getting to their territory in the high mountain valleys of northern Afghanistan in winter could be a challenge. There was no airport, and any helicopters used for delivering troops and supplies would have to negotiate 24,000-foot snowbound passes as they crossed the Hindu Kush. Once there, any Americans would be at the mercy of the Alliance, a fractious, backstabbing bunch. Al-Qa'eda had assassinated the one figure of national standing, defense minister–turned–Alliance leader Ahmad Shah Massoud, the day before 9/11.

If there was a bright side, Tenet said, it was that the Taliban was just as unruly. Some of the Pashtun tribes upon whom the Taliban relied for support could be bought, although a core of bearded zealots remained around the movement's spiritual leader, Mullah Omar. The Taliban might be persuaded to part ways with al-Qa'eda if the regime's survival depended upon it, but Tenet feared that the harsh brand of Islam that had brought together Mullah Omar and bin Laden would not be broken. The CIA paramilitary teams who would exploit the rollback of the Taliban under Black's scheme had to expect they would be fighting all the way to bin Laden's lair, in the middle of a brutal winter, with unreliable Afghan allies and an entrenched foe.

Bush looked suitably daunted as he listened to Tenet's presentation that September morning. Black took that as his cue for a little bombast. He leaped from his chair as he started to talk about the coming battle, throwing down markers on the floor to represent the two sides.

"Mr. President," he said, "we can do this. No doubt in my mind. . . . But you've got to understand, people are going to die. And the worst part about it, Mr. President, Americans are going to die—my colleagues and my friends."

"That's war," Bush said.[14]

Black concluded his presentation with a ghoulish claim: "You give us the mission—we can get 'em. When we're through with them, they will have flies walking across their eyeballs," he said. He promised to bring victory within weeks.

Bush lapped it up. Black became a regular at the president's morning intelligence briefings. In the White House Black became known, with a certain awe, as "the flies-on-the-eyeballs guy."[15]

Under normal circumstances Black would not have shaped US policy single-handedly, but the turmoil within government agencies presented powerful opportunities for those with strong convictions. The ambiguous nature of 9/11—more than a crime but not a conventional act of war—had created a gray area where the CIA's leadership should have trodden carefully given its history of overreaching at the whim of earlier presidents. Instead the organization embraced its role at the heart of what a week later Bush would call the "War on Terror."

Black would play a key role in shaping the objectives of this broader war and in distorting the administration's thinking about Afghanistan for years to come. While he was drawing up plans for Afghanistan, Black also envisioned the CIA conducting global covert operations against terrorist organizations. He wanted a free hand to create paramilitary teams to assassinate suspects and detain and interrogate others—whatever it took to stop the next attack. What Black was describing were counterterrorism operations that were ultimately limited in their scope (albeit employing unprecedented levels of violence). Yet in Afghanistan, Black's covert means against a terrorist group were being employed for a very overt objective: a war to overthrow a government and install a new one, carrying with it grave and ill-discerned implications.

CHAPTER 2

Bloody Hell

On September 15, 2001, four days after al-Qa'eda attacked America, Bush brought together his advisers at Camp David, the president's country retreat in rural Maryland. Much of the morning's discussion was dominated not by talk of Afghanistan but by the subject of Iraq. There was no clear link between Iraqi president Saddam Hussein's regime and al-Qa'eda, but some top officials saw the opportunity to target a country that had routinely provoked America since the first Gulf War in the early 1990s. The Pentagon's number two, the deputy secretary of defense, Paul Wolfowitz, went as far as suggesting that the US skip a potentially difficult campaign in central Asia in favor of toppling Hussein.

Bush eventually grew irritated with the digression and asked the group to stay focused on Afghanistan. "What are the worst cases out there? What are the real downside risks?" he asked them at one point.[1]

National Security Advisor Condoleezza Rice had already looked at a map of Afghanistan spread out on a conference table and recoiled. The country evoked every negative association in Rice: distant, remote, treacherous. She wondered aloud whether America would make the mistake of being drawn into such a nest of vipers.

Rice was right to be cautious about Afghanistan. There was the country's most recent, bloody history. Two decades of war—starting in 1979 with the Soviet occupation and ending with the desperate civil war of the 1990s—had turned the country into one of the poorest on earth. Afghanistan was defined by its mountains, which covered four-fifths of its land, and fractured the country along ethnic and tribal lines. The Pashtuns in the south were the largest ethnic group, representing a little over half the country's 30 million inhabitants. Afghanistan's rulers had traditionally come from its highly conservative tribes as did the Taliban. The country's second-largest group was the Tajiks in the north and west, whose members spoke Dari, a version of Persian, and opposed Pashtun hegemony. They formed the bedrock of the Northern Alliance's support. On one level, the recent civil war was a sectarian conflict between the two groups, with the country's Uzbek and Hazara minorities siding with the Alliance against the Pashtun majority. There were plenty of other reasons to fight besides ethnicity, however; each group had a brittle sense of tribal honor, which often led to clashes within each clan and family. As a young Winston Churchill observed while stationed in one Pashtun valley in 1897, "a continual state of feud and strife prevails through the land. . . . Every man's hand is against the other, and all against the stranger."[2]

The complexities of Afghanistan's tribal culture had thwarted powerful foreign invaders throughout history. The British arrived in Afghanistan in 1839 near the height of their empire. Members of the jodhpur-wearing ruling class were unhinged by the thought of Russia, which was expanding rapidly across central Asia, seizing Afghanistan and thereby threatening British holdings in India and present-day Pakistan. A few on the British side voiced their concerns about the venture. For example, veteran diplomat William Elphinstone warned that victory over the Afghans might be swift, but the idea of imposing a puppet ruler and garrisoning such a poor and remote country would be "hopeless."[3]

But the British had talked themselves into the necessity of occupying Kabul, and were soon pleasantly surprised by the salubrious setting they found. American adventurer Josiah Harlan, who arrived in Afghanistan in 1827, the country's first visitor from the US, later recalled that, "Kabul, the city of a thousand gardens, in those days was a paradise." In the heat of the summer, the evenings were often cooled by air blowing off the Hindu Kush mountains. The winters were frigid but the snows melted rapidly in the spring, as daisies, forget-me-nots, and purple gromwell blossomed on the hillsides, and beds of roses, hyacinths, and narcissi filled the compounds of notable families.

Harlan was not impressed by the arrival of "senseless stranger boors," as he called the British, whom he accused of being "vile in habit, infamous in vulgar tastes, callous leaders in the sanguinary march of heedless conquests."[4] There was plenty of evidence to support Harlan's views. Having installed themselves in Kabul and with a hapless former king, Shah Shuja, on the throne, the British set about re-creating a peculiar colonial idyll, consisting of the starched formality of military parades, manly endeavor on the cricket pitch, and, more dangerously, amorous abandon with the locals. Kabul had long had a red-light district, in the town's Indian quarter, but the arrival of the 5,000-strong army sent demands soaring, and Afghan women in their full-length burkas were soon spotted entering the British camp, lending another meaning to Harlan's complaint of "heedless conquests."

British Deputy Envoy Alexander Burnes was "especially shameless" and kept a harem of local and Kashmiri women, wrote Mirzat Ali, an Afghan chronicler of the period. "In his private quarters, he would take a bath with his Afghan mistress in the hot water of lust and pleasures, as the two rubbed each other down with flannels of giddy joy and the talc of intimacy," wrote Ali, adding that, "Two memsahibs, also his lovers, would join them."[5]

Whatever the truth to such lurid affairs, the apparent British wantonness symbolized the rapid and deep malaise of the colonial experiment in Kabul. The cost of occupying Afghanistan had largely drained the coffers of the Indian government as what was intended as a short stay inevitably dragged on. Instead of reining in their own luxurious lifestyles, the British leaders in the capital chose to cut subsidies they were giving to the tribal chieftains in an effort to bolster the regime. The British also eliminated the long-standing custom of tribal levies, in favor of creating a professional standing army, further weakening the ties between the colonial government and the country it purported to govern.

The British, relaxing amid the sweet peas and geraniums they had imported to their small enclave in Kabul, took their pleasant lives to mean the deeply conservative and tribal world beyond its gates had accepted them as rulers.[6] From the British perspective, village life didn't appear to be a threat but hopelessly backward and prone to anarchy. Yet in these communities, powerful principles ensured justice was served between individuals and clans, whether by brokering a deal involving the elders or by taking up arms. The British wisely stayed away from interfering with such affairs, but they failed to realize that their very presence as an invading force was an affront to tribal mores.

The British soon experienced Afghan justice for themselves. In November 1841, angry residents attacked Burnes's private house in Kabul and hacked him to pieces. His death sparked a national revolt the British garrison in Kabul proved incapable of dealing with. Some 3,400 men, women, and camp followers staged a desperate retreat to India that winter, harried by vindictive tribesmen the whole way, and were finally butchered in the snowy passes of Gandamak, in southeastern Afghanistan. Only a few survived, among them the British army medic Reverend G. H. Gleig, who later commented bitterly that the first Afghan war was one "begun for no wise purpose, carried on with a strange mixture of rashness and timidity, brought to a close after suffering and disaster, without much glory attached either to the government which directed, or the great body of troops which waged it."[7]

Their humiliating defeat in 1842 didn't stop the British from meddling. They were back in 1879, once again to prevent what they thought were Russian moves on Afghanistan. This time they invaded the country with 40,000 troops, mostly Indians, and installed another puppet ruler in Kabul. The following year, the Afghans rose in revolt. The son of the deposed ruler, Ayub Khan, assembled an army of 12,000 tribesmen and set off to confront the British, who sallied from their garrison in the southern city of Kandahar to meet the Afghans with their own, much smaller force of around 2,000. The local Afghan governor had urged the British to confront Ayub Khan and offered to provide troops to support them, but this turned out to be a ruse. The governor's fighters switched sides shortly before the battle.

The two armies met on a desert plain outside the village of Maiwand outside Kandahar. Unused to the terrain's exposed flats and plunging ravines, the British were quickly outflanked by Khan's horsemen and forced to retreat back to Kandahar, losing almost a thousand men in a few short days. British forces rallied only to withdraw back over the mountains to India a year later, having extracted a treaty from the Afghans and not much else.

In the end, the British learned to live with the bloody frontier that divided their empire from the Afghans, discovering that with the right management of tribal politics they could afford to limit their military involvement in this hellishly intractable region. "If we knit the frontier tribes into our imperial system and make their interests as ours . . . and as long as we are able and ready to hold our own, we can certainly depend upon them being on our side," wrote Robert Sandeman, one of the young officers who went on to man the border the British had drawn through the Pashtun heartlands in the south to divide and rule the tribespeople.[8] This job required a substantial knowledge of the tribes themselves, sensitivity to their mores and forms of government, and a certain bloody-mindedness.[9] Sandeman spent his career enticing tribesmen to join British-backed militia forces or launching punitive attacks when they rebelled. The best the British got in the Pashtun borderlands was a simmering insurgency, occasionally flaring up into all-out war—a constant reminder of the limits of the colonial enterprise.

With the decline of the British Empire after World War II, the US began its own tussle with Russia in central Asia, and Afghanistan became an important front in the Cold War. Throughout history, successful Afghan leaders had often kept avaricious neighbors at bay, and this period proved to be no exception. In the 1950s and 1960s, the Afghan King Zahir Shah played the two superpowers off each other. The result was a brief golden age in Afghanistan, though the period contained the seeds of its own destruction.

During this period, both the Russians and the Americans invested millions on infrastructure projects to win over the Afghans. In Helmand province, the Americans spent years building the Kajaki dam and an extensive system of irrigation canals. The rationale for the dam was twofold: First, it would provide a long-term, sustainable water and electricity source for southern Afghanistan. A second, more ambitious goal was to use the dam's irrigation to transform the Pashtun from seminomadic herders into farmers. The Afghan government would award them newly irrigated land in the hopes of engendering loyalty and a sense of private ownership essential for capitalism to flourish. Neither the Afghan government nor the Americans consulted the herders themselves, and somehow ignored the fact the sheepskin pelts they produced constituted Afghanistan's main source of export revenue.[10]

Over the 1950s, the Americans had built a whole new town, Lashkar Gar, to house the western engineers working on the dam. The town was every bit as odd as earlier British experiments. It was laid out on a grid system like a US suburb, with wide boulevards and traffic lights. Houses were single-story bungalows rather than the traditional high-walled compounds, with open lawns facing the street. There was also a tourist office, cinema, and clubhouse, the very trappings that had inspired historian Arnold Toynbee, visiting the town in 1960, to write about an "America in Asia," although that phrase fails to capture the town's pioneering ethic and almost defiant sense of itself. Paul Jones, an engineer working for the Morrison Knudsen firm building the dam in Afghanistan, captured it best in a work of history that bordered on the allegorical and visionary. "Yes," he wrote, "all about is life and an air of hopeful expectancy, and the beginning (we Americans watch and in our own humble way fervently pray) of a new Afghanistan rising from out of the mysteries of forgotten centuries to become truly a modern 'Star of Asia.'"[11]

The dam, completed in 1953, did not have the desired effect. Pashtun nomads were skeptical about the offer of land, forcing the government to instead hand out land to rival Tajiks and Hazara, creating a dangerous tribal brew between the groups. In addition, Helmand's soil was heavy clay that was susceptible to waterlogging, and the resulting marshy fields drew salt deposits to the surface, making the soil unsuitable for farming. Crop yields began to fall. When the US tried to improve drainage by removing families from the afflicted fields and leveling land with bulldozers, locals provided armed resistance. As a *New York Times* article at the time noted, the US may "have unwittingly and indirectly contributed to driving Afghanistan into Russian arms."[12]

That turned out to be an exaggeration when it came to the tribal areas of the south. But the Russians did have greater success in Kabul winning over the country's elite to the virtues of communism. During their own building boom in the 1960s, the Russians had helped establish the Polytechnic Institute, largely staffed by Russian teachers. It wasn't long before revolutionary talk was building among Afghan students there and at Kabul University. By 1968, a proto-communist party in the capital had 1,500 members. Unlike the British before them, the Russian leadership was painfully aware of the disconnect between the Kabuli elite and the agrarian society beyond the city. Out in the countryside, the Russians' revolutionary theory had little relevance. But when a communist faction seized control of the country in 1978, proclaiming its undying loyalty to the Soviet Union, the Russians had little choice but to back it. Their Afghan disciples sought to reassure Moscow. One of the new leaders in Kabul told the Russians, "Comrade Stalin showed us how to build socialism in a backward country: it's painful to begin with, but afterwards everything turns out just fine."[13]

By then, trouble was brewing in the Afghan countryside, already disturbed by King Zahir Shah's willingness to embrace foreign ideas, the cosmopolitanism of Kabul, and the general prevalence of well-meaning westerners—including thousands of long-haired hippies—who were perceived as a cultural threat to the country's conservatives. All-out insurrection broke out in March 1979 in a village outside the eastern town of Herat, where according to one account peasants were incensed by local communists forcing the villagers to school their daughters. In Herat a mob tore through the streets, sacking communist offices, tearing down red flags, beating up anyone not wearing traditional Muslim clothes, and murdering any Russians they could get their hands on. The Afghan government succeeded in establishing control a few weeks later, but the violence set in motion the events that led to the Soviet military invasion that December.

In light of the British experience a hundred years before, the Russians at first were wary about invading. To several members of the Politburo, the Soviet leadership council in Moscow, it was clear that Afghanistan's problems would have to be solved politically and that "Soviet bayonets" could not provide the answer.[14] Ironically, in the end it was the Communist Party in Kabul that precipitated the Soviet invasion. Party chairman Hafizullah Amin detained and then murdered Afghanistan's president, a Moscow favorite, before launching into fresh purges. Moscow felt it had to intervene to save the local party from its unbalanced leadership.

On December 27, 1979, Soviet special forces stormed the presidential palace in Kabul and executed Amin. At the same time 80,000 troops crossed into Afghanistan from neighboring Soviet states. The troops were to replace the country's president with a figure more pliant to Russia's wishes and then quickly withdraw, leaving a residual force to develop the Afghan army. Almost at once, however, they were sucked into a battle with tribal malcontents already fighting against the government. Soviet columns were attacked along the main supply roads, obliging the Russians to set up a system of guard posts between cities—targets that served only to draw more attacks. The Russians responded by launching assaults into the mountains to root out the insurgents, with sadly predictable results. By April 1980, around 150 Russian soldiers were being killed each month.

Early in the war, the Russians hoped Afghans would recognize their efforts to establish law and order and to introduce the benchmarks of the Soviet economy: collectivized farms and heavy industry. They would soon discover, however, that the Afghans had little interest in what they had to offer. It was the worst kind of war: The Soviet forces recognized that they could not win, yet they continued to intensify the fighting, bombing villages and strafing any fleeing Afghans with helicopter fire. In 1986, Soviet troops began to withdraw, but it took until the end of the decade for the last soldiers to leave. The war had exacted a terrible toll on all sides: Over 14,000 Russian troops had

The Afghan capital of Kabul was once called "the city of a thousand gardens." Three decades of war had devastated the city by 2001. (Photo by author)

been killed, and an estimated $128 billion spent, and the Soviet Union was on the verge of collapse, at least partly due to the fighting. As for Afghanistan, the country lay in ruins, with 1 million war dead, and 5 million forced to flee their homes.

The US had begun funneling cash to the mujahideen resistance before the Soviet invasion, and stepped up their support once it became clear that Moscow was struggling to contain the insurgency. "There are 58,000 dead in Vietnam, and we owe the Russians one," said Congressman Charlie Wilson, who helped organize over $3 billion of government funding for a motley crew of Afghan warlords fighting the Soviets.[15] In doing so, Wilson became the latest westerner to project his own desires onto the Afghans. In this case, he saw the mujahideen as devout and freedom-loving warriors battling the godless communists. CIA officers on the ground had a less than rosy view of those they were empowering, or of the extreme brand of Islam promoted in Afghan refugee camps along the border by their chief allies, Pakistan and Saudi Arabia. So long as the Soviet Union was suffering, however, they were happy to ignore the emerging mess.

Once Russian forces had withdrawn, Washington cut its funds to the warlords, and left them to fight it out among themselves. Afghans refer to this period as the "mujahideen nights," which marked a particular nadir in the country's fortunes. Any man with a gun might claim power, if he was prepared to butcher his rivals, shake down the locals, and stake his claim to Afghanistan's rapidly growing opium trade, which entrepreneurial warlords had helped foster during the resistance. Between 1981 and 1994, opium production grew fourteen-fold—from 250 tons to over 3,500 tons, making up almost half the global supply of opium and its more refined derivative, heroin.[16]

Fighting for control of the opium trade only accelerated the country's dissolution. In Kabul, rival warlords were at one stage shelling each other and the city indiscriminately from the surrounding hills, destroying what remained of the once-elegant capital. Millions of Afghans fled the country to live in refugee camps in Pakistan. Washington largely turned its back.

The anarchy ended only with the arrival of the Taliban in 1994. Like the warlords, they were also a product of the Soviet invasion, but they rejected—or at least claimed to reject—the warlords' greed. The Taliban's leader, Mullah Omar, was a former mujahid-turned-preacher who espoused a stringent form of Islam. His views were rooted in the customs of village life but they had been charged with religious fervor by the war. He came from the Ghilzai tribe, traditionally looked down upon by the other tribes, but Mullah Omar's lowly status gave him an outsider's view of warlord rule. His solution was to cast the whole lot aside, a call to arms that rapidly found favor among his weary countrymen. He shot one notorious warlord dead, and strung up another from the barrel of his own tank.

The uprising he sparked soon drew the attention of Pakistan's spy agency, the Directorate of Inter-Service Intelligence, or ISI. The Pakistani government in Islamabad had been America's principal ally during the war against the Soviet Union in Afghanistan. The US had outsourced the management of the networks of mujahideen fighters to Pakistan. After Soviet forces withdrew, the ISI had championed a succession of warlords who might seize the country, and thus extend Pakistani influence over its neighbor. Islamabad saw the country through the prism of its rivalry with India: Afghanistan was in its backyard, and if they didn't draw it into their sphere of influence, then India surely would. Factors, like the Northern Alliance, had received support from both New Delhi and Tehran, casting the war into a broader regional struggle.

In the end, the warlords Islamabad backed had failed to seize Kabul, and their bloody tactics appeared to have permanently fractured the country. The rise of the Taliban provided a fresh opportunity for Pakistan to extend its interests. Mullah Omar was a prickly character, but he was focused on a religious agenda and seemed ready to accept Pakistan's guidance on more worldly matters, such as foreign affairs. In return, the Taliban received an influx of arms and money from the ISI. The Taliban were never beholden to the ISI, but neither were they independent.

Over the next few years, the Taliban swept across Afghanistan, seizing one city after another. The Taliban's ascendency marked a familiar reaction of the country's conservative hinterland against the corruption of Afghanistan's rulers. Afghans welcomed the Taliban's eviction of the warlords; the harsh brand of Islam the group espoused was less popular.

In the past, the country's tribal elite had used such populist surges to dislodge their rivals in Kabul before carrying on as before. Mullah Omar's ascension marked one of the first times that a villager had gained power himself. When he promised to restore Afghanistan to the Islamic values of the Dark Ages, he meant it. Men risked flogging if they did not grow long beards or wore western clothes like jeans or suits. Girls were not allowed to attend school and women could be stoned to death if they were charged with adultery. Afghanistan was increasingly conforming to the bizarre and brutal fantasies of village mullahs, albeit a vision supported by modern weaponry and influxes of Pakistani cash.

This was the country President Bush was contemplating invading as he met his inner circle at Camp David on September 15, 2001. They weighed the military's two plans—missile strikes or a massive ground invasion—against the CIA's paramilitary option. Everyone in the room thought a ground invasion was a bad idea. Bush dubbed the military's thinking "unimaginative," and the argument swung decisively toward the CIA's lighter approach.[17]

Most of the group stayed at Camp David for the evening and drove to the retreat's main lodge in golf carts. Attorney General John Ashcroft, who was about to play a crucial role in facilitating the torture of captured al-Qa'eda operatives and members of the Taliban, sat down at the piano in the wood-beamed reception room and banged out "Nobody Knows the Trouble I've Seen" and "America the Beautiful" for an impromptu sing-along. Bush sat quietly to the side, at work on a jigsaw puzzle.

Five days later, on September 20, Bush stood before Congress and announced that the "War on Terror" had begun. This speech cemented America's distorted understanding of Afghanistan by conflating al-Qa'eda, a malevolent terrorist group, with the Taliban, a movement with a claim to represent significant swathes of southern Afghanistan. Bush demanded that the Taliban hand over the al-Qa'eda leadership, dismantle terrorist training camps, open Afghanistan's borders for US inspections, and free eight recently detained Christian aid workers. "From this day forward, any nation that continues to harbor or support terrorism will be regarded by the United States as a hostile regime," he warned Americans during the address. This speech was the most aggressive formulation yet of what became known as the Bush Doctrine, and it set the stage for a war against the Taliban that promised to endure long after the paramilitary forces had removed them from power.

CHAPTER 3

Good Taliban

At the end of September 2001, a few days after President Bush's speech announcing the "War on Terror," Robert Grenier, the CIA's station chief in Islamabad, arrived at a five-star hotel in Quetta in western Pakistan to give the Taliban a final chance to give up Osama bin Laden. Grenier was liaison with the Taliban's second in command, Mullah Osmani. The liaison between the dapper CIA officer and the turban-wearing Taliban had the potential to end the war before it began. Yet Grenier also knew that any chance of avoiding conflict hinged on the Taliban displaying more pragmatism than they had so far. The US demands were straightforward enough, as was the threat of noncompliance: Hand over Osama bin Laden or face military intervention.

Grenier dispensed with the pleasantries and got to the point. "The Americans are coming," he warned Osmani. "You need to do something to dodge this bullet."[1]

He had the credibility to speak this bluntly to the Taliban's number two because he understood Afghanistan better than perhaps anyone in the agency. A cool, shrewd diplomat, Grenier was a Cold War–era throwback to when spies dressed in tailored suits, and the Yale men took on their Harvard counterparts at tennis on the embassy lawn. Grenier eschewed such self-conscious trappings, but he brought an intellectual rigor to the job that marked him out as different from the more recent intake of ex–special forces types.

For much of the past year Grenier had been sending his staff to the Afghan borderlands or for secret meetings with tribal chiefs and former mujahideen commanders, trying to engineer a split between the Taliban and al-Qa'eda. The potential for division was clear to Grenier. Mullah Omar, the Taliban's spiritual leader, had inherited al-Qa'eda's presence in the country from the previous government and was increasingly annoyed by bin Laden's independent declaration of war against the US, which exposed his country to American retaliation. Mullah Omar likened the Saudi dissident to a "bone stuck in my throat."[2]

What's more, Grenier knew that more moderate members of the Taliban's leadership like Osmani felt that al-Qa'eda's espousal of global jihad was endangering the regime, and that the movement should engage with the international community, including the US. At one stage in 1998, the Taliban had appeared to countenance the idea of handing over bin Laden to the Americans. They had asked the US to provide proof of his role in the attacks that year on the US embassies in Kenya and Tanzania. In 2000, the FBI dispatched Patrick Fitzgerald, the federal prosecutor of the southern district of New York, to Islamabad with a thick dossier of evidence to meet Taliban representatives, only for the Taliban to backtrack. Instead, the Taliban suggested that bin Laden be tried by an Islamic court in Kabul. That was a non-starter as far as Washington was concerned.

Grenier had come to believe the Taliban were simply toying with the Americans, and that Mullah Omar was unlikely to betray his guest. Tribal honor partly motivated Mullah Omar; another factor was his shared sense of religious conviction with the al-Qa'eda leader. He wouldn't hand over a fellow Muslim to an infidel government, no matter what his crimes. To some, Mullah Omar's decision to protect bin Laden in the face of international and domestic pressure implies that the Taliban and al-Qa'eda shared a common cause. Indeed, while it's unclear whether members of the Taliban were aware of the details of the 9/11 attacks, they likely knew the basic plot. Al-Qa'eda's assassination of Northern Alliance leader Ahmad Shah Massoud the day before the attacks suggested a certain quid pro quo.[3] For these reasons, Grenier was not particularly hopeful that the Taliban would hand over bin Laden and be spared attack. The Taliban duly rejected the offer.

But Grenier did not give up. On October 2, 2001, he met Mullah Osmani, the Taliban's second in command, again in Quetta, with a second American proposal, one intended to exploit the gap—if one existed—between hardliners and moderates within the Taliban: Would Osmani consider seizing power himself? The CIA would help in the coup, provided that Osmani agree to hand over bin Laden afterward. Osmani could explain the action to the rest of the leadership by saying he moved against Mullah Omar to save the Taliban movement from the deleterious effect of foreigners like bin Laden. Mullah Osmani appeared to respond positively, and suggested he and Grenier continue their talks.

A week passed, and it became clear to Grenier that Mullah Osmani would not go through with the coup idea. Grenier suspected that Osmani could not see the Taliban surviving without its iconic figurehead.[4] The CIA officer also wondered what role Pakistan had played in Osmani's decision. Islamabad was giving off mixed signals. Pakistan's military dictator Pervez Musharraf had told the US ambassador to Islamabad, Wendy Chamberlain, that his country would support the US "War on Terror," even if that meant turning against Pakistan's longtime allies, the Taliban.[5] Yet questions remained over how deep Musharraf's commitment actually was. For example, when the dictator had dispatched Mahmud Ahmed, the head of ISI, Pakistan's spy agency, to Kandahar in a last-ditch attempt to get Mullah Omar to hand over bin Laden, one Taliban official recalled that Ahmed urged the movement's leaders to stand firm.[6] Ultimately, the Taliban did just that—and thus Grenier's warning came to pass. On October 7, President Bush announced to the American public that the first US air strikes against Afghanistan had begun. The Taliban would "pay a price" for its failure to hand over bin Laden, the president warned.

Still, Grenier hadn't given up on winning over moderates within the Taliban: His instincts told him that as the war progressed, pressure to negotiate

Robert Grenier (right), CIA station chief in Pakistan, on the border between Pakistan and Afghanistan in April 2002. Grenier advocated building support among the tribes of the Pashtun south, including moderate members of the Taliban. (Photo courtesy of Robert Grenier)

would only increase the movement's leaders. At the same time, Grenier would need Pakistan's help in finding an alternative to the Taliban to represent Afghanistan's Pashtun south. Pakistan wanted to host a conference of Afghans to put together a new national government, an offer that Grenier was wary of—he knew it would give Islamabad scope to manipulate the process—but he recognized the importance of engaging with Pakistan.[7]

It was a tough proposition. Under US pressure, Musharraf had replaced ISI chief Ahmed—a notorious advocate for the Taliban—but he stopped short of promising to sever ties between the spy agency and militants on both sides of the Pakistan-Afghanistan border. The ISI also failed to produce Taliban defectors who would be able to form a "southern alliance" to complement the Northern Alliance as the latter advanced on Kabul. The limited cooperation from Pakistan could have been a form of prevarication, or it could reflect the genuine difficulties Islamabad faced as it sought to reposition its policy. Grenier decided the wait was worth the risk. Nonetheless, after the first CIA team arrived in northern Afghanistan at the end of October 2001—code-named Jawbreaker—the clock was ticking for Grenier and his negotiations.

Gary Schroen, the leader of the first Jawbreaker team, arrived in Afghanistan on October 20, 2001. As he saw it America was already living on borrowed time. Schroen was a veteran of the CIA's operation against Soviet forces in the 1980s, and had witnessed firsthand how the mujahideen had driven out a much greater invading force than the Americans. Of course, American objectives were far different than those of the Russians, he believed, but any foreign army ran the risk of pushing the Afghans into revolt.

Where Grenier was arguing for patience to get the politics right, Schroen was urging a speedy prosecution of the war. He was disappointed by the first two weeks of the bombing campaign. So far, American bombs had targeted Afghanistan's limited military infrastructure around Kabul but had held off from attacking the Taliban's front lines to give Grenier more time. That was a mistake, Schroen believed.

"Do we want to defeat the Taliban quickly?" Schroen asked his bosses in Washington from his makeshift headquarters in the Panjshir valley, the small sliver of Afghanistan the Northern Alliance controlled. If the answer was yes, Schroen said, then the US needed to bomb the Taliban front lines in the north, then turn loose the Northern Alliance.[8] As the CIA man saw it, the Northern Alliance would inevitably seize Kabul, so there was no sense in the Americans running the risk of inflaming local animosity by trying to delay the takeover.

He made another good point: Until the Taliban was rolled back, no Pashtun was going to dare to join a southern alliance or seek to overthrow Mullah Omar.

In Islamabad, Grenier pushed back. In an increasingly testy exchange of memos with Schroen via the CIA headquarters in Langley, Virginia, he warned that should Kabul fall to the Northern Alliance, Tajik tribal militias might well ransack the city, resulting in a "bloodbath."[9] Grenier saw an additional challenge: If the Northern Alliance seized the Afghan capital, they might claim the whole country, thereby alienating the country's Pashtun south, whose residents would see the US as having chosen sides in the country's ongoing civil war. Far better to buy time for both sides to reach a negotiated settlement.

Grenier's view prevailed in Washington, at least for a few more weeks. Yet, his efforts to prize away moderates from the Taliban or find a credible alternative were failing. Pakistan's spy service, the ISI, had not contributed to his idea for a southern alliance of tribal leaders. In mid-October, Pakistan had hosted an ISI-approved "peace conference" in Peshawar, which delivered plenty of platitudes from the 1,500 Afghan exiles and tribal leaders who attended but few volunteers to take on the Taliban. Later that month, the ISI also held secret talks with the Taliban's foreign minister, Mullah Wakil Ahmed Muttawakil, but again, Grenier was unimpressed with the results. The Pakistanis leaked details of the talks to the press, and Grenier, among others, wondered whether the discussions were little more than window dressing for Islamabad to appear to follow the American agenda. The ISI seemed to be playing the long game in the belief that it was only a matter of time before the US withdrew and handed management of the country back to Pakistan, just as it had done after the Soviet collapse in Afghanistan.[10]

By early November 2001, it was clear that the regime had begun to totter. Mullah Omar was hunkering down in his Kandahar stronghold, as bin Laden prepared to flee Kabul for his mountain redoubt in Tora Bora. On November 9, Mazar-e-Sharif, the Taliban's northern stronghold, became the first city to fall to the Northern Alliance, after the Uzbek warlord Abdul Rashid Dostum and a detachment of US special forces charged Taliban positions outside the city on horseback. The victory confirmed Afghanistan's otherworldliness and the wisdom of adapting western ends to Afghan means.

Just as significantly, Mazar-e-Sharif's capture opened the road to Kabul as US bombers turned their attention to Taliban positions outside the capital. Grenier continued to urge caution, but Bush's team wanted to take advantage of their momentum.[11] The victory emboldened the White House and also coincided with the arrival of US special forces teams that pushed the chain of command to target Taliban positions. Having ceded the early leadership of the war to the CIA, the Pentagon was now attempting to reassert its control over the campaign. CIA Director George Tenet had been sympathetic to Grenier's view that bringing together a southern alliance required more time; Defense Secretary Donald Rumsfeld had less patience.

A few days later, the Northern Alliance advanced on Kabul and the remaining Taliban leadership fled. The Jawbreaker teams on the ground extracted promises from the Northern Alliance leadership that their forces would remain outside the city to give the international community time to organize a peacekeeping force, and prevent what Grenier feared would be a bloodbath once the Tajik militias descended. But on November 13, the Northern Alliance drove into the capital anyway and seized key buildings, including the presidential palace. Grenier's worst fears went unrealized. Having established control, the Tajik militias didn't tear apart the city or seek to exact revenge on Taliban sympathizers who remained. Yet their symbolic conquest of the capital gave the Northern Alliance leaders far greater sway in determining who would rule the country now that the Taliban leaders were in retreat.

The fall of Kabul accelerated the debate in Washington over what post-Taliban Afghanistan should look like and America's role, if any, in shaping that future.

In its discussions immediately after 9/11, the Bush team had dismissed getting sucked into the messy business of rebuilding failed states. During the election campaign the team had referred derisively to the Clinton-era reconstruction effort in the Balkans as an example of how the US military's fighting spirit was diminished by the international wrangling and petty bureaucracy of such endeavors. As late as September 26, Bush continued to insist that the US was "not into nation-building; we are focused on justice." The State Department, however, increasingly recognized that the US must help shape Afghanistan's next administration, and that installing a pro-western regime after the Taliban would require some form of limited reconstruction—"nation-building light," as UN officials dubbed it. A key question was what sort of force should occupy Kabul after the Taliban left.

At an October 11, 2001, National Security Council meeting, Secretary of State Colin Powell suggested they hand over the knotty problem of Afghanistan's political future to the United Nations. He argued Kabul should become a UN protectorate, manned by a peacekeeping force that would ensure that Kabul remained outside the control of any one faction while the international community helped form a representative government.[12]

Early on in the conflict, the UN had indicated its readiness to play a lead role in Afghanistan. The organization had maintained a presence in Afghanistan during the 1990s, one of the few international entities to do so. While the US had largely ignored the country's civil war, the UN had done its best to engage both sides in peace talks, led by veteran Algerian diplomat Lakhdar Brahimi. In early October 2001, UN Secretary-General Kofi Annan turned to Brahimi to forge a new settlement between the Afghan factions.

Brahimi belonged to an earlier generation of Arab nationalists who had embraced modernism after an empire's collapse. His background battling the French for Algeria's independence in the 1960s had given him an acute sensitivity to the perils of colonialism, while his country's subsequent travails against Islamic extremism had left him wary of a younger generation of Arab politicians who sought the ready legitimacy of religion. Brahimi had already held the post of UN special envoy to Afghanistan in the late 1990s but had resigned in frustration after talks between the Northern Alliance and the Taliban broke down. The Taliban had launched a major assault in the midst of the cease-fire, and Brahimi blamed Pakistan for encouraging the movement. Even after Annan reappointed him special envoy in September 2001, Brahimi refused to speak to the Pakistanis, delegating the job to his deputy, Francesc Vendrell, and the envoy's sense of distrust lingered.[13]

That fall of 2001, Brahimi favored a light international footprint for Afghanistan, reflecting his cautious assessment of what westerners could achieve amid the country's extreme poverty and complex politics. He supported providing a small peacekeeping force to keep Afghan factions apart while a new government was established. But he agreed with Rumsfeld that there was little that international forces, with limited experience in the country, could achieve if they were deployed more widely. Afghanistan's problems had to be solved with politics, he believed, which is where his attentions settled.[14]

By mid-October, Brahimi had laid out a political framework that started with a conference to bring together all sides of the conflict in Afghanistan, as well as countries with a vested interest in the outcome, including Pakistan and Iran. The UN leadership argued over when to hold the conference, with Vendrell urging them to have it as soon as possible, preferably before the Northern Alliance seized Kabul and unbalanced any deal with the Pashtun south. Others in the UN wanted more time to assemble as broad a set of delegates as possible. In the end, Brahimi settled on the end of November, which would give the UN enough time to bring together delegates from the country's varied factions and from Pakistan and Iran, among other countries in the region.

As Brahimi's team compiled the conference list that fall, it was obvious that the organizers must include a delegation from the Tajik-dominated Northern Alliance. The ragged militia had initially made slow progress against the Taliban, but were the most powerful indigenous force in the country, and as they neared Kabul, their clout was only increasing.

Another, altogether better-dressed, delegation was drawn from the followers of the former king, Zahir Shah, who had been driven to Italy in exile in 1973. Over the years, restoring the king to power had remained a consistent refrain of many leading Pashtun families. But it gradually became clear that the idea of the king's return contained as much nostalgia for a lost past as it did hope for the future. In 2001, the king was a frail eighty-five-year-old who spent his days pottering around his Italian mansion watering his bougainvillea. His courtiers also suffered from their long absence from their home country. They would likely struggle to connect with Afghanistan's fractured tribes from which the Taliban drew its support, which left open the question: Who could represent these Pashtuns?

On this front, the UN had no more luck than the CIA in finding alternatives to the Taliban. Yet Mullah Omar's inner circle was at last ready to engage in earnest as the Northern Alliance approached Kabul that November. Taliban foreign minister Muttawakil had yet to return to Kabul from his talks in Islamabad, but his deputy contacted the UN office in the Afghan capital to introduce the prospect of handing over the city to a UN peacekeeping force. "It was a bold suggestion that could only have been made with the support of the Taliban's leadership," recalled Michael Semple, a UN official working at the UN's Peshawar office at the time, but in regular contact with Kabul.[15]

Offering the Afghan capital to the UN had the virtue of sidestepping the Taliban having to deal with Pakistan and America. But the offer came too late. On the same day the UN Security Council was due to meet to endorse Brahimi's plan and to authorize a 5,000-strong peacekeeping force for Kabul, the Northern Alliance seized the capital. The British military—which had volunteered to contribute the bulk of the soldiers for the peacekeeping—had only a small vanguard at Bagram airfield outside the city, and were powerless to stop the Tajik militia.[16]

Whether the Taliban was prepared to deliver on their promise is unclear, yet it seems entirely possible. As the mullahs' power faded, they appeared ready to seek compromise and negotiate a withdrawal from their remaining strongholds. Yet at the same time they also became easier for the West to ignore. Ultimately the choice to spurn the Taliban had tragic consequences.

Washington, its mood increasingly triumphant, set the tone for the approaching UN conference. The thought of including Taliban representatives seemed preposterous to the recently appointed American envoy to the talks, James Dobbins. "Out of the question," he recalled thinking at the time. "They have been defeated. Why would they be included?"[17]

For Dobbins, a veteran diplomat who had implemented the peace accords in the Balkans in the late 1990s, the dangers of imposing a victor's peace on Afghanistan should have been all too apparent. Instead he chose to label the Taliban a "spent" force. The future now lay with those promising to build a brave new future for the country.

Dobbins was not alone in his conclusions about the Taliban. The UN Envoy Lakhdar Brahimi, in drawing up the invitation list for the Bonn conference, could have pushed for Taliban inclusion, or indeed any real voices from the Pashtun heartlands. After his last experience trying to broker peace in Afghanistan, he was skeptical of the Taliban and nursed a deeper distrust of the rise of Islamist movements that sought political power, and a bitterness—shared by other modernizers—that the region was heading in the wrong direction.

Brahimi has since recognized his mistake. "The Taliban should have been at Bonn," he said later. "This was our original sin. If we had had time and spoken to some of them and asked them to come, because they still represented something, maybe they would have come to Bonn. Even if none came, at least we would have tried."[18]

But in late 2001 the West didn't see the point of including the Taliban in Afghanistan's future. As UN officials and regional delegates gathered at Bonn to decide what that future would be, they were about to place their hopes on the unlikeliest of figures seeking to challenge the Taliban for Pashtun allegiance and become the country's new ruler.

CHAPTER 4

The Man Who Would Be King

Shortly before 9/11, Hamid Karzai was preparing to fly from Pakistan to Baltimore, Maryland, to join his family's restaurant business. Once he had dreamed of becoming a great Afghan leader, an unlikely ambition for the fourth son of a chief of the Popalzai tribe in southern Afghanistan. But by 2001 even he could see that the only political power that mattered in the country was that of the Taliban.

Karzai loathed the Taliban and their harsh and aberrant interpretation of the Quran that kept women locked away and men subservient to illiterate village mullahs. He had grown up with the seasonal rhythm of tribal life on his family's ancestral land in the rich Arghandab valley, with its dense groves of grapevines and pomegranate trees. The mudbrick reception room of his family's home in Karz had filled up with supplicants every day to resolve, over tea and tart cherries, marriage and land disputes. The Popalzai were one branch of the largest tribal confederation in the south, the Durrani, from which most of the country's kings had been drawn. The Karzais were a lesser clan that had wisely kept their ambitions in check. What power they wielded was drawn from the same sources as with every other ruling family: wealth, custom, and an intimate knowledge of the tribe's vast genealogy, and the network of debts and obligations that tied families together.

The Soviet invasion in 1979 upended the traditional order that had sustained the Karzais. The family opposed the occupation, and fled to safety in Pakistan. In exile the family retained a degree of its luster. The Karzai compound in Quetta was well attended by Popalzai tribesmen who traveled for a day or more from the Arghandab to resolve their disputes, revealing a hidden robustness to Afghan life during the occupation. By then Karzai's three elder brothers had departed for America. Karzai went to study at university in Simla, India, an old British hill-station where he immersed himself in English literature, and took to strolling on the Mall, wearing pressed suits with a folded umbrella under his arm, just as an educated Indian might in the days of empire.[1] He seemed fascinated by the cultural attraction of that bygone era and repelled by its inequalities. That latter impulse ultimately drew him back to Pakistan, and to his roots as a tribal chieftain's son and heir, now that his brothers had left.

Pashtun culture dictated that the young Karzai take up arms against the Russians, but that wasn't his style. Instead he became the spokesman for Sibghatullah Mojaddedi, the mildest of the warlords the CIA was bankrolling. As the war against the Soviets wore on across the border, Karzai proved quite adept at keeping warm the plush leather couches of the Pearl Continental hotel in Peshawar, a predominantly Pashtun city that like Quetta, two hundred miles away, had become a center for Afghan refugees and exiles. He would gossip for hours with spies, diplomats, and journalists in relative luxury. He had lost his hair early, and the effect was to extend the broad expanse of his olive-brown forehead and indelicate nose, strong features offset by his hunched carriage and stiff, overly precise movements. His almond-shaped eyes offered a soft counterpoint to these coarser aspects, as if he had a wry question on his lips. Karzai could be headstrong, vain, and in his darker moments surly and obtuse. Yet he was also ebullient, gregarious even—a man of flickering charisma more likely to join the flow of conversation than to seek to dominate it.

Karzai's career appeared to have peaked in 1992 after the Soviet ouster and the creation of a short-lived national unity government in which he had served as deputy foreign minister. As the country subsequently began to fracture along ethnic lines, Karzai was hauled before the National Security Directorate for questioning. His background may have gotten him into trouble; Karzai was a Pashtun from the south, but in 1994—the year of Karzai's fall from power—the state's security apparatus was in Tajik hands. The two ethnic groups had a long-standing rivalry, exacerbated by the perception among many Pashtun that the Tajiks had sided with the Soviet Union against them.

It's not clear whether Karzai was beaten during the interrogation, or whether his life was in danger. But in the middle of his ordeal, a rocket from a routine exchange of fire between warlords struck the building in which Karzai was being held, stunning his captors and knocking Karzai off his chair. In the dust and confusion that followed, Karzai escaped, ultimately finding his way back to Pakistan.

Back in Peshawar, Karzai rallied support for the ascendant Taliban movement, raising $50,000 for their cause, a huge sum for the fledgling outfit.[2] Karzai saw the Taliban as unworldly foot soldiers content to kick out the warlords and leave the politics to sophisticated men like himself. However, as the Taliban's victories mounted on the other side of the border, they showed little interest in relinquishing power. When Kabul fell in 1996, Mullah Omar offered Karzai a token role as ambassador to the United Nations. Karzai turned it down, put off by the Taliban's increasing intolerance and what he judged to be Pakistan's controlling influence on the group. Karzai knew that this rebuke was not lost on Taliban leaders. Three years later a gunman killed Karzai's father outside the family home in Quetta. Karzai blamed the Taliban, although the Pakistanis surely bore some of the blame; the killing was unlikely to have been carried out without the knowledge of ISI, the Pakistani spy service. Still, there was little that Karzai, with his small band of followers and limited reputation, could do.

By September 2001, Karzai's mounting criticism of the Taliban and his contacts with the Northern Alliance had proved irritating enough for the ISI to ask him to leave the country. Seeing the smoking towers in New York stirred his flickering ambitions once again. He canceled his ticket to Baltimore, and instead began plotting his return to Afghanistan.

Karzai suspected that the Americans would try to oust the Taliban, and he saw an opportunity to throw his name behind the cause and become the leader he'd always dreamed of becoming. In reality, his options were limited. He could rally a band of followers around Kandahar, but they would not be enough to topple the Taliban. He hoped that through his actions he could inspire a broader revolt. More pragmatically, he recognized that his chance of doing so depended on whether he could win American backing for his mission, and with it, the appearance of power that would do more to win over his countrymen than his soft words. In early October, he visited the CIA headquarters in Islamabad.

Grenier, station chief, was still pushing to create a southern alliance that would include tribes prepared to take on the Taliban, as well as moderate elements from within the movement itself. The idea of including members of Mullah Omar's inner circle had all but disappeared. In the Pakistani cities like Quetta, close to the Afghan border, Grenier's staff had met a steady stream of middle-aged mujahideen commanders to see if any might be capable of leading such an uprising, but none of the paunchy, gout-ridden fighters had appeared likely candidates. Several had walked away from the meetings with thick wads of money, but the only result so far had been greatly expanded fleets of SUVs with tinted windows bought with the cash.[3]

The CIA reached out to Karzai, too. The elegant Pashtun didn't fit the most basic CIA criteria: the ability to fight. One American officer handed him a satellite telephone and told him to keep in touch. It was not exactly the ringing endorsement Karzai had imagined. On October 7, 2001, the day after the US began bombing Afghanistan, he decided to take matters into his own hands. Karzai called a tribal leader from northern Helmand province named Sher Mohammed Akhundzada, whose father had pioneered the drug trade in southern Afghanistan, only to be gunned down by a rival. Akhundzada Junior had fled to Pakistan and married one of Karzai's half sisters. The diminutive warlord was one of a few Karzai family allies in exile who also maintained a strong network, allegedly supported by the family's drug trafficking; Akhundzada could provide a safe haven for Karzai in the mountains that connected the provinces of Helmand and Oruzgun.

That same day, Karzai called the Pakistani journalist Ahmed Rashid to tell him he would be returning to Afghanistan shortly to lead an armed revolt against the Taliban. Then he clambered into the back of a cargo truck with three of his supporters and headed for the border, knowing that many shared his desire to overthrow Mullah Omar's regime—but that his chances of success were slim.

At the Chaman border crossing, the four men switched to two motorcycles under the noses of the Taliban guards before riding for six hours over the potholed road to Kandahar. Stiff and layered in desert sand, Karzai arrived at the house of a family friend on the outskirts of the city. Two days later he reached Tarin Kowt, the gritty capital of Oruzgun province, a hundred or so miles northwest of Kandahar, where Karzai hoped to begin his resistance campaign. It was a smart choice: Mullah Omar had been born nearby, making the province the Taliban's symbolic home. At the same time, it was far enough from Kandahar that the regime's hold over the area was weak.

The only problem was that the tribesmen of Oruzgun province were less than convinced by Karzai's offer to join his cause. At an early meeting between Karzai and the local elders, one of them pointedly asked: "Do you have the Americans with you? Are they behind you, as they are behind the Northern Alliance?"[4]

Karzai showed them the satellite phone and said he had been promised support—although he had no idea how much. The elders were skeptical: "Have the Americans bomb the Taliban here," they instructed, jabbing thick fingers at a map laid out before them. When Karzai shrugged in response, the leader responded, "Then you will never win."[5]

Karzai stayed on awkwardly for over a week at Tarin Kowt's small airfield with about a hundred tribesmen before the Taliban finally got wind of his presence. On the satellite phone the CIA had given him, he tried to garner some enthusiasm, declaring he had a thousand men under arms. US satellite imagery showed a fraction of that number. When Karzai was forced to flee into the mountains with the Taliban's approach, no more than a dozen of his men followed. Karzai could now at least claim to the Americans that he was on the run from the Taliban. On the phone with his CIA contact, he managed to arrange an airdrop of food supplies.

It was a start. "The Americans are finally taking me seriously because for the moment there is no one else resisting among the Pashtuns," Karzai told the journalist Ahmed Rashid. But both men knew how far he still had to go to turn his gang of fighters into a nationwide revolt.[6]

K arzai's quixotic quest was transformed by the arrival in southern Afghanistan of another would-be king, Abdul Haq. Unlike Karzai, Haq was the quintessential mujahideen commander, right down to his garrulous bustling persona and his missing right heel that had been blown off during a battle against a Soviet tank column in the 1980s. He conducted his later battles against the Russians from horseback as a result of his injury, which only added to his swashbuckling image. Haq also spoke flawless English, and had a professed western bent that included a taste for Johnnie Walker whiskey.

Toward the end of the war against the Soviets, Haq had fallen out with the ISI over its growing support for Islamist warlords, at the expense of Afghans with more nationalist and secular inclinations. He knew why: The ISI found Islamists to be blinded by their religious views and more easily manipulated. Soon Haq was also at odds with the CIA, which he blamed for deserting Afghanistan. The CIA, for its part, considered Haq a loose cannon, more interested in grandstanding on the sidelines than in fighting. "Hollywood Haq" became his nickname after he was pictured with President Ronald Reagan and British Prime Minister Margaret Thatcher.

Such grandstanding sometimes worked against Haq. After 9/11, he had attracted the support of several well-placed Republicans and two millionaire commodity traders from Chicago, Joe and Jim Ritchie. At the CIA headquarters in Islamabad, the whiff of Washington politics was unlikely to endear Haq to those running covert missions inside Afghanistan. When he presented himself in Islamabad in October, the CIA treated him with skepticism. No matter that Haq shared Grenier's view that, given time, moderate elements within the Taliban might be persuaded to switch sides, provided the bombing campaign didn't push them into the hands of the hard-liners. Like Karzai, he was offered a satellite phone, and not much else.

On October 24, a little over two weeks after Karzai had headed back to Afghanistan, Haq entered southeastern Afghanistan near Jalalabad on horseback with a handful of followers. He'd spent the previous weeks in touch with Taliban commanders in Kabul and the eastern part of the country. Several of these men had fought with Haq against the Soviets, and he believed they could be persuaded to switch sides without a fight.

Haq was in for disappointment. He had barely crossed the border before he was detected by Taliban fighters. The ISI may have tipped them off to dispose of an awkward critic, Haq's supporters later alleged. Attempting to flee up a steep hillside, Haq dismounted, and as his retreat turned to a hobble on the rough terrain, he surrendered. The next day the Taliban took Haq to Kabul and subsequently hanged him near the site of a recent US air strike.

Haq's death had one enduring significance: It alerted Washington that moderate Pashtun leaders prepared to stand up to the Taliban were in short supply. After Haq's demise, only one remained: Hamid Karzai.

By early November, Karzai and his remaining men had split into small groups to avoid capture. The Taliban had sent fighters into the mountains to track him down. Karzai hid out in villages he thought to be safe, but the Taliban soon found him. It was clear to the CIA officer keeping tabs on Karzai's movements from Pakistan via satellite phone conversations that Karzai's rebellion was petering out.[7] With few men, limited supplies, and grudging local support, it was just a matter of time before he would be killed or captured.[8]

The CIA officer feared that Karzai would meet the same fate as Haq unless the US intervened. Over a series of phone calls to his bosses, including CIA director George Tenet, he urged action. Karzai was not as charismatic as Haq; neither did he command a large following. Yet, during his phone conversations with Karzai, the spy had detected a rare and sophisticated understanding of American policy—even as the Taliban was hot on his heels. Karzai might not have the strength to oust Mullah Omar himself, but the US military was taking care of that. Karzai might be the Afghan to turn to once the fighting stopped.[9]

Staging a rescue mission was not as easy as the CIA officer had hoped, an operation that should fall under the purview of US special forces. The US military had taken weeks to deploy even its elite forces to the region, and the teams that had arrived in Afghanistan under Colonel John Mulholland were acting too cautiously in the opinion of many CIA officers as well as the unit's own soldiers. The spy who was in touch with Karzai urged Mulholland to take more risks, and after waiting a few agonizing days, the colonel agreed.[10]

On November 3, US special forces in Blackhawk helicopters were sent to pick up Karzai and return him to Pakistan. A few hours later, a shaken Karzai and seven Afghan fighters arrived at Jacobabad air base just over the border in Pakistan. He had dreamed of winning American support, and at last he had it.

The US military wanted to keep secret Karzai's presence in their compound on the Jacobabad base, lest the Pashtun tribes interpret his flight to safety as a sign of weakness. The subterfuge lasted barely a day before Donald Rumsfeld let slip Karzai's location at a press conference. Rumsfeld quickly backtracked, although if anything the revelation bolstered Karzai's bid: For Afghans looking to oppose the Taliban, the only candidate worth backing was the one the US was already behind. The same day, UN Envoy Lakhdar Brahimi raised Karzai's name as a possible leader as foreign ministers gathered in New York ahead of the Bonn conference scheduled for a few weeks later, where they were to endorse Brahimi's plan to create a new Afghan government.[11]

Karzai's reputation was rapidly growing among western officials, but back at the air base in Pakistan he was still establishing his credentials with the soldiers, who were cut off from diplomatic gossip. Karzai was assigned an eleven-man team of special forces and CIA operatives, similar to those deployed with the Northern Alliance. The unit's commander was a rangy thirty-year-old officer from Honolulu, Hawaii, Captain Jason Amerine. Before meeting Karzai, Amerine had expected a typical Afghan warlord, power-hungry and unscrupulous; he had even bought a large military knife (which he dubbed "the big fucking knife") to present to Karzai, a typical gift for an Afghan warlord. Amerine was surprised when he first bumped into Karzai in the hallway of the American base on the evening of his arrival. The Afghan was delicate and middle-aged, with a neatly trimmed beard; he seemed to be lost in thought and not a man to whom you gave a knife.[12]

The next morning, Amerine formally met Karzai and his small band of tribal followers in the building's conference room. The young officer earnestly laid out his mission: "We're here to learn what it is that you want to accomplish in southern Afghanistan and how we can support you."[13]

Karzai closed his eyes, raised his chin, and let out a deep breath. Lowering his face, eyes open again, he said, "That is something I have waited a long, long time to hear."[14]

Over the next two hours, Karzai laid out his plan to return to Tarin Kowt. The fighting would be limited, he said. The Taliban were not a monolithic enemy. Most were compelled by circumstance into taking arms. Karzai remembered the crowds of young men that used to form outside his family's home near Kandahar, seeking service or help raising funds for a dowry.

"These young men will be the first to lay down their weapons and join us," he insisted.

Amerine admired Karzai's vision but was not sure Karzai would be able to avoid a fight upon returning. Even with the support of his special forces team, Amerine suspected that Karzai's limited band of followers would not be enough. They would need to raise a guerrilla army to fight their way into Tarin Kowt and beyond—and hope they could get enough men together before the Taliban realized what was going on and came to get them. It was a high-risk strategy, even with American backing.

A few days later, as they were preparing to depart for Afghanistan, Karzai received a phone call from a member of Mullah Omar's inner circle, Tayib Agha, which seemed to raise the prospect of a negotiated settlement with the Taliban. Agha wanted to find out where Karzai was, and how he saw the fighting ending.

The conversation was certainly not unusual. War in Afghanistan was rarely waged between strangers. Savage and capricious though outbreaks of violence might be, a back channel was always open, enabling combatants to parlay should one side weaken. Of course, if Mullah Omar did get hold of Karzai, the Taliban would probably string him from a tree, hence the interest in his current location. But if Karzai should prove successful with his rebellion, then they would talk. Karzai had already chosen an old tribal ally from the Arghandab, a grizzled former mujahideen commander named Mullah Naquib, to serve as an interlocutor.

"What do you think?" Karzai asked Amerine when he next saw him. In the few days the two men had spent together on the base, they had formed a ready friendship. Amerine, the son of an anthropologist, was not a man to push his point of view, but when asked, he offered a deep current of thought.

Amerine replied cautiously, aware that he might be making US policy on the fly: "If they are willing to negotiate, then maybe you should talk to them further. Once the Taliban collapses in Kandahar, many of them are going to keep fighting as insurgents if you can't find a way to achieve some kind of reconciliation."

"Rumsfeld expects unconditional surrender," Karzai said, "and so does the Northern Alliance. I might be able to calm the Northern Alliance, but I can't risk alienating the US by negotiating with the Taliban."

Amerine countered: "Ask yourself, Hamid: once the Taliban are defeated, do you think they will go away? Or do you think they will regroup and do exactly what we are doing—fighting against the government your Loya Jirga [traditional tribal gathering] elects?"[15]

That was their last significant conversation before the operation began. On the evening of November 14, two Blackhawk helicopters touched down in a storm of dust on a deserted hillside in southern Afghanistan. In the darkened hold, squeezed between his tribal supporters and bulky American soldiers, sat Hamid Karzai, wrapped in a woolen shawl. It wasn't quite the triumphant return to southern Afghanistan at the head of a Pashtun army he'd envisioned, but he was right that once the tribes saw he was backed by the US military they'd flock to his cause. The following day an uprising began in Tarin Kowt. The Taliban governor was hanged from a lamppost and his supporters driven out. That same evening, Karzai was installed in the province's main government headquarters.

Karzai had also been correct to place his faith in US force. After he was ensconced in Tarin Kowt, the Taliban dispatched a fifty-strong convoy of trucks packed with fighters from Kandahar to retake the town. When they emerged from the high mountains, US F-18 fighter jets picked them off with laser-guided missiles. A single Taliban truck made it to the outskirts of the town before being forced back by the makeshift defense of special forces and tribal supporters that Amerine had organized.

Karzai wisely kept his head down during the fighting, although that didn't stop wildly inflated stories about his role fending off the Taliban from spreading around the town. Indeed he was about to be reminded that the perception of strength often matters more than the reality.

The following day Karzai called Mullah Naquib, an ally and the leader of the Alakozai tribe outside Kandahar who was in regular contact with the Taliban. He sensed from Naquib's excited tone that Mullah Omar's calculations were shifting. Naquib confirmed that the pressure on the Taliban was mounting in Kandahar and they were ready to talk, possibly even negotiate surrender. It wasn't just Karzai's victory in Tarin Kowt that was forcing Mullah Omar's hand; the US bombing raids around Kandahar were also taking their toll. Mullah Omar had sent his family into exile, and ever since US special forces had raided his compound on the edge of the city, he had become a ghost, flitting between safe houses in the city. US air strikes had forced the rest of the leadership into hiding. The regime's defense minister, Mullah Obaidullah, and Mullah Abdul Ghani Baradar, a key military adviser from the same Popalzai tribe as Karzai, were leading the discussion with Naquib.[16]

The Taliban just needed a little more prodding, Naquib insisted. Karzai and Amerine made plans to push south to the Arghandab River, in the valley from which Karzai's family hailed—and within striking distance of Kandahar.

On November 27, 2001, as Karzai glimpsed victory, delegates began arriving in the sleepy German town of Bonn to shape Afghanistan's political future. Karzai's name was already on everyone's lips. In Turkey and Pakistan, the recently appointed US Envoy to Afghanistan, Jim Dobbins, heard Karzai mentioned as a possible leader as the American toured the region ahead of the conference. Karzai's popularity reflected some regional players' desire to support, at least publicly, whomever the US favored. Karzai's earlier weakness—his relatively anonymous career during the Soviet occupation and mujahideen period—now became a virtue. Because outside powers had never deemed Karzai worthy of funding, he was no one's stooge. In Dobbins's mind, that meant Karzai could be the Americans' man.[17]

On the opening day of the conference in Bonn's baroque Petersberg hotel, the UN arranged for Karzai to address delegates from the US special forces' dusty command post in Tarin Kowt. The besuited exiles and gnarly warlords listened dutifully as Karzai's disembodied voice filled the conference room: "We are one nation, one culture. We are united, not divided. We all believe in an Islam that is a religion of tolerance."[18]

Dobbins knew there was still plenty of arm-twisting to be done before the delegates lined up behind Karzai. A veteran of the Balkans, Dobbins was a man of quiet intensity, who was more likely to wear down his opponents than win them over with the force of his oratory. At fifty-eight, Dobbins had been preparing to leave the Foreign Service when he received the Afghan brief. After his success in the Balkans implementing a peace deal, and then a stint in Haiti, it was his highest-profile assignment yet. He liked to think of himself as a pragmatist, although like many Balkans veterans he brought to Afghanistan a number of assumptions about the West's ability to nation-build.

Dobbins's priority at Bonn was to reach a power-sharing agreement between the two main factions gathered there. On one side there was the Tajik-dominated Northern Alliance, whose militias held the Afghan capital. Kabul was theirs for the time being. However, some of the leadership had conceded that the head of the country's new government would have to be led by a Pashtun, given the historical precedents and their majority in the country. The foreign minister, Abdullah Abdullah, had already indicated that Karzai would be an acceptable candidate, but the Northern Alliance would have to cede considerable power— namely key cabinet positions—if the agreement that emerged were to be credible. In addition, there was the prickly subject of the one-time Afghan president Burhanuddin Rabbani, nominally of the Northern Alliance faction, but really a force unto himself. He had recently reoccupied the presidential palace in Kabul, and indicated he considered himself Afghanistan's rightful leader.

On the other side of the room were supporters of the king, known at the UN as the "Rome group." Their outlook was not quite as pragmatic as the Northern Alliance's. The Rome group had a long-cherished dream of restoring the king to power. But Dobbins and his counterpart from the White House, Zalmay Khalilzad, had met the eighty-five-year-old monarch before the conference and concluded that the old man had little to offer a future government. Instead, he would be conferred the right to nominate his successor. Unfortunately, the king's followers at Bonn showed little inclination to hand over the throne to a distant ally like Karzai, perhaps realizing that if they gave up their claim now, their limited following within Afghanistan gave them little chance of reclaiming power. Instead the head of the royalists, an urbane Uzbek named Abdul Sattar Sirat, promptly nominated himself, in the face of opposition from the Northern Alliance.

The resulting standoff between the royalists and the Northern Alliance dominated several days of the conference, with Sirat giving up his claim only in the early hours of the last day after Khalilzad, an Afghan émigré himself, locked the two groups in a conference room and by turns threatened and cajoled them.

The international community hailed the agreement that finally emerged from the Bonn conference as a success. Karzai was appointed head of the interim government, a decision that appeared to install in Kabul a moderate Pashtun who could unite the country's south without antagonizing its other ethnic groups. At the same time, the Northern Alliance relinquished several cabinet positions, reducing the impression that a Tajik cabal had taken over. Rabbani, the troublesome former president who had recently occupied his old quarters at the palace in Kabul, had also been persuaded to drop his claims.[19] In addition, a political timetable was set, starting with a Loya Jirga, or tribal council, to ratify the government in the summer, followed by the drafting of a constitution and elections.

Yet amid the congratulations there was some criticism of the Bonn agreement. The loudest protests came from the influential western proponents of humanitarian intervention and the aid world. They had grown into a powerful constituency in Washington and London in the 1990s following the West's perceived failures to respond to the acts of ethnic cleansing in the Balkans and Rwanda. They shared a belief in universal human rights and the duty of developed nations to help less fortunate societies. To many in this community, the mere presence at Bonn of warlords like Dostum, the Uzbek leader who was accused of corruption and human rights abuses, including the deaths of hundreds of Taliban prisoners of war, was a dangerously retrograde step that would pave the way for the Taliban's return. "From the start, I had suspected warlordism was going to be the most serious problem facing the new Afghan-istan," wrote Sarah Chayes, a prominent journalist–turned–aid worker.[20]

Others like Thomas Ruttig, who served on UN Envoy Lakhdar Brahimi's team, felt that an Afghan settlement may not have been possible without the warlords. A former East German diplomat and fluent Pashtu speaker, Rut-tig understood that the most important constituencies in Afghanistan were represented by men with guns.[21] The UN duly set up a process to disarm the militias and bring them into the political process. Indeed Ruttig argued that Bonn's failure was that it did not include *enough* warlords—that is, those tribal and religious leaders from the Taliban heartlands.

Haji Qadir, one of the few attendees who commanded a sizeable following among the southern tribes, promptly quit in protest at the lack of Pashtun representation. His worst fears were confirmed by the eventual shape of the agreement: Although the Northern Alliance had given up several ministries, they still had seventeen of the twenty-nine cabinet posts, including the key triumvirate of defense, interior, and foreign affairs. The other posts largely went to well-educated technocrats. The only recognition of the Taliban and the Pashtun tribes aligned with them was added at the last minute as a clause requesting help in reintegrating mujahideen fighters into any new Afghan security forces.

Ruttig argued in vain to increase Pashtun representation, in particular to give greater powers to the king, a Pashtun himself, who commanded genuine respect in the south, and whose empowerment might have offset the appear-ance of a Tajik takeover of the national government.[22]

Other initiatives largely petered out or were ineffective. One bunch of delegates at the conference—the so-called Peshawar group—was meant to bring together southern tribal leaders and moderate Taliban, but few leaders of any real standing in the south had been forthcoming. The closest appears to have been a mooted invitation to the conference for Jalaluddin Haqqani, a powerful former mujahideen commander and former Taliban minister whose tribe controlled crucial territory on both sides of the border. At one stage in the autumn of 2001, Haqqani had appeared ready to attend the conference, only to withdraw when he saw that a rival militia leader from his clan—one of the few armed followers of the king—had been invited. Haqqani refused to switch sides, with damaging consequences for the coun-try's future.[23] A group of moderate ex-Taliban also set up a political party, the Jamiat-e-Khuddam ul-Furqan, with some support from the ISI, but they were largely ignored.[24]

The result of the West's ultimate disinterest in finding Pashtun voices seeded the idea that the Bonn agreement was a victor's peace, and that by excluding the Taliban, the international community and the new government in Kabul were also turning their backs on the Pashtun. The Taliban had been given the opportunity to hand over bin Laden before the Americans had entered Afghanistan, and the regime had demurred; now the south of the country was reaping the consequences.

I f the failure to include the Taliban at Bonn was the "original sin" of the effort to restore Afghanistan, as Brahimi later put it, a far greater omission was to ignore the Taliban's unilateral offer of peace when it came.

Just as Grenier had predicted, the prospect of their imminent demise had finally brought the Taliban to the negotiating table. By early December, Taliban control barely extended beyond Kandahar. Karzai was advancing on the city from the north, while another CIA-backed warlord, Gul Agha Sherzai, was making progress toward Kandahar from the south. Fighting had been limited, although that didn't stop Sherzai from boasting of smashing the Taliban, to the apparent delight of his American advisers.[25]

Confronted by the two usurpers, Mullah Omar made clear he'd rather do business with Karzai than with the Americans. He instructed defense minister Mullah Obaidullah to seek out Karzai and "do what needed to be done" when it came to negotiations, according to one source privy to the discussions.[26] Obaidullah arranged to meet Afghanistan's new leader in the town of Shah-wali Kot, one hundred miles north of Kandahar. The meeting was scheduled to take place on December 5, the same day the Bonn delegates were to appoint Karzai as their interim president. The timing proved inauspicious. In the past two weeks, since the capture of Tarin Kowt, Karzai's forces had made slow progress. US special forces did not want to expose their prize asset to a risky campaign, and Karzai himself was content to rally the tribes and reach out to the Taliban. But Sherzai's rush to Kandahar had changed that equation. Karzai knew that whatever titles might be bestowed upon him at Bonn, it was just as important that he build on his reputation among Afghans. It was crucial that he be seen delivering the city from the Taliban. Whoever occupied the principal city of the south, and the capital of the Pashtuns, would hold considerable sway.

Karzai had reached the town of Shahwalikot on December 2, a few days before his scheduled meeting with the Taliban defense minister. Local forces had put up a fierce resistance—the town controlled a key crossing over the

Arghandab River as it wound across the desert to Kandahar—but they had ultimately given way to US special forces and the swelling ranks of Karzai's militia.
Karzai's new headquarters was an abandoned school on the town's outskirts, behind which rose a small hill with a dilapidated mudbrick compound at the crest.
The US special forces accompanying Karzai had dubbed these ruins "the Alamo."

Karzai's American entourage had undergone a crucial change just before
this operation. There had been concern in Washington that a lowly captain,
Amerine, was not senior enough to deal with Afghanistan's interim leader, so
a higher-ranking officer, Lieutenant Colonel David Fox, and his headquarters
staff had recently helicoptered in to take over as Karzai's mentor. Amerine
took the news stoically, but his worst fears about the arrival of a headquarters
eager to prove its credentials were soon confirmed.

On the morning of Karzai's scheduled meeting with Obaidullah, Fox's staff
was busily calling in air strikes on a ridgeline a mile away, despite little evidence that the Taliban were anywhere near. A newly arrived twenty-five-year-
old sergeant, Jim Price, was crouched over his radio in the roofless remains
of the compound on the Alamo, coordinating with the F-18 jets overhead.
Several of Karzai's Afghan militia had climbed onto mudbrick walls of the
Alamo to watch; even Karzai himself made a brief appearance before heading
back into the school building to meet a tribal delegation.

The first of the two bombs headquarters had called in hit the ridge, but
then Price's GPS batteries went dead. He replaced them and repowered the
device without realizing the coordinates had reset to his own location. After
he read out the numbers to the B-52 pilot circling overhead, the pilot asked
him to confirm his own location. Price refused; the previous week a bomber in
Mazar-e-Sharif had accidentally dropped a bomb on the sender's coordinates.
He wasn't about to make the same mistake.

Thirty seconds later a 2,000-pound bomb landed on the Alamo with a
shattering roar that ripped a crater in the floor of the roofless building and
sent a shower of earth, guts, and body parts spraying into the air. Amerine had
been twenty yards away, planning the next stage of the advance toward Kandahar. The blast threw him to the floor. Staggering to his feet, he confronted
a hellish bombscape of body parts, covered with gray dust and blood that was
pooling at the bottom of the crater. Survivors amid the tangle began to move
and groan. Despite being peppered with shrapnel, Amerine raced down the
hill looking for medics and to call in helicopter support. He spotted Karzai
emerging from the school building with his bodyguard, looking dazed but
unhurt. Thank God, Amerine thought, before ducking into the makeshift
medical center beside the school building.

"What happened?" Karzai asked a special forces soldier in his entourage. He could glimpse the horror up the hill, but he was wisely kept away as medics tended to the injured. Two US special forces had already been confirmed dead, as well as half a dozen Afghan militiamen.

Fifteen minutes later, Karzai was nervously pacing when his satellite phone rang. It was BBC reporter Lyse Doucet, a friend from his days in Pakistan, informing him that the Bonn conference had just concluded and he had been appointed the interim leader of Afghanistan. Karzai mumbled a brief reply. His first thoughts were with his dead and dying men, although he could be forgiven for dwelling on what would have happened had he stepped outside to take the call a quarter of an hour before.

As Amerine and the wounded were evacuated by helicopter, Karzai's thoughts slowly turned to the Taliban delegation that even now was driving along the Arghandab River to Shahwalikot. Mullah Naquib, accompanying the Taliban, was soon on the phone seeking assurance that the distant bomb blasts they could hear were not US efforts to target them. Karzai assured the Taliban that they were under his protection, although he double-checked with Fox just to be sure. He didn't want to jeopardize the most important meeting of the war to date, and he knew from Amerine that US attitudes toward the Taliban had only hardened since hostilities had begun.

A few hours later, Karzai greeted the Taliban delegation as they climbed out of their dusty SUVs and adjusted their turbans. The defense minister, Mullah Obaidullah, led the delegation, courteously referring to Karzai as "Chairman," the title just bestowed on him at Bonn. The group moved to a dusty schoolhouse nearby for their meeting.

The fact that the Taliban had been trying to kill Karzai only a few days ago—even putting a 10 million Pakistani rupee ($110,000) reward on his head in late November—lent a certain tension to the gathering. Yet it soon became clear that the Taliban's thinking had been transformed. Obaidullah had carried with him a letter from the Taliban that accepted Karzai's leadership and acknowledged that "the Islamic Emirate [the official name of the Taliban government] had no chance of surviving."[27]

The subject of what would happen to senior Taliban members, and in particular Mullah Omar, arose early in the meeting. The Taliban was prepared to relinquish all claims to the country, and in return they wanted to be allowed to return to their villages. Karzai was magnanimous. Provided Mullah Omar also agreed to these terms, Karzai said, he would be allowed to remain in Kandahar under the supervision of Mullah Naquib.[28] He made the offer to every Taliban member in the room.

Obaidullah had brought with him the long, pear-shaped breads of Afghanistan. He now signaled for them to be fetched from his truck and shared as a token of the agreement. As plastic sheets were laid on the floor to serve as a tablecloth and tea poured, a delighted Karzai led the discussions, which ranged from the size of the state pension Taliban leaders might get as former officials, to the number of bodyguards they would receive, to whether they would get either one or two government vehicles.

There has since been debate over the exact terms of the deal, with Karzai later denying that Mullah Omar was offered amnesty.[29] But perhaps the terms didn't matter so much as the fact of the deal itself. For the experienced Afghan watcher Michael Semple, this is certainly the important point: a deal was cut, Afghan-style. "Karzai was being pragmatic," said Semple later. "The Taliban had surrendered, so why not bring them into your camp?"[30]

The real question was whether the US would support the deal, so for the moment, the American officers on the ground were at least allowing the discussion to take place. Outside the school building, Taliban fighters and American soldiers were viewing each other with curiosity. "One minute you're shooting at them, and the next minute they are now your allies and your friends," recalled Fox, the special forces commander. "We've got these former Taliban looking at us and going, 'So this is what an American looks like. Oh, he's got two legs and puts his pants on the same way we do.' So it was just kind of an unnerving situation."[31]

But once Obaidullah had left after the customary flurry of handshakes and kisses and Karzai informed the Americans of the terms of the deal, Fox expressed skepticism, as did his chain of command.[32] After learning of the discussion, US Defense Secretary Donald Rumsfeld appeared to reject the idea at a press conference. Letting Mullah Omar "live in dignity" as opposed to in custody was "unfeasible," Rumsfeld said. Under the rubric of the "War on Terror," Mullah Omar was the enemy, and making deals with him and his ilk would only embolden other rogue nations. For Karzai the message was painfully clear: The Americans expected to call the shots, even as they espoused a hands-off approach.

Fox was directed to tell Karzai that such an arrangement with the Taliban was not in American interests.[33] Karzai could have pushed back. But he remained silent. Perhaps his sense of indebtedness to the US discouraged him. What is certain is that this was the first indication that the new Afghan president could be easily compromised. Indeed Karzai swiftly fell for the American hype that the Taliban had been vanquished. After the Taliban leadership departed for Pakistan and their military threat disappeared, he seemed to forget about the deal he had struck in that Shahwalikot schoolroom.[34]

Even if Karzai had fought back against American pressure to disavow the deal, the terms of the agreement may not have been deliverable. This is not to say that the Taliban would have reneged on their end of the bargain; quite the opposite. The fact that there were subsequent Taliban peace initiatives in January 2002, and again the following summer, suggests the Taliban's genuine desire to make peace. Of course, they might still have turned against Karzai's government at some later date, but restarting a movement that had symbolically surrendered would have been difficult, and Karzai could have ensured that many of those who reconciled with the Afghan government stayed firmly in its pocket.

O n December 6, Karzai's rival, Gul Agha Sherzai, had reached the outskirts of Kandahar. The special forces team with Sherzai was meant to keep him beyond the city limits to allow Karzai to claim the glory of liberating Kandahar. However, Sherzai's chief US adviser, known as Captain Smith, appeared only too happy to give his charge free rein. "The whole team was itching to get into the city," special forces team leader Captain Smith later recalled.[35]

That evening, Sherzai seized the governor's palace in Kandahar, and the Taliban's leadership fled the city. The following morning, Karzai called Sherzai and ordered him to leave the palace, but according to one account, Sherzai scoffed at the idea. "I don't take orders from Hamid Karzai," he said.[36]

When Karzai arrived in Kandahar on December 7, he was forced to take up residence in Mullah Omar's compound on the outskirts of the city. A potentially dangerous standoff ensued. Karzai had promised the governorship to Mullah Naquib, but Sherzai wasn't about to give up his prize. Neither was the US military prepared to weigh in on one side or the other. At a humiliating meeting in the governor's palace, Sherzai greeted Karzai as he would a supplicant, rather than the country's head. When Sherzai waved his pudgy fingers at Naquib and accused him of being a Taliban, Karzai was silent.

Karzai left the meeting fuming and ready to turn on Sherzai, but ultimately Fox placated him. "Do you want to start a civil war?" the special forces officer asked Karzai. "You are on the verge of starting a war."[37] The Afghan leader relented.

The aid worker Sarah Chayes later judged this moment to be one of the key battles that determined Karzai's legacy and "the kind of Afghan nation

Captain Jason Amerine guided Hamid Karzai from fugitive guerrilla leader
all the way to his appointment to become the country's first leader after the
Taliban. Here the two men are reunited in the president's palace following
Karzai's elevation. (Photo courtesy of Jason Amerine)

that will be built under US aegis."[38] In her interpretation, Karzai represented
a progressive future that so many Afghans were striving for, while Sherzai
was a return to the bad old days of the "mujahideen nights." Yet while the
stakes were certainly high that December morning, it's a mistake to project
too closely western notions of the dichotomy between anarchic warlords and
the virtues of Afghan government. From Karzai's perspective, the battle with
Sherzai was a blow not because a warlord gained control of Kandahar, but
because a warlord outside his network of tribal patronage had done so. His
chosen candidate, Mullah Naquib, would have been more conciliatory toward
the Taliban but may not have ruled any differently than Sherzai, judging by
the allegations of corruption that surrounded Naquib's clan.

The showdown in Kandahar revealed a fundamental misunderstanding on
Karzai's part as to where power lay in his relationship with the US. A different,
more daring leader might have called upon the Americans to support him,
whether in his dealings with the Taliban or in his battle with Sherzai. Instead,
Karzai betrayed his own agenda—and in doing so revealed his callowness.

But at the start of that indispensable relationship between Karzai and the
West, neither side saw the other's shortcomings—or realized that the Taliban
they'd so effectively shoved off the stage would be biding their time in the wings.

CHAPTER 5

At the Gates

As the international community celebrated Hamid Karzai's rise to power and the Taliban's demise, the man who had waged war on America had eluded capture. Ever since the fall of Kabul to Tajik militias on November 13, 2001, the Northern Alliance had been tracking Osama bin Laden's movements. On November 10, bin Laden was spotted in the Saudi-funded Islamic Studies Institute in Jalalabad, eastern Afghanistan, giving an apocalyptic speech to his admirers with his usual softly spoken vitriol. The day of Kabul's fall, the Northern Alliance's tribal connections in the east spied the al-Qa'eda leader's convoy fleeing the city on the unpaved roads that led toward the Tora Bora mountain range.

Gary Berntsen became the CIA's station chief in Kabul soon after the city's fall on November 13. As soon as he heard where bin Laden was heading, he knew how the battle was going to play out. In 1987, bin Laden had made his name fighting off a Soviet assault from a mountainous hideout near Tora Bora. Bin Laden had chosen the same area to make another last stand, Berntsen reckoned.

A hulking Long Islander, Berntsen had recently taken over from Gary Schroen as the CIA's point man. He'd been on bin Laden's trail for years, most recently as part of a CIA snatch team that had tried to capture the Saudi dissident in 2000—a scheme that had reduced the Clinton administration to its usual indecision. After 9/11, the instructions of Cofer Black at the National Counterterrorism Center couldn't have been clearer: Bring me bin Laden's head in a box packed with ice.[1]

The initial plan to kill or capture bin Laden called for special forces to train Afghan pursuit teams. However, Berntsen had already identified one Afghan warlord named Hazrat Ali, whose Pashai tribe came from the south but was affiliated with the Northern Alliance and was ready to accept a CIA team or US special forces unit, whichever came first. The special forces were playing an increasingly influential role in the war, but in Berntsen's opinion they were still being used with excessive caution. He wasn't prepared to wait for the military to get their act together, not when he had a promising lead like Ali waiting to be exploited. The twenty-nine-year-old Ali had provided most of the intelligence so far on bin Laden's whereabouts, although his help hadn't come cheap: The CIA handed over $4 million in cash to the warlord, who flounced around Jalalabad with a posse of young men decked in flowers.

On November 18, Berntsen dispatched an eight-man Jawbreaker team to link up with Ali's rough outfit in Jalalabad, believing that while they would not be enough to take on al-Qa'eda, they could pin down bin Laden until more forces arrived. "If we don't take care of this final part for ourselves, it won't get done," Berntsen reflected, given the CIA's earlier trouble corralling local forces, and his own preference to stick in the knife himself.[2]

Ali's men guided the CIA team up the rock-strewn valley that led to Tora Bora. Afghanistan's uplands can be densely wooded with chir pines, larch, and junipers, along with thickets of rhododendrons and hawthorn bushes. But here the trees were stunted, and the greenery limited to a few patchy fields on either side of a river. The rough track the American and Afghan contingent had been on followed one side of the river as it split and rejoined among islands of pebbles. Just before one sharp river bend, the contingent slowed. Edging over a shoulder of land that blocked their view up the valley, they spied a cluster of mudbrick buildings in the distance. Command posts and machine-gun nests marked the entrance to a military camp on the opposite embankment. Armed fighters milled around outside. Above the valley floor there were gloomy openings in the rock-faced hillsides that suggested caves lay beyond.

The small CIA team sent back a hurried and elated message to Kabul. They'd found bin Laden's headquarters. Berntsen wasted no time in ordering an air strike within twenty minutes. The team on the ground in Tora Bora briefly glimpsed the first rocket, a streak of light against the darkening mountain walls, before a ball of flames ripped through the camp. As bombers joined the queue circling overhead, a succession of missiles followed. In Kabul, Berntsen slammed his fist on his desk as the news came in. He doubted they'd killed bin Laden with their first strikes—he surely had hollowed out some bunker inside the mountain—but the payback had started.

Berntsen's efforts were appreciated back in Washington. The next day he received a belated call from the deputy head of the National Counterterrorism

Center, Henry Crumpton. "Gary," he said, clearing his throat, "it's apparent that you have a team up near Tora Bora and they're calling in a lot of air strikes."

So far, Berntsen had not asked for higher approval for the strikes, figuring it was better to take action than to risk politics getting in the way. "Yeah," he replied. "That's us."

"Good job," Crumpton said with a chuckle. "I'm proud of you. Keep it up."[3]

Berntsen didn't mind the plaudits but what he needed was boots on the ground. The bombing had driven al-Qa'eda fighters from the valley floor into cave complexes high up the mountain's southern flank. But as Berntsen had feared, Hazrat Ali's pursuit was halfhearted: His men would engage al-Qa'eda fighters in the occasional skirmish before mounting a full-scale retreat as night descended. It was the Islamic holiday of Ramadan, Ali sheepishly explained to the Jawbreaker team, and his fighters needed to return to their families for tea, pomegranates, and prayer.

To make matters worse, by late November 2001, British intelligence had muscled in on Berntsen's operation, introducing into the fray another warlord named Haji Mohammed Zaman Ghansjarik. A dissolute former mujahideen commander, Zaman had been marinating in Dijon, southern France, for the past decade. The British intended for him to link up with Hazrat Ali as part of an "eastern alliance." Other members of this unsavory band included self-confessed al-Qa'eda sympathizers such as Mohammed Younes Khalis, who had invited bin Laden to return to Afghanistan in 1996, and whose son was a prominent militant. Some of Zaman's own Khungani tribe had been on al-Qa'eda's payroll at one time.[4] The presence of Zaman's and Ali's men in a US-backed coalition suggested the extent the old order had been turned upside down. Their rapid shift in allegiance also raised questions about how deep their new loyalties were.

The only quality the Americans could count on from these men was their own self-interest and petty rivalry. The two self-styled generals Zaman and Ali promptly were soon bickering. On any given morning, they were usually show-boating before the television cameras of the small press pool that assembled at the valley entrance. When the warlords' men did venture up the valley to al-Qa'eda positions, they were just as likely to end up pointing their guns at each other as at the presumed mutual enemy. The tribal fighters also shook down US units for any loose change, brazenly robbing their erstwhile allies in the knowledge the Americans wouldn't fight back when so much rested on their alliance.[5]

This was fighting, Afghan-style: "More symbolic than savage, more duty than deadly, more for spoils than scalps," noted a special forces commander

Osama bin Laden hid in the Tora Bora mountain range after 9/11 and managed to escape US and Afghan forces when they confronted him. (Photo by Specialist Ken Scar)

involved in the events who later wrote a book under the pen name Dalton Fury. "It was not intended for anyone to really get hurt. The skirmishes would last a few hours, then the fighters would do some looting and call it a day and retreat back down the ridgelines, giving back to al-Qa'eda any of the day's hard-earned terrain."[6] Neither did they want to weaken their forces by engaging in actual combat. The real prize for the warlords was not bin Laden but control of the nearby city of Jalalabad, along with any money they could pressure out of the opposing factions.

Unless US forces were quickly deployed, bin Laden was going to slip away, Berntsen believed. At that point, the most readily available supply of troops was US special forces, a branch of the army, which acted under its own chain of command. Berntsen had already asked the contingent's commander, Colonel John Mulholland, for a unit to accompany his CIA team into Tora Bora. Mulholland had refused, citing safety concerns. Now that the bombing in the valley had commenced and Washington had begun to take note, Mulholland agreed to send thirty men to the front—but insisted they partner with local forces to boost their manpower and give the semblance that the Afghans were leading the operation.

Berntsen could scarcely hide his frustration, and instead turned to the army itself. On December 3, he wrote a request for eight hundred US Army rangers to seal the area, principally the mountain passes behind Tora Bora that led to Pakistan. The 3rd Battalion, 75th Ranger Regiment, was stationed three hours away by plane in Oman. Two hundred of them had already positioned themselves outside Kandahar, having conducted a parachute assault on Mullah Omar's compound at the start of the campaign, and had spent the past two weeks guarding an airfield. The rest of the rangers could be deployed to the country within forty-eight hours.[7]

Berntsen's boss, Henry Crumpton, took his request to General Tommy Franks, the Centcom commander of the overall campaign. A self-styled "good ol' boy" from Texas, Franks had risen far on the strength of his back-slapping bonhomie. He opposed deploying the rangers, however, arguing that the "small footprint" approach had worked so far, and it was important for the locals to be seen siding against al-Qa'eda. He was also aware of the dangers of sending in hundreds of foreign troops.[8] As Franks explained later to the US Senate Armed Services Committee on July 31, 2002: "I was very mindful of the Soviet experience of more than ten years, having introduced 620,000 troops into Afghanistan, more than 15,000 of them being killed, more than 55,000 of them being wounded."[9]

Even had Franks acted on Berntsen's request, subsequent studies of the battle at Tora Bora suggest that eight hundred rangers would not have been enough to trap al-Qa'eda, given the dozens of possible escape routes—106 passes led to Pakistan, according to Michael O'Hanlon of the Brookings Institution—and the ease of hiding in the boulder-strewn landscape. At least 3,000 American troops would have been necessary, and even then there was no guarantee they would catch bin Laden. The al-Qa'eda leader would almost certainly have been aware of the influx of troops and sought to escape before they got into position.[10]

As it turned out, bin Laden didn't need to sneak along perilous mountain passes to escape. He most likely walked straight through US lines, back down the valley toward Jalalabad courtesy of America's Afghan allies, before heading east toward Kunar province.[11]

If bin Laden did slip through American lines, then some sort of under-handed deal with either Hazrat Ali and Haji Zaman or some of their minions was surely to blame. Neither man wanted a fight to the death, not when money could be made helping the terrorist group's members escape. Both were in regular contact with al-Qa'eda on walkie-talkies. As soon as they had closed in on the cave complex, it appears that the warlords began seeking to outmaneuver each other to help bin Laden escape.

The warlords' easy exchanges with the terrorist group were disconcerting for the special forces team that arrived in Tora Bora on December 7. Ali at least had the tact to play up to his special forces counterpart, promising over the radio "surrender or death" for al-Qa'eda whenever the Americans were with him. Zaman, on the other hand, made little pretense of his desire to reach a cease-fire.

The CIA officer Henry Crumpton made one final attempt to send more troops to Tora Bora. He was so concerned by lack of focus that he raised Berntsen's request with President Bush. At a White House briefing in early December, he warned, "We're going to lose our prey if we're not careful."

Bush, seemingly surprised, pressed him for more information. "How bad off are these Afghani forces, really? Are they up to the job?"

"Definitely not, Mr. President," Crumpton responded. "Definitely not."[12]

Nothing came of the exchange. Instead, the US continued to push on with its air strikes and rely on its Afghan allies. On December 9, the Americans dropped a massive 20,000-pound bomb on Tora Bora. In the resulting mayhem, US special forces urged the warlords to attack al-Qa'eda positions higher up the mountain. Until then, Zaman had been wary, even downright obstructive, of such advances. The following morning, much to the surprise of the American soldiers accompanying them, Zaman led a practical footrace with Ali to reach a hill that commanded access to the front line. Reaching the peak first, Zaman's men quickly expanded their perimeter, pushing his rival back down the mountain.

The reasons for this burst of enthusiasm were about to become painfully apparent to the special forces. By seizing the peak that December afternoon, Zaman now had direct access to al-Qa'eda's front line. That evening, Zaman called his American partners to tell them he was agreeing with al-Qa'eda to a cease-fire until eight o'clock the following morning.

The US special forces commander was immediately suspicious when he joined Zaman on the hill.

"This is the greatest day in the history of Afghanistan," the warlord declared.

"Why is that?" asked the soldier.

"Because al-Qa'eda is no more. Bin Laden is finished!" he boasted.[13]

In Kabul, Berntsen was furious when he heard about the truce, insisting there would be no negotiations.

"My response to al-Qa'eda is, 'Screw you! We're going to kill all of you,'" he bellowed down the phone. "And that's our final position. Make sure [that's translated] clearly."

Even as Berntsen raged, bin Laden was almost certainly heading right past American positions to safety in eastern Afghanistan. In one of his last radio transmissions the CIA picked up, bin Laden addressed his followers. "I am sorry for getting you involved in this battle," he told them. "If you can no longer resist, you may surrender with my blessing."[14]

Did Zaman mastermind the Saudi's escape? The US special forces certainly thought so, although Philip Smucker, one of the few journalists to reach the front lines and who was with Zaman during some of the negotiations, believes it was one of Hazrat Ali's subcommanders, Ilyas Khel, who led bin Laden to safety. Smucker points out that Ali had only recently hired Khel: The latter's previous boss had been Khalis, the prominent al-Qa'eda supporter.

Whichever warlord ultimately betrayed the Americans, both men were no doubt looking to exploit their presence. What is certain is that by the time the special forces finally cleared the last of the caves, the al-Qa'eda leader was long gone, and with him any prospect of an early closure to the "War on Terror."

I n the aftermath of bin Laden's escape from Tora Bora, the Bush administration went into full denial mode. The White House told the press that bin Laden had never been there in the first place, and that even if he had been, the Saudi was probably buried under a ton of rock.

Its refusal to confront reality was a missed opportunity for the administration to draw important lessons from the Americans' failure to capture or kill bin Laden. Partnering with Afghan forces had brought success when the westerners had been working with the grain of local interests, namely attempting to topple the Taliban. Yet the US had been powerless to corral the Afghans into confronting bin Laden. Much blood would be spilled before the US learned that however hard it tried to impose its vision on Afghanistan, the country would resist those aims unless they coincided with those of its people.

Indeed the Americans and their allies drew a conclusion from Tora Bora that was to muddle future western thinking about Afghanistan: more troops were the answer. Berntsen came to believe that a special forces strike force of several hundred men that could have tackled the cave complex within days of its discovery might have had a better chance of success. But that option was not on the table in 2001, and in its place grew the belief that greater force rather than greater sensitivity was necessary when it came to the country's tangled interplay of tribal loyalties.

CHAPTER 6

Warlords

With the end of the fighting in Tora Bora, the Pentagon concluded that America had largely won the war. Kabul was in the hands of the Northern Alliance and a recently arrived United Nations peacekeeping force. In Kandahar, American special forces and a favored warlord were in charge. Al-Qa'eda and the Taliban had fled. In Washington that Christmas of 2001, there was a sense of relief, triumphalism, and anticipation, as Defense Secretary Donald Rumsfeld and his inner circle turned their sights on Iraq.

Rumsfeld's stock was riding high. The CIA might have developed the plan for invading Afghanistan, but US special forces had delivered the war's dramatic successes, whether partnering with the Northern Alliance to seize Kabul or ensuring Hamid Karzai's survival and emergence as Afghan leader. Indeed the special forces' success seemed to justify Rumsfeld's vision of a new military characterized by highly mobile units, backed by air support and precision weapons. Rumsfeld wanted to maintain only a small residual force in Afghanistan concentrated along the Pakistan border to hunt down lingering terrorists. He believed that locals would not support a larger, enduring western presence in Afghanistan and it could provoke a backlash. Besides, any invasion of Iraq was likely to demand the military's full attention.

The British, who had sent 500 troops to Kabul for the UN peacekeeping force, had a different take on where American priorities should lie. They sent the Pentagon a proposal in early December 2001 to greatly expand the number of peacekeepers in the country from the 500 already in Kabul to 25,000 stationed in major cities around the country.[1] British Major General John McColl, head of the UN-authorized peacekeeping force for Kabul, initiated the idea. McColl, a trim, erudite officer, had served extensively in Northern

Ireland and witnessed the British military evolve into a sensitive peacekeeping force that set the stage for the Good Friday Agreement in 1997 that ended the sectarian conflict there. He believed that peacekeepers in Afghanistan could similarly secure Karzai's fledgling government by giving it time to establish itself in the delicate post-conflict situation.[2]

Karzai's arrival in Kabul on December 14 had underscored for McColl just why he needed more western troops. A delicate calm had prevailed in the Afghan capital since the Northern Alliance's entrance. Even so, Karzai had appeared vulnerable when he had touched down at Kabul's airport in the back of an American C-130 transport plane with just a few US special forces for protection. The first snow had just fallen, turning the barren ridges around the city white, and the wind whipping across the airstrip was icy. Northern Alliance leader Marshal Mohammed Fahim had shown up at the tarmac with several hundred militiamen and struggled to keep his men from exuberantly mobbing Karzai. When Fahim finally reached Karzai he asked, "Where are your men?" If he had wanted to, Fahim could have ended Karzai's presidency right there and then. Instead he stared amazed as Karzai calmly replied, "You are my men."[3] His American escort carefully steered him to the presidential palace.

When McColl met Karzai a few days later in a reception room at the drafty palace, the British general brought his own proposal for more peacekeepers. This was one of Karzai's first official meetings as the country's leader. He made sure he was dressed for the part, resplendent in a costume that would become his signature: the handwoven green and blue silk robe, or *chapan,* draped over his shoulders in the style of Uzbek chieftains, the baggy pants and long tunic of the Pashtun south, and the high lambskin hat once common among Kabulis.

"Masterful" was how McColl later recalled Karzai's unique formulation.[4]

Yet, McColl also sensed a certain vulnerability behind the facade, and a leader who was in need of a generous western hand. The two men quickly struck a rapport: McColl offered crisp military advice, and Karzai warmed to his role as president.

The Afghan leader was only too happy to accept more troops. His gravest concern at this stage was that the West would once again turn its back on Afghanistan, just as it had during the 1990s. "Karzai saw troops as a way to guarantee the international community's engagement," said Said Tayeb Jawad, who became Karzai's chief of staff in 2002.[5]

McColl's intention for the thousands of peacekeepers he wanted to station outside the capital was to patrol the country's towns and villages; this would buy time for the Afghan government to establish itself. Much of the country was free of violence at that point. However, both McColl and Karzai felt the symbolism was important.

The proposal could not proceed without American buy-in. When the US envoy to Afghanistan, Jim Dobbins, brought McColl's proposal to Rumsfeld's attention during a December 16, 2001, visit, the defense secretary asked how many men it would take, and narrowed his eyes when he heard the 25,000 figure.[6] Dobbins supported the proposal, given his experience in the Balkans working with a large peacekeeping force. The British, Dobbins explained to Rumsfeld, were offering to provide the majority of additional troops for the first six months. There was a downside. The Americans would be required to provide logistics—foot the bill, in other words—and air support in the event of fighting. If British forces got into trouble, US forces would have to bail them out.[7] Rumsfeld was immediately skeptical. By underwriting the campaign, the US would effectively be taking military ownership of the effort. Rumsfeld turned down the proposal.

In February 2002, US Secretary of State Colin Powell raised the issue again at a National Security Council meeting. Dobbins noted with disgust that Elliott Abrams, a special adviser to President Bush on the NSC, had circulated a paper before the meeting that asserted that peacekeeping was, in fact, a failed concept, one that throughout the 1990s had been tried and found wanting.

"Such was the prevalent prejudice against nation-building within the Bush administration . . . that his ludicrously misleading paper went unchallenged," Dobbins later reflected.[8]

Both Powell on one side of the debate and Rumsfeld on the other recognized the potential for volatility across Afghanistan. CIA Director George Tenet confirmed there had been skirmishing among Afghan commanders, although so far the special forces teams embedded with the warlords had mediated between the factions. Rumsfeld took this as a sign that his approach was working, and again dismissed the peacekeeping suggestion.

When Powell told Dobbins, who had been waiting outside the NSC meeting, of the decision, he looked dismayed. "It's the best I could do," said Powell. "Rumsfeld promised he would handle the problem. What more could I say?"[9]

Rumsfeld was prepared to authorize one large-scale operation. Criticism of how he handled Tora Bora, and the perception that the lack of troops may have allowed bin Laden to escape, had been growing in the media. Therefore, when news that a pocket of al-Qa'eda fighters—possibly including the fugitive leader—was holed up in southeastern Afghanistan, he sought to destroy them with what he hoped would be the first and last major military operation of the campaign.

The CIA had detected al-Qa'eda massing in the Shah-i-Kot valley near Gardez, a large town on one of the key roads linking Afghanistan's southeastern border region with Pakistan. The area was under the control of Jalaluddin Haqqani, the leader of a tribal network that had fought the Soviets with the CIA's and ISI's help, and whom Pakistan's spy agency had once touted as an alternative Pashtun voice to the Taliban. The CIA had linked the Haqqani family with bin Laden's escape from Tora Bora, a claim the clan strongly denied.[10] The Haqqani clan had since been targeted by American air strikes, and the family driven over the border into Pakistan. But the al-Qa'eda fighters who had sheltered in the family's tribal lands remained after the Haqqanis departed.

The operation—which the US military called Anaconda—began on March 21, 2002. The military intended airlifting 1,700 US troops into Shah-i-Kot. The plan was to use Afghan auxiliary forces to push up the valley toward al-Qa'eda positions, while American troops blocked off escape routes.

It got off to a bad start when the AC-130 gunships supporting the mission mistook the Afghan fighters and their special forces counterparts for al-Qa'eda and strafed them as they drove up the valley, leading to more than forty casualties among the Afghans. As a result of the confusion, the air force then shied away from a bombing operation against actual al-Qa'eda positions. At that point the Afghan forces fled. US troops setting up the perimeter defenses also found themselves in trouble when they discovered that a large number of the enemy had based themselves in the caves and ridges high up on the mountain slopes, from which they now bombarded the arriving American forces.

Two days into the operation, a navy SEAL force was dispatched to outflank an al-Qa'eda's position, but one of its Chinook helicopters was hit by a mortar round shortly after landing, causing navy SEAL Neil Roberts to tumble out of the craft's open rear hatch. Though it's not clear whether he survived the fall, six special forces soldiers were killed trying to rescue him. Roberts's body was never recovered.

After a tactical retreat and a week of heavy bombing, the US persuaded Afghan forces to return to the valley. This time they found the place deserted. With telltale hyperbole, US General Tommy Franks told reporters that the operation was an "unqualified and absolute success."[11] The truth, as the bloodied American and Afghan units well knew, was quite the opposite.

The bungled mission appeared to confirm many of Rumsfeld's worst fears about the large-scale use of American troops in Afghanistan. As far as he was concerned, the broader war was now over, and US special forces could be left to mop up any Taliban or al-Qa'eda stragglers.

The British General John McColl was certain that Washington's failure to approve more troops to secure the peace was a catastrophic mistake. The American tactic of using warlords to oust the Taliban had worked, but now these men were becoming the country's power brokers. Some of the commanders were popular figures, with strong tribal connections, but others relied on US power to support their rule, which was frequently harsh and despotic.

McColl believed the Afghan president was ill-equipped to confront the warlords and that only western troops would allow Karzai to establish government control outside Kabul. "The warlords undermined what we were trying to achieve. We promised the Afghans government, and instead they got them," he reflected later.[12]

Karzai's own take on warlords was more subtle. He told advisers that he recognized the dangers to his own rule that the competing power structures of warlords and various tribal leaders represented. He espoused the same vision for modernizing the country as the international community, but that was a long-term goal. In the meantime, he was pragmatic enough to realize that he needed to work the country's tribal networks if he was to develop his power base. After all, he had been raised to be a chieftain, a job that entailed balancing his own aspirations with the mores of clan life.[13]

Karzai was particularly eager to shore up support in the south, his tribal heartland and the production center for the country's main export, opium. Karzai would have known that controlling the opium trade was a prerequisite to controlling the country, although he has maintained he has no links to the opium trade himself. He had already lost the battle to install his own favorite in Kandahar after the US special forces had sided with his rival, Gul Agha Sherzai. However, the Americans had yet to make it to neighboring Helmand province, an epicenter of opium production, with a trade worth over $1 billion. He needed to act quickly to ensure Helmand fell under his influence.

On December 13, his first day in office, Karzai ordered the removal of the tribal consortium that had occupied the governor's palace in Helmand's provincial capital, Lashkar Gah. In its place he installed as governor his ally Sher Mohammed Akhundzada, the scion of the Alizai tribe from northern Helmand. Sher Mohammed's father, Mullah Nasim, had risen to prominence in the 1980s by butchering his clan rivals in the midst of the anti-Soviet resistance and blaming many of their murders on the Russians. At the same time, he had roped his followers into growing poppies, the opium produced from which was only used as a palliative for local consumption. Under Mullah Nasim's coercion, poppy-growing shifted from northern Afghanistan's narrow gorges to the rich banks of the Helmand River valley. In 1981, Mullah Nasim even issued a religious

Karzai appointed Sher Mohammed Akhundzada to run the opium-rich province of Helmand on his first day in office. Akhundzada was to have a powerful impact on the course of the war. (Photo by author)

decree ordering his men to plant poppies. His efforts were successful for a time, but he was ultimately gunned down by a rival, and his family—including Sher Mohammed—fled to Quetta, Pakistan, once the Taliban showed up.[14]

Sher Mohammed sensibly used his time kicking around Quetta to cultivate relationships with western intelligence agencies, chiefly MI6, and the Karzais. He married off his sister to Karzai's half brother, Ahmed Wali, and regularly visited the Karzai compound with bouquets of flowers and other gifts. After 9/11, he also offered men and weapons for Karzai's rebels. When he returned to Afghanistan after the Taliban's overthrow and found his brother-in-law, Karzai, running the country, Sher Mohammed undoubtedly felt that his investment had been well worth it.[15]

Sher Mohammed's appointment as Helmand governor in December 2001 led to a flurry of wheel greasing and allegiance shifting within the province. His sometime rival, Abdul Rahman Jan of the Noorzai tribe, was elected police chief. Dad Mohammed Khan of the Alakozai, who had presided over the province's largest opium bazaar in the northern town of Sangin, was brought to Lashkar Gah as head of the secret police. In his place he appointed one of his own followers as the Sangin district governor.[16]

All of this reshuffling was sure to result in tension. The locals in Sangin had already elected as district governor a popular former jihadi commander, Maulavi Atta Mohammed Isheqzai. The Isheqzai tribe had supplied many of the Taliban's local commanders, although some, like Maulavi Atta, had remained neutral and well respected. Nonetheless, he was hastily dumped, after Sher Mohammed realized he could exercise a little spite and get away with it.[17]

Karzai's appointment of warlords, such as Sher Mohammed, set him on a collision course with the international community. Western officials belatedly came to recognize the Afghan president's role in creating and managing a system of patronage and corruption. In the early days, however, westerners largely ignored Karzai's pragmatism in favor of their own agenda. If they had properly understood Karzai's moves at the time, it might have allowed for some international acceptance—and oversight—of the networks he was empowering. Instead the international community fixated on what their nation-building plans could achieve.

CHAPTER 7

National Solidarity

The debate about whether to send more troops to Afghanistan matched a similar conversation within the aid world over the size and scale of the country's reconstruction. At the conference in Bonn, Germany, the international community appeared to have agreed to a "light footprint" approach, leaving it to the Afghan government to manage the reconstruction effort. Yet even at Bonn, the aid world had begun to lobby for a broader mission, one that would replicate the perceived success of the Balkans in the 1990s.

The Balkans effort had been a massive, internationally led and financed mission. A patchwork of aid organizations, such as the United Nations, the World Bank, government aid agencies including USAID, and the British government's Department for International Development. This top-down approach reflected that for emerging states in the Balkans region, such as Bosnia and Kosovo, no national administrations had existed before. Entire governments needed to be started from scratch.

Afghanistan presented different challenges that could be read as evidence either for or against implementing a Balkans-style enterprise. Those in the aid world with Afghan experience favored a smaller effort pointing to the country's long-standing history as a sovereign state. Even during the dark days of its civil war, Afghanistan's government ministries had operated. The government had little control beyond the major cities and their environs. But in a country that was overwhelmingly agricultural and rural, leaving justice, and most everything else, in the hands of local communities made sense. Some villages in the mountains hadn't seen a government official in a generation.

Yet western officials coming fresh from the Balkans held up their work there as a model for a more robust effort, one of which was to develop civil society and democratic institutions, establish the rule of law, and begin reconstruction work. The sheer scale of Afghanistan's needs was staggering. The nation was one of the poorest on earth, with 98 percent illiteracy and infant mortality rates of five per thousand. The United Nations estimated in 2002 that the country needed $10 billion over the next five years, and some officials speculated that developing the country might require as much as $25 billion.[1] The Afghans themselves held a tangible desire for change post-Taliban. Kabul residents in particular wanted to rejoin the international community and embrace the modernity they had been denied for so long. Afghans in the provinces also wanted development, but of a more basic kind: schools, clinics, and greater access to running water.

Confronted with such overwhelming demand, those seeking to create a Balkans-style reconstruction effort won out. In January 2002 the UN convened a donors' conference in Tokyo to raise $1.8 billion for Afghanistan for the coming year. The attendees, including representatives from sixty countries and two dozen aid organizations (and a handful of Afghans), were, on the whole, an idealistic bunch who believed in their agendas for transforming the country. However, they were also driven by a more subtle and self-serving motive: Humanitarian interventions kept them in business. Mark Malloch Brown, head of the UN Development Programme, was heard saying during a preparatory meeting before Tokyo that it would give his organization funding for the next twenty-five years.[2]

In response to Afghanistan's poverty, many in the aid world advocated a nation-building effort similar to that carried out in the Balkans in the 1990s. (Photo by author)

From the outset of the Tokyo conference, it was not clear how much of the money from donors, such as the World Bank and individual countries, the UN would spend on the Afghans, and how much would go toward funding the costly business of establishing the aid community in Kabul. Every international aid agency and nongovernmental organization had to bring a posse of consultants and security contractors, rent villas and guest houses at inflated prices, buy electrical generators, install Internet and satellite television, and scramble to hire local staff who spoke English and understood the language of development. By virtue of paying high salaries, the aid community succeeded in poaching many of the most capable Afghans from their jobs as teachers, doctors, and engineers.[3]

Just as the debate about the role of peacekeeping troops had largely taken place in western capitals, far from the reality of Afghanistan, so too did the discussion of reconstruction largely take place without input from Afghans. The one man who could be said to be an expert on the subject, the country's de facto finance minister, Ashraf Ghani, did not even attend the Tokyo meeting. He was too busy trying to pull together the country's shattered finances from a cramped and icy office on the grounds of the presidential palace in Kabul.

If Ghani had attended the conference, the aid world would have been disturbed to hear what he had to say. Ghani was adamant that not a penny of donor money should go directly to aid organizations. Rather, he felt, the funds needed to be spent through the Afghan finance ministry, that is, him. A veteran of the World Bank, Ghani had seen enough of the reconstruction projects in Bosnia and East Timor—where the UN had effectively established a protectorate as a new country was forged—to realize that without an Afghan lead, the country was liable to be swamped by aid agencies and donors whose desire for showcase projects and deliverable targets for their stakeholders was likely to confuse and overwhelm the fledgling country.

Ghani had been born in Afghanistan and had attended the American University in Beirut, Lebanon, before gaining a scholarship to Columbia University in New York. A sharp-tongued intellectual, he was acutely sensitive to western condescension and was not prepared to let Afghanistan become a glorified hobbyhorse for the West. The whole purpose of the reconstruction project, as he saw it, was to build up Afghan capacity. Giving funds to the Afghan government to spend on reconstruction not only ensured that projects were scaled to, and sensitive of, Afghan society, it also reinforced the administration's legitimacy. By contrast, if international aid agencies dominated the rebuilding work, their agendas could easily dominate proceedings—and much of the money earmarked for Afghans would end up in western contractors' pockets.

Ghani wasn't even asking for a lot of money to fulfill his vision. Before Tokyo, Ghani had requested $240 million to fund Afghan ministries and pay the salaries of bureaucrats, doctors, and nurses. He received only $20 million and a succession of resignation letters from Afghan officials leaving their posts to join higher-paying aid organizations. At one point a furious Ghani tried to block visas for UN officials before he was persuaded by the organization to relent.[4]

Ghani had also requested that the UN create a trust fund for donor aid, to centralize the reconstruction project and avoid duplicating efforts to ensure that reconstruction work followed a single strategy. Donors paid lip service to the idea but were reluctant to contribute. Instead, Ghani was dismayed to learn that western donors would "adopt" Afghan government ministries with only limited provisions for coordinating between themselves or with his ministry.

The potential for confusion and replication of efforts was high, and exacerbated by the fact the US was leery of taking the lead. The Bonn conference had placed the UN in charge of the international community's rebuilding mission, but Ghani had hoped that Washington, as one of the largest donors, would still pull the strings. In his opinion, the United Nations lacked the ability—and the clout—to coordinate the array of countries offering assistance, each with its own national interest at heart. If anything, agencies such as the World Food Program and the World Health Organization only added a competing layer of management.

The White House did not step up and the resulting piecemeal arrangement would bedevil the reconstruction effort for years to come. "Anarchic" was how one British general later characterized it.[5] The US took charge of building the army, the UK counter-narcotics, Japan disarmament, Germany the police force, Italy the justice system. Diplomats joked about some of those countries' suitability to perform their duties in light of past records. "The major donors were more interested in carving out their own fiefdoms to look good back home than they were about Afghanistan itself," noted one disgruntled western observer.[6]

US Envoy Jim Dobbins blamed both the US and the UN for not taking more of a leadership role at Tokyo. Whether or not one agrees with his assessment that Afghanistan needed large-scale investment at the outset, western guidance and a clear set of expectations were obviously necessary over the long term. "Without that framework," noted Dobbins, "there was always a danger of chronic waste, corruption and failure."

The disastrous projects that ensued overshadowed the potential of a smaller, remarkably successful Afghan-led aid program that illustrated

Ghani's vision. While the international community was devising grand schemes for reconfiguring the justice system and countering the poppy trade, Ghani was attending to a small-scale development program already operating in Afghanistan, which consisted of community-appointed forums that selected, designed, and implemented rebuilding work such as wells and building repairs. By the time the Taliban fell, five forums in major cities and two more in the countryside had been set with help from a UN subsidiary.[7]

The program had cost less than $3 million since its inception in 1993. It might have languished in obscurity but for Clare Lockhart, a redoubtable twenty-eight-year-old British lawyer who had worked for Ghani at the World Bank before being assigned to Afghanistan. In 2001, she had spent some time in Indonesia working on a World Bank project that had independently used the same model as in Afghanistan, though the Indonesian version had operated on a much larger scale. The World Bank had backed it with a $200 million grant, and the project had established thousands of community councils across rural Indonesia.

The potential of this approach in Afghanistan, as an alternative to the expensive and uncoordinated aid system, had already occurred to Lockhart when she was introduced to Samantha Reynolds, a UN aid worker who had worked on the Afghan version throughout the 1990s. Lockhart was stunned to discover the Afghans' version. All they needed was the technical know-how to scale up the project. After an exhilarating evening at the UN guest house in Kabul exchanging ideas, Lockhart raised the scheme with Ghani, who immediately backed the idea of expanding the Afghan version.[8] The obvious thing to do was to bring in Scott Guggenheim, who had pioneered the Indonesian model to create a national program in Afghanistan.

The National Solidarity Program (NSP) was thus born in November 2001, when Lockhart called Guggenheim, who was halfway up a mountainside in Indonesia, and asked him to come to Afghanistan. Guggenheim and Ghani had been friends since the 1980s, when they'd had the same adviser for their PhDs: Eric Wolf, a leading anthropologist who had studied peasant societies in Latin America and Europe. Guggenheim was a year younger than Ghani, naturally outgoing, gregarious even, in contrast to the Afghan with his darker humor. Guggenheim had been instrumental in getting Ghani a job at the World Bank, which Guggenheim had joined a few years earlier.

The World Bank wasn't hiring many anthropologists when Guggenheim and then Ghani joined—math hotshots were usually preferred to fuzzy social scientists. However, the institution was undergoing intense self-reflection in the early 1990s after a series of damaging revelations about its approach to foreign aid. The bank had been set up at Bretton Woods, a financial summit held in 1944 to drive postwar reconstruction, but had soon turned its resources to the countries emerging from the wreckage of empire. Large-scale infrastructure projects were popular early recipients of World Bank loans. Yet, by the early 1990s the damaging social and environmental consequences of projects like the Sardar Sarovar Dam in western India, which evicted hundreds of thousands of families from their homes, resulted in an international outcry.

Guggenheim was part of a team in 1993 that oversaw a far-reaching internal review of the World Bank's policy toward large-scale infrastructure. He made sure Ghani joined the review team, along with several other anthropologists. The subsequent report led to an immediate shift in the World Bank's development approach, finding that the organization was "institutionally incapable" of measuring the social impacts of large-scale projects. Along with the corruption such big loans engendered, and the reliance on western contractors for delivery, the report questioned whether projects like Sardar Sarovar Dam benefited the poor. The World Bank called an immediate moratorium on funding future dam projects.

In scaling back its investment in major infrastructure projects, the World Bank was catching up with an emerging train of thought on delivering aid. In 1983, British social scientist Robert Chambers had published an influential paper expressing frustration at how little development helped the poorest residents of affected countries. He urged the aid world to focus instead on small-scale projects, where they could more readily ascertain the links between investment and a community's well-being.

As a result of his research, Guggenheim had reached a similar conclusion. In 1997, four years after submitting his report, he found himself in the remote jungles of Indonesia, having persuaded the World Bank to back a village-based program. Starting with twenty-five communities in the Kecamatan district of northwestern Indonesia, Guggenheim's staff organized town hall–style meetings to ask villagers what they would like to spend any aid money on. Villagers held local elections—neatly bypassing the government-appointed officials—and the elected leaders were responsible for managing the budget after completing bookkeeping classes. Devolution of power delivered results: Local ownership over projects increased once villagers realized it was their money to lose. Corruption was basically "non-existent," noted Guggenheim.[9] This was the program Ghani wanted Guggenheim to re-create in Afghanistan in 2001.

Guggenheim arrived in Kabul in January 2002, a few days before the Tokyo conference. Few places are less forgiving than Kabul in the grip of winter. A single rocky headland—Sher Darwaza, the Lion's Gate—runs across the city from the northwest to the southeast, with a rugged defile cut by the Kabul River linking the two halves of the city. To the northwest lies the traditional heart of the capital, with the presidential palace and its ancient cedars, and old city walls running along the ridgeline above. After that comes the commercial hub of Wazi Akbar Khan. Farther north lies the pockmarked runway of Kabul airport, and the towering peaks of the Pamir mountain range; to the south, the Hindu Kush and the riches of the Indian subcontinent.

The city had once drawn wistful paeans to its beauty. Two hundred years and several conquests later, however, only the grandeur of Kabul's snow capped ridges endured. The previous decade of fighting had been particularly savage. Rival warlords had occupied opposing hilltops and shelled one another indiscriminately, and though the warlords' artillery was quiet now, the city retained the air of a siege only recently lifted. The foothills around the city center, long since denuded of their covering of larch, spruce, and oak trees for firewood, had become vast slums of stone and mudbrick shelters for the dispossessed. The tributary rivers of the Kol-e-Hashmat Khan wetlands to the south, once a sanctuary to 30,000 migratory birds, had been dammed, and the area was now a barren mudflat. On most days a grimy pall from wood smoke and car exhaust hung over the city, along with a faint whiff of excrement from the open sewers in the slums and the flat metallic smell of blood from the flocks of sheep slaughtered on the city's outskirts.

Ghani met Guggenheim at Kabul's rudimentary airport, which had recently reopened to civilian flights, although planes landing there had to stop abruptly due to an unexploded bomb at the end of the runway.

"Welcome to my home," said Ghani, with his usual mixture of pained self-awareness and irony.[10] The two men shared a brief greeting before clambering into Ghani's jeep for the drive into the city center. The roads were already clogged with traffic. Within weeks of the Taliban's departure, a veritable flotilla of cheap junkers had arrived from Pakistan, reminding Guggenheim that even in war-torn societies, local networks operate with far greater efficiency than anything the aid community could create. Just as instructive were the torn hulls of tanks and mangled artillery pieces stacked along the road, evidence of the precision of US air strikes from the recent war, and earlier battles against the Russians.

Ghani dropped off Guggenheim at the villa where the United Nations housed its staff, and the two men agreed to meet for lunch at a local restaurant the next day. That evening, Guggenheim fell asleep huddled next to a steel drum of smoldering packed sawdust that warded off the cold for a few hours before the last smoke cleared from the chimney that fed out of a hole in the wall.

They met the next day for lunch in Herat restaurant, a Kabul institution that had continued serving kebabs throughout the recent US bombing campaign. Ghani picked at a plate of rice; ever since an operation to remove a tumor in his stomach, he rarely ate more than a few mouthfuls at a meal. Guggenheim tucked into a regulation kebab with gusto.

"How quickly can you set this thing up?" Ghani asked, although he already seemed to have an answer in mind as they discussed the small-scale Afghan version. Extending the program into the countryside, as Ghani wanted, would require a dramatic expansion. He knew well that the Indonesian program had taken years to set up, and he took pleasure in needling his counterparts, whether old friends or besuited development consultants, about the need to move faster in his country.

"You've got six months," Ghani informed Guggenheim.

The next day, Guggenheim began work in the spartan finance ministry office at the palace. Ghani had assembled a small team of experts, including Clare Lockhart and Michael Carnahan, a wry Australian economist who'd worked in East Timor. Even leaving aside the National Solidarity Program, Ghani's plan for the next few months was ambitious. The items on his to-do list included introducing a new Afghan currency, centralized tax collection, and a computerized banking system to allow money into the country electronically. At that point, Afghanistan's budget had to be flown in from the donor countries as bundles of cash.

For westerners such as Guggenheim, the early days of their work in Afghanistan brought the rare thrill of embarking on a project where the need was great—the grim office was a reminder of that—and the mandate clear. Guggenheim had spent enough time in pointless meetings with foreign bureaucrats over the years to realize the unique potential of the situation: Here was a government ready to embrace a bold departure in delivering aid, as if the social scientists and philosophers had staged an unlikely coup against the bureaucrats who usually ran the show.

The Afghans in the office shared in the excitement, although—perhaps inevitably after three decades of war—they were restrained by an awareness of the thin divide between order and collapse. Guggenheim traveled with several members of the team and Samantha Reynolds to see the Afghan version of the project in Bamyan to the west of Kabul, and he was struck by participants' hunger to manage their own destinies. Upon returning to Kabul, Guggenheim began the framework for scaling up the program. It really took off a few months later with the appointment of Hanif Atmar as minister for rural affairs, under whose jurisdiction the village program would fall.

F ew Afghan lives have been untouched by tragedy since 2001, and in his own way Atmar, one of the most talented administrators of his generation, was to be a victim too. Atmar's career and his attitudes toward the West would chart the war's progress and the views of many Afghans from an almost reverential hope in reconstruction to a drastic loss of faith. Just thirty-three years old at the time of his appointment, Atmar had a thin, hawkish nose and dark eyes that held a bookish reserve. For much of the 1990s his lanky frame could be spotted in the windblown refugee camps of Peshawar and Quetta, surrounded by refugees as he listened, with his quiet empathy, to their woeful stories. At that time, interest in Afghanistan's hundreds of thousands of refugees was limited to a few international aid agencies. Atmar found a job in Peshawar with the Norwegian Afghanistan Committee. He soon distinguished himself from other local hires through his crisp English, unhurried thinking, and apparent disdain for tribal politics. He was selected for a scholarship to a master's degree program at York University in the United Kingdom, specializing in post-conflict reconstruction and development.

Atmar rarely revealed that his past contained a dark secret. His father had been a district official working for the Soviet-backed governments of the 1980s. That in itself was fairly uncontroversial. What was less well-known was that a young Atmar had joined a branch of the secret police toward the end of the Soviet occupation, and in 1988 had fought with a special unit against US-backed mujahideen fighters besieging the western city of Jalalabad. He had lost part of his right leg in the fighting and walked with a limp. When asked about his background by other students at York, he usually explained that he'd been accidently caught in a rocket attack.[11]

Atmar's supervisor at the university was Professor Sultan Barakat, himself the son of Palestinian refugees. Barakat had done much to translate Robert Chambers's ideas about community-driven development into a post-conflict setting, when the absence of government only reinforced the need for strong local networks. He imparted these lessons to his promising pupil. Atmar was a diligent enough student, but he shone in seminars, where he brought a gravitas to discussion that eluded most of his western classmates.[12]

Atmar had been appointed to his ministry position after the Bonn conference when several NGO leaders had vouched for his talents.[13] It was an
unfashionable assignment, but that proved to be an advantage. The warlords
at Bonn had squabbled over the major posts that offered power and prestige,
like the ministries of transport and energy. By contrast, the ministry of rural
rehabilitation and development appeared to offer neither. It was nominally in
charge of delivering services in the countryside, but other ministries had their
own officials in the provinces for that sort of thing, so past incumbents had
been content with the illusion of power and a minister's perks.

With Ashraf Ghani's support, Atmar took a different approach to his re-
sponsibilities. Ghani had made clear at Bonn that he considered most of
the other appointed ministers, many of them warlords, to be incompetent
administrators. That's where the nature of the "rural rehabilitation and development" took on a new meaning. Ghani might have struggled to launch a
reconstruction program through the other ministries, but the national reach
of Atmar's ministry meant he didn't need to bother with warlords and their
bureaucratic fiefdoms.

After the Tokyo conference, Ghani had argued for, and received, an initial
$25 million to launch a pilot for the NSP, the pilot which would be expanded
nationally later in the year if it proved successful. Given his background in
development, Atmar enthusiastically embraced the village program concept
when Guggenheim presented it to him. However, it was clear to Atmar that
significant alterations would have to take place—prime among them a change
to the program's local organization.

In Indonesia, the program called for citizens to elect a community development council to select and manage grants. Yet the very idea of using
a secret ballot in Afghan villages had revolutionary potential. Most villages
contained a *shura*, a council of elders drawn from family groupings. The
shura is used mostly for local conflict resolution, although its unspoken role is
to enforce age-old customs. The elected community groups Atmar wanted to
create would have a very different function: awarding contracts and managing
projects, tasks that likely would require younger and more savvy members of
the community. Whether such an organization would be seen as threatening
the traditional power structure was unclear, but Atmar knew he would have
to be extremely sensitive in presenting the program to outlying communities.

Atmar's solution was to drop one of the clearly contentious aspects of the
elections—the requirement for a turnout of more than 50 percent. The quota
was intended to dilute local landowners' and religious leaders' power, but it

was more deeply significant for many conservative Afghans. A 50 percent quota implied that women would also have to vote. Atmar knew this would be a step too far for many villages, and yet he also knew that suggesting a lower threshold would open him to criticism from the international community. One of the iconic images of the war to date had been the blue burka, the full-body veil that restricted a woman's view to a tiny grille, and that had become a symbol of the Taliban's totalitarian regime.

So Atmar decided to forgo elections entirely and use local shuras to act as community councils. It would dodge the issue of female empowerment, and make the program easier to manage. But when Atmar suggested dropping elections, he was surprised members of the existing network of councils pushed back. They believed elections were the only way to ensure accountability. Atmar ultimately suggested a compromise: a male shura council and a smaller female one.

Five villages were selected for the pilot scheme. Once each community had voted in a council and had established reconstruction priorities, it would receive a block grant of $200 per family, up to a total of $60,000. Atmar persuaded his NGO partners to manage the disbursement of funds—$7 million for the initial pilot—but gave budget oversight to the villages' respective shuras, which would contract out the desired project to local workers.

"The beauty of the project was its simplicity," Atmar later reflected. "It was everything else that got complicated."[14]

What is life like in a poor Afghan village? The answer to that question in 2002 was often only dimly understood by the aid world. Yet the realities of everyday life in the villages for Atmar's pilot development program would effectively determine whether the plan succeeded or failed—and whether it stood a chance of being replicated elsewhere in the country.

One of the first villages to join the scheme was Bala Karz, on the outskirts of southern Kandahar. Managing the contract on the government's behalf, UN-Habitat had selected this village of 330 families for its proximity to Kandahar, a dozen or so miles away. The village was close to the relative sophistication of the city. Yet culturally it was part of the tribal belt linked by the waterways that fed the Arghandab River and the densely cultivated fields of the Panjwei. The area had been a bastion of the mujahideen during the Soviet occupation, and remained something of one since. The lowlands were dominated by the Popalzai tribe, which had produced many of the country's Pashtun leaders, including Hamid Karzai. The Noorzai tribe controlled the hills, some branches of which had supported the Taliban.

Mohammed Lal was a local farmer from the Noorzai, who lived outside Bala Karz. He had fought for the Taliban in the 1990s but wasn't particularly ideologically driven; everyone else in the village had grabbed their guns to fight, and he'd gone along. But now he had a wife and three children, and a small patch of land where he eked out a living. The land around Bala Karz had always made for poor farmland: desiccated hillsides of sagebrush and wormwood that forlornly overlooked the richer valleys of the Panjwei. Lal, a tall, angular man who would have looked older than his thirty-five years if not for his wolfish grin, grew watermelons and poppy, which earned him around $100 a month.

The last three years of Taliban rule had coincided with a drought that had reduced harvests of wheat and fruit to subsistence levels. Lal was happy to see the retreating backs of the Taliban, which he considered a nuisance. "They were always forcing us to gather in the village and listen to their orders," said Lal.[15] They had also banned poppy cultivation in their final year in power.

Yet so far Lal's only experience with the new authorities was considerably worse. Twice US special forces looking to capture Taliban leaders had raided the village. The local mechanic-cum-handyman had been hauled off, a major inconvenience as the community's three decrepit pickup trucks and collection of motorbikes were in constant need of servicing. "When my family's truck broke down I had to pay Abdul Razzak [a local landowner] to take me to Kandahar for spare parts," Lal complained. (There was considerably more amusement when Governor Sherzai's men took away one of the wealthier shopkeepers, from the rival Popalzai clan.)

Also irksome from the Noorzai's perspective was the new district police chief, a Popalzai, whose goons set up checkpoints on all the roads leading to Kandahar. These men were a constant menace, stealing money and making rude comments. Lal almost took a beating when he told the police at one checkpoint, after they'd taken most of his money, that the Taliban would be back soon.

Lal and other Noorzai were slowly coming to wish for a return to the old order. When staff members from UN-Habitat, one of the organizations overseeing the NSP, visited Bala Karz in early 2003, the villagers' level of distrust surprised them. Reform was viewed as dangerous, a potential plot to undermine the very resilience that had allowed the community to weather so many storms. "We have no interest in change," said Lal.

Nonetheless, the village's two dozen men gathered outside the mosque one bitterly cold winter's morning and reluctantly agreed to form a council, a sad commentary on their own desperate plight. In reality, the war had already hollowed out the village; the traditional shura rarely met, Lal admitted, and when it did it was riven by divisions between the Noorzai clansmen and the Popalzai.

When UN-Habitat workers polled the villagers on their priorities, drilling for a well was at the top of the list, with a health clinic or a new school a distant second and third. The prospect of a well raised the uncomfortable possibility that the UN team overseeing the project would be promoting

The National Solidarity Program gave Afghan communities control over reconstruction work in their area and was a rare success story. Here villagers vote to elect a council to manage a small government grant. (Photo courtesy of Samantha Reynolds)

poppy production, dependent as it was on a good water supply. The first post-Taliban harvest had seen a boom in poppy cultivation as farmers sought to recoup the previous year's losses. It was no coincidence, Lal believed, that outsiders had started showing up in villages such as Bala Karz claiming to be hunting Taliban. In fact, he surmised, they were seeking to muscle in on the drug trade.

But the villagers went ahead with the well project, despite UN workers' reservations. By the end of 2003, Bala Karz had elected both men's and women's councils, contracted out a $60,000 well project to local builders, and settled on a development plan for further reconstruction, including a school. In return, there was shocked recognition in the village that "NSP was for real," according to one villager.[16] Outside intrusion did not have to be predatory. "We still didn't trust the government or want outsiders in our village," said Lal. "But we were prepared to continue their work."

The World Bank was sufficiently impressed with the pilot that in 2003 it announced a $117 million grant to expand the program to 20,000 villages, with additional funding from Denmark and Japan. Indeed, the program's early success was such that communities across the country were clamoring to be included in the first round of funding, leaving Atmar with the tough decision of whether to expand the program to villages that it had not yet reached or to offer follow-up grants to those already participating. In the name of fairness he opted for the former, thereby limiting what was meant to be a steadily deepening relationship between government and countryside.

"More money early on would have made a difference," Sultan Barakat said.[17] But rather than pump more money into a scheme whose effectiveness was readily apparent, the international community continued to find more ways to undermine Ghani and expand their own programs in the mistaken belief that they knew better than he where the country's best interests lay.

CHAPTER 8

A Convenient Drug

Nowhere were western ambitions for Afghanistan more disconnected from Afghan reality than the subject of opium. By the late nineties, the country was responsible for around three quarters of the global trade in heroin. The idea of tackling the supply at its source appealed to British Prime Minister Tony Blair. He liked the grand gesture of connecting the war in Afghanistan with the domestic war against drugs. So, at his urging, the UK had volunteered to take charge of Afghanistan's counter-narcotics policy at a G8 meeting of world leaders in April 2002, vowing to end the opium trade once and for all.

The announcement took Michael Ryder, the UK's special representative on drug issues, by surprise. The British government had not consulted him even though the job now fell to him. In his late forties, with thinning hair and thick glasses, Ryder was the sort of diplomat with whom the British Foreign Office was well stocked: a man of deep intelligence and probity who tried to balance his own views with official government policy, knowing he'd likely come out the worse. When it came to counter-narcotics policy, Ryder admired the prime minister's ambition but viewed the task as almost impossible.[1]

Over the past twenty years, Afghanistan had become the world's largest poppy cultivator. The country's drug trade had started almost innocently with marijuana, a business that flourished in the 1960s after the hippies discovered the high-grade hashish that grew around Mazar-e-Sharif. The great-grandson of one Afghanistan's kings, Mohammed Durrani helped pioneer the trade with the Oxford graduate and pot smuggler Howard Marks, who brought hash into Europe rolled up in Afghan rugs.[2] It didn't take long for other, harder operators to move onto the scene and for the drug of choice to shift from hashish to opium. The global opium trade had been dominated by the so-called Golden Triangle in Southeast Asia. However, the early 1980s saw a collapse in production in the hills of Thailand and Burma as a result of a sustained eradication effort and a shift to making methamphetamine. In Afghanistan, the Soviet invasion of 1979 dispersed the hippies to be replaced by the warlords, who quickly took advantage of the anarchy and high demand for narcotics to carve out their own drug empires.

Afghan farmers had traditionally avoided anything to do with poppy, viewing the drug trade as un-Islamic. But in a war-torn country, poppy had undeniable advantages over other crops. The cabbage-like plants needed little tending, with the opium resin collected from its seed head capable of being stored for years—an important advantage, as fighting often made travel difficult. With a price at the farm gate of approximately $125 per kilogram for dry opium, an Afghan farmer could make seventeen times more profit growing opium poppy than growing the traditional mainstay of Afghan agriculture, wheat—$4,622 per hectare for poppy, compared to only $266 per hectare for wheat.[3] Warlords also lent farms money each season to cover costs, providing much-needed assistance to the poor while guaranteeing their loyalty to that particular kingpin. Between 1981 and 2000, the country's opium production grew tenfold: from 250 tons to 3,275 tons, around 75 percent of the global supply of heroin, and almost all of the drug found on British streets.[4]

The Taliban's rise to power ended the free-for-all, introducing an unprecedented level of central government control over the country's principal industry. The Taliban government succeeded in collecting a tax from farmers,

Poppy cultivation flourished after 2001. Here a poppy crop grows along the Baghran River valley in northern Helmand in 2005. (Photo courtesy of Jim Hogberg)

couched as a religious levy or *usher*, ranging from 10 percent to 20 percent of their income from poppy cultivation. The government levied a similar toll on the traffickers exporting the processed heroin. This was the first time an Afghan government had collected an agricultural tax. In 2001, their final year of rule, the Taliban had instituted a poppy ban, ostensibly as a concession to the international community, although many suspected that the mullahs were simply trying to drive up the price of opium after growing too much the year before.

As Ryder prepared to formulate Afghanistan's counter-narcotics policy following the 2002 Tokyo conference, some absurdities of the effort soon became apparent. Ryder had visited Afghanistan the year before as part of the UN team sent to verify the poppy ban and had drawn a few conclusions about tackling the trade. The Taliban had enforced the ban with its typical brutality, killing off a few farmers as an example to all. Such drastic measures could work—the empty fields were proof of that. It was clear to Ryder that enforcing the ban was not sustainable in the long term without a program to provide alternative livelihoods to farmers.

After the G8 meeting, Ryder's team was set to receive a large budget—later announced as $125 million—to build on Afghanistan's legitimate agricultural economy, which at the time earned around $100 million in exports. By the recent standard of the cash-strapped Foreign and Commonwealth Office, the counter-narcotics budget appeared vast. Yet it was miniscule compared to the $1 billion in revenue that Afghanistan's first poppy harvest since the Taliban was about to rake in. With such a bonanza looming, persuading the country's poppy growers to switch to different crops was a dim prospect.[5]

Part of Ryder's problem was that the Americans, who had more resources than the British to throw against poppy cultivation in Afghanistan, had come down strongly in favor of doing nothing at all. US Secretary of State Donald Rumsfeld had decided early on in the bombing campaign that the US military would stay out of Afghanistan's war on drugs. The British had urged air strikes against the opium labs, but Rumsfeld disagreed—the move might jeopardize US relations with the warlords. There was also a deeper philosophical point to his refusal: If US forces helped destroy the opium trade, they were liable to get drawn into the question of what should replace it. They would inadvertently get roped into nation-building, in other words.

For top officials in London, nation-building was precisely the point. Here was an opportunity to transform Afghanistan permanently; all they needed were resources—and the only coalition members who could provide the adequate resources were the Americans. But London would carry on regardless of whether Washington shared its vision—and so it was that Ryder and his team holed up in their cramped office in the Foreign and Commonwealth Office and devised a plan.

The resulting document was one of hundreds of such plans western diplomats would produce in the years ahead: pages of hazy, never-to-be-fulfilled goals, documents that papered over the gaping cracks in the coalition's efforts in Afghanistan with quasi-scientific development-speak about "stakeholder buy-in" and "positive feedback loops." Yet even by the genre's standards, Ryder's paper was a triumph of unreality. He knew that given Afghanistan's grinding poverty, a realistic counter-narcotics policy likely would take twenty or thirty years to be effective. However, he also understood that Blair's team would be dismayed by a long time frame. Politicians and even civil servants struggle to think more than a few years ahead, he surmised.

Ryder opted for a ten-year plan, a length of time that suggested the gravity of long-range thinking without dropping off the edge of the horizon. The plan's centerpiece was the revamping of Afghan agriculture, whether boosting the production of staples like wheat or introducing high-earning crops like saffron. Conspicuously absent from the first steps was any mention of measures to actually eradicate the poppy crop.

The officials at Number 10 Downing Street in London were delighted with the scheme, which promised an end to opium production without coercing anyone into doing it. In his heart, Ryder knew that the chances of meeting his self-imposed deadline were dim. Occasionally he also dwelled upon the bigger picture. Even if they persuaded Afghan farmers to grow other crops, history suggested that the poppy trade would simply move to another corner of the globe. "Opium production can't be tackled by fixing the supply side," Ryder later reflected. "It's all about demand." And demand, as he knew, had only one solution. "The only effective counter-narcotics program is to persuade people to stop using heroin."[6]

Finding out what motivated the UK's 100,000 heroin users appeared as complex as the Afghan mission. At least his scheme could do no harm, Ryder surmised, a conclusion American officials also seemed to reach. What Ryder didn't anticipate was his own government subverting his mission.[7]

For a week in early April 2002, Ryder reveled in Number 10's interest and the respect that a potentially large budget for counter-narcotics conferred upon him in Whitehall, the district of government offices in central London. A steady stream of visitors had begun filtering through his usually neglected office. Unfortunately, the vultures were also circling overhead.

By the end of the month Ryder was summoned to the permanent under-secretary's office to learn that British intelligence had claimed half of his budget for its own program to tackle the opium trade.[8] In the name of national security, British intelligence could get away with most things, including raiding aid budgets. If that wasn't likely to annoy the usually mild-mannered Ryder, he was sure to be furious when he learned what the money was for: British intelligence intended to launch a crop-eradication program by handing out millions to its favored warlords. Among those set to receive a $13 million payment was none other than Haji Zaman, the warlord whom US special forces accused of allowing Osama bin Laden to escape from Tora Bora just a few months before receiving a bribe from al-Qa'eda.

Ryder said later the money was not taken from his budget, and that they used their own funding. But he recognized the dangers of British intelligence's approach. By paying warlords like Zaman to eradicate crops, it was potentially creating a perverse incentive for the warlords to grow more poppy. The more they planted, the more they could get paid for destroying the crop—if, indeed, they did chop down any poppy plants. Moreover, Ryder noted that program oversight was likely to be limited, given the rough terrain and the negligible resources for inspecting the fields. In effect, Britain's counter-narcotics policy could be about to give a $62 million boost to the industry for the next poppy harvest. There were already worrying signs that large swathes of the south had been planted with poppy.

Ryder took the matter to UK Foreign Secretary Jack Straw, pointing out that British intelligence was effectively giving money to the very warlords who were pressuring poor farmers to grow poppies in the first place. Straw was noncommittal, however, explaining that this payment was merely a one-off.

Ryder later reflected that additional factors might be involved in this decision, such as the need to use the money to promote stability in the area. Zaman remained influential outside Jalalabad, although he was persona non grata to the US military. By giving Zaman a cash handout, the British might be accused of trying to buy the warlord's silence for his, and by proxy Britain's, role in bin Laden's escape.

British intelligence ended up paying Zaman and the other warlords, and while Ryder never got a clear sense of what the money had actually bought, he gravely doubted its effectiveness. In later reporting, the UK claimed that up to 15 percent of that year's crop had been destroyed, a figure that was never verified. Some Afghan officials traveled to eradication sites with cameras and took pictures holding up GPS devices to record time and location. But as one of the local inspectors admitted, they only photographed the corner of a field where the poppy had been flattened—the rest of the crop was untouched.[9]

The Americans shared Ryder's displeasure with the program's outcome and were less reserved in their criticism. A US embassy report assessed the British effort as inadequate "both conceptually and operationally," and pointed to the harsh fact that opium production went from 185 metric tonnes in the Taliban's last year to 2,600 metric tonnes in the summer of 2002.[10] By 2004, the crop had doubled again, a global record for the biggest harvest, which earned around $2.8 billion, more than the entire Afghan budget.[11]

The one counter-narcotics strategy the coalition members did not seriously discuss was the one that might have brought at least a measure of success. Even the most precise targeting of drug traffickers and most sensitive of aid programs to farmers was unlikely to prevent the aggressive return of poppy cultivation to Afghanistan. As commentators like the aid worker Sarah Chayes have pointed out, the problem with the drug trade wasn't simply that it buttressed the warlords' power base: The trade was so large that drug money pervaded every aspect of the economy. By championing counter-narcotics policies, the British were ensuring that this money stayed in the black market. As the drug trade grew, so did this shadow economy, which rapidly outstripped the legitimate one.

There was only one way to escape the trap, and that was to do as the Taliban had done: effectively legalize the industry. Legalization had powerful precedents in both Turkey and India. After failing with their own eradication drives in the late 1960s, these countries had tried licensing farmers to grow poppies for the morphine trade. The US had supported the earlier effort, granting Turkey and India protected-market status that obligated the US to buy a combined 80 percent of the raw material for American painkillers from both countries. The illegal trade in both nations rapidly shriveled.[12]

It wasn't clear that these models would be able to work in Afghanistan, however. The success of the legal markets in Turkey and India still required a degree of national enforcement to stop poppy farmers outside the program from feeding the demand for illegal heroin. Afghanistan could not ensure that farmers would grow the crop only for the legal trade, and thus legalization ran the risk of dramatically *increasing* overall opium production, as farmers took advantage of both the legal and illegal markets. The farm gate price for poppy sold to drug traffickers, furthermore, was likely to outstrip the legal one. There was a simple solution: Western governments could subsidize the legal crop so that farmers received more money for it. This idea wasn't as outlandish as it may have seemed, given that the cost of eradication was nearly $16,000 per acre. By contrast, buying up the poppy even at a cost of $177 per kilogram of opium would cost half that.[13]

Incorporating Afghanistan's illegal business into the international market for legal opium derivatives, such as the hospital staple morphine, presented challenges. Large western morphine producers, such as Canada and Australia, vigorously protected their market shares and could be counted on to oppose any legalization of the Afghan poppy trade. Yet the advantages of aligning a legal industry with the interests of the Afghan government—just as the Taliban had done—would compensate for these drawbacks. With suitable incentives, officials would seek to incorporate as much of Afghanistan's opium trade into the legal system so that they could better exploit it. Whatever inevitable kickbacks arose to grease the wheels would enforce the process. At the same time, the Afghans themselves were much more likely to target drug traffickers outside that system.

In this approach, an element of window dressing is unavoidable. How different would a legal system be from the one that existed—one in which every level of the Afghan government was already complicit? Legalizing the poppy trade would most likely have just conferred the illusion of legality to it—yet appearances can be important.[14] But the Americans and British never seriously entertained the model. Instead the UK's counter-narcotics policy set the West on a collision course with Afghan farmers that would prove far more injurious to westerners and Afghans than anyone predicted.

CHAPTER 9

Homecoming

After the Taliban's leadership abandoned Kandahar in December 2001, most of its members fled to Pakistan. There was scarcely time to reach contacts within Pakistan's spy service, the ISI, and several senior members simply crossed the border with the throngs of other Afghans fleeing the fighting, ministers reduced to refugees in a few hours. The only one who had no intention of leaving, at least not at first, was Mullah Omar. Even in defeat, he remained sullen and defiant. As the American missiles fell around Kandahar, Mullah Omar fled into the northern Helmand mountains from where Karzai and his US-backed forces were advancing to depose him.[1]

Yet even that bitter moment held the promise of redemption for Mullah Omar. For he knew well that brutish as Afghan politics may be (all but one twentieth-century Afghan king has been either murdered or deposed), it had a certain enduring form that favors exiled leaders. If he could escape capture and execution, he was positioned to launch an insurgency by playing on the divisions between the country's fractious tribes.

That first summer after falling from power, Mullah Omar shuttled from one desolate village to the next, agitating against the Americans and their Afghan supporters but receiving little support. Among the villagers he met, some of them his own commanders, there was also a powerful feeling that the ideology the Taliban represented had been proved a failure. In Pakistan, his inner circle was seeking both as a group and individually to make peace with Karzai's government. As for the ISI, which had nurtured the movement over the years, there was little support. Everyone had turned their back on him except for a few die-hard tribesmen.[2]

Mullah Omar's only solace came from an unlikely source: the Americans. Over the course of 2002, US special forces had waged a campaign against the low-ranking Taliban commanders who had remained in southern and eastern Afghanistan. Yet the Americans had little knowledge of the country, and often relied on their Afghan proxies to tell them whom to target. Warlords like Gul Agha Sherzai in Kandahar readily exploited such ignorance to pursue their own vendettas against rival clans.[3] Frequently Sherzai would submit a tribal leader's name to the Americans and the US would target the man's home with an air strike or special forces would kick in his doors, ransack his home, and drag military-aged men off into the night.

The occasional value of these raids paled in comparison to the damage they inflicted. Night raids were particularly loathed in Afghanistan, where the home held a special sanctity. After their arrest, prisoners faced further indignities. The lucky ones were handed over to Kandahar's overflowing prisons, where their release depended on their families paying a hefty bribe. The less fortunate were taken away by American interrogators for further questioning. In early 2002, the White House had yet to issue its secret directives on the use of so-called enhanced interrogation techniques against detainees. Nonetheless, the Bush administration refused to recognize those detained during the "War on Terror" as prisoners of war, who would therefore have been protected by the Geneva Conventions that prohibited torture. CIA and US special forces interrogators took this legal gray area to be a license to routinely maltreat detainees through starvation, sleep deprivation, and physical abuse such as breaking kneecaps, crushing genitals, and hanging of prisoners by their arms until their shoulders dislocated.

Drawing sketched by Thomas V. Curtis, a reserve MP sergeant, showing how detainees were tortured at Bagram air base in 2002. According to the army documents from the investigation into the abuse—which include more drawings like this one—new prisoners were often hooded, shackled, and isolated for twenty-four to forty-eight hours.

In the absence of accurate figures on the scale and nature of the abuse, the death of a taxi driver, Dilawer, at the hands of American soldiers in December 2002 represents the fate of many.[4] Dilawer and three passengers were detained by a warlord allied to the Americans as he drove past a military base. The men were handed over to the US interrogators who promptly hand-cuffed them to a fence so they would be unable to sleep. Dilawer was later taken to a room and suspended above the ground by his wrists for four days, during which time he was subjected to vicious beatings that, according to a subsequent post-mortem, snapped his shoulder joints and turned his legs to "pulp." Two soldiers were later sentenced to up to three months in prison in connection with the case. The US military later suspected that to win American trust and lucrative contracts, the friendly warlord, Jan Baz Khan, was himself orchestrating attacks against the US base and then handing over innocent Afghans he claimed were responsible.

Most US troops were not involved in this sort of torture; in fact, many special forces teams formed important bonds with local communities, often shielding them from the warlords' predatory behavior. Yet the abuse was persistent enough to create the impression among Afghans that maltreatment at the foreigners' hands was common. Furthermore, by torturing detainees—even selectively—the Americans lost any authority they might have had to rein in Sherzai's own brutal behavior.

By endorsing torture, American policy in Afghanistan appeared designed to goad the remnants of the Taliban into armed revolt. Indeed, given the scale of the persecution, it is extraordinary that the insurgency took so long to materialize. A typical case in which one former Taliban commander's persecution became a rallying point is the story of Mullah Ahmed Shah. A low-level commander from the Mushan district south of Kandahar, Shah had returned to his village after the Taliban's overthrow. Like many Afghans, he blamed the Taliban for leading the country to defeat at America's hands. Having spent half of his forty years at war, he was ready to hang up his AK-47.

In January 2002, Sherzai's men dragged Shah from his home and beat him before releasing him. The same thing happened again later in the year. Only after his third detention at the end of 2002 did Shah reluctantly leave his home for the hills and armed rebellion, persuaded that he would have to fight to drive out the warlords and foreign devils, just as he had done for much of the previous two decades. In areas of southern Afghanistan like Panjwei, Shah's experience was the norm for Taliban commanders.

For Mullah Omar, hiding in the bony hills above Helmand, the persecution of former Taliban commanders was reason to hope. He began receiving a succession of his former comrades, who urged him to resume the fight against the invaders and their allies.[5] He was getting similarly encouraging messages from Pakistan, where other Taliban leaders were giving up on their efforts to negotiate with the Karzai government.

In February 2002, Wakil Ahmed Muttawakil, the foreign minister under the Taliban, offered to return to Afghanistan to serve as an intermediary between the Taliban and Kabul, only to be detained by the Americans and sent to Guantánamo.[6] Jalaluddin Haqqani, an influential member of the Zadran tribe on the border with Pakistan, also sought a deal with the Karzai government, but when his younger brother traveled to Kabul in early 2002, American forces ignored his overtures and subsequently arrested him, and allegedly tortured him as well.[7] The absence of Taliban representatives was particularly striking at the Loya Jirga, or tribal gathering, outside Kabul in June 2002 to confirm Karzai's presidency.[8]

At some point in 2002, Mullah Omar appeared to have attracted enough support to launch a rebellion against the forces that had pushed him from power the previous year. However, the logistical challenges of managing an insurgency from the hills of northern Helmand were considerable, as was the risk of the Americans hitting the Taliban's leadership. The precise impetus behind Mullah Omar's departure from Afghanistan is unknown, but according to one source, whose version of events could not be verified, he received an invitation from Brigadier Sultan Amir, one of his former handlers connected to the ISI, to come to Pakistan.

Amir informed him that Islamabad's policy was changing. Officially, the country had turned against the Taliban, just as President Pervez Musharraf had promised the Americans. Behind the scenes, Islamabad was calculating that American interest in Afghanistan would soon pass, allowing Pakistan to resume suzerainty over its neighbor. The Pakistanis were already deeply suspicious of Hamid Karzai's regime, with its strong representation of Northern Alliance interests, which Islamabad saw as an ally of India. It was time for the Taliban to reunite and cast out this puppet of their enemies. Amir informed Mullah Omar that a villa had already been prepared for him in Quetta, and that the rest of the Taliban leadership was waiting for him there.[9]

Re-forming the Taliban would require the utmost caution if Pakistan were to avoid the Americans' wrath, but Amir, often known by his nom de guerre of Colonel Imam, was a man of rare abilities. Early in his career, in 1974, he had trained with the US special forces at Fort Bragg, North Carolina, and had returned to Pakistan with the lessons of Vietnam ringing in his ears. After the Soviets invaded Afghanistan, he worked with the CIA to coordinate the resistance, overseeing fighting around Jalalabad, where a young and wiry Mullah Omar had also fought. At one point Amir had shown Texas Congressman Charlie Wilson and then–Deputy CIA Director Robert Gates around the front lines.

After the Soviet Union left Afghanistan in 1989, Amir served as Pakistan's consul in the western Afghan city of Herat, which fell to the Taliban early in the post-Soviet civil war. The warlord that the Taliban ousted from Herat later blamed Amir for orchestrating his overthrow. Whether or not this was true is unclear, but Amir did go on to advise Mullah Omar, as the Taliban seized Mazar-e-Sharif, Jalalabad, and Kabul.[10]

By the time of the September 11 attacks, Amir had retired from the ISI but was part of a cadre of former officers the spy agency relied upon to manage its relationships with Islamist groups. A burly fifty-year-old, Amir still dressed like a mujahid, with a white *shalwar kameez*—a long shirt and baggy pants— and a scruffy commando jacket, and kept his graying beard long in accordance with strict Islamic tradition. After the attacks he had rushed to Mullah Omar's side until the American bombing began and the Taliban leader fled Kandahar.

Pakistani President Pervez Musharraf's initial decision to side with the Americans against the Taliban outraged Amir. Like those of many ISI officers then and since, Amir's own views about the superpower had shifted over the 1990s. He'd come to view America as a malign force that sought to curtail the Islamist movement in Afghanistan and Kashmir, where jihadists backed by Pakistan were battling Indian forces over one territory they both claimed.[11] The Pakistani military's alliance with these Islamists had served Islamabad well in its rivalry with India, but there were questions over how much control the ISI truly exerted over these groups.[12] In the days after 9/11, large demonstrations broke out across Pakistan in support of al-Qa'eda, with militant groups such as Harkat ul-Mujahideen proving prominent organizers. Within Pakistan's urban areas these groups were widespread, with networks of safe houses, arms caches, and training camps. In some cities they controlled entire districts. The ISI had to deal with these groups carefully to avoid exposing the limits of its influence.

Musharraf's decision to join the "War on Terror" threatened to expose rifts between the Pakistani state and the militants. He was forced to walk a fine line as he sought to appease Washington and pacify the country's Islamist community and its substantial Pashtun population in the border areas with Afghanistan, many of whom were sympathetic to the Taliban. Opinion polls also suggested there was widespread opposition to Pakistan collaborating with the US.[13] At a meeting of the country's senior generals in Islamabad on September 12, 2001, Musharraf warned that America was a "wounded bear" and that Pakistan risked marginalization and even an attack if it continued supporting Islamist movements whose religious creed was now seen as a threat to the US and its allies.[14] If the Pakistanis sidestepped American anger now, however, he believed they could turn the situation to their advantage. His spy chief Mahmud Ahmed predicted that the US would give Islamabad a free hand to manage Afghanistan once its own short-term interests had been fulfilled.[15]

Musharraf decided to bow to some of America's demands and promised a crackdown on militants and to allow the use of Pakistani territory to stage attacks into Afghanistan. When it came to publicly condemning the Taliban, however, he pointedly refused despite Washington's best efforts to get him to choose sides. In a televised address to his country at the end of September, Musharraf even promised to use whatever leverage he could with the Americans to prevent "any damage to Afghanistan or the Taliban." Even his promise to tackle militants only went so far.[16]

Musharraf was happy enough to work with the CIA in targeting al-Qa'eda. After Tora Bora, what was left of al-Qa'eda had streamed over the border into Pakistan. That country's security forces picked up many of them to sell to the Americans. Occasionally Pakistan's nets caught big fish; in 2003, the architect of 9/11, Khalid Sheikh Mohammed, was detained in Rawalpindi in a joint operation involving Pakistani police and the CIA. When it came to homegrown Pakistani militant groups such as Harkat ul-Mujahideen, the spy agency's clampdown was negligible. The ISI was prepared to arrest some militants and banned half a dozen organizations. Yet the fundamental belief in Islamabad that radical Islamist groups were the ultimate protection against Pakistan's main threat, India, never changed.

As for the Taliban, Pakistan would shelter the group, which the ISI regarded as the only cogent political force left in Afghanistan that would still follow its orders. In December 2001, the ISI held a meeting in Peshawar with the Taliban's newly exiled leadership and prominent Pashtun tribal leaders from the borderland to reiterate their support for the Taliban and assure them they would not turn them over to the Americans. They discussed how to agitate against Hamid Karzai's new government, but plans were still inchoate compared to the following year when Amir contacted Mullah Omar.[17]

The CIA was aware of the ISI's outreach to the Taliban but was focused on dismantling al-Qa'eda's network. Pakistan's cooperation was considered essential to that effort, and the US was prepared to turn a blind eye to ISI's links to other groups, including the Taliban, to take down the group that had perpetrated the 9/11 attacks. As Islamabad station chief Robert Grenier admitted, "The Taliban wasn't our top priority. Al-Qa'eda was."

In early March 2003, Mullah Omar reconvened the Taliban leadership in Quetta. It was the first time the Taliban's inner circle had been together since their ouster from Kandahar, and tears were shed in the dusty compound of the modest villa the ISI had selected for the occasion. Since they had last met, their views on Afghanistan had been repeatedly upended: from despair after their apparent rejection by the country to a renewed belief in the righteousness of their cause. According to one account, Mullah Omar greeted his inner circle with the customary handshakes and kisses and an air of expectation that these men would form the operational command of the resurgent Taliban in the years ahead.[18]

They included Mullah Obaidullah, the former defense minister and the man who had once delivered an order of surrender to Hamid Karzai, who would oversee the Taliban's daily operations in Afghanistan. He and Mullah Omar fought together against the Russians in the 1980s and had worked at the same religious seminary outside Kandahar before the Taliban's launch. Mullah Baradar, another founder, was to become the Taliban's managing director, recruiting commanders inside Pakistan and marshaling the movement's troops. And Tayeb Agha, formerly on the Taliban's financial committee, would raise funds.

Also present at the springtime meeting in Quetta were the men who a few weeks later would return to Afghanistan to lead the offensive, notably Mullah Dadullah Akhund, a one-legged former mujahid who had made his name in the 1980s for beheading captured Soviet troops. When US forces had entered Afghanistan in 2001, Dadullah had been in charge of the northern front around Kunduz, narrowly escaping the town's encirclement by General Abdul Rashid Dostum by bribing his way through Northern Alliance lines. Within the Taliban leadership, Dadullah represented a new generation of the movement that was more closely aligned to al-Qa'eda's ideology of global jihad.[19] Dadullah was to promote in Afghanistan the practice of suicide bombing, borrowing techniques of the Jordanian al-Qa'eda leader in Iraq, Abu Musab al-Zarqawi.

The rise of this new, jihadist strain of the Taliban was to prove unpopular with Afghanistan's local tribes, which soon pushed back against the excessive brutality. But overall, the Taliban leadership was remarkably effective at cajoling, threatening, and motivating Afghans to join their cause. It helped that the Taliban could tap into public discontent, whether it stemmed from the national affront of the American invasion, or the tolls exacted by Afghan national police at roadside checkpoints, or the brutality of the newly installed warlords. They also benefited from a simple declaration that served as a rallying cry to disaffected tribes across the south. As Mullah Omar announced following that meeting in 2003, the war was not over. In fact, it was only just beginning.[20]

A month or so later in May 2003, Mullah Dadullah and a dozen fighters gunned their motorcycles through the border crossing at Spin Boldak, waved on by Pakistani policemen. Naturally enough, they were heading for the Panjwei area of southern Afghanistan, home to many of the Taliban commanders who had recently been roughed up by Sherzai's men and the seat of the Noorzai tribe that had lost out to other clans in the domestic political shake-up the western invasion caused. The landscape through which Dadullah and his men passed showed signs of rebirth. That season's poppy crop had just been planted, and already the bare fields were bursting with the dark green variegated leaves of the young seedlings.

With a typical lack of fuss he got to work, reactivating the Taliban's *andi-wali,* or network of former colleagues, coaxing those who had hung up their AK-47s to dust them off. As he grew in confidence, he instructed mosque imams, or clerics, to use their loudspeakers to hail villagers, calling out, "You will not be free. Your wives and your children will not have rights. Your country is under the occupation of infidels."

Given the presence of US patrols and Sherzai's militia checkpoints around Kandahar, Dadullah didn't stage large-scale attacks there. He didn't have to take the risk; as his fighters fanned out from Panjwei to neighboring provinces, they encountered other opportunities to strike at the new government and its foreign allies. In March 2003, Ricardo Munguia, an engineer from Ecuador working for the International Committee of the Red Cross, was driving with three local staff members when their white Toyota Land Cruiser was stopped at a Taliban roadblock in a narrow valley defile on the road leading to Oruzgun. A few other cars had been stopped, but Munguia's vehicle, with its distinctive red cross on the doors, was singled out. By several accounts, the Taliban commander at the checkpoint spoke with Dadullah on his satellite phone to confirm their target, then lined up Munguia against his vehicle and pumped his body full of bullets.[21] Corpse and vehicle were then set alight.

There were few clearer symbols, in the spring of 2003, that the Taliban was returning. Those western intelligence agencies that wanted to dig a little deeper could discover the ISI running training camps for Taliban recruits along the border, funds and arms shipments arriving from the Gulf countries, and shopping sprees in Quetta and Karachi in which the Taliban bought hundreds of motorbikes, pickup trucks, and satellite phones.

Yet few in the West were paying attention to Afghanistan. The week before Munguia's death, the US had invaded Iraq, and the entire international apparatus—military, intelligence, diplomatic, and development—that had previously been fixated on Afghanistan was pivoting westward toward the Middle East. When the West turned its attention to Afghanistan a few years later, the insurgency was in full bloom.

PART II

A DANGEROUS ALLIANCE

2004–2007

CHAPTER 10

Imperial Vision

I t took the US just three weeks to overthrow Saddam Hussein's regime in
Iraq. The March 2003 invasion was as resounding and rapid a success as
the campaign in Afghanistan. The Bush administration had intended to use
the same plan in Iraq that it had applied to Afghanistan: a quick handover
of power to a local administration headed by a favored Iraqi exile, Ahmed
Chalabi. But the differences between the two wars soon became apparent. In
the capital city of Baghdad, Iraqis began a frenzy of theft and destruction, as
the country's poor and downtrodden grabbed what they could from ministry
buildings, schools, and hospitals.

Even as the looting began, the White House's thinking about nation-building
had started to change. Before the war, US Secretary of State Colin Powell had
suggested that the US would need to take an active role in framing whatever
government replaced Saddam's regime. Defense Secretary Donald Rumsfeld
rejected the idea, but Powell continued to insist on some sort of international
oversight, whether from the US or the United Nations. The White House
considered his suggestions seriously once the invasion was under way.[1] In early
April, Rumsfeld approved the creation of the Coalition Provisional Authority, a US-led administration that put America firmly in the business of nation-building that it had so studiously avoided in Afghanistan.[2]

It's not clear what caused this shift in the defense secretary's thinking. The
CPA's mandate was being formulated before the looting in Baghdad began,
yet even the sight of Iraqi government buildings being ransacked didn't sway
Rumsfeld: "Stuff happens," he said at a press conference, by way of comment. Harder for Rumsfeld to take, however, was the growing appearance
of ineptitude. On some level, the Iraq war had been intended as an exercise

in American power, but the sight of the senior US official in Baghdad, retired general Jay Garner, flapping away at press conferences while the city
burned revealed just how little control the US had over the situation. The
Coalition Provisional Authority, in part, became a means to alleviate that
embarrassment.[3]

Rumsfeld personally selected Paul Bremer to lead the new administration.
Bremer had little experience of the Middle East but was an energetic manager
who could be relied upon to project authority. Rumsfeld did not give Bremer
detailed instructions on what to do in Baghdad, and the defense secretary
remained wary of embracing a full-blown nation-building agenda.[4] Yet by
approving the CPA, Rumsfeld had opened the door for those who, like Jim
Dobbins, the former special representative to Afghanistan, called for more
robust efforts in Kabul.

A few months after the US invaded Iraq, Dobbins coauthored a widely
read paper titled "America's Role in Nation-building from Germany to Iraq."
Since leaving the White House in 2002, Dobbins had taken up a directorship
at Rand Corporation, a military-sponsored think tank. Still rankling at what
he saw as the Bush administration's dismissive attitude toward the international rebuilding effort in the Balkans and Washington's failure to back a
similar campaign in Afghanistan, Dobbins set out to debunk the "light footprint" approach. He argued for large-scale reconstruction efforts, citing the
scale and ambition of the Marshall Plan in postwar Europe and the positive
effects of the international mission in the Balkans as examples of what the
Bush administration could do in Iraq and Afghanistan with more troops and
money. He neglected less encouraging examples, such as Vietnam. The paper
was readily embraced by a coalition of liberal and neoconservative interven-
tionists in Washington. The former seized the opportunity to criticize Bush
for underresourcing the effort in Afghanistan and the ill-conceived blunder
into Iraq; the latter of whom were glad to have their faith in America's transformative power reaffirmed.

Bremer, a neoconservative, took an early version of Dobbins's paper with
him to Baghdad in May 2003, which informed his activist approach to reconstruction. Bremer likened Saddam Hussein's Iraq to Nazi Germany, and
believed the country needed a complete overhaul similar to the one the US
had given Germany after World War II—an example that Dobbins held up as
the gold standard of nation-building. "The country needed to be rebuilt from
the bottom up," Bremer claimed.[5]

He promptly disbanded the Iraqi military, sacked government officials
who had belonged to Saddam Hussein's Ba'ath party, and declared that the
country's state-run industries would be opened up to outside investment and

global market forces. He also began creating his own bureaucracy to manage the reconstruction. Soon 1,600 American officials were managing their own budget of $20 billion, bypassing the oversight of not just the Iraqi ministries but also such established aid donors as USAID.[6]

Dobbins's views on Iraq also refocused Washington on what was going wrong in Afghanistan. He went on to argue that invading Iraq had fatally drained resources from Afghanistan.[7] If the US had deployed to Afghanistan a peacekeeping force with greater reconstruction funds sooner, he claimed, the country wouldn't now be struggling. Hamid Karzai would not have had to rely on corrupt warlords for power, and the country could have spent money on projects—roads, bridges, schools, and the like—that could have cemented Afghans' loyalty to their new president. "If more resources were directed to Afghanistan, we'd be looking at dramatically different outcomes," said Dobbins.[8]

Dobbins suggested that one peacekeeper for every fifty civilians—the same ratio that had been used in the Balkans—should be the norm for Afghanistan and Iraq.[9] He also suggested the US boost reconstruction funds to Balkan levels. Bosnia had received sixteen times more money than the $5 billion allotted to the Afghans over a five-year period. Boosting Afghan funds to the same level would mean providing Afghanistan with $75 billion. In Dobbins's view, the more troops and money you put in, the more you got out.

Dobbins was by no means the only voice urging for greater resources for Afghanistan. Rumsfeld himself showed signs of embracing a broader mission in Afghanistan as he had done in Iraq. In December 2002 he had hired Martin Strmecki to develop a plan to train the Afghan military to buttress Karzai's government. The US had taken on that task at the Bonn conference, but so far its efforts in the field had been nonexistent. Strmecki was an academic and a former Nixon aide, who had researched a book for the disgraced president called *No More Vietnams* and had written his doctoral thesis on the illusory nature of Soviet power in Afghanistan, a subject that sat uneasily with his own recommendations for a more hands-on approach. He believed the US had been too cautious and that its lack of engagement was preventing Karzai from establishing his rule.

The idea of helping Afghans help themselves appealed to Rumsfeld and his conservative credo.[10] Rumsfeld told Strmecki to wrap his plan for the military into a new strategy the Bush administration was planning for Afghanistan called "Accelerating Success."

In May 2003, the Bush administration offered Zalmay Khalilzad, the White House's principal expert on the Muslim world, the ambassadorship to Kabul and $1.7 billion in additional funds to launch his own nation-building

program in Afghanistan. Khalilzad had been born in Mazar-e-Sharif before
emigrating to the US. His hawkish views on the use of American power contrasted with an acute understanding of the region's politics. He had opposed
creating the CPA, arguing that instead power should be handed over to Iraqis
quickly.[11] But Afghanistan posed a different challenge, he believed. There
was a role for nation-building given the inadequacies of Karzai's administration and its weak government structure. While he had been against a more
hands-on approach in Baghdad, he felt that elements of the model were essential in a less-developed country like Afghanistan. The open question was
whether the money would be well spent.

By the time Khalizad arrived in Kabul in November 2003, the US had
spent a total of $500 million on reconstruction over the preceding two years
with little to show for it. The flagship school and health clinic program of
USAID was a case in point. In 2002, a $73 million contract had been awarded
to the US engineering firm Louis Berger to construct 1,000 schools and health
clinics across Afghanistan within two years—"a school and clinic in every district" was the claim from USAID's press office. Yet from the start the program
revealed a startling naïveté from the aid agency. Louis Berger was directed to
build schools to American standards, including walls capable of withstanding
California-scale earthquakes and wheelchair-accessible entries. Yet many areas
of Afghanistan lacked roads capable of transporting the heavy cranes needed
for such buildings.[12]

When USAID dropped its high standards, quality control plummeted. The
resulting schools were so shoddily built that their walls were soon collapsing
and their roofs caving in. Two years into the contract, only one hundred buildings had been completed, most of them refurbished structures; the prospect
of Louis Berger completing the contract looked dim. USAID eventually got
around to checking some of the potential building sites, only to discover that
some were sheer mountain slopes, riverbeds, and in one case a local graveyard.[13]

Such incompetence raised questions about the West's ability to carry out
its reconstruction mission in Afghanistan and served to underscore the point
repeatedly made by Finance Minister Ashraf Ghani during this period—the
reliance on western contractors was overshadowing the Afghan government's
own efforts to rebuild the country. During this period, he continued to lack
the resources—some $200 million—to pay basic salaries for the country's
240,000 government employees, including engineers, teachers, doctors, and
police. The Afghan trust fund he advocated for—the one meant to provide
a central repository for international donor funds—had never received the
amount that Ghani had hoped. Instead the bulk of money had been spent
by government agencies like USAID on western contractors or funneled to

aid the UN's agencies. In 2003, the UN had launched an appeal for a further $900 million, on top of the $1.8 billion already given at Tokyo in 2002. Much of that money went toward paying overheads and international staff— at the same time that Afghan officials were going unpaid.

The international reconstruction effort wasn't just starving the Afghan government of funds. It was also fueling corruption. Ghani had pointed out the year before that if the West tried to do too much at once, they would end up creating a parallel bureaucracy that would flood the country with money while lacking accountability and local knowledge. This not only would lead to failed projects, it would also undermine the government's authority.

Indeed, the influx of cash almost immediately fueled corruption. Washington would later blame the Afghan government for rampant graft, but what is striking about the early years of the US reconstruction effort is how often it was *American* firms ripping off their own government. Louis Berger was later revealed to be overbilling USAID tens of millions of dollars—the exact figure is still not known, and may never be ascertained given the complex web of subcontractors the firm used.[14] Even the Maryland-based nonprofit relief agency hired by USAID to monitor Louis Berger's work was itself revealed to be shaking down an Afghan contractor for $50,000 in return for passing their schools in inspections.[15]

The West got considerably better value by giving money directly to the Afghan government. Louis Berger charged on average $226,000 per site, in contrast to the $40,000 the Afghan government said it was spending on its own school and refurbishing program that delivered far more schools for less money. What's more, government-spent money was more likely to be circulated within the Afghan economy instead of being paid out to foreign contractors.[16]

USAID was an easy scapegoat for these early failures. From a Republican point of view, the agency appeared to fit every negative stereotype of a government aid organization: It seemed to be stacked with bureaucrats who, when they weren't pushing paper around desks, were trying to give away money on hopelessly idealistic projects in the developing world. In fact, USAID's approach to flawed subcontracting was largely the result of the Clinton administration's attempts to introduce competition into overseas aid through outsourcing government-funded projects to large engineering firms. USAID lacked the manpower or expertise to hold these firms accountable or to identify failing projects.

These early setbacks should have revealed the limits of America's ability to rebuild Afghanistan. Instead USAID officials—like their military counterparts— embraced the view that their early failures were due to lack of both manpower and money. "If only we'd had more money, we could have done so much more," said Jim Bever, USAID's chief representative, in 2003.[17] Corrupt contractors weren't the only ones hoping to turn on the Washington spigot, so it seemed. Organizations such as USAID also stood to gain power and prestige once the money started to flow.

Upon arriving in Afghanistan in 2003, Khalilzad was aware of these problems and had a number of possible solutions. Drawing on some of the lessons of Iraq, the ambassador sought to create yet another administration—his own—staffed with businessmen and entrepreneurs who would supplant the USAID bureaucrats and the warlords in government ministries. This new body was called the Afghanistan Reconstruction Group, made up of a dozen or so American businesses and consultants with political connections in Washington. The ARG, as it was called, set itself up at the embassy.[18] Khalilzad intended for the group to become a conduit for all reconstruction decisions while unlocking the country's economic potential, although it lacked the mandate to run ministries or the ability to actually manage projects.[19]

Ashraf Ghani recognized that the arrival of a miniature American government threatened to bypass his own finance ministry, and braced himself for yet another battle over who should control the country's reconstruction. His rivalry with Khalilzad had a further undercurrent. Both Afghan émigrés aspired to lead their country, and each knew that whoever could claim to have rebuilt the country would win widespread support for a presidential bid.

Ghani and Khalilzad's relationship stretched back years. They had attended prestigious high schools in Kabul before pursuing academic careers in the US, and had enjoyed a mildly competitive acquaintance ever since. Their paths had crossed at Columbia University in New York in the late 1970s. Ghani was beginning his doctorate at the same time that Khalilzad was taking up a teaching position.

Despite their similar backgrounds, the two men held very different political beliefs. Khalilzad was fresh from his tutelage at the University of Chicago under Albert Wohlstetter, one of the godfathers of neoconservatism, who had advocated a more aggressive approach to the Soviet Union at the beginning of the Cold War. Wohlstetter had rejected what he saw as the nihilism underpinning early American thinking on the nuclear deterrent—namely that each side needed enough bombs to ensure the other's destruction—in favor of taking on the Russians with conventional weapons. The Reagan administration later favored the approach, and Khalilzad soon had a job at the White House, where he pushed the US to support the mujahideen resistance to the Soviet invasion of Afghanistan.

Ghani had also opposed the Soviet invasion, but he was naturally skeptical of the claims his rival made for the mujahideen and was more self-conscious about shopping around his Afghan credentials. He settled into a more prosaic, steady career at the World Bank, while Khalilzad's star burned brightly in the neoconservative firmament.

The presence in Kabul of both the progressive, if cantankerous, Ghani and the florid and right-wing Khalilzad was a recipe for confrontation. Ghani wanted to place more power in the people's hands. Khalilzad had faith in a top-down approach. "They were temperamentally and ideologically different," said Scott Guggenheim, the World Bank official who had helped set up the National Solidarity Program in Afghanistan in early 2002. "Put another way, they just didn't like each other very much."[20]

Their designs for the country inevitably clashed. Ghani had set up a considerable power base at the finance ministry. President Karzai was often absent, and when he was around he feigned to know little about numbers. So at cabinet meetings Ghani was left to oversee the financial affairs of other ministers, some of whom were sympathetic technocrats but most were traditional warlords who didn't take to being lectured to by the US-educated finance minister.

Ghani's mixture of self-confidence and venom also irked Karzai, who had grown weary of his badgering for reform. Ghani had set the stage for the sinuous, smooth-talking Khalilzad, who immediately became the president's confidant. With his reconstruction money and influence at the White House, Khalilzad

The Afghan minister Ashraf Ghani advocated a more limited role for western agencies in reconstructing the country and insisted that Afghans knew best regarding their country's priorities. (Photo courtesy of Staff Sergeant Ryan Crane)

all too readily relieved Karzai of much of the burden of government, massaging the political system, dispatching troublesome warlords, and commandeering the reconstruction effort. Khalilzad might not be so grandly imperial as Bremer in Baghdad, but he appeared to be equally enthralled by his newfound power.

Ghani tried to fight back and push his own, more limited view of reconstruction with Karzai and the Americans. He pointed to the considerable achievements from this approach. There were the tangible successes in health care and education; almost half of the country had access to basic medical care, compared to 9 percent under the Taliban, and 5 million children were in some form of education, up from 1 million in 2001. A third of those were girls, after the Taliban's ban on female education was lifted. Then there were victories that were harder to quantify, such as the creation of a free press and a vibrant media scene. Afghans' ability to speak openly about the country's past and its current troubles spoke to the underlying strength of their civil society.

Yet Ghani was unable to stop the ARG's flood of grand plans in 2004: a pipeline across the country to take gas from central Asia to Pakistan, mines that could tap into Afghanistan's rich metal deposits, the creation of multi-million-dollar saffron and pistachio nut cultivation.[21] Ghani was not opposed to all of their schemes—some, such as a ring road linking together the country's main cities, he had long supported—but only if they developed Afghan autonomy.

Initially Ghani's inklings were proven right: The ARG's ambitions represented a radical overreach. Many of their most fantastical projects died on delivery. The ARG team of former executives and industry experts cut increasingly isolated figures on the embassy grounds where they lived in spartan temporary housing that resembled a rehabilitation facility. When they weren't convening endless meetings at the embassy to the exasperation of USAID officials, they took to lecturing unsuspecting Afghan officials on the benefits of trickle-down economics.

But there was one project the ARG championed that would have an enduring impact on the country's future. The Kajaki dam and hydroelectric plant in northern Helmand province, built by American engineers in the 1950s and '60s at the height of the Cold War, was barely functioning, so shortly after arriving in Kabul in November 2003, Khalilzad urged USAID to complete work on the dam. The early Bush administration might have balked at getting involved in such a large infrastructure project, but the benefits of repairing the dam's two 16.5-megawatt turbines and installing a third unit, along with refurbishing the transmission lines and substations to Kandahar, were undeniable: The dam could meet a sizeable chunk of southern Afghanistan's energy needs.[22]

One of Khalilzad's first acts as ambassador was to sign off on a $20 million contract for a preliminary study on the repair work. The project was slated to cost $125 million. Neither Khalilzad nor any other US representatives consulted Ashraf Ghani or the local government in Kajaki about the project. If the US embassy had done so, they would have discovered Ghani had already carried out his own assessment of the dam and concluded that its two functional turbines could be rehabilitated for just $500,000.

Ghani's frustrations over being sidelined on issues like Kajaki represented a growing rift between the finance minister and the rest of Afghanistan's power structure. The Afghan cabinet had taken to ignoring him and held their meetings when they knew he could not attend. He had to rely on the likes of Hanif Atmar, the rural affairs minister, and other members of the "reform team" to brief him on the warlords and members of the Northern Alliance, who retained a vice-like grip on the government.

Ghani also found that many in the international community who had once supported him had turned against him for his opposition to the United Nations and much of the international reconstruction effort. He still retained the backing of the UN senior representative Jean Arnault, who was sympathetic to his views on how Afghan ministries had been sidelined and starved of funds. In late 2004 they jointly sent a memo to the White House and other governments asking them to reallocate money from poorly performing aid projects to essential expenses such as wages for government employees. They were informed that the US was already spending enough on Afghan reconstruction and that they preferred to use USAID and their system of contractors.[23]

It turned out to be one of Ghani's last acts. Khalilzad had begun suggesting to Karzai that it was time to replace his troublesome finance minister. A few months later, in January 2005, Karzai would do just that, removing an important brake on expensive pipe dreams and rampant corruption, two bugbears of the reconstruction effort that would soon undermine the dream that many foreigners and Afghans alike had for the ravaged country.

PRTs

A s American money began to pour into Afghanistan upon Ambassador Zalmay Khalilzad's arrival in November 2003, the US confronted a fundamental challenge facing all the country's rulers. It was easy enough to draw up grand plans in Kabul, but Afghanistan's far-flung provinces had no local administrations to implement them. As project after project conceived in the capital struggled to take off outside the city, it slowly became clear that the Afghan government—and its international sponsors—had limited control over the country.

Afghanistan had no history of a strong government. The kings in Kabul had traditionally relied on consent rather than coercion of their tribal allies across the country's thirty-two provinces. Since King Zahir Shah's time, each province had had a veneer of central control in the form of a governor's office and local branches of each main ministry. When Hamid Karzai took power in 2001, the provincial government consisted of little more than a presidentially appointed governor and his own private militia. Their budgets were minimal, with governors usually viewing their position as an opportunity to make money by extracting profits from local industry.

This gave new fuel to those American and British officials, who continued to argue that soldiers should be used to establish greater control over the country, especially its more remote regions where the Taliban and even al-Qa'eda could regain a footing. In the summer of 2002 Colonel Nick Carter, an ambitious British officer who had been assigned to the US military headquarters as chief planner at Bagram airport, drew up a fresh scheme to push western troops into the provinces in the name of good governance. The forty-two-year-old Carter was embarking on his first staff job at a headquarters run by a three-star general. But he operated at several ranks higher than the decorations on his lapel indicated. He knew that the American commander Lieutenant General Dan McNeill was focused on counterterrorism and on rounding up any last pockets of Taliban resistance. That gave him free rein to expand the reach of Karzai's administration into the provinces.

The question Carter faced was how to create an effective peacekeeping force without significantly stepping up troop levels. The solution, he decided, was to create small teams of civilian and military advisers to work along-side provincial governors, delivering reconstruction projects and liaising with the local security forces. He was all too aware of the American reluctance to engage in nation-building, hence the cleverness of his plan: Western troops wouldn't actually be "walking children to school," as Condoleezza Rice had once famously characterized such involved work. They would merely link Kabul and the provinces, offering funds, advice, and logistical support.[1]

The units Carter created over the fall came to be known as Provincial Reconstruction Teams, or PRTs, and while they were largely a British officer's innovation, they would transform the US military's approach to the wars in both Iraq and Afghanistan and usher in a program of nation-building not seen since Vietnam.[2] Their significance lay not in their size—although they eventually would swell in number—but in the change in mind-set that PRTs entailed for the military, one that matched the Bush administration's evolving thinking. The military's job was no longer confined to offensive operations in Afghanistan; they had a duty to supervise the disparate provinces they were now effectively in charge of. That many of these areas had never known strong government and preferred tribal governance over national control was often not understood.

In the beginning, PRTs existed nowhere other than a two-page strategy paper, "The Role of Coalition Humanitarian Liaison Cells" (the name for the first iteration of the PRT organization). Carter first won over Lieutenant General McNeill, who quickly saw how boosting local government would complement his efforts to drive out the Taliban and ensure they could not return. In September 2002, the American commander pitched the idea to Donald Rumsfeld as the defense secretary was realizing the US military had a role to play in developing the Afghan government's capacity to look after itself.

Rumsfeld was also impressed by the limitedness—and cost-effectiveness—of Carter's demands.[3] The US military already had civil affairs teams deployed around the country to smooth relations between its forces and the locals, primarily through so-called quick impact projects, such as building wells. Civil affairs officers were typically reservists, well-meaning and usually irrelevant to a field commander's plans. Under the PRTs, regular officers and diplomats were to be drafted and could expect to have a more prominent role coordinating reconstruction with local governors and aid groups. The combined budget for the launch of three pilot PRTs in the cities of Gardez, Bamyan, and Kunduz was peanuts, around $10 million.

Rumsfeld was sold. Less enthusiastic were many of the western aid agencies in Kabul, who were invited to play a supporting role in the PRT scheme. Somewhat unwittingly, Carter's plan had placed the military on a collision course with the aid community and reopened a long-standing debate about the principles underlying humanitarian works and the military's motivations in pursuing them.

When Carter's deputy, the American Lieutenant Colonel Jim Dickens, presented the PRT idea to an assortment of aid representatives in Kabul in November 2002, they reacted angrily to what they saw as a takeover of their own reconstruction work in the provinces. Military-sponsored nation-building, they argued, would destroy their carefully maintained neutrality and could turn aid workers into targets—whether they cooperated with the program or not. In February 2003, Caroline Douillez, a spokeswoman for the International Committee of the Red Cross in Kabul, said, "As a general position, we feel it creates confusion in the minds of those who receive the aid and creates confusion among those who carry out military and humanitarian missions at the same time."[4]

The PRT concept did not merely threaten the aid community. Douillez, among others, warned it also risked overpowering fragile local governments. PRTs had a mandate for rebuilding work that western officials could use to bypass the governors they were meant to empower. Given the circuitous and sometimes corrupt practices of Afghan officials, PRT commanders might be tempted to use money to create a parallel system of reconstruction, dominating and even superseding their Afghan partners.

The critical question for the aid community was whether to partner with the military in the hope of bringing greater cultural sensitivity to PRTs, or whether they should turn their backs and preserve their independence. In many ways the question cut to the heart of the Good War ideal, the nature of western intervention, and the fragile coalition of voices from the Left and Right that the Afghan war was to do much to rent asunder.

In the 1960s and '70s, the Vietnam War threw into question how to use armed forces to intervene on humanitarian grounds. Yet the ashes of that conflict bore a new doctrine of humanitarian intervention that would reach its apogee in Afghanistan. In 1968 Bernard Kouchner, a young French doctor, arrived in Biafra in eastern Nigeria to help refugees from a bloody insurrection. Kouchner had grown disillusioned with his work for the ICRC and what he saw as its failure to openly criticize the Nigerian government's brutal repression of rebel groups. Upon returning to Paris that year, Kouchner created Médecins Sans Frontières (Doctors Without Borders), or MSF, an organization that would blend medical assistance with a worldview unconstrained by traditional political considerations. Wherever there was suffering, MSF would take the victims' side, irrespective of where their allegiance lay. This championing of the world's unfortunate presaged the rise of modern human rights and had a powerful effect on the West's approach to war zones.

Kouchner and his acolytes were self-styled Marxists who believed that the aid community needed to be clearly segregated from the military. However, the Bosnia crises sparked a rethink, spurred on by the feeling among many humanitarian groups that their work was a convenient excuse for inaction among western governments, which could point to their charity but avoid getting involved. A watershed for the humanitarian movement arrived in 1995 when Dutch UN troops stood to one side as Serb paramilitaries massacred 8,000 Bosnian Muslims at Srebrenica. As José Maria Mendiluce, a UN special envoy, noted, "You don't fight fascism with relief supplies."[5]

Out of Srebrenica came the strange hybrid that some have called "armed intervention." The concept was immediately tested by Kosovo in 1999, when British Prime Minister Tony Blair, a keen adherent to this new way of thinking, convinced US President Bill Clinton to join in a North Atlantic Treaty Organization (NATO) bombing campaign against the Serbian government's persecution of ethnic Albanians in the area. The bombs had the unintended consequence of speeding up ethnic cleansing by both sides, although ultimately the Serbs were defeated. Bernard Kouchner became head of Kosovo's international administration that year.

The military adventurism of the Bush administration after 9/11 led many humanitarians to question their views about the compatibility of aid with armed intervention. The aid world had largely welcomed the US military's role in overthrowing the Taliban. The Iraq war, however, proved divisive. Bush's evocation of the humanitarian case for ousting Saddam Hussein appeared to many aid workers to be a cynical cover for his war aims, and placed them directly in the line of fire, as the truck bombing of the UN mission in Baghdad in August 2003 had shown. Ill feelings toward the American mission in Iraq bled into how the aid world interpreted the US military's involvement in Afghanistan. Every missile strike gone astray, every ill-informed night raid, strengthened the feeling among humanitarians that the Americans were the aggressors and the Afghans the victims.

These increasingly negative views were exacerbated by the relative isolation of aid workers and soldiers—a gap that showed no sign of closing. The military was cut off from the country on their bases, except when out on patrol. By contrast, many internationals involved in the aid effort lived in a different kind of bubble in central Kabul. They were chauffeured daily from office to guest house, and ate in garden restaurants that declared at their entrances "No alcohol will be served to Afghans." At night, the distant sound of dance beats revealed the location of the latest party and annoyed the local imams. Aid workers insisted they were more in tune with the sentiments of the country, and developed a disdain toward anything to do with the military.

Few organizations were more vocal in their criticism than MSF. Its head in Kabul, Pierre Salignon, regarded PRT as a military takeover of the aid mission, and threatened to withdraw his staff if the program proceeded. "The Americans want to turn us into soldiers," he told US Ambassador Robert Finn.[6]

In fact, MSF was making a distinction that didn't exist for most Afghans, as the tragic killing in March 2003 of International Committee of the Red Cross worker Ricardo Munguia revealed. Many Afghans presumed foreigners, whether civilian or military, were working for the same cause. The general exodus of aid organizations from southern Afghanistan after Munguia's death further weakened MSF's arguments that aid could be delivered without military assistance. Except for a few brave aid workers, such as Sarah Chayes in Kandahar, by 2004 the PRTs became the main vehicle for western aid in southern Afghanistan. Chayes recognized the aid world's particular dilemma: beholden to the military's intervention but opposing its excesses. She chose to work with her military counterparts in Kandahar to temper, if not prevent, the desperate waste of the years ahead.[7]

The aid community took an ethical stand against PRTs, fearing the consequences of associating their work with the military. Yet by doing so, they lost the opportunity to moderate the military, and increasingly left the work to soldiers with no aid training or experience to rebuild the country. Here lies the particular failure of MSF's—and other aid agencies'—principled stance in this period. Vast sums of money were committed to Afghanistan and yet so little of it was put to good use.

The first PRT launched in February 2003.[8] US Ambassador Robert Finn arrived in Gardez by Blackhawk helicopter on a bleak winter morning to announce to local residents that US forces had come to rebuild Afghanistan. There was a reason military planners had selected Gardez, a dusty town of 70,000 six hours' drive south of Kabul, for the inaugural PRT. In 2002, US troops had fought Operation Anaconda nearby, and the region had strong ties with the Zadran tribe of Jalaluddin Haqqani, who the US was convinced had sheltered Osama bin Laden. Zalmay Khalilzad, Bush's special envoy at the time, had called the region one of the three most troubled in Afghanistan in terms of warlord violence.

The PRT was meant to serve the local governor in Paktia province, Raz Mohammed Dalili, and strengthen his connections with Kabul. However, US military commanders simply saw the units as souped-up civil affairs teams of the type they were familiar with, and used them to hand out money in the form of quick cleanup contracts following operations. That reconstruction was seen through the prism of the military severely limited the PRT's scope and meant that the projects it launched were rarely undertaken in the service of a political strategy, and with all too little input from the Afghans.

Having promised the locals in Gardez that the PRT would deliver a more meaningful reconstruction process than it in fact could, Finn departed in his helicopter in a cloud of dust and raised expectations. The man left behind to deliver on his promises was Thomas Praster, an American career diplomat with fifteen years' experience, including a stint working for Finn in Croatia after the Balkans conflict. At forty-eight years old, Praster was the PRT's

Tom Praster helped set up the first Provincial Reconstruction Team in Afghanistan in the eastern town of Gardez. PRTs helped shift American priorities in the country from counterterrorism operations to nation-building. (Photo courtesy of Tom Praster)

energetic political officer, and honest enough to admit his shortcomings. He had limited experience of reconstruction work and none of Afghanistan, beyond a hasty reading list that included James Michener's *Caravans*, a lurid adventure story set in 1940s Afghanistan.

Praster's disadvantages paled in comparison to the obstacles beyond his control. Despite assurances to the contrary from the embassy in Kabul, he arrived in his gritty compound on the outskirts of Gardez without a cent to spend, a situation that hardly changed throughout his tour. What the US base in Gardez did have in abundance were boxes of donations from American church groups and charities. With his military counterpart, Praster started driving around the city's bustling streets handing out Old Navy clothing cast-offs, bubble gum, and American footballs. It wasn't clear what the Afghans made of these gifts, but they were good for the morale of the troops who accompanied Praster.

Another glaring problem for Praster was the cold shoulder he received from the half dozen NGOs stationed in Gardez. "I tried reaching out, but they didn't reach back," he said.[9] The NGO workers had apparently concluded that even meeting a PRT representative might lead Afghans to start associating their aid mission with the military's counterterrorism operations. Praster knew of the concerns the international community in Kabul had raised about the PRTs, but he was nevertheless surprised to discover the depth of their hostility in the field. Some charities required their employees to sign letters stating they would not associate with US troops—or, apparently, their civilian counterparts.[10]

The local UN office was also aloof. The recently expanded UN mandate for Afghanistan had established advisory teams in a dozen provinces to report on regional political developments, liaise with the local governments, and foster good relations with the community. The UN team was everything the early PRT officers were not: knowledgeable, proficient, and with a fine ear for local politics.

The outgoing UN representative in Gardez, Thomas Ruttig, was a case in point: His last job had been advising UN Envoy Lakhdar Brahimi at the Bonn conference; he had worked extensively in Afghanistan and spoke fluent Pashtu. Ruttig had already done much to talk one of the area's chief trouble-makers, Pacha Khan Zadran, into a tentative peace deal. He had begun to contemplate a broader regional initiative. However, Ruttig did not want to stop there. He'd known from the start that any deal with Pacha Khan would be of minimal value if it did not include other elements of the Zadran tribe, principally the Haqqanis. Here was an opportunity to launch a wider reconciliation process, with the aid money used to build goodwill.[11]

Unfortunately, the US special forces had other ideas. For much of the past year they had been trying to kill Pacha Khan Zadran, even as Ruttig was negotiating with him. The Haqqanis were also targets. The special forces contingent based in Gardez, ODA 2121, had already established a reputation as one of the most brutal and unhinged operations in Afghanistan. "They were cowboys," recalled Praster. "You know, shaggy beards, shades, bandanas. There was an obvious lack of discipline which the Special Forces at the time seemed to embrace." Christopher E. Coffey, an army investigator assigned to Afghanistan in the wake of prisoner abuse scandals at Abu Ghraib prison in Iraq, agreed. "Gardez is the worst facility—it is three or four times as bad as any other base in Afghanistan," he said.[12]

In March 2003, ODA 2121 had arrested a contingent of Afghan soldiers it believed were allied to Pacha Khan Zadran. The Afghans were brought back to the base at Gardez, where they were subjected to seventeen days of abuse that left one soldier, Jamal Nasir, dead and seven others bloody and bruised, according to reports.[13]

In the middle of this episode, the UN office got wind that the men were being held at the base. On March 10, they organized a meeting with the Americans to obtain the men's release, or at least their transfer to Afghan custody. A special forces interrogator known by the UN staff as "Crazy Mike" reportedly warned local commanders present that he would kill them if they released his Taliban prisoners. One official in attendance said he stood up and interrupted. "Mike, sit down. This is the United Nations. We don't talk about shooting or killing people here."[14]

For the moment, the UN intervention seemed to work; the seven heavily bruised soldiers and Nasir's dead body were subsequently handed over to the Afghan police. But a few days later, on March 23, a detachment from ODA 2121 appeared to gun down Pacha Khan Zadran's son as he drove to meet them to discuss peace terms, according to UN officials who conducted an after-action report.[15] The US military claimed they were involved in a firefight at the time and acted in self-defense. This shattered any chance of reviving the UN-sponsored peace talks.

The PRT commander Thomas Praster found himself uncomfortably wedged in the middle of this standoff between the UN and the US military. In many ways, this should have been an opportunity for the PRT to back the UN, thereby asserting the primacy of political action over military. To his credit, Praster recognized the danger the special forces posed but when he urged the embassy in Kabul to take ownership of the peace process the UN had begun, he heard nothing. Ambassador Finn was not prepared to get

involved in what he viewed as a military matter, and without a strategy to rec-
oncile with the Zadran tribe, there was no way to parse through the events in
southeastern Afghanistan and seize on a chance for peace. The PRTs in Gardez
proved powerless to stop a breakdown of relations between parties. It is hard
not to see in this organization's floundering start an early indication of what
was wrong with western attempts to rebuild the country. Far from bringing
together the US military and international community to empower the local
Afghan administration, the PRT had been left on the sidelines.

In May 2003, as Praster was leaving his post, the UN published a review of
the three Provincial Reconstruction Teams in Gardez, Bamyan, and Kunduz.
Perhaps the most damning criticism of PRTs was not of the limited effectiveness
of the projects they had commissioned; rather, it was that the PRTs gave the
impression of progress while diverting attention from the problems confronting
local government. As Barbara Stapleton, an aid expert, later noted, PRTs "distracted from the dire state of governance in many provinces." In fact, Stapleton
concluded that PRTs main role had little to do with Afghan needs. One UN
official excitedly told her that the PRTs' purpose was to draw in greater numbers of international forces. If that was their goal, they were all too successful.[16]

The US military had not embraced Provincial Reconstruction Teams with
any zeal. The Pentagon rightly discerned that PRTs straddled the line
between their original, limited mission and a larger, nation-building effort.
But if US planners were concerned about "mission creep" in Afghanistan, that
prospect suited other observers just fine.

At NATO headquarters, Secretary General George Robertson sensed an
opportunity. Since the end of the Cold War, NATO had been struggling to
find its role in the world. Set up in 1949 to shelter Western Europe from
communism—or to "keep the Russians out, the Americans in, and the Germans down," as one British general put it—the organization had foundered
for much of the 1990s.[17] Its military headquarters in Brussels, Belgium, had
become a cushy posting for suites of trimly saluting officers from two dozen
nations. First Bosnia, and then the Kosovo war in 1999, had provided NATO
with the first combat operation since its founding, and thus a renewed sense
of purpose. Robertson, who became the organization's secretary general
shortly afterward, was keen to find the next mission to continue NATO's
rehabilitation.

A bluff, well-liked Scot, Robertson had been Tony Blair's first defense minister, and he shared with the British prime minister a readiness to use force.
The day after 9/11 he had quickly convened the representatives of NATO's

member countries to invoke the organization's founding principle, that an attack such as the one on the World Trade Center represented an assault against
each member country. Yet, when Robertson approached Donald Rumsfeld
with an offer to help overthrow the Taliban and hunt down al-Qa'eda, the
Pentagon told him, in effect, "Don't call us, we'll call you," according to
Robertson.[18]

The American response went down badly among the other members.
NATO had been founded on the principle of collective security, and although
American military power underpinned that idea, at least during the Cold
War, the sense of togetherness was important. European foreign ministers
complained that by ignoring NATO, America was slighting its allies.

A few months later, Rumsfeld did get back to Robertson to request European troops for the peacekeeping mission in Kabul. Robertson refused on
the grounds that it might create the damaging impression—at least as far as
NATO was concerned—that American forces did the "heavy lifting" while
other countries did the cleaning up.

In reality, peacekeeping was the only type of mission that many NATO
nations were capable of. Except for France and Britain, member countries
lacked the logistical network to maintain forces in Afghanistan during combat
operations. Rumsfeld appeared to realize that for all NATO's tough talk, most
of its member nations were really looking for an extended photo opportunity
while the US military picked up the tab for shipping and supplying these
forces. At the time, the US provided 63 percent of the organization's funding
and most of its military capability.

By January 2003, Robertson swallowed his pride and asked Rumsfeld to
hand over to NATO the 5,000-strong peacekeeping force in Kabul. His suggestion came with a kicker: Why not expand the NATO mandate to other
parts of the country as the situation allowed? Rumsfeld scoffed but a few
months later the invasion of Iraq and the ensuing chaos began to change his
thinking. The need to maintain large numbers of troops in Iraq was straining
American resources. Outsourcing some of the war effort to America's allies
seemed attractive.[19]

Robertson hadn't given up on expanding NATO's mandate in Afghanistan
either. The willingness of many countries to contribute to such a mission had
taken a knock because of Iraq. NATO had split down the middle over its support for the war, with countries like France and Germany bitterly opposing
the invasion, and every other aspect of the "War on Terror." Robertson hoped
that Afghanistan—widely seen in Europe as a legitimate war—could reunite
NATO countries and serve as the organization's next campaign.

The way to bring America's NATO allies into the war was provided by . Major General John Vines, who in May 2003 had succeeded Dan McNeill as commander of US forces in Afghanistan. His headquarters occupied the same threadbare tents at Bagram air base that had been pitched at the start of the war—Rumsfeld refused to allow the headquarters to be housed in portable structures, concerned that more permanent buildings would send the wrong message to Americans and Afghans alike. In this rough setting Vines and his team struck upon an idea that promised to extend the stay of western, if not American, forces a little longer. If a NATO country objected to joining the US war effort, why not give it a Provincial Reconstruction Team to run instead? Doing so would allow American troops to focus on what they did best, killing Taliban and al-Qa'eda members, as well as free up resources for Iraq. Meanwhile, NATO could focus on rebuilding Afghanistan.[20]

The idea was embraced by NATO members that summer, with Germany—a staunch critic of the war in Iraq—announcing it would take over a PRT in Kunduz, northern Afghanistan. Robertson sought to take the idea one step further. In October 2003 at an informal gathering of defense ministers at Colorado Springs, Robertson pitched to Rumsfeld the idea of putting the new PRTs under NATO command. Robertson also made a more radical suggestion: As the PRTs established themselves in successive regions of Afghanistan, first in the north, then west and south, it would make sense to combine this expanding NATO mission with the American one. Overall responsibility for the country would then fall under a single command, which would be NATO led. Robertson was offering to take over the war entirely.

Predictably, Rumsfeld chewed out Robertson. "How dare you tell me how to manage the war?" he yelled.[21] But the following morning, over a breakfast of orange juice and eggs and after further persuasion from the American commander of NATO, General Jim Jones, Rumsfeld acquiesced. The PRTs had been intended as a limited tool for enabling reconstruction in Afghan provinces. The agreement Robertson and Rumsfeld reached turned the teams into something more ambitious: a vehicle for internationalizing the war effort, and in so doing, greatly expanding PRTs' scope.

In December 2003, two hundred Germans arrived in Kunduz, northern Afghanistan. These were some of the first NATO troops to be responsible for a PRT, and while their mission had just begun, the international community was watching their progress keenly. If the PRT in Kunduz was successful, others would be offered to American allies as the program expanded. The British had also recently taken over a PRT in Mazar-e-Sharif. Twelve more scheduled to open in 2004. How the PRTs would quantify their success was not clear, although the Bundeswehr, or German military, had set itself a single, unofficial objective: to avoid casualties at all costs, and thus the appearance that its soldiers were going to war.[22]

This aversion to casualties required some contortions by the Germans. Cooperating on counterterrorism operations with the Americans was out of the question. Furthermore, German troops could use lethal force only if fired upon, and should not fire on retreating attackers either. Troops were not allowed to stay overnight outside their camps, and would have to be accompanied by an armored ambulance at all times. A large field hospital also had to be deployed to enable injured soldiers to be treated quickly. This required complex logistics and large numbers of medical personnel. By the time the Germans' medical facilities were set up, doctors and nurses at the hospital outnumbered the soldiers actually engaging with Afghans.

Given the restrictions on overnight travel, these troops relied heavily on air support to bring supplies into Kunduz. The Germans had three CH-53 transport helicopters stationed over the border in Uzbekistan. Much to the annoyance of their NATO partners, the Germans refused to allow the helicopters to be used on any other mission. Such stipulations, known as "national caveats," would frustrate NATO operations over the coming years, with often quasi-comic effect as headquarters staff had to anxiously page through the rules—over one hundred by 2006—that governed what each unit could do during operations.[23] "You'd have thought we were going to a royal ball, not a war," quipped one Canadian officer of his NATO allies.[24]

As it happened, there was plenty of bloodshed around Kunduz at the time, as Ghilzai Pashtun battled with Uzbek militants for dominance. There were also signs of the Taliban's return. In June 2004, gunmen killed eleven Chinese construction workers as they slept in their tents in Afghanistan. Yet, the German troops remained resolutely in their camp even as the suspected Taliban members ran riot—a response that led one local development worker to accuse the Germans of "locking the door from the inside."

This edgy position was captured in the contorted reasoning of Colonel Reinhard Kuhn, an early German PRT commander. "There is an absence of enemy military actions, but no peace," he noted. "The situation is quite stable but not really safe. There is potential danger, but I am comfortable so far that we 'are in control' of the situation."[25]

It turned out that simply getting into the field was the main benchmark of success for NATO members such as the Germans. Crucially, the apparent calm could be maintained for the NATO summit in Istanbul, Turkey, at the

end of June 2004. The Istanbul conference is best remembered for the moment when Condoleezza Rice handed George W. Bush a note announcing
that Iraq had gained its sovereignty, on which the president had scrawled,
"Let freedom rule," and showed it to British Prime Minister Tony Blair sitting
beside him. The handover of Iraqi sovereignty was in keeping with the hollow
showmanship of such summits: a largely meaningless gesture and one that,
far from signaling the end of American involvement, only presaged an ever-
deepening commitment as the country slid into civil war.

Nonetheless, this illusion of progress in Iraq bolstered the summit attendees'
confidence as they contemplated sending more NATO troops to Afghanistan.
The "success" of the PRT in Kunduz—that is, its deployment—prompted
other countries to offer troops. Discussions also returned to the timetable for
NATO's taking charge of whole sections of the country. NATO announced in
Istanbul that it would take over five more PRTs in northern Afghanistan. The
organization also confirmed that it would assume responsibility for security
over the north in October 2004, the first step to expanding NATO's mandate
across the whole country.

Some of the more ambitious militaries, among them the British, were also
pushing for PRTs and NATO control to expand to the south, where the
pockets of Taliban fighters had returned and were proving a nuisance. With
America's allies eager to take the lead in Afghanistan, the temptation was
strong to let them do just that.

CHAPTER 12

A Special Relationship

In 2004, the United Kingdom sought to play a greater role in Afghanistan for several reasons: supporting the Afghan government, defeating terrorism, and eradicating poppy, to name a few. But the most important belonged to Lieutenant General Robert Fry, the new head of strategic planning at the British Ministry of Defense, who believed that Afghanistan presented a critical strategic opportunity to secure the British military standing in the world.

Fry was responsible for identifying Britain's long-term military interests and he believed that its armed forces were facing a moment of historic importance. Over his thirty-two-year career he had witnessed Britain, like most European countries, radically shrink and reinvent its military into a force that mostly did peacekeeping. Even the military's success in Northern Ireland had seemed to confirm to lawmakers and the public alike that British soldiers were better at policing wars than fighting them. The "War on Terror" promised to reverse that process and reestablish the British military's long-sought global standing.

The credit belonged to Tony Blair. After 9/11, the British prime minister had been the first to offer troops for Afghanistan, and he had done the same in Iraq, providing 40,000 personnel, almost a third of manpower of the initial invasion. That decision had proven controversial at home but Blair defended his adherence to US foreign policy by arguing that he was making the most of the special relationship between Britain and America, and guaranteeing the country a "seat at the table." Blair's political influence over the Bush administration was debatable. But there was no doubt that his robust support of the Americans had boosted the British military's stature. For the first time in half a century, British military planners could contemplate storming an Iraqi city like Basra or embarking on an expedition to Afghanistan, confident that they commanded the world's attention.

What's more, the "War on Terror" had compelled the British government to expand the military budget. A 2002 spending review had reversed some of the UK's defense cuts of the 1990s. Furthermore, the war provided over $800 million in emergency military funding from the UK's treasury in the run-up to Iraq that went beyond the operational budget.[1] Unsurprisingly, the top brass were soon working out what parts of their basic expenses they could pass off as a so-called urgent "operational requirement." As Major General Richard Dannatt, assistant chief of the general staff, effectively the army's managing director, noted, "Many of the things that were added back in as urgent operational requirements at the start of Iraq were things that had been taken out of the equipment program, the savings in earlier years."[2]

Iraq threatened to undo these gains. British popular support for the Iraq war, barely a majority at the outset, rapidly collapsed as it became clear that Blair had misled the public over the threat Saddam Hussein's regime posed. Casualties were front-page news. The mainstream press accused Blair of having "blood on his hands." The damage to Britain's military establishment was huge.[3] For Fry this meant his first strategic priority was to ensure that Iraq did not derail the military's expansion.[4] It was this sense of the big picture that set Fry apart from his fellow officers. Most generals talked easily of the pros and cons of specific battlefield strategies. But Fry, who combined an attorney's talent for prosecuting a case with a flair for the dramatic, believed that the ultimate purpose of military strategy must be to express and consolidate maximum state power. By that rubric, he had to find a way to assert the military's strength, while identifying an exit strategy from Iraq.

The deteriorating situation in Afghanistan provided the perfect solution. As far as Fry was concerned, the British had mostly accomplished their mission in Basra, which was relatively peaceful compared to Baghdad, and they were ready for a new challenge. He calculated that taking the lead in Afghanistan would enable Britain to swap an unpopular war for one that still enjoyed widespread support. Equally important, the shift would keep the UK at the forefront of America's "War on Terror" and avoid the accusation that it was abandoning the US in its hour of need.

A few weeks before the 2004 Istanbul summit, Fry saw his chance to act. The Pentagon had asked the British to deploy more troops to Iraq, along with a larger headquarters that would expand the UK's remit across the country's south. Fry proposed sending the British-run headquarters in question along with the Allied Rapid Reaction Corps to Afghanistan instead. The Americans understood that Britain wanted out of Iraq. Holland, Italy, and several eastern bloc countries were sending troops from the Iraq theater to Afghanistan as well. As far as the US was concerned, these promises of troops for Afghanistan were mostly just a way to save face. "NATO countries were rushing for the exit. It was a stampede," said Lieutenant General Tom Metz, the US commander in Baghdad.[5] What the Americans perhaps failed to understand about the British military was that it had believed its own hype over what had been achieved in Iraq, and had an inflated sense of what could be achieved in Afghanistan, both in terms of defeating the Taliban and asserting its renewed sense of global mission.

Former US Secretary of State Dean Acheson had once caustically commented that Britain had "lost an empire and has not yet found a role" other than clinging to the idea of a special relationship with the US. Fry had finally found a riposte to Acheson: It didn't matter if British power derived from the Americans; what mattered was that the British had power to wield, and he didn't mind admitting that he rather enjoyed wielding. The British could never hope to ascend to full partnership with the Americans in terms of troops, money, and influence in Afghanistan. However, by taking responsibility for the southern part of the country—the epicenter of the poppy trade and the critical borderland to Pakistan—they would play an equal role in shaping the war's trajectory during the next several years.

O ver the summer of 2004, Fry's team began planning the deployment on the top floor of the defense ministry's main building opposite the cabinet office in Whitehall. At the Istanbul conference in June, the British had agreed that any additional troops they might send would be as part of a NATO force, to which other allies would also contribute. One way to harness this international contribution was to give each interested country its own Provincial Reconstruction Team, which the US military was currently running, along with security responsibility for the surrounding area.

Discussions between allies that summer concerned who got which part of the country. It was widely believed in London that the Canadian military would partner with Italy to establish a NATO presence in western Afghanistan, which likely would leave southern Afghanistan open for the British, for both a PRT and a peacekeeping force. There was more Taliban activity in the south than in other parts of the country, and the British military wanted a challenge that would bolster its reputation as a war-fighting nation.

In September, Fry presented a twenty-page strategy paper to the chief of the defense staff, Michael Walker, and the other service heads. The work's most eye-catching feature was a graph. On one axis, it showed troop numbers in Iraq steadily decreasing; on the other they steadily rose in Afghanistan. On Fry's

Lieutenant General Rob Fry (center) was the British strategist who conceived of the UK deployment to Helmand as a
way to get British forces out of Iraq while maintaining the
reputation of the British military and the UK's special relationship with America. (Photo courtesy of Rob Fry)

PowerPoint slide, the graph lines marked a bold cross that would have profound consequences not just for the British military but for the Americans too.

Fry's scheme contained a dangerous assumption. The British military was
set up to only field one expeditionary force at a time. The switch from one
war zone to the next would need to take place swiftly and relied on the British territory in Iraq remaining calm. Otherwise the UK would be confronted
with the awkward situation of having sent troops to Afghanistan, only to
find they were needed back in Basra. If the Afghan deployment encountered
a more testing situation as well, then the British faced the very real danger of
being caught in two battlefronts 1,000 miles apart.

This risk of plunging into two wars at once didn't go unnoticed. When
British Defense Secretary Geoff Hoon learned of the plan, he immediately
highlighted the awkward moment at the center of the graph's "cross," when
the British military would be most exposed. Michael Walker told him to
"speak up" if he had any objections; in other words, Hoon should put his
doubts into writing to Tony Blair.[6] Unlike in the US, where the chairman of
the Joint Chiefs plays an advisory role and real power lies within the Pentagon, the British chief of the defense staff is at the top of the chain of command. Walker, a strained patrician nearing the end of his career, was known to
hold the left-of-center Labour Party politicians in low regard. Working with
Hoon on Iraq had softened his impression, but he wasn't going to put up with
politicians prevaricating. Hoon shut up.[7]

The British military's top brass were also content to kick the actual decision down the road. By ordering the next round of more detailed planning, they didn't need to come to an immediate conclusion over Afghanistan. The predominant mood among the defense chiefs was often one of inertia. By ordering the next round of more detailed planning, they didn't need to come to an immediate conclusion over Afghanistan. Furthermore, the slow-burning rivalries of the service chiefs, who had spent years vying for the top job while jealously guarding their own turf, did not want to take risks. In such a system, officers like Fry who had more than an ounce of passion and rhetorical flair could be particularly transformative.

In October 2004, Brigadier Barney White-Spunner—the British officer charged with scouting out southern Afghanistan and suggesting how many troops to send—arrived in Kandahar, the region's principal city. The Americans, who had 20,000 troops in all of Afghanistan, had stationed only 1,200 in the southern part of the country. White-Spunner, a heavy-set man who had once backpacked around Afghanistan during the hippie era (he had stayed with the British ambassador while in Kabul), had been put out to discover shortly before he arrived in Kandahar that the Canadians might have beaten the UK to the punch by claiming Kandahar as their own.

Like their British counterparts, Canadian strategists were also seeking a global role for their military. Canada was happy enough to embrace peacekeeping. One of the reasons Ottawa had defied the Americans and not taken part in Iraq was that the operation had appeared too aggressive. But this lonely stand had stirred up an age-old insecurity among Ottawa politicians about opposing America and losing status in the eyes of Washington.[8] Afghanistan provided the perfect opportunity to seek rapprochement with the US, while demonstrating Canada's capacity to execute a large-scale peacekeeping mission.

Jean Chrétien's government initially pushed to take over a PRT slated for the relative obscurity of western Afghanistan before the Canadian ambassador in Kabul, Chris Alexander, suggested they put the PRT in Kandahar. If Canada was serious about its commitment, it needed to choose a "pivotal province," Alexander reasoned.[9] The considerable US presence would make the task easier as American troops would remain at the Kandahar airport, a major logistics hub.

The Canadian defense chiefs were eager to demonstrate that theirs too was a top-tier military by taking on a more ambitious area. Personally, though, Alexander was less interested in how Kandahar would change Canada's fortunes on the world stage than he was in improving the Afghan nation.[10] He had faith in the Afghan people, the moral mission of the United Nations, and the West's ability to help this suffering nation. His suggestion was accepted in Ottawa, and an offer to deploy troops more quickly than the British could manage ultimately won US support for Canada taking on Kandahar.

That decision left the British scrambling for a place to put its forces. By then, the British military was contemplating a deployment of some 3,500 troops, an expedition-size force that could be sustained over multiple tours. One option was to create a combined Canadian and British headquarters in Kandahar, but neither capital wanted to lose the potential kudos that came with an individual effort. The idea of sending a UK force to Helmand wasn't discussed during White-Spunner's three-day trip.

Yet within a few weeks of returning to London, Helmand was under consideration. In February 2005, White-Spunner's chief of staff, Colonel Gordon Messenger, returned to Kandahar, this time to specifically assess the option. Upon his arrival, Messenger pored over a map of southern Afghanistan with his American counterparts at the dusty air base where the US maintained its small headquarters in the city. Any military planner looking at Helmand was likely to be daunted by the province's expanse, which was roughly the size of West Virginia. Helmand's main feature was its eponymous river, which emerged from the Hindu Kush mountain range in the north and provided a thin ribbon of greenery as it flowed west and south through the Dasht-e-Margo—the "desert of death," as the Afghans called it. Since 2001, that sliver of farmland had nurtured one of the biggest opium-producing regions in the world. The Taliban were also believed by western intelligence to have a presence in the mountainous northern regions. Beyond this, however, military planners knew little about Helmand. At the time, just two hundred American soldiers were in the province, including a PRT and a small special forces contingent that was building schools around the provincial capital, Lashkar Gah.

Messenger's visit was brief, as was a further trip by Air Commodore Mark Leakey. Yet armed with this scant knowledge of the region, the British were forced to make one of the most significant calls of the war and commit their forces to Helmand. The question of whether local Afghans wanted the British or would welcome them as allies didn't arise until May 2005, when the officer who took over the planning, Brigadier Andrew Kennett, raised the point with the Deputy Chief of Joint Operations, Peter Wall. He was told that the plans were the plans, and that there would not be any backtracking.[11]

In July 2005, Whitehall's thinking about engaging with the Islamic world had taken on new urgency when three British-born Pakistanis and a Muslim convert of Jamaican ancestry had carried explosives-filled backpacks onto the London Underground subway that summer. Three had detonated their bags on commuter-packed trains departing from King's Cross station on different lines, killing thirty-nine; a fourth blew himself up on a double-decker bus in Tavistock Square, killing thirteen more.

Much like 9/11 in America, the London attacks provoked the British to defend their national values and to ask in outrage why the bombers would attack them. Early on, British Prime Minister Tony Blair linked the attacks to the "War on Terror." He told reporters outside his office at 10 Downing Street in London, "When they try to intimidate us, we will not be intimidated. When they seek to change our country or our way of life by these methods, we'll not be changed. When they try to divide our people or weaken our resolve, we will not be divided and our resolve will hold firm."

The bombers claimed that the attacks were in response to British involvement in Iraq and Afghanistan. In a martyrdom video filmed before the attacks, Sherzad Tanweer, one of the bombers, threatened, "What you have witnessed now is only the beginning of a string of attacks that will continue and become stronger until you pull your forces out of Afghanistan and Iraq."

As the smoke began to clear, literally and metaphorically, a more nuanced and disturbing picture of the attacks began to emerge. Two of the bombers had trained in camps run by Islamist groups in Pakistan before 9/11, and had even traveled to the Taliban front lines in the battle with the Northern Alliance before returning to the UK. The men underwent further terrorist training in Pakistan's border region with Afghanistan in 2003 and 2004. For the British government, the London attacks underscored the link between such "ungoverned spaces" and terrorism.[12] The mission to southern Afghanistan would fill in what looked like a large blank spot on the map. As Whitehall phrased it, the task was to "out-govern" the Taliban. This wasn't going to be war, in the British estimation, so much as it was a wrangle over which side—the western-backed Afghan government or the Taliban—could prove the better administrator.

To ensure that the British were prepared for the challenges they faced, the UK government had created a special organization, the Post Conflict Reconstruction Unit, or PCRU, to envision what could be achieved in Helmand. One of the lessons the British government claimed to have taken from Iraq was the need for proper planning before sending in troops. The PCRU was meant to be the answer, but it ran up against Whitehall's petty infighting. Most government departments were reluctant to cede their own planning authority to the PCRU—and many bureaucrats were not even aware it existed.[13] As a result the PCRU was not sent to southern Afghanistan until the autumn of 2005, a few months before the deployment to work out what the British and to some extent NATO could achieve.

In October 2005, the PCRU arrived at Kandahar air base, its home for much of the planning. The PCRU had received from the cabinet office a list of objectives for the team to plan toward. The British approach was to ask not what the Afghans would like western forces to do for them, but what western forces could do to transform Afghanistan. Objectives included introducing a functioning criminal justice system where none existed and curbing, if not stopping altogether, the narcotics industry.[14] As if that didn't sound challenging enough, the British had three years to complete the mission and a $1.6 billion budget. That sum had to cover the military deployment and the overall reconstruction mission, for which the PCRU was establishing a plan. That deployment, scheduled for the spring of 2006, would include a PRT and up to 5,000 soldiers.

Getting all this done in such a short time frame and with such a tight budget was a tall order—but it wasn't the only challenge the PCRU faced. The five members of the planning team that began work that autumn in a frigid army tent at Kandahar's air base quickly realized their biggest task was simply to "manage expectations back in London," according to Mark Etherington, the team's operations manager.[15] The military had encouraged these high expectations inside 10 Downing Street as a way to generate enthusiasm for the venture, and to "sell" the deployment across other branches of government. Rob Fry at the defense ministry had taken the lead in this, as part of a committee chaired by Secretary of State for Defense John Reid. Fry appreciated there was considerable skepticism within government about another overseas adventure and that the military needed to "make the whole thing sound as palatable as possible" to other Whitehall officials, hence the high-blown talk of governance, short time frame, and shoestring budget.[16]

As the launch date approached, even the defense ministry was starting to get nervous about the exact nature of the mission. Reid had begun to question just whether this could be termed a peacekeeping operation, given recent attacks against government officials in Kandahar and the local security forces. Fry did his best to calm nerves. At a September 2005 meeting, Fry reassured Reid that the British presence, at least initially, would be limited to operations in and around Lashkar Gah, the provincial capital of Helmand. Camp Bastion, the British military headquarters where most troops would be based, was twenty miles away, in the middle of nowhere. Fry used this as a selling point: The desert would insulate British troops from disturbances, and if the Taliban did make an appearance, "we'll see them coming over the desert," Fry asserted in a meeting that the head of British intelligence, John Scarlett, and other department heads also attended.[17]

With the deployment only a few months away, British understanding of the situation didn't extend much further than these vague misgivings and self-assurances. As Jock Stirrup, shortly to be appointed head of the British military, reflected later, "I can recollect a number of discussions around the Chiefs of Staff Committee table that essentially were along these lines—I have used these very words myself, so I can recollect them well—'We don't know much about the South, but what we do know is that it's not the North. It's real bandit country.'"[18]

Meanwhile, in Afghanistan the PCRU had begun to make a number of uncomfortable discoveries. The first came courtesy of Minna Jarvenpaa, an erudite Finn who had also worked in the Balkans and Northern Ireland. Before heading to Kandahar as part of the PCRU, she had decided to canvass opinion among Afghans as to the British mission's likely reception. She had interviewed, among others, Ashraf Ghani, who had recently been ousted as finance minister. His insistence on an Afghan-led reconstruction had been increasingly at odds with the nation-building agenda the US was supporting.[19]

Ghani had landed on his feet as the new head of Kabul University and was in a characteristically acerbic mood when Jarvenpaa asked him about the arrivals of 3,500 British troops in Helmand. The Afghan replied that was exactly the wrong approach to take in Helmand, and brought some historical perspective to the issue: "If there's one country that should not be involved in southern Afghanistan, it is the United Kingdom," he declared. The British might have forgotten their own colonial history, he explained, but the Afghans had not. In fact, the defeat of a British army outside the village of Maiwand in 1880, a stone's throw from Helmand, was still celebrated nationally. In one well-known poem the battle inspired, an Afghan woman named Malalai, seeing Afghan forces falter, used her veil as a banner and stirred the courage of her compatriots by shouting, "Young love if you do not fall in the battle of Maiwand / By God someone is saving you as a token of shame."

If the British deployed to Helmand, Ghani warned, the locals were likely to see it as just the latest colonial intrusion by their old foes. Nothing was more likely to stir up a rebellion than the sight of the Union Jack fluttering over a desert outpost in Helmand. "There will be a bloodbath," Ghani warned.[20]

Though shaken by Ghani's assessment, Jarvenpaa wasn't in a position to call off the mission, and such an apparently obscure historical analogy was unlikely to sway her superiors. She did make a point of visiting Helmand to continue her straw poll of locals, although it was hard to get them to open up to her the way Ghani had. Few Afghans were able to offer such frank assessments.

Jarvenpaa understood that without further detailed study there was no way to judge the scale of the problem or the likely impact of the projects the British had planned. The only conclusion she and the PCRU could draw from their research was that the job was huge, even if they focused only on Lashkar Gah and the nearby town of Gereshk. It certainly would take far longer than the three years Whitehall demanded. As another member of the PCRU, Mark Etherington, pointed out to Jarvenpaa, how could they expect to make a real impact on governance when even Helmand's education minister was illiterate and signed his name with a cross?

This was not what London wanted to hear. When the PCRU team presented their report in the British capital in December 2005 before a packed meeting of the cabinet office, their call for more time was greeted with hostility by Margaret Aldred, the combative deputy director of the Security and Defence Committee. "What do you mean we don't know anything?" snapped Aldred. "We've been there [in Afghanistan] since 2001."[21]

She and others in the establishment were not prepared to admit an unspoken truth of government planning: that once momentum begins to build behind a project, it becomes almost impossible to stop. There was plenty of evidence in the autumn of 2005 that the deployment was a bad idea; if the PCRU's work was too anecdotal to have an effect, the evidence from Iraq suggested the British would struggle to have a positive impact. In September 2005, the police in Basra, long suspected of being in league with Iranian-backed Shia militias, had seized two British special forces soldiers and refused to let them go. The standoff ended only when the British sent tanks barreling through the gates of the station where the men had been held while troops fought a pitched battle against Shia militias and rowdy locals outside. The British project in Iraq was clearly in trouble. The chief of the general staff, Mike Jackson, even warned of "strategic defeat."[22]

To rectify the situation in Basra, the British would have to send more troops. And yet their pivot to Afghanistan required them to do the exact opposite and withdraw. Rather than confront this gaping hole in their strategy, the British opted to do nothing. The deteriorating situation in Iraq and its effect on Afghanistan were not raised during the cabinet office meeting, and neither were they discussed at a subsequent ministerial vote in January 2006.

"We had made commitments . . . they are not the sort of thing you back away from," said Mike Jackson later.[23] Such lack of strategic vision was about to turn southern Afghanistan into the bloody fulcrum of the war.

CHAPTER 13

Eradication

The British government needed assurance that it had a local partner in Helmand who at the very least wouldn't obstruct or embarrass them. An important aspect of the mission was how it was portrayed in the UK media. So they had sent Ambassador Rosalind Marsden to Helmand province in May 2005 to assess the Hamid Karzai–appointed governor and alleged opium profiteer Sher Mohammed Akhundzada, who also happened to be a long-term asset of British intelligence.[1]

By the time the formidable Marsden, with her steel-rimmed glasses and penchant for floral shirts, met Akhundzada at the governor's residence, she had already gleaned that overt support for the diminutive warlord with his pointy shoes and nervous grin would undermine the whole purpose of the British mission to create accountable and transparent government.[2] Some believed he was particularly ruthless, even by Afghan standards. He had a reputation for empowering his tribe over others while exacting retribution on those who opposed them. A private militia believed to be under his control had ransacked villages that resisted his rule.

Akhundzada had surrounded himself with tribal allies who seemed to be particularly loathsome. The police chief, Abdul Rahman Jan, allegedly used his men to shake down locals at checkpoints and snatch young boys for sex—a popular practice among some Pashtuns. Meanwhile Dad Mohammed Khan, the governor's intelligence chief and alleged opium impresario, was a torture specialist. Marsden surmised that this dastardly behavior likely played a role in the Taliban's newfound popularity in the region.

Akhundzada also controlled much of the province's opium trade, Marsden believed. Indeed, some diplomats in Kabul speculated that Karzai appeared to have made him governor of Helmand, in part so that Akhundzada could aggressively expand his interest, and by inference, that of the Karzai family, in the opium business. Karzai repeatedly refuted the claims, although Akhundzada was often more coy. It was hard to deny that under the warlord's leadership, poppy cultivation was booming, with Helmand home to half the country's production.[3] The suspicion that most of the revenue may have gone into Akhundzada's pocket was another factor fanning Helmand's tensions.

Marsden saw at once that dealing with Akhundzada and what looked like his sordid affairs could undermine the British mission from the outset. The drug trade had clearly corrupted Helmand and was facilitating the Taliban's return, she wrote in a strongly worded cable to the Foreign Office that was passed on to MI6. They all agreed with her assessment: Akhundzada had to go.

The issue of poppy cultivation was an acutely embarrassing one for the British, given their role overseeing the country's counter-narcotics policy. In the three years the British had guided the policy, poppy cultivation had flourished, with the British inadvertently subsidizing warlords to plant more poppy. Washington regarded the UK's handling of the brief as a disaster.

Subsequently, the UK had set up an Afghan commando unit to work alongside British special forces to target drug traffickers. But as the Brits discovered in 2002, going after traffickers was fraught with politics. There was a good chance that any name on their list was linked to the Afghan government, was a paid informant for the CIA or Pakistan's ISI, or was a bewildering combination

The British Ambassador Rosalind Marsden explains British intentions for Helmand province to a room of dignitaries in Lashkar Gah in June 2005. Akhundzada's ouster occurred a few weeks later. (Photo courtesy of Jim Hogberg)

of all three, with some Taliban connections thrown in.[4] Either way, the Afghan commando unit spent a lot of time sitting on helicopter landing strips waiting for authorization to proceed, which they rarely received.[5]

In the end, the British focused on eradication. It was the only way they could be shown to be having an impact. They sought to temper the ill effects of such a campaign by having provincial governors manage the program, which they hoped would lead to greater sensitivity to farmers' plights. Coordinated by the counter-narcotics directorate in Kabul, this effort established small Afghan teams in each province to be used at the governor's discretion. The British included an incentive in the program, whereby the governor would receive $100 for each destroyed acre of the poppy crop. These eradication drives had been hailed as a success: In 2004, governors like Sher Mohammed Akhundzada claimed tens of thousands of acres had been destroyed.[6]

The actual results were far more modest. "In the best case scenarios, governor eradication teams merely destroyed one corner of a field but claimed they'd done the lot," said Bashir, who worked on the UN monitoring program in 2005 and asked not to be fully identified. Farmers could be spared a visit by paying off a governor, a profitable extortion racket. In the worst-case scenario, explained Bashir, whole fields *were* actually destroyed, usually because they "belonged to a rival tribe of the governor."[7]

Eradication thus extenuated tribal divisions, giving the favored access to opium wealth while destroying the livelihoods of others. Large-scale eradication drives in Nangarhar province in 2005—heralded as a success in Kabul— led to thousands of farmers being driven off the land and forced to look for a job planting poppy in other areas of Afghanistan, inadvertently boosting the harvest there. "It's no coincidence that the large-scale poppy eradication program in Nangarhar in 2005 led to a huge surge in production in Helmand the following year," said Nick Lockwood, a British diplomat who worked on counter-narcotics in 2006.[8]

By the time of Rosalind Marsden's visit to Helmand, the opium trade in Afghanistan had grown to such proportions—from a few hundred acres in 2002 to 86,000 in 2005—that the Bush administration had been forced to change its hands-off attitude toward counter-narcotics.[9] This change had come into focus during a November 2004 White House meeting to reassess a drug strategy for Afghanistan for the first time since Defense Secretary Donald Rumsfeld had declared at the war's outset that the US would not get involved. What was changing the Bush administration calculation was the apparent link between the growth in the drug trade and increasing attacks against western forces and the Afghan police, which suggested that the Taliban were benefitting from the business. This approach mistakenly singled out a single strand of the poppy trade and missed the key point that money from opium touched all aspects of Afghan life. Furthermore, many communities were aligning themselves with Taliban fighters to protect their crops *from* eradication efforts.[10]

Robert Charles, head of the US Bureau of International Narcotics and Law Enforcement Affairs, attended the meeting as the official who would lead any potential drug war the White House decided to launch in Afghanistan. He had not visited the country and knew little of village life. That didn't stop him from insisting that "you can't tackle [the Taliban] without going after [poppy cultivation]."[11] He had already won over his boss, US Secretary of State Colin Powell, to this line of thinking. Powell, who was also at the meeting, favored "going big" and eradicating Afghanistan's entire crop by aerially spraying herbicides. He touted Colombia's perceived success in combating drugs with such tactics.[12] Bush liked the idea. Rumsfeld did his best to talk the president back around, insisting that the US military, which might be expected to provide the air support for any such aggressive counter-narcotics operation, should not be distracted from their primary mission in Afghanistan to rout out al-Qa'eda and the Taliban.[13]

In the end, the White House reached a compromise whereby the US State Department would contract out eradication to DynCorp, a US security firm with a track record in South America. Aerial spraying, Powell's preferred tactic, was put on the back burner, after the Afghan government (along with the British) expressed strong reservations about such a measure. The alternative was "manual eradication." This involved teams of DynCorp contractors and Afghan police hacking down poppy stems one field at a time, a beefed-up version of the earlier British approach.

Doug Wankel, a Harley-driving former US drug enforcement agent from Missouri, was brought in to manage the program in December 2004. He didn't believe the US or British could ever fully eradicate poppy. His aim, as he put it, was simply, "Let farmers know there was a risk to planting poppy, that they should think about another option."[14]

The *New Yorker* writer Jon Lee Anderson memorably described one of the eradication drives in southern Afghanistan that started in 2005. The two hundred–strong Afghan Eradication Force arrived in the former Taliban stronghold of Oruzgun at the height of the poppy-growing season. Afghan members of the team, who were predominantly ethnic Tajiks from northern Afghanistan and ancient rivals of the Pashtun, drove ATVs dragging metal chains behind them to knock down the poppies. Others used shovel handles to whack at poppy plants while Wankel and twenty gun-wielding DynCorp contractors—in "redneck heaven," according to one—supervised the destruction.[15]

One of the local farmers whose crop was being destroyed looked on silently, until Wankel approached and awkwardly asked him how much money he was losing as a result of the AEF's handiwork. Between $500 and $700 per acre, the man replied—compared to $33 for wheat. The farmer pointed out that the ATVs had also destroyed his wheat crop for the year. Wankel apologized. "But you have also damaged my watermelons," the farmer insisted, pointing to another part of the field. "Now I will have nothing left."[16]

Wankel had little to offer and was already walking away when the farmer called out, "Are you destroying all the poppies or just my field?"[17]

The next day the AEF was ambushed outside a nearby village while conducting a similar operation. One Afghan policeman was killed and four others critically wounded. The AEF and DynCorp contractors returned fire into the village with heavy machine guns and rocket-propelled grenades (RPGs) and reportedly killed eight Afghans, including an old woman and a twelve-year-old girl. Wankel later discovered that the AEF had been directed to fields belonging to the Alakozai tribe, leaving untouched those of the Popalzai—Karzai's tribe.

Some carrot was meant to go with the stick. In 2004, USAID had extended a program called Alternative Livelihoods to Helmand to encourage farmers to grow other crops. The agency awarded the contract to Chemonics, a company that, like DynCorp, was a prolific grant-writing operation that fell alarmingly short in delivering on its promises. The project boiled down to creating the equivalent of 2.5 million workdays in Helmand in 2004–2005, with locals receiving roughly $3 an hour. The problems in executing the program were manifold. For starters, the company had no idea where to apply so much manpower. In their desperation to find projects, the Chemonics team hit upon repairing drainage ditches, known locally as *karezs*. It subsequently transpired that Afghanistan had a long-standing tradition of doing just that for free, and by introducing money Chemonics was turning a shared community endeavor into a system of patronage that inevitably favored one clan over another.[18]

The program was ripe for other forms of corruption as well, whether it was Afghan subcontractors claiming more workers than they had really hired or Chemonics logging more work hours than they had actually paid out. The American company's primary objective was to spend as much money as they could, so they could justify an even bigger budget when they applied to renew the grant. "It was all about the burn rate, how quickly we could burn through money to give the appearance of progress," noted Joel Hafvenstein, a member of the Chemonics team who later wrote a scathing account of this period. (The program was abandoned in May 2005 after some of its workers were ambushed by the Taliban and two Afghan staff killed.)

US counter-narcotics policy almost certainly would have done more damage to the Afghan people and the western cause had it not ultimately failed to take off. The military refused to cooperate with DynCorp, leaving the contractors to make their own way to each province.[19] Under considerable pressure from the State Department, the military did airlift bulldozers and other equipment into southern Afghanistan, although these would sometimes "disappear" for weeks at a time at Kandahar airfield and elsewhere. Such obstruction by the military—both US and British—in Afghanistan succeeded in disrupting the eradication drive; in 2005, DynCorp had eradicated only 220 hectares of poppy out of a planned 10,000–15,000, mostly in Helmand, where Akhundzada made a great show of assisting the Americans. He would call Wankel and the PRT commander and invite them to visit his compound, where he revealed sacks of opium resin he claimed to have seized from drug lords. He invited the Americans to watch him dispose of the stash, and they routinely accepted. "We knew he was deep in the drugs trade and that he was probably running rings around us," said the PRT commander, Jim Hogberg.[20]

The Americans had little choice but to turn a blind eye to much of the trade. With his small detachment and limited budget, Hogberg decided to go with the grain. He supervised the stash burnings but made a point of not inquiring too deeply into the warlord's other activities. For Wankel, it was a frustrating time. "We took some hits, actually we took a lot of hits, but we kept on rolling," he said.[21]

America's new counter-narcotics strategy, such as it was, added urgency to Rosalind Marsden and her efforts to remove Akhundzada, the governor of Helmand. The challenge she faced was twofold: The first, and in some ways the easier task, was to envision who and what would replace the warlord's regime. The British had already lined up a possible replacement as governor: a technocrat from Helmand named Mohammed Daoud who had worked extensively with the aid community in Kabul. That he was not a tribal leader was a positive for Marsden, and reflected a prevalent view among the international community that the sort of clannishness and warlordism that Akhundzada represented was at the root of the country's problems. Daoud would be less prone to corruption and amenable to the sort of inclusive, transparent government the British sought to install.[22]

The graver challenge Marsden faced was how to get rid of Akhundzada. The warlord had a tenacious grip on power in Helmand, was close to the Americans, and was protected by Karzai. When she first broached the subject to Karzai, he delivered a definitive no. The Afghan president considered Akhundzada to be his indispensable ally in Helmand, the first tribal leader to rally to his side in 2001, and a man who knew how to manage the province's tribal dynamics. In reality, Akhundzada's track record was mixed when it came to Helmand's politics. He had won over Taliban sympathizers like Abdul Waheed Baghrani, the warlord from northern Helmand who had helped shelter Mullah Omar after his ouster. At the same time, he had alienated those he saw as rivals, like the linchpin of central Helmand, Mir Wali. Instead of pressing the president to make Akhundzada behave more inclusively, the British appeared intent on sweeping the warlord aside.

When Karzai described to Marsden a list of Akhundzada's achievements, she countered with all the ways in which the warlord was failing to live up to her ideas of how a provincial governor should behave. The UK would not be able to countenance spending millions of dollars in Helmand with such a partner. Even then Karzai remained intransigent.

"Prove that he is corrupt," Karzai sullenly declared at one point.

The British took Karzai up on his challenge. On June 22, 2005, the Afghan commandos that the British had set up and continued to supervise, swooped

The Afghan government burned large quantities of seized opium stores, but that did little to stop the rampant trade, which was the country's largest source of income other than aid money. (Photo courtesy of Jim Hogberg)

down on the governor's compound in Lashkar Gah. Jim Hogberg, the PRT commander, had just left the building, where he'd been inspecting Akhundzada's latest haul of drugs. Since the start of the 2005 poppy season, Hogberg had supervised the destruction of tons of poppy resin by Akhundzada and his men. He sent regular briefs to Kabul outlining when a stash was about to be burned. This time, the governor had around nine tons wrapped in plastic bags and tarpaulin to be destroyed outside the compound later that day.

At first, Hogberg thought a US special forces raid was in progress—they were the only sort of flights he wasn't informed about—but as he prepared his men to potentially provide backup he received a call from Akhundzada telling him that the British had come to seize the drugs and asked for his help. The PRT commander explained there was nothing he could do. It was only the next day, when he heard the news declaring the British had uncovered the largest drug haul in Afghanistan's history in the governor's compound, that Hogberg began to suspect a ruse: Hogberg had written a report about the drugs the day before about the upcoming burn, which the US embassy in Kabul had passed on to the British. With that information, the British may have seen the opportunity to paint Akhundzada as the country's worst drug dealer.

"Was it a coincidence that the British raided Akhundzada that day when we all knew he'd have a large amount of opium in storage?" he asked later. "I don't think so." A British official later confided to Hogberg that the occasion was "simply too good to pass up."

In Kabul, Marsden made little effort to hide her satisfaction at the news of the drug haul. She later denied the operation was set up, although if Hogberg's suspicions of a set up were correct, it is not clear Marsden would have known about it. It was a high-risk game; if Karzai didn't remove Akhundzada now, the British had potentially undermined the mission by publicly declaring that the governor, their principal partner in Helmand, appeared to be a major drug baron.

In the end, Karzai went against his judgment to appease the international community and sacked Akhundzada.[23] Western diplomats would later complain about Karzai's weakness, yet they readily exploited it to suit their needs.[24] The consequences were larger than Marsden or the Americans imagined. For while Akhundzada may have been out of the governor's palace in Helmand, he was by no means out of the struggle for power in southern Afghanistan. He was simply beyond western influence at the very moment they needed his help to counter the Taliban's gathering insurgency.

CHAPTER 14

Friendly Advice

As the British were rearranging the political landscape in Afghanistan's Helmand province in 2005, NATO was readying its forces to deploy to southern Afghanistan. For the first few months, NATO troops would fall under American command. Once the international contingent had found its feet, the plan was for NATO to take responsibility for the south. But not if Major General Ben Freakley, the American commander of the 10th Mountain Division, had anything to do with it. He was about to take charge of troops in southern and eastern Afghanistan, including the first batch of NATO soldiers. In December 2005, Freakley traveled to Fort Wainwright, Ontario, to review NATO's preparations.

Freakley was a classic product of the post-Vietnam military, an era when America turned its back on messy insurgencies in favor of the certainties of conventional warfare. A hearty, red-cheeked, exuberant man in his mid-fifties with thinning hair and a well-padded midriff, he had been prepared to cut NATO slack. After all, the headquarters had only just been assembled, and the organization had never deployed outside Europe. But even he was shocked by the level of disorganization he found during training exercises for NATO's brigade headquarters.[1] The NATO headquarters he saw that bleak and chilly morning wasn't capable of managing a marching band, much less a major military operation.

To start with, there was the petty rivalry between the two lead nations, Britain and Canada. Since both countries had declared their interest in heading the NATO mission to Kandahar, there had been some inevitable squabbling over rank and prestige. Both nations wanted their own brigadier to lead their national contingents; neither was prepared to leave its own general at home.

The result was a sometimes difficult and confusing relationship between the Canadian Brigadier David Fraser and his British counterpart, Ed Butler, that was about to worsen in the months ahead.

Then there were the Dutch, who had unexpectedly asked to take charge of a Provincial Reconstruction Team in the south. The UK and Canada acquiesced, albeit with a certain hesitation. The Dutch military had been wracked with existential guilt since Srebrenica, when peacekeepers from Holland had stood aside while Serb militias massacred 8,000 Bosnian Muslims. Nonetheless, one month before they were due to deploy to Afghanistan, the Dutch had suddenly gotten cold feet. Attacks against Afghan security forces had increased over the fall of 2005, and the Dutch were concerned that the peacekeeping mission they had signed up for was becoming a warfighting one. Holland's NATO partners scrambled for a solution. In the end, the Australian military reluctantly agreed to effectively become the Dutch contingent's bodyguards.[2] Even then politicians in the Hague required constant reassurance, leading to British Defense Minister John Reid's remarkable statement in January 2006, ahead of a Dutch parliamentary vote to approve the mission, that NATO forces would be "perfectly happy to leave in three years without firing one shot because our job is to protect the reconstruction."

As a result, NATO headquarters was a medley of nations, competing national prerogatives, cavalier egos, and political calculation, with only a cursory knowledge of one another's military systems, and in the case of some Italian

US Major General Ben Freakley opposed the NATO deployment to southern Afghanistan in 2006 on the grounds that the international force was not prepared to tackle a counterinsurgency. (Photo courtesy of Ben Freakley)

officers roped in, not even a shared language. Its leaders were unable to co-ordinate air support and lacked basic equipment, such as a device to track the disposition of friendly units. Furthermore, the Dutch intelligence officer could not review US traffic due to a lack of security clearance.

Freakley found the petty bickering at headquarters as alarming as its dis-organization. The operation, it seemed to him, had been cobbled together by contributing nations more concerned with meeting their domestic political imperatives than securing the Afghan peace. Indeed, most of the leadership at NATO headquarters—except a few Canadians and British officers—seemed unaware they were entering a nation struggling with an insurgency. "That headquarters should never have been allowed to deploy," said Freakley.[3]

Freakley held no illusions about Afghanistan. Over the summer of 2005, violence had increased noticeably, including attacks on American forces and Afghan police. The exact nature of the threat was unclear. But Freakley's in-telligence officer at the 10th Mountain Division was sure the Taliban had returned to the country in force. Freakley planned a series of offensives in the eastern province of Kunar and expected heavy fighting. On June 28, 2005, the Taliban had shot down a special forces helicopter carrying nineteen men in the Pech valley, and the area was believed to be a staging ground for attacks elsewhere in the country. Freakley knew NATO forces were likely to find sim-ilar problems in southern Afghanistan, and he believed large-scale operations were necessary to preempt Taliban attacks.

After visiting Canada, Freakley sent an urgent memo to the commander of US forces in Afghanistan, Karl Eikenberry, warning that the NATO headquar-ters was nowhere near prepared for deployment. He asked Eikenberry to con-sider deploying his own 4th Brigade headquarters to Kandahar to support the NATO effort. Eikenberry gave him a pat reassurance: "Don't worry, NATO would only take over in Kandahar if and when they were deemed ready."[4]

Freakley did achieve one small victory. As a result of his misgivings, he persuaded Eikenberry to push back the handover to NATO from May to July to more fully assess their capabilities.

While NATO played war games in Canada, the Taliban prepared its own campaign after a year of subtle networking, soapbox preaching, and intimidation in the form of night letters, daubed insults on walls, and—in a few instances—public executions of government officials. The loosely co-ordinated spate of attacks across southern Afghanistan escalated through the winter of 2005. They were a significant tipping point that marked the first sustained attacks against government forces.

Abdul Waheed Baghrani was a
staunch supporter of Taliban leader
Mullah Omar in 2001. He later sided
with the Afghan government only to
play a role opposing the British arrival
in Helmand. (Photo courtesy of Jim
Hogberg)

Mullah Dadullah, the Taliban commander Mullah Omar had dispatched
to southern Afghanistan the previous year, had played an important role in
the Taliban's resurgence as he flitted between southern provinces rallying support. Starting in Zabul province to the east of Kandahar, Dadullah and other
mullahs reestablished their networks of followers in the disgruntled southern
communities. As they grew bolder, they staged attacks against moderate clerics and government officials in Kandahar.

US intelligence later attributed the uptick in violence in southern Afghanistan solely to Dadullah, but in fact the increasing number of attacks—which
rose from a dozen a month in 2003 to over a hundred by 2005—reflected
numerous local grievances, small fires with their own sparks. In the Panjwei
region south of Kandahar, protests the year before by members of the Noorzai
tribe had prompted the provincial government to send in a rival clan's militia,
which provoked an armed confrontation.[5] "In our area, the Taliban went from
40 people to 400 in just days," recalled Neda Muhammad, a Noorzai elder.[6]
By January 2006, small bands of Noorzai tribesmen struck at local government offices around Kandahar.

In northern Helmand, tribal groups staged similar revolts against the hated
rule of local intelligence chief Dad Mohammed Khan, with police officers

from Khan's own clan, the Alakozai, ambushing his convoy on several occasions in 2005. In Musa Qala, local factions booted Sher Mohammed Akhundzada's brother out of power. Meanwhile, the British in Helmand began to feel the consequences of their decision to depose Akhundzada. While they were right that the warlord had alienated many tribal allies of the Taliban, he also knew how to appease such militants as Abdul Waheed Baghrani, whom he had brought over to the government's side. After Akhundzada's ouster, Baghrani attacked local government offices in the towns of Musa Qala and Now Zad that winter. Akhundzada stood aside, and may even have teamed up with him, a common tactic of spurned warlords.[7] Whatever the truth to such claims, the British were left without a local interlocutor to help them in the critical task of negotiating with the tribes to secure the peace.

Tribal grievances and armed opposition to the government were nothing new in Afghanistan. The perpetual problem facing the country was whether the warring tribes and clans in places like Panjwei and northern Helmand could be brought into equilibrium through a patchwork of deals and accommodations. As the attacks escalated that winter, with suicide attacks on government offices in Kandahar, the assassination of prominent officials, and the ransacking of police checkpoints, the time had arrived when Afghanistan needed its president to exercise his subtle feel for tribal politics and soothe his agitated nation.

In 2005, Hamid Karzai was arguably at the height of his power. He had just won a landslide victory in the country's first presidential elections. Troublesome warlords like Ismail Khan and Gul Agha Sherzai had been forced out of their positions of power, and parliamentary elections in September 2005 offered an opportunity to incorporate other malcontents (among them Pacha Khan Zadran and Sher Mohammed Akhundzada). In Kandahar, Karzai's own brother had been installed as a virtual overlord of the south to manage the family's business interests.

These political developments were largely due to US Ambassador Zalmay Khalilzad, who had sweet-talked, cajoled, and bullied one warlord after another into siding with Karzai, America, and its allies. Even the most thuggish chieftain, like the Uzbek warlord Abdul Rashid Dostum, a great bear of a man, seemed mesmerized by Khalilzad's spidery approach.[8] A handful of diplomats in Kabul questioned whether Khalilzad had gone too far in sidelining warlords and disbanding their militias at the very moment they might be needed to combat returning Taliban.[9] There were those, too, who speculated about Khalilzad's motives and whether he was priming the country ahead of his own run for the presidency. In typical fashion, Khalilzad appeared to enjoy the speculation, which only strengthened his hand. His eye for a deal might have allowed the ambassador to manipulate the new political order he was creating and pull together a political compromise to offset the growing insurgency. But in April 2005, the Bush administration tapped Khalilzad to become ambassador in Iraq.

This was the moment for Karzai to manage both the expansion of the western presence and the country's fractious tribes. On both counts he failed. With regard to the military, it's possible to excuse some of his lassitude. He could, indeed should, have pushed for a role in planning NATO's arrival, but he appeared to accept his long-standing position on the periphery. Not until the following year did the military actually involve Karzai in detailed military discussions, an unfortunate oversight given the West's limited understanding of the region it was about to invade.

What is less comprehensible is why Karzai ignored the chorus of discontent that winter of 2005. Karzai was nothing if not a tribal leader, and yet he was ready to outsource the crucial issue of engagement with regional tribes to western troops. His reconciliation efforts during this period were feeble. A peace council he established in 2003 to reach out to Taliban leaders became little more than talking shop for a few former officials. The crucial task of addressing Pashtun disengagement went unresolved. At the same time, the Tajik-backed Northern Alliance, which had dominated over proceedings at Bonn, retained their grip over key ministries. They were widely seen as corrupt and, along with the warlords brought on board by Khalilzad, evoked for many Afghans memories of the mujahideen nights of the 1990s that had first inspired the Taliban—and appeared to be doing so again.

No peace imposed at the barrel of a foreigner's gun was ever likely to be sustainable in Afghanistan, as Karzai knew well. Yet at this crucial juncture he revealed the narrowness of his concerns; a willingness to "take a backseat in a car speeding off a cliff," as one Canadian diplomat put it.[10] One possible explanation was that NATO's presence obviated the need for Karzai to take risks bringing tribal groups together or in standing up to the Northern Alliance. "He didn't have to, not with thousands of troops and millions of dollars arriving," theorized EU diplomat Michael Semple.[11]

Indeed, all sides appeared to gain by the coming deployment: Karzai got western engagement that would flood the country with billions. Western militaries got the mission they wanted to establish their credentials. And of course, there was another beneficiary: the Taliban, whose members were spoiling for a common enemy to unite the south.

A s Taliban attacks in southern Afghanistan continued over the spring of 2006, it wasn't Karzai who formulated Afghanistan's response, but Ben Freakley. The scale of the violence in and around Kandahar and Helmand upon his arrival had forced Freakley to change his priorities. He was still planning an offensive in the eastern province of Kunar, but as he told Colonel John Nicholson soon after the attacks began in April, the east was no longer the "main effort." The priority lay in the south.

From what he had seen of NATO in Canada, Freakley was concerned that the international forces would not have the wherewithal to respond should the Taliban target them, as appeared likely. The first step was to get the NATO troops into the country without bloodshed. The Canadians arrived first only to lose the head of their Provincial Reconstruction Team to a roadside bomb. That had put the jitters on the Dutch. The US commander Karl Eikenberry had informed Freakley that if they incurred casualties, the Dutch would pull out, an embarrassment for NATO and a victory for the Taliban. Yet, the Dutch refused to accept direct US supervision outside the NATO chain of command, apparently fearing they would be dragged into offensive operations they were seeking to avoid.

The solution was to use Canadian forces to secure the road from Kandahar to Oruzgun. The commander, Colonel Ian Hope, was a rakish tank commander whose readiness to go roaring into enemy territory set him at odds with the under-pressure Canadian hierarchy. After an elaborate operation that was weeks in the preparation, the Canadians succeeded in escorting the Dutch to Tarin Kowt, the provincial capital of Oruzgun, without a shot being fired. The relief in NATO headquarters was tangible.

At the same time that NATO forces were inching their way to Tarin Kowt, a US special forces team deployed into the mountains of Oruzgun and northern Helmand to distract the Taliban as NATO forces arrived. Freakley had received intelligence assessments that suggested the Taliban had established a base of operations in the warlord Abdul Waheed Baghrani's territory. In fact, Mullah Dadullah, the Taliban commander, had been Baghrani's guest for several weeks. In February 2006, Dadullah had led a three hundred–man assault against the local government building, known as a district center in Sangin, a small market town on the Helmand River, half a day's drive from the provincial capital. The attack was arguably the Taliban's largest since their overthrow. It was eventually repulsed by the arrival of the US special forces team.

At this sensitive juncture, Freakley was informed by his chain of command that DynCorp and its Afghan Eradication Force intended to start destroying poppy around the town in what was meant to be its largest destruction of the poppy crop to date. Predictably, the attempt had started badly when DynCorp contractors targeted a small agricultural town called Dishu south of Lashkar Gah. Word of the impending drive had already reached the locals by the time the first Afghan police and contractors rolled up with an assortment of pickup trucks, ATVs, and armored bulldozers. Swarms of local defenders managed to push back the invaders, with limited damage to their crops. Undaunted, the contractors proceeded north to the larger town of Garmsir. Here the locals had taken the reasonable step of reaching out to the Taliban. They, too, were able to repulse the eradication team.[12]

Freakley was alarmed to discover that DynCorp's next destination was Sangin. He expressed his reservations to Eikenberry, only to find that this was a political decision that came straight from the White House. The scale of poppy cultivation in 2006 was to be a key benchmark of success that year, in both Washington and London. That so far the Afghan Eradication Force had destroyed only a few fields while uniting the countryside against the Afghan government had yet to sink in.

It was clear, however, that eradicating poppy around Sangin would require more muscle than DynCorp could provide. Whatever Freakley's reservations, he had little choice but to comply. He instructed the Canadian Lieutenant Colonel Ian Hope to head over to Sangin, ostensibly to provide backup to a US special forces unit stationed in the town. Hope sought assurance that his men would not be involved in any poppy eradication programs. He was happy to pick a fight, Hope said, but only when necessary. Freakley assured him that his men would not be involved in eradicating poppy.

The next day, as his light armored vehicles rolled into Sangin, Hope was furious to see the Afghanistan Eradication Force forming up on the other side of the river, where lush green fields of poppy stretched across the valley. "Freakley set me up. I was not happy about it one bit," he later reflected.

Hope knew a fight was coming. Sangin's outskirts were deserted, and there was a hushed stillness in the air. He tensed in anticipation as his convoy pulled up outside a patrol base, still on the outskirts. Before long the first bullets started to crackle, distantly at first, and then closer. Hope watched as the eradication team started to scramble for cover. It's not clear who these particular attackers were: US intelligence had implicated Dadullah in earlier assaults, although it's just as likely the shots were coming from local tribesmen protecting their livelihoods. That distinction was easily lost in the heat of battle.

"Should we go over there to help them?" Hope asked his brigade commander, David Fraser, watching the eradication team take cover from the unseen assailants.

"It's not our fight; stay out of it," Fraser advised.[13]

That was easier said than done. The eradication team had rapidly retreated under fire, but rather than falling back themselves, the attackers now turned on the district center in Sangin where, it turned out, a detachment of US special forces remained. As the evening shadows lengthened and the sky began to light up with tracer bullets, Freakley ordered Hope and his men into town to repel the attack. They found the government building, a two-story structure, beside a fast-flowing river, under fire from all sides as Afghan fighters flitted between buildings and among the dense shrubbery around the river. The fighting lasted most of the night. Amid the confusion, the US special forces opened fire on their Canadian allies, killing one. An American was killed in another brief exchange of fire. Several locals also died, and more were injured. The exact number was never established.[14]

"We lost control of people in the camp. At night, people were scared," said Fraser.

The violence died down the next day in Sangin, but Ben Freakley was convinced that NATO forces would not be able to cope with the volatility of the situation in Helmand. Driving out the Taliban would require a US-backed operation involving an entire brigade.

In May 2006, Freakley briefed the head of the British contingent, Brigadier Ed Butler, on his plan. The meeting with Butler did not go well. American and British commanders enjoy very different cultural relationships to their subordinates, with US generals expecting their officers to "follow the mission," while the British tolerate, even expect, a discussion. As the military historian John Keegan notes, those differences extend beyond the operations room: "The British notoriously exhibit an unhurried and amateur manner, while Americans are formal and conscious of rank. The British officer's tendency to wear odd clothes and use Christian names to other officers strikes Americans as unserious."[15] In Butler's case, there was the added friction of what Freakley perceived to be the British officer's hauteur.

The American general was under no obligation to include Butler in his deliberation. Technically Butler had no formal role in the chain of command in the south. He had been removed from direct supervision of his men after the Canadian one-star general in Kandahar, David Fraser, had objected to having a British officer of the same rank stationed in Helmand, which was meant to be subordinate to his headquarters. Fraser didn't want "too many swinging dicks" in the south.[16] That left Butler in the odd position of being the head of the British military contingent in Afghanistan, without being in actual command of the soldiers in Helmand. The result was an awkward system whereby Freakley could issue an order to NATO that would be passed down the chain to the British. At the same time, the British would check with Butler on whether the mission met national objectives.

When Freakley finished describing the brigade-size operation, which concluded with 2,000 soldiers converging on the troubled town of Sangin, Butler simply shrugged and issued the crisp response that this was not what was needed.[17] To him, it looked like Freakley was trying to launch a conventional military assault. Butler preferred lighter and more nimble raids, which would pose less risk of needlessly provoking the local population. He also wanted the UK to retain control over their own battle space. The British had already insisted, as a condition of their deployment, that US special forces would not be allowed into Helmand because of their overly aggressive approach.[18]

Butler's style of debate and dismissive attitude angered Freakley. He was seeking input from the British officer, not approval. According to Freakley, when he pushed Butler to explain himself, he replied, "We fought in Northern Ireland. You did Vietnam. We've got this."[19]

It was exactly the sort of reply guaranteed to rile the American. Freakley was later reported to have said, "I nearly punched that damn Limey's lights out, he was so arrogant"—a claim he later denied, although he recognized that he was "as mad as hell at that arrogant bastard."[20] Butler denies making the comment, but acknowledged that there was a fundamental disagreement between them that he thought stemmed from Freakley's failure to appreciate his advisory role and the UK's subtler approach.

Freakley was now in the awkward position of having to go to his superior, Karl Eikenberry, and the head of the US Central Command, General John Abizaid, and explain that if the operation were to go ahead, the Americans would have to do it themselves.

Abizaid was understandably cautious, telling Freakley, "If Butler doesn't want to support it, I'm not sure we're going to do it."[21] The general had been informed of the delicate nature of the NATO headquarters, and, with the handover looming, the last thing he wanted to do was strain relations.

Eikenberry expressed his concerns about whether Freakley's operation would stir up trouble, not tamp it down: "What happens if this operation does not have the intended effect?"[22]

Eikenberry knew that Washington wanted American involvement in Afghanistan to start winding down, and he was determined not to disappoint. In the name of normalizing US relations with Afghanistan, the general had already scaled back his meetings with Karzai and pulled his headquarters out of the embassy in Kabul to return to the flapping tents of Bagram. He told Freakley he might have to reconsider his plans. The meeting broke up without a clear resolution.

Freakley didn't think that Afghanistan was normalizing—far from it. On the other side of the country, Freakley's strategy of pushing forces into eastern Afghanistan along its mountainous border with Pakistan was a move he knew would be a gamble. The first area he wanted to seize was the Korengal valley, close to where nineteen US special forces soldiers had been killed the previous year. One rationale for the operation was to kill the perpetrators, believed to be hiding in the valley; the other was to establish a permanent US presence in the Korengal and elsewhere along the Pakistan border to prevent militants from entering the country.

Freakley and the officer leading the operation, Colonel John Nicholson, also hoped to do so with a different approach to the war. Nicholson's brigade was unusual in that it had started from scratch eighteen months before in the knowledge that Afghanistan would be its first operational tour. Nicholson used that time to read up on British imperial history. One of his distant relatives, also called John Nicholson, had fought in the imperial British army against the Afghans in 1840, and was briefly taken prisoner by them.[23] He asked his men to read up on Vietnam, and invited Lewis Sorley, the author of a history of the largely ignored lessons of that war's final years, to speak to his headquarters.[24]

From the outset of his tour, Nicholson recognized that broad sweeps and house raids were proving counterproductive. They needed to separate the people from the Taliban, and the only way to do that was by having his men live among them.[25] As Nicholson saw it, Afghanistan was emerging as a classic counterinsurgency campaign. In 2004 Lieutenant General Dave Barno had tried to implement a national plan along those lines, but the White House was reluctant to call it that, and thus be forced to tackle the problem. The following year, US Secretary of State Condoleezza Rice went as far as referring to "clear, hold, build," a phrase often associated with the approach, only for her to be reprimanded by the Pentagon for straying onto its turf.[26] For Nicholson, defining the campaign was less important than devising an approach that could tackle the Taliban threat and do so in a sensitive and humane manner. He believed that Afghans and Americans could benefit once they got to know each other.[27]

The initial operation to seize the valley—dubbed Mountain Lion—provoked only limited resistance. The problems came when American units sought to build combat outposts in the area, and American intentions to stay

US Colonel John Nicholson (second from right) was an early pioneer of counterinsurgency tactics in eastern Afghanistan and went on to play a key role in deciding the direction of the surge. (Photo courtesy of Sergeant Amber Robinson)

beyond a few days became clear.[28] The Afghan contractors building one of the bases were attacked by locals with machetes and axes who killed eight and mutilated their corpses. Once Nicholson's men moved into the outposts, they were under fire from the surrounding hills, patrols were regularly ambushed, and booby traps were laid, apparently with the connivance of the locals.

When Freakley visited the Korengal valley in June 2006, his helicopter was shot at upon its return and unable to land. Freakley spent an uncomfortable few hours hunkered down at the base, scratching at the sand fleas and gazing nervously at the surrounding hills, before the fighting died down and his transport could pick him up. The position was exposed to sniper fire from the ridges on either side. As he learned from talking to Nicholson's men, you could see the flashing muzzle of a Taliban gun but still not be able to move out of the way before it hit you.

Freakley knew the sort of grinding warfare American soldiers were engaged in, but believed that Nicholson's experiments would bear results. He returned to Kabul for a second meeting with Eikenberry to discuss his proposed operation in Helmand, only to be put out by the senior officer's dismissive attitude. Don't think that "one battle in the south is going to defeat the Taliban," Eikenberry told him. Freakley listened to him in disbelief. Of course, there wasn't going to be some "Battle of Hastings" to decide Afghanistan's fate, he retorted, whether in the south or the east. The uncomfortable reality was that once western troops showed up en masse, they would have to wrest control from the Taliban and every other disgruntled tribesman one town at a time. They wouldn't stop until the insurgents surrendered.

Freakley's fixation on crushing the Taliban may have lacked nuance at times, but unlike Eikenberry, he grasped the fundamental danger of the US position: They were sending unprepared, under-resourced NATO troops into one of the war's most active fronts. His superiors might believe that the British could pad softly around Helmand, but Freakley considered that to be an illusion. Once the US had opted for a military solution in the south, armed confrontation with the Taliban was inevitable, Freakley believed. That the soldiers in question were NATO and not American was likely only to make the fighting longer and messier.

Abizaid ultimately approved Freakley's operation. But he refused to address the deeper concerns over the suitability of NATO command in the south. In May 2006, just as the British were arriving in Helmand, General Jim Jones, the American in charge of NATO's overall headquarters in Brussels, arrived in the country and Freakley again listed his concerns. Jones responded that the decision to hand over to NATO was no longer condition-based. It was a firm date: July 31, 2006. Freakley gave a stiff salute and left.

CHAPTER 15

Fly-Fishing in the Hindu Kush

As the US and NATO forces were stepping up operations in 2006 to crush the insurgency, the UN had spent the previous year brokering a peace deal in one area of the southeast that had so far removed the need for military intervention. Loya Paktia was a mountainous area spread over three provinces in the country's southeast. The Zadran tribe was one of the region's preeminent clans, and its scions included the troublesome warlord Pacha Khan Zadran. The UN had shielded Zadran from the Americans, who at one stage had wanted to kill him, and Zadran had ultimately reconciled with the Afghan government after being elected to parliment. After a few tour rotations the US military had largely forgotten about him.

But other branches of the tribe around Gardez still posed considerable challenges to the UN's efforts in the region—not least among them another, more powerful member of the Zadran tribe, Jalaluddin Haqqani. The Haqqanis controlled territory on both sides of the border with Pakistan, and Jalaluddin had been one of the CIA's favored warlords during the Soviet occupation, before Pakistan's ISI spy agency took over his handling. Haqqani had served under the Taliban as minister for tribal areas before seeking peace talks with President Hamid Karzai following 9/11. The Americans had rebuffed that overture, accusing the clan of sheltering Osama bin Laden and, more recently, launching attacks against American bases.

There was some truth to the American claims that Haqqani and his family posed a threat to American soldiers and Afghans alike. According to US intelligence, in 2003 Haqqani's son, Sirajuddin, brought Arab and Iraqi fighters to their stronghold at Miranshah in northern Waziristan, Pakistan, a dozen miles from the Afghan border. The result was a migration of bomb-making technology into Afghanistan, and a dramatic increase in suicide bombings there in 2005. Miranshah was also becoming the hub for a perilous alliance of tribal leaders, Taliban fighters, and al-Qa'eda remnants that US tactics had done much to reinforce. Western military and diplomatic leaders agreed that talking with Haqqani, let alone winning him over to the western cause, was impossible.

Tom Gregg thought they might be wrong.[1] He was a twenty-six-year-old Australian who in February 2005 had been appointed UN representative to the region. Most diplomats struggled to leave Kabul, whether due to security concerns or their own predilections for the comforts of the capital. The US military's interest in local politics was also limited. Members of the UN mission, by contrast, were still able to travel freely, and connect with rural Afghans to understand their hopes and grievances. The UN had a mandate to act on their findings and broker peace where possible.

Gregg had already gleaned from his predecessors that members of the Zadran tribe were open to discussion, although no one from the UN had yet contacted the Haqqanis. Gregg, fresh from graduate school in Canberra, Australia, with a few books on Afghan history, a Pashtu primer, and a certain devil-may-care attitude, seized his moment. When a tribal delegation from Jalaluddin Haqqani's home village of Gerda Tserai on the Afghan side of the border visited Gardez, Gregg decided to invite himself back to their village.

The elders looked alarmed at the suggestion. The local government officials who would accompany him insisted that the elders come with them for the three-hour drive into lush but remote mountain valleys south of Gardez. The elders asked for a couple of hours before setting out because, it later transpired, they needed to remove a roadside bomb that had been laid on the road to kill the likes of Gregg.

They made it safely to Gerda Tserai later that day, where Gregg was greeted by a motley crowd of bearded locals who emerged from a mudbrick compound. It was a poor village even by Afghan standards, lacking schools, health clinics, and a district center. The elders were conscious of their miserable conditions but were caught between their desire for help, their own pride, and the considerable dangers that came with talking to foreigners. Up on a hill, overlooking the town, was Haqqani's house with a gaping hole in the side, courtesy of a US missile strike the year before.

Gregg and the elders sat outside beside a smaller river that divided the village. Birch, larch juniper, spruce, silver fir, and mountain ash bounded the banks, along with a river cover of wildflowers, yellow barberries, and dwarf rhododendrons. Afghanistan's rich ecology had led the great Russian botanist Nikolai Vavilov to conclude in the 1920s that the country was an epicenter for plant life, where many of the world's first crop plants were domesticated.

The valleys of the Hindu Kush, remote and inhospitable for some, had sheltered plant life for millennia. The country had over 1,700 species of flowers that grew nowhere else.[2] Gregg could almost imagine reclining on the bank to listen to the trickle of the river.

"Look, we want to talk; we're open for business," Gregg told the elders. Unlike other UN regional offices, the team in Gardez had a small amount of money for reconstruction from the German government, money his predecessors had used to foster goodwill with the tribes.[3] The response he got was noncommittal, possibly, he surmised, because Haqqani would have to sign off on any arrangement.

As evening fell, Gregg moved to a tea shop in the village bazaar where he had dinner with some of the elders and was even considering spending the night, when one of his hosts' radios started crackling. Gunmen had ambushed a checkpoint down the road and were on their way to them. Gregg and his UN colleagues sprinted outside and into their car. It was arguably more dangerous to take to the roads after dark, but if Haqqani's men knew they were at the village, they had little choice. To take his mind off the tension of the moment, Gregg counted the bumps in the road as the convoy sped through the night. The lights of Gerda Tserai finally disappeared around a bend in the valley. A few hours later he reached the relative safety of a village controlled by Zadran's gunmen.

Gregg's foray had skirted with disaster and yet, in the Afghan way of things, he'd won a certain respect from his would-be killers for daring to show up at Gerda Tserai in the first place. Ten days later a tribal delegation arrived at Gardez, led by a former Haqqani commander in his early thirties named Haji Sangeen. Sangeen apologized for the earlier "misunderstanding" and gave an impish smile, which Gregg returned.

Over the coming weeks, Gregg began to negotiate a deal with Sangeen and tribal leaders from neighboring districts to begin reconstruction work in their communities in return for guaranteed security. He found that as he struck a deal with one group, the others followed suit. The hill country in question outside Gardez was particularly interconnected, with no ethnic or tribal rivals. That didn't mean there wasn't plenty of internecine fighting. However, the Zadran clan there and elsewhere across Loya Paktia lacked the simmering tensions that made other regions of Afghanistan so challenging for western peace brokers. In these districts, the main barrier to success was overcoming the tribal leaders' distrust and sense of neglect. Given that two of the three districts were the heartland of the Haqqanis, the political payoffs of bringing that family in particular into the process were potentially large.

The first and most conventional step in the UN's efforts to forge peace was to build local government offices in Gerda Tserai and the other districts. But a building wasn't enough to secure peace. Aid agencies in Kabul were slowly realizing that large-scale building programs were meaningless if they didn't include locals capable of staffing the buildings and providing a tangible link between the community and the national government. The difficulty they faced was that appointees from Kabul were rarely accepted in tribal areas, so Gregg hit upon an elegant solution. He asked the tribal shura in Gerda Tserai for three names of potential district heads, and stipulated that the governor would be able to choose any one of the three. That ensured a modicum of control on the government's part, but would also yield a leader the community had clearly endorsed. That most of the appointees were former Haqqani sub-commanders lent the process credibility among the locals. "They were probably reporting straight back to the old man in Miranshah," reflected Gregg. "I thought that was a good thing."

Borrowing from the success of the National Solidarity Program, the reconstruction initiative that placed project control in Afghan hands, Gregg let the tribal shura in Gerda Tserai choose how to spend some $1.3 million of German and USAID money. Schools, clinics, water projects, and roads were at the top of their priority list. The shura, religious leaders, and the government all signed reconstruction contracts.

Gregg's suggestions made good sense and built on best practices established in Loya Paktia and elsewhere before he arrived. But not all of them went down well with the US military. His most controversial initiative was to give the tribes responsibility for their own security—an arrangement that would involve creating a local defense force of up to fifty men to guard reconstruction projects and secure the area. Most of these villages were already well-armed, so Gregg was merely seeking official recognition of that fact through the Afghan government. The provincial police chief would pay and supervise the men. In many villages, guards drawn from local communities offered more security than the police, who were often corrupt and predatory. "It was an obvious solution, because it was already in place," said Gregg.

This was hardly a new idea in Afghanistan. Knowing his history, Gregg recognized militias as a mainstay of British colonial-era policy.[4] There were more modern precedents as well. Karzai's administration had experimented with the system as early as 2001 by extensively using tribal levies to guard polling stations in 2004 and 2005. American contractors had also recruited several Afghan tribes to defend stretches of the US-funded Kandahar–Kabul road. However, these programs, largely ad hoc, were opposed by some officials, including the US commander Karl Eikenberry, who believed that creating militias was a backward step that would undermine western efforts to create a central police force. This led to a similar but less refined (or promising) approach. In February 2006, the Karzai administration proposed creating an Afghan National Auxiliary Police, meant to supplement local police with locally mustered forces, but the interior ministry was soon hiring without vetting recruits and the US blocked further payments for them, and the effort subsequently petered out.[5]

In resurrecting the militia idea, Gregg was forced to confront an awkward reality that at least some of those involved in Paktia had staged attacks against the US military. It was one thing to build schools in Haqqani territory, and another to empower the locals to take up arms. Gregg doubted that the US military would sign off on a scheme that organized some of the Americans' former enemies into militias. Fortunately for Gregg and his militia program, one of the consequences of working through local Afghan power structures was that he wasn't required to directly seek American approval for his initiatives. He answered to the Afghans and his own supportive bosses in Kabul. To sign off on the agreement, he enlisted the three governors whose territory touched the Loya Paktia. On March 20, 2005, an elaborate ceremony in Gardez marked the inauguration of the Zadran Arc Stabilization Initiative.

As the summer drew to a close, Gregg had great hopes that he had established a model that could be replicated across the region to create a rough and ready sort of peace. He celebrated in the spirit of his colonial forebears: On the way back from a meeting with one local tribal leader, Gregg spotted a surprisingly fast-flowing river. The area was more arid than some of the lush mountain valleys he had seen, but there was still a dense thicket of trees, and higher up on the hills a rich covering of scented shrubs and herbs—vetchlings and other types of pea flowers, thistles, dandelions, daisies, forget-me-nots, and purple gromwell. Many rivers along the border are seasonal, running as the snow melts before drying up entirely by the end of the hot season. This river seemed to run throughout the year and thus had potential for a sport not seen in those parts since British imperial officers were nosing around: Fly-fishing.

Gregg had brought to Afghanistan an account of an 1857 expedition to Afghanistan by Henry Bellew, a British army medical officer. In his leather-bound copy, Gregg was intrigued to discover a reference to "flogging," or fly-fishing, in a nearby river for a fish known locally as the *mahisa* and to westerners as the snow trout. As Bellew enthused, "The 'Mahisa' is very good eating and has somewhat the flavor of salmon when large of size, but the smaller ones are more akin to the taste of trout. They afford capital sport to those who are fond of angling, and are generally easily taken by a hook baited with a bunch of yellow feathers."[6]

Fishing was relatively unknown to contemporary Afghans, and after years of drought few still bothered. British soldiers in Sangin, northern Helmand, had taken to fishing in the irrigation canal that ran past their base, finding that ration pack cheese was useful as bait. They would hand their catch over to the Afghan National Army contingent billeted on the other side of the canal.[7] The Afghans were happy enough to accept the offerings, which they grilled over open fires, but few joined the soldiers dipping lines into the fast-flowing water, explaining that the Afghan "way" of fishing involved dynamite or electricity to stun the fish. As Gregg noted in his diary after hearing a similar explanation, this was an Afghan twist on the old development adage, "Give a man a fish and he'll eat for a day, teach him to fish and he'll eat for a lifetime."

By the riverside outside Gardez, Gregg spotted a shepherd boy and through his translator asked him whether the river contained fish. The boy said he and his uncle had seen some, a fact confirmed by the *spin girees* or "white beard" in the local village. Understandably, Gregg, an avid fisherman, had not brought his line and rod to Afghanistan—but once back in Gardez, he sent a note home to ask his family to send his gear. In the meantime he decided to fashion his own rod from one of the region's threadbare trees, which he later replaced with a military radio antenna. For a line he used twine from a neighborhood cobbler, and he found a fishhook in a survival kit he borrowed from the nearby special forces base.

Given his rough tools, Gregg wasn't going to try fly-fishing, using instead some gouda cheese and old salami from the UN compound (salami was generally forbidden in Afghanistan because it contains pork) for bait. Trout are notoriously picky eaters, unlikely to be tempted by either of these delicacies. Yet catching fish wasn't the point of the exercise.

Over the following months, Gregg's fishing expeditions became a means of escape and a chance for a quiet communion with the country. Such moments were fleeting; the peace accord he'd brokered was under pressure within weeks, as one sub-tribe after another tested the agreement's limits by launching sporadic attacks against local government forces. There was talk, too, of increased Taliban infiltration from over the border in Pakistan, and swirling conspiracy theories among the Afghans about why the Americans weren't doing more to address the problem. Many believed that the US was deliberately seeking to prolong its stay in Afghanistan.

Gregg's work as a political officer was in some ways similar to the art of fishing: part patience, part timing, and part luck. As he reflected on this period after leaving Loya Paktia to take a job with the UN in Kabul in 2008, "As in all things tribal, success will always be relative rather than absolute. Indeed, cementing and keeping a degree of consensus in a given tribal community requires constant nurturing." It was slow, painstaking work, and Gregg wondered whether he wasn't also mimicking his colonial predecessors and their hunting trips. Was he merely a precursor to a much larger military effort, one that would render meaningless his connection to the country and its people?

It wasn't until his gear arrived from Australia that Gregg actually caught a trout. It happened on a clear, cold morning in September 2005, the sunrise lighting the mountain peaks, and steam rising from the stream; Gregg felt like he was getting a glimpse of what Afghanistan at peace might look like. The scene was interrupted when one of Gregg's Afghan police escorts started firing his AK-47 into the air, followed by the sound of the *attan*, the Pashtuns' tribal song and dance. His commander told Gregg his men had been overcome by the beauty of the morning.

By the autumn of 2005, it was becoming increasingly clear to Gregg that he needed to switch out his fly-fishing rod for more conventional Afghan tools. For his work to achieve broader acceptance in the region, he would need more overt clearance from Jalaluddin Haqqani himself. So far, the old

The United Nations diplomat Tom Gregg revived the art of fly-fishing in eastern Afghanistan, last practiced in the region during the days of the British Empire. (Photo courtesy of Tom Gregg)

warlord's presence had hung over every one of Gregg's meetings with the tribal elders, threatening, and yet perversely intriguing. After one incident in Gerda Tserai, in which a police checkpoint was ambushed, Gregg informed one of his tribal interlocutors that he wanted Haqqani's clearance for future projects. Gregg was startled when, after a brief phone call, his contact suggested he travel to Kabul and meet Haqqani's brother, Ibrahim Omari, in person.

Omari had been involved with tentative negotiations with Karzai's government in 2002, only to be arrested during Operation Anaconda and held in US detention at Bagram air base, where he alleged he was tortured before being transferred to a government facility in Kabul. Thomas Ruttig, one of Gregg's predecessors in Gardez, was among those who had pushed to engage the Haqqanis and to hold open discussions with the Taliban, only for the initiative to peter out in the face of US disinterest. Omari was eventually released.

Omari was predictably uninterested in meeting another westerner. Yet Gregg's tribal contacts prevailed on him to meet in a Kabul safe house just before Christmas. Gregg stood outside the gates for half an hour in the frigid cold of a Kabuli winter before the door opened. Omari looked irritated. He allowed Gregg inside but sat half turned away from his visitor in a scarcely furnished reception room and did not offer tea, the ultimate Afghan insult. Instead, Omari complained about kidney and back problems. Gregg didn't dare ask whether those injuries were a result of his beating in US custody.

Gregg began the meeting by asking Omari about the history of the Zadran tribe and his brother's role in fighting the Soviets, a line of questioning that seemed to catch the Afghan off guard. "It was one of the more hostile meetings I'd had in Afghanistan and I was trying to be as non-threatening as possible," Gregg recalled. Omari relaxed somewhat as he recounted the family history of bloodshed and mayhem.

Tea was finally served.

Gregg laid out what the UN was trying to achieve in the Zadran area. As luck would have it, Omari had a personal connection to one of the roads and a school that Gregg mentioned. "My brother and I built that very road and school twenty years ago," said Omari.[8]

"We can't continue work without your blessing," reasoned Gregg.

Omari gave a quick nod of his head, and raised his hands as an offering. "It's yours," he said. "Just keep working with the people and you will have success."

Gregg felt like he was on the cusp of a breakthrough that could pave the way for deeper talks between the United Nations and the warlord. Could an

understanding with the Haqqanis form the basis of a deeper political settlement, one that might bring tribes on both sides of the border into the fold?
Even without a grand bargain, extending the program to other sub-tribes in
the area would offer a measure of reintegration and would give the tribes a motive for resisting the Taliban's incursions. Such deals had the potential, as Gregg
put it, to "stitch together" a tribal alliance in Loya Paktia, one that, given
sufficient support, could bring the Haqqanis back to the negotiating table.

Still, the UN officer knew the deal was a long shot. There was no guarantee that any one thread of this presumptive tribal alliance would hold. Such
tribal diplomacy also needed to take place as part of a broader reconciliation
process that recognized the root causes of Pashtun disillusionment driving
the insurgency. Gregg hoped that with constant effort, his fledgling model
for tribal diplomacy could be proven effective and replicable. Yet Afghanistan
has a way of disregarding dreams. Gregg's were about to be shattered by events
a hundred miles to the west, in a part of southern Afghanistan where NATO
forces led by the British and Canadians were about to arrive with little interest
in negotiating peace.

CHAPTER 16

A New War

The British Brigadier Ed Butler might have objected to following American orders upon arriving in Helmand in April 2006, but he had few qualms about approving operations at the Afghans' bequest provided they made military sense. Butler was one of the brightest stars of his military generation; a former commander of an elite unit, and one of a few officers to have actually seen combat in Afghanistan after the fall of the Taliban. Forty-five years old, Butler shouldered the high expectations many had for the British mission while recognizing that he needed to close the gap between hope and reality.

One of the unforeseen repercussions of the UK decision to remove the warlord Sher Mohammed Akhundzada from power in Helmand province and replace him with a functionary lacking a power base in the region was that the British now found themselves as Helmand's custodians. Every time a local government office was attacked, Butler received requests from the new governor, Mohammed Daoud (and sometimes from President Hamid Karzai himself), to send in British troops. "If the black flag of the Taliban flies over any village it jeopardizes the authority of the Afghan government," Daoud would say.[1]

Butler advised Daoud that the British weren't as all-powerful as the governor seemed to think, and that the 3,500-strong British contingent only amounted to seven hundred or so frontline soldiers. However, there was no denying that Butler's paratroopers were well-suited to airborne assaults on potential Taliban strongholds. Butler saw the use of helicopters as the only safe means of gaining access to Helmand's far-flung communities. Butler had been briefed on the earlier plan by the British Post Conflict Reconstruction Unit to limit British efforts to Lashkar Gah, but he regarded it as "unrealistic" due to their lack of resources for development work.[2] Instead of focusing on reconstruction, Butler was increasingly preoccupied with Daoud's requests to combat the Taliban. According to the Afghan governor, the entire north of the province was in danger of falling into enemy hands.

Butler shared his concerns and believed that if the Taliban weren't stopped in the north they would soon be challenging for control of Lashkar Gah. He also knew that he didn't have enough forces to deal with every threat, so they would have to manage a careful balancing act between his obligation to help the Afghan government and the judicious use of his forces. Then there were the requests from the US military to take part in their own operations, as well as whatever tasks came from the NATO headquarters in Kandahar to which the British also answered.

As the UK's senior military representative, it was Butler's job to vet these requests, and while he turned some down, the operations he did take on soon committed the British to a frenetic schedule that took them far beyond their original plan to focus on the center of the province. Lieutenant Colonel Stuart Tootal, the commander of the 3rd Battalion of the Parachute Regiment that provided the bulk of the fighting troops, had estimated that the British could perform one or two operations a month involving a company-size force of one hundred men. By May 2006, a little over a month into the operation, they had already conducted a dozen such raids across the province.[3]

When it came to overseeing these missions, Butler operated with considerable freedom. He remained outside NATO's command structure, and thus was not obliged to meet requests from the likes of US commander Major General Ben Freakley. At the same time, the commanders he did answer to were based 3,500 miles away at the UK operational headquarters in a sleepy suburb on the outskirts of London. Butler sought to brief the HQ daily, but his superiors were far removed from the reality on the ground, and were eight and a half hours behind Kabul anyway. This gave Butler a high degree of autonomy with which to steer operations during his regular contact with officers in Helmand.

The principal problem he faced was that once his soldiers arrived in Helmand's far-flung communities, they found it difficult to leave. The local police had a tendency to disappear at the first sign of trouble, and despite promises from Kabul, Afghan army units were rarely dispatched to support the British troops. The US military had only belatedly turned its attention to rebuilding the Afghan army. In 2005, just 2,500 Afghan soldiers had been trained, and those who did deploy were ill-disciplined and prone to desertion. None were stationed in Helmand.[4]

There was a further twist: The local government officials the British were being asked to protect were often deeply unpleasant characters, whom the

Brigadier Ed Butler was the senior British military official in Afghanistan when NATO forces deployed to the south of the country in 2006. (Photo by Heathcliffe O'Malley)

villagers would have liked to send packing. The arrival of foreign troops in support of predatory officials was all the inspiration some locals needed to pick up their guns to start attacking the British. Once they did, the Brits were then obliged to fight until the area was pacified. "We can't withdraw and let the Taliban think they had got the upper hand," Butler told his staff.[5]

Yet despite the problems these operations presented, Butler felt he had no option but to continue them as he came under increasing pressure from the Karzai administration and the US military to do more. British soldiers were soon manning outposts with platoons of a few dozen men in Musa Qala, Now Zad, Gereshk, Kajaki, and Forward Operation Base Robinson. For the Kajaki operation, the Americans had gone as far as threatening to withdraw their contractors working on the dam if the British did not intervene.[6]

At first the violence was limited, but Butler knew this "platoon house" strategy, as it became known, was stretching his forces thin, not least because he only had half a squadron of helicopters to ferry them around: eight Chinooks that could transport troops and accompanying Apache helicopters. The issue of helicopter allocation was to prove particularly contentious for the British military. The need for more helicopters had been apparent since 2004, when the defense chiefs had agreed on a budget for $1.4 billion for up to one hundred aircraft, but the chiefs had tried to extract the money from the Treasury using an accounting sleight of hand, and their ploy was quickly spotted by then-Chancellor Gordon Brown who told them to make cuts. The military chose to eliminate the one line item that the services contributed to, thus limiting the pain to each branch: helicopters. Ever after, the military vilified Brown for forcing these "cuts," partly to distract the media from its own role in the disaster to come.

Butler had asked for more helicopters before deploying to Helmand, but he knew none were available. Yet instead of operating cautiously, within the limits of his force, the British appeared to do the exact opposite, deploying their troops across the province in a disposition that would challenge their ability to support them in an emergency. At times, Butler tried to limit the number of outposts, yet he also supervised on their expansion. Butler later said that this approach was not part of a deliberate strategy, and that for each mission, contingencies were made to support the soldiers.[7] The consequences of British forces becoming overextended soon became clear. In mid-June 2006, Butler received a worried call from Daoud about the security chief in Sangin, whom the locals had attacked. Daoud demanded that Butler send another detachment of troops to the town.

"I'll see what we can do, but it is going to be very difficult," said Butler.

S angin was to be one of the war's bloodiest venues, for both the British and American military, and it would take on an outsize significance in western discussions of how to manage the war in the years to come. Yet before so much blood was spilled over Sangin, it was just another dusty town in Helmand. Its main feature was a marketplace through which the poppy harvest of much of the surrounding hills and *wadis*, or valleys, was sold. Local strongmen frequently contested for control of the market, and in 2006 Sangin was under the grip of a particularly unpleasant one: Dad Mohammed Khan, the head of Helmand's secret police. Even members of his own tribe, the Alakozai, had little good to say about him. According to Mullah Sadiq, a Sangin local, Khan had turned the town into a private fiefdom, systematically stealing from the population and maintaining a private jail where he caroused, got drunk or stoned, and raped his prisoners.[8]

Sadiq was one of many Sangin residents who had had enough of Khan. By the summer of 2006, Sadiq had signed up with the local Taliban commander to try to kill the secret police chief. In early June, Sadiq and the Taliban assassinated Khan's brother in an ambush. The next day, as Khan and his family were driving to the site of the first attack, Sadiq was among those who ambushed the convoy. Several men and boys, many related, were killed, and Khan's own son was shot in the stomach. Khan managed to escape with his injured offspring. The reporter Elizabeth Rubin was visiting Taliban leaders in Quetta a few days after the attack and found them filled with "energy and bombast," a reminder of how local were the motivations of many of the Taliban.[9]

But Khan had friends of his own: the Afghan government, and by proxy, the British. The UK contingent received a flurry of calls from Daoud and even

Karzai, who said that Khan's son was in need of medical attention and insisted the district center was under attack and in imminent danger of falling.[10]

Butler knew that the situation was more complex than Daoud implied. In April, Minna Jarvenpaa, the Finnish planning expert who was working with the PCRU in Helmand, had specifically warned Butler about sending soldiers into Sangin. The fighting there wasn't between the government and the Taliban, she explained; rather, it was between two prominent local tribes for control of the drug trade. By wading in to support one tribe, the British would be taking sides in a battle over drugs. Butler recognized the dangers of getting involved in such a sordid tribal dispute but felt the British needed to give a strong show of force in support of the Afghan government.[11]

Butler continued to hold to this view regarding Sangin, even after the Afghans themselves had concluded that the British would be better off staying out of the town. Governor Daoud, who had initially supported the operation, realized a few days later that it would be easier to fix the situation by bringing together the town elders rather than dividing them by throwing British support behind a single faction. "We don't need the British forces in Sangin," concluded Daoud.[12]

According to Tom Tugendhat, a British civilian adviser assigned to Daoud, Butler chose to ignore the governor. Butler insists that Daoud did not backtrack. Either way, on June 20, Butler ordered Stuart Tootal of 3 Para to prepare an operation to briefly occupy Sangin's district center and rescue Khan's son.

By coincidence, the deputy head of British military operations, Major General Peter Wall, was on a trip from London to visit Helmand and assess the mission. Wall urged caution but deferred to Butler as the senior British commander Afghanistan. That left it to Butler to give the final go in ahead for the assault. Butler says he spent six hours resisting Afghan government requests to conduct the operation, before relenting after he was told that Khan's son was on the verge of dying.

At the last moment, however, he appeared to have doubts and ordered Tootal to prepare another risk assessment of the operation as the paratroopers from A Company, 3 Para, waited on the helicopter landing pad. Butler was in Lashkar Gah at the time. By the time he was satisfied, dawn was less than three hours away. He asked Tootal if his force could deploy within ninety minutes.[13]

The British experience in places like Musa Qala and Now Zad—where UK forces had already established small outposts in the midst of hostile communities—had led Tootal to question another operation that might lead to a further expansion of the mission. They were concerns that Butler shared and he fully intended their presence in Sangin to be brief. Tootal said he needed twenty-five minutes to ready his men.

T he horizon had lightened from black to a thin shade of gray as the thump of helicopter blades echoed across Sangin. In the back of two Chinooks sat the 120 soldiers of A Company, 3 Para. The troopers had been ready to deploy since sundown, but whatever grogginess they might have felt was being replaced by the special dread of combat. Dimly lit by green lights, transport helicopter holds have a liminal quality—as if the men, rocking on the currents of the desert sky, were already aboard a ferry to the underworld.

As the choppers landed, the men dashed down the rear platform and onto the hard-packed desert floor. On one side of the landing zone was the bullet-ridden district center on the eastern edge of town, along with the entrance to the drug bazaar and the narrow streets of the marketplace; on the other, open farmland stretched to the Helmand River half a mile away behind a screen of trees.

Company commander Major Will Pike had expected to arrive in a hail of bullets, but instead his men dashed over to the district center without trouble. Pike and his chief medical officer entered the building, and inside found Khan's son in stable condition and needing only a shot of antibiotics to prevent what was a minor stomach wound from becoming infected.

The helicopters took off shortly after daybreak, leaving Pike to hastily shore up the building's defenses with sandbags as best he and his men could. The plan was for the Paras to stay a few days, and help the local security forces control the situation. Governor Daoud had promised to send Afghan forces to guard the city center, but they hadn't shown up. It was beginning to look like they would have to hold the center and protect Khan's family all by themselves.

A day after arriving in Sangin, Major Will Pike held the first British shura in Sangin and was politely asked to leave by the elders. The next eight years of violence in the town claimed 107 British and 115 American lives. (Photo courtesy of Will Pike)

A delegation of locals approached the headquarters mid-morning, and Pike held a shura. When the elders asked why the British had come, Pike gave them a pat response: to help rebuild the country and establish security.

"How much money have you brought?" one of the white-bearded men asked him.[14]

Pike was forced to admit he had none. The British Provincial Reconstruction Team had only recently deployed to Afghanistan, and much of its staff was based in Kandahar, far from Sangin. The PRT's pre-deployment plan had focused on Lashkar Gah, and the team lacked the capability to deploy elsewhere. Indeed, PRT head Wendy Phillips plainly opposed the operation to Sangin.[15] Such conflicts between civilians and the military would bedevil the western effort in the years ahead. The military criticized the often poor quality of diplomats sent into the field, claiming that they lacked knowledge of local tribes, generally disdained the military, and refused to share the same risks as soldiers. The PRT countered that there was little point in meddling in village affairs unless the military planned to be there for a very long time.

Either way, the result was that Pike had nothing to offer the elders, who politely explained to him that if the British remained in Sangin, the Taliban would certainly attack them. Fearing the town would be caught in the crossfire, the elders kindly requested that the British leave. Pike had no choice but to refuse.

That night, the first mortars landed in and around the district center of Sangin, followed by occasional small arms fire. As dawn broke on the second day of the UK occupation, potshots continued, building up over the course of the morning and didn't let up for days. The soldiers fired back into the shuttered shops on two sides of the district center. At several points, the British dispatched Apache attack helicopters to fire on the assailants. The choppers' 50mm machine guns ripped through the buildings' mudbrick walls.

During lulls in the fighting, the elders came to beg the British to leave. The para commander was anguished. "It was a mockery of the idea that we were there on a peacekeeping mission," said Pike.

The violence had left Butler frustrated by what he saw as Daoud's duplicity, both in terms of misrepresenting the condition of Khan's son and by promising to send Afghan troops that didn't show up. "We went into Sangin. It's a complete fucking mess; you've got to get back here," he told Tom Tugendhat, Daoud's British adviser. Tugendhat had gone on leave believing the operation had been canceled.[16]

The mess only got worse. On July 1, 2006, a 105mm rocket struck a British sentry position on top of the district center, killing two soldiers and wounding half a dozen others. They weren't the mission's first British casualties, but their deaths did underline the British position's growing precariousness. The media in the UK had begun to pick up the unfolding disaster after London *Sunday Times* reporter Christina Lamb was ambushed while embedded with British troops elsewhere.

Butler was caught in a bind. He wanted to withdraw, but he risked an embarrassing loss of face in Afghanistan and at home. At this point, Butler turned his attention to Ben Freakley's operation to rout the Taliban from northern Helmand, which he had initially opposed and which had been launched with relatively little planning input from the Brits. The operation was meant to conclude with American and Canadian forces entering Sangin in mid-July, which was a couple of weeks away. It appeared to offer Butler a way to extract his men from Sangin when Freakley's forces arrived, but Butler remained wary. In the end there was nothing he could do to stop American and Canadian forces from moving into position. He reluctantly agreed that the UK would contribute a two hundred–man airborne assault on the Sangin town center.

On July 16, British forces were to assemble at Camp Bastion's helicopter landing pad, but when the hour to launch arrived, the Canadian Brigadier David Fraser, who was commanding the operation, was incensed to learn that Stuart Tootal was requesting permission from Butler to go ahead. Having approved the operation, at the last minute Butler appeared to be changing his mind.

Fraser had a number of conversations with Tootal, at the end of which he was informed that 3 Para was standing down.[17]

"Do not stand down," Fraser insisted. "This operation is on. Repeat, do not stand down."

"Whose fucking order am I meant to follow?" a confused Tootal asked.[18]

At this critical juncture, the British communication equipment failed, not for the first time that day. In the enforced lull, Fraser called the recently arrived NATO head, British General David Richards. Richards had yet to take charge of NATO operations, but he was British and technically outranked Butler. "Get rid of Butler, or put him under command," Fraser told Richards. "This can't go on."

By the time the radio network was working again, Butler had consulted with London and the operation proceeded, although with dawn imminent it was considerably more dangerous. After a short, intense fight on the outskirts of Sangin, the combined western forces entered the town and imposed a peace of sorts after suffering only a few minor scrapes. Once the bulk of the troops had left, however, the British position in the town came under fire yet again.

A few days later, Ben Freakley arrived in Helmand to confront the British over their perceived flouting of the chain of command. Ed Butler was not at the meeting. In his place, Tootal bore the brunt of the American's frustration. "Get off your asses!" Freakley shouted, furious about the UK's failure to follow his orders or grasp the basic nature of the challenge in Sangin.

The explosive meeting was soon reported back to both capitals. General Eikenberry's deputy, a Brit, called Freakley the next day. The British military leadership lives in perpetual fear of just such American reprimands. "I heard you used scathing language about [our] performance in Helmand," said the British officer nervously.[19]

"That would be a wonderful classification of the meeting," said Freakley. "One of you needs to go down there and sort it out."

CHAPTER 17

Medusa

R estoring British pride and NATO's reputation in the eyes of the Americans fell to Lieutenant General David Richards. A forty-eight-year-old Brit, Richards had long been on the gilded path to the top of the British military establishment, and his appointment as commander of all NATO troops in Afghanistan in July 2006 was the latest step on his ascent. He was neither overbearing nor self-consciously grand. Instead he had the air of a schoolmaster, ready to extol his pupils to greater acts of courage or to quietly express his disappointment when his own high standards weren't met. Yet even Richards's patience had been stretched by the British Brigadier Ed Butler, whom he believed had made a grave error in allowing the UK mission to expand into towns such as Sangin that summer.[1]

Richards's American counterpart, Ben Freakley, continued to oppose handing over US control of the south to NATO forces. But Richards went some way toward mollifying him by promising to rein in the British operation in Helmand, which had become dangerously overstretched. That in itself was no easy task. One of the problems that Richards identified was with what he saw as Butler's free role outside the direct military chain of command in the south. "He'd gone rogue," concluded Richards.[2] Butler refutes the characterization and later said that it was by following multiple and conflicting sets of orders, from London, Kabul, and NATO, that the British had gotten into trouble, along with a poorly defined mission and not enough forces.

Richards recounted that he only brought Butler to task by issuing an ultimatum to London: He would refuse to deal with British troops in Afghanistan if the command situation wasn't resolved. The new head of the British military, Jock Stirrup, intervened, and it was decided that Butler would set up

The British NATO commander Lieutenant General David Richards realized that UK forces in Helmand were overstretched and sought to de-escalate the fighting. (Photo courtesy of Tom Tugendhat)

his headquarters in Camp Bastion with the rest of his troops, and to take his orders from Richards as a subordinate commander in Helmand.[3]

Repairing the damage caused by the British deployment proved more difficult. Richards was desperate to get back to the original plan for southern Afghanistan. The 3 Para expansion into northern Helmand had dragged attention away from towns where it really mattered, such as Kandahar, where the Canadians maintained a tenuous grip on the principal city of the south. "We had invested significance in the wrong places," Richards recalled.[4] He agreed that towns like Sangin and Musa Qala were not strategically important, but he had come to believe in the symbolic imperative in following through on NATO's commitment to hold them.

At the same time, Richards needed to figure out how to maintain peace in Kandahar, where the postwar tribal settlement was unraveling. In the Arghandab region to the north, Karzai's erstwhile ally, Mullah Naquib of the Alakozai, was a waning force (he would die of a heart attack the following year). Power was shifting to the Panjwei region east and south of the city, where the Noorzai had responded to heavy-handed government interventions by arming themselves and creating a virtual enclave, complete with fortified positions and checkpoints manned by former Taliban commanders and their tribal followers. The region of dense farmland that supplied Kandahar with grapes, melons, and pomegranates had also been a bastion of the resistance during the war with the Soviets.

Karzai had done little to reach out to the Noorzai and include them in the region's power structure. In 2005 he had removed the unpopular governor of Kandahar, Gul Agha Sherzai, only to install a weak replacement, while real power shifted to Karzai's half brother, Ahmed Wali, the head of the provincial council. The move unsettled tribal groups like the Noorzai, who already felt that their voices weren't being heard.[5]

In August, Richards's commanders began planning for a brigade-scale NATO offensive into Panjwei to smash the Taliban, even if it meant further antagonizing the locals.[6] Richards knew it could prove to be the largest battle of the war as well as an ultimate opportunity to prove NATO's competence. The American and NATO commands were due to combine later in the year, provided all went well. Panjwei fell under the Canadian area of operations in Kandahar, so they would direct Operation Medusa, as it was soon dubbed.

A recently arrived Canadian officer, Lieutenant Colonel Omar Lavoie, was due to lead the mission. On his first day in command, Lavoie had sent a company to a rocky promontory called Masum Ghar that overlooked the Arghandab River and, on its northern banks, the verdant heart of the Panjwei. Within hours the Canadians were attacked by several hundred militants. They managed to fight off the assault without casualties, but the scale of the attack suggested to Lavoie that pacifying the Panjwei would require extreme levels of force. His plan called for conventional tactics against what he assessed to be dug-in enemy positions: an artillery bombardment, followed by an armored advance. The shelling he planned would be the largest in Afghanistan since the Russians fought the mujahideen. In fact, the Canadian military had to order so many rounds of ammunition that NATO suppliers were overwhelmed. "There simply weren't enough ammo supplies in the NATO logistics system," recalled Fraser.

The enormous quantity of ammunition on order raised concerns for Freakley over whether Lavoie had grasped the nature of the fighting and the need to limit damage to Afghan homes and livelihoods. He asked Fraser directly if he thought the colonel was right for the job. Fraser insisted Lavoie was competent but quietly scaled back plans for the artillery bombardment while keeping the basics of the plan in place. He then left for a break in Canada.

While he was on leave, US intelligence suggested that an earlier strike might snag several Taliban leaders, including Mullah Dadullah, believed to be hiding in the Panjwei. Richards flew to Kandahar in Fraser's place, inspected Lavoie's men, and told the colonel: "The fate of NATO is resting on your shoulders."[7]

Lavoie's more modest assault plan had gotten the green light. It still called for a three-day bombardment of the Panjwei before advancing on enemy positions, believed to center on a collection of villages in the district known as Pashmul. The largest of these was Bazaar-e-Panjwei. The first step was to occupy the high ground at Masum Ghar. Fraser arrived back in Kandahar just in time to witness Canadian forces occupy the promontory without trouble at dawn on September 2.

From that vantage point, Lavoie's men were to ascertain whether any civilians were present in the town before the first air strikes went in. This proved hard to do, at least to Fraser's satisfaction, and he canceled the bombing run. Instead Lavoie's men used the cannons on their armored vehicles to blast away at the opposite bank, receiving sporadic return fire.

That afternoon, Fraser arrived at Masum Ghar to find the area quiet. He decided to scrap the bombardment plan entirely and ordered Lavoie's men to cross the river and attack that night. Lavoie was skeptical about advancing into unknown enemy territory. He wanted to target buildings on the opposite bank that provided cover and to conduct smaller sorties over the river to expose enemy positions. Fraser told him that dropping bombs wasn't going to add to his knowledge of the area, and that they needed to take advantage of the lull. Every officer felt the pressure to show the Canadian military's prowess.

Lavoie reluctantly sent an engineer detachment down to the river to work out where best to ford. At that point, the Arghandab was a half-mile-wide series of rivulets divided by banks of pebbles. Fording the river was possible, but they would have to proceed slowly to avoid deep spots. As darkness fell, however, Lavoie was once again having doubts. When the launch hour arrived in the early hours of September 3, Lavoie refused to send his men across the river. He told Fraser over the radio that it would be safer to cross during the daytime, when they could gauge river depths more clearly and spot enemy positions. That was an advantage that worked both ways, Fraser pointed out, because the Taliban would be able to see them. He finally got Lavoie moving across the river by dawn.

Major Matthew Sprague of C Company of the Royal Canadian Regiment and a small team of Afghan soldiers crossed the river in a convoy of armored carriers and utility vehicles. They made it to the other side without incident. As they established a beachhead, a platoon from C Company advanced farther inland toward a school building several hundred meters away. Then the bullets started to fly from the school's direction. A rocket-propelled grenade struck a lightly armored utility vehicle at the front of the column, instantly killing

The Canadian Brigadier David Fraser sought to take
on the Taliban outside Kandahar during Operation
Medusa. (Photo courtesy of David Fraser)

Sergeant Rick Nolan in the front seat and grievously wounding a medic and
an Afghan interpreter at the rear. Another soldier died as he returned fire. In
the confusion, one Canadian vehicle, hastily stuffed with injured soldiers, reversed into a ditch and was riddled with RPGs as soldiers scrambled for cover.[8]
Over an hour after fording the river, C Company retreated under fire, shocked
and dispirited. In total four soldiers had died and ten more were injured.

The following day, as Lavoie was preparing for another assault over the
river, disaster struck again. This time Fraser had approved US air support
before the advance. As Lavoie waited for it to arrive, his men got out of their
vehicles. In the distance, an A10 Warthog sped into view. The Warthog was a
heavily armored jet designed by the US military in the 1960s to fly close air
support for ground forces. It was armed with a 30mm cannon, the largest ever
mounted on a jet, capable of firing 4,000 bullets a minute. It was a fearsome
complement to any ground operation. But on this day, the ground troops
found themselves on the wrong side of its guns.

Lavoie was in his command vehicle when he felt an ear-shattering set of
explosions. He staggered outside to see torn metal, smoking tree stumps,
and a writhing mass of bloody bodies on the ground. It took him a second
to realize that his entire command post had been destroyed by the Warthog's
bullets, which had mistaken their position for the enemy's. Dashing back into
his vehicle, he screamed into the handset: "Call off the Warthog, call off the
Warthog."[9]

Once he was sure his surviving troopers were safe and that medical evacuation helicopters were on their way, Lavoie rushed back outside to tend to

the injured and dying. One soldier had been killed outright, and thirty-three more were seriously injured. Fraser had no choice but to call off the attack, not least because he thought Lavoie might be cracking under the pressure. "Get [Lavoie] out of there," ordered Fraser.

To make matters worse, the Canadians' NATO allies were falling short in their duties. The Dutch, who had been roped in to provide outer cordon duty for the Canadian advance, had announced they would withdraw shortly, and the Danes refused to take over Canadian positions and were falling back too. At the last minute, an American National Guard officer in Kandahar, Colonel R. Stephen Williams, was scrambling whatever men he could find—aging civil affairs specialists, fellow reservists, and others simply passing through—to fill the gap in the NATO lines.

That afternoon, Fraser and Lavoie met in NATO headquarters in Kandahar. Lavoie accused Fraser of sending his men to their death, before tearing up and leaving the office. Half an hour later he returned, calmer.

"Look, I know it's hard. It's shitty," said Fraser. "But you've got to finish this thing off. Can you do it?"

Lavoie agreed, but only if Fraser promised to revert to his plan for a massive aerial bombardment and this time to tackle Panjwei from the north along more established routes. Fraser accepted, knowing full well that replacing his main commander would be a public announcement of Canadian failure. The media was already beginning to point out the obvious—that NATO was in trouble.

But for the heroics of the American officer Colonel Williams and his irregular force, the operation would have collapsed altogether. Like extras from *The A-Team,* his newly christened "Task Force Grizzly" crossed the Arghandab River that night under heavy fire. At one point, the forty-six-year-old Williams got out of his Humvee to urge on his men and a contingent of Canadians across even as bullets puckered the river. Half an hour later they had made it to the far side, where they established a base, from which they were skirmished deep into Noorzai territory with Williams' favorite rock music blasting out of a Humvee set up with a loudspeaker.[10]

By the time General Richards made it down to Kandahar a few days later, with NATO Secretary General Jaap de Hoop Scheffer in tow, Fraser's headquarters was able to hail Williams's ad hoc force as an "American bridging force." More than a week later, Lavoie's men began their aerial offensive, launching tons of artillery rounds to cover their advance as more Canadian troopers splashed across the Arghandab to join Williams's men in Panjwei. Richards claimed victory from the jaws of disaster. Crucially, NATO assumption of overall command of the war could go ahead. "Operation Medusa has been a significant success and clearly shows the capability that Afghan, NATO and Coalition forces have when they operate together," Richards said.

In reality, NATO had succeeded only in strengthening the insurgency. The campaign had destroyed extensive swathes of local farmland and done little to address the Noorzai's political grievances. The Taliban leadership, which had fled by the time Lavoie's men bombed their way into the Panjwei, was soon back again.

In September 2006, NATO could not hide how bad the situation had become in Helmand, where the British were still battling for their lives and the province was slipping into anarchy. Pockets of UK troops were stationed in half a dozen outposts across the province, most of them under steady attack by Taliban and tribal forces. These "platoon houses" of only a few dozen men relied entirely on helicopter support to bring in food and water. Some weeks, when desert storms raged or the Taliban prevented helicopters from landing with small arms fire, the soldiers' supplies dwindled to a bottle of water a day per man. They had little choice but to raid local marketplaces.[11]

In this dire predicament, British soldiers fell back on gallows humor and the camaraderie of squaddies in trouble. The objectives of the war, the motivations, even cold, wet England, lost relevance in the rush to the rooftop and the discharge of bullets. On patrol, the dense groves of pomegranate, apricot, and mulberry trees interspersed, and narrow paths between irrigation ditches and compound walls were known simply as the Green Zone.[12] Their enemy was renamed "Terry Taliban," and inspired some verse, too. In one of the Sangin guard towers, someone had scribbled a short poem on a scrap of cardboard from a box of rations:

> *Watch out Terry, we're hunting you down*
> *There's nowhere to hide in Sangin Town*
> *You shit yourself when the .50 cals are fired*
> *No point in running, you'll only die tired*
> *Got A10s on call for brassing you up*
> *No food or water, we don't give a fuck*
> *So do one Terry, you've plenty to fear*
> *We run this town now. The Paras are here.*[13]

Adding to the troopers' worries was the fact that they badly needed helicopters to ferry away the steadily mounting British casualties. One of the miracles of military logistics since the Vietnam era was the ability to airlift wounded soldiers to hospitals within the so-called golden hour, during which time medical intervention can dramatically increase the chance a patient will survive. Air evacuation had effectively become part of the military covenant. "I always said that if we couldn't look every soldier in the eye and say we can get you to medical facilities in the right time, we'd have to pull the plug on the operation," recounted Butler.[14] He was directly in charge of British operations in Helmand since Richards had insisted he be placed under NATO command.

With only six helicopters available for airlifts, and one or two of those needing maintenance or repairs from Taliban attacks at any one time, multiple casualties raised the prospect of soldiers being left stricken on the field. Butler, who had been shaken by the scale of fighting and the inability to guarantee casualty evacuations, wanted to withdraw. Yet General Richards at NATO headquarters couldn't countenance a withdrawal. "We can't pull out of these towns; that would be a major defeat of the British Army," Richards told him.[15]

On September 6, the British skirted disaster. That day, a patrol near the Kajaki dam wandered into an old Soviet minefield. A single soldier, Lance Corporal Stu Hale, lost his left leg below the knee. What happened next is a subject of controversy. Canadian Brigadier David Fraser said he immediately called Butler to offer UH-60 Blackhawk helicopters for the rescue that were at his disposal at Kandahar airfield, and would have taken less than forty-five minutes to reach the stricken men. Fraser was concerned that a British Chinook, a large transport helicopter with twin blades, might touch off more mines if it landed.[16]

According to Fraser, Butler insisted that the British had the situation under control and that he would use his own British helicopters, stationed at Camp Bastion. Butler said later that Fraser did not make this offer, and that furthermore, the Canadian didn't have the authority to send any. Butler's own headquarters was in direct contact with the officer tasking helicopters for southern Afghanistan, to whom he made repeated requests for a Blackhawk fitted with a winch to rescue the men without getting a response. As it was, Tootal decided to send in a British Chinook from Bastion to rescue Hale. The stricken patrol was forced to start clearing a path out of the minefield to a rocky ridge, where the patrol leader, Corporal Mark Wright, adjudged the Chinook sent to evacuate Hale would be able to land safely. At that point, a second British soldier stepped on a mine and lost his leg, before a third went off, seriously injuring another soldier.

Wright realized the dangerous extent of the minefield, and that there was no way a Chinook could safely land. By then the patrol could hear the helicopter rapidly approaching, but the British lacked the equipment that would allow them to directly speak to the pilot and tell him to back off. The Chinook briefly landed on two wheels, before the pilot spotted the soldiers waving him away. When the helicopter took off, the wash of air from its blades kicked up a loose mine, which struck Wright in the chest and exploded, mortally wounding him. Three hours later, Blackhawk helicopters did eventually arrive, but Wright did not survive the return to Camp Bastion.

As the rescuers at Kajaki struggled to save what remained of the patrol, reports emerged of further casualties in Musa Qala and Sangin. With only one other Chinook available, the British mounted a second, desperate rescue effort that required the single transport helicopter to evacuate wounded from both places, and made rescuing the injured inside the golden hour all but impossible. In both locations, the aircraft came under heavy machine-gun fire, which at one point forced the helicopter and its Apache escort back to Bastion. A second soldier died by the time the helicopters were able to get back to base. At one point, two rocket-propelled grenades passed within ten feet of the helicopter on either side—the closest yet the British mission in Helmand had come to losing a helicopter and an even more catastrophic loss of life that might call into question the entire British mission in Afghanistan.

Butler soon concluded it was only a matter of time before a helicopter was downed. He started planning to pull out all British troops from Musa Qala, the most perilous of the outposts. General Richards opposed the move: The UK and NATO had staked their reputations on holding these towns, and it was essential they make good on those bets. But Butler's concerns appeared to have infected London, where the head of the British military, Jock Stirrup—who had questioned the wisdom of deploying to Helmand the year before—was prepared to sanction the move. "We didn't have a choice," he noted later.[17]

At this excruciating juncture, Richards sought an awkward compromise. From the start of the tour he had held meetings with Sher Mohammed Akhundzada, the former governor of Helmand whom the British had worked so hard to remove from power. Richards didn't have a firm opinion on removing Akhundzada in the first place, but he knew the warlord was instigating violence in Musa Qala and, given the right incentives, could be persuaded to stop.

The British foreign office opposed even talking to Akhundzada, which would signal to the Americans and Karzai that they had blundered in removing him. However, Richards brushed aside such narrow concerns. He met Akhundzada that September to ask him to use what influence he had to calm the situation. Richards did not have the power to offer him back his former position as governor. But he promised he would lift British objections to Karzai's giving Akhundzada a political position elsewhere. "Maybe we could get you a governorship somewhere else," Richards suggested. "Then you can work your way back to Helmand." Akhundzada said he would contact tribal leaders and ask them to stop fighting. It's not clear what sway Akhundzada had over Musa Qala at that point, but Richards had sent a signal that the British were interested in reconciliation.

At the same time, Helmand's provincial governor, Mohammed Daoud, and his British adviser, Tom Tugendhat, held a series of talks with tribal leaders in Musa Qala that would prove even more controversial than Richards's outreach to Akhundzada. Ever since the British had arrived in Musa Qala, the elders there had been asking them to leave. The fighting had destroyed every house within a two hundred–meter radius of the district center, the local mosque was on the verge of collapse, and the market was filled with shuttered shops.

Butler was quickly brought into the talks. He consulted with Daoud and Tugendhat as they spoke to the elders and a deal began to emerge. If the British left, the elders would assume responsibility for the town and keep the Taliban out. Tugendhat was aware that many of their clans had been fighting against the British and, according to Tugendhat's sources, were closely affiliated with the Taliban. Tugendhat was one of the first British officials to realize that this fact should not prevent negotiations. "These were tribesmen with legitimate concerns, which had been neglected by Kabul and the British military," he said later. "It was time we listened to them."[18] Indeed it was a vast oversimplification to identify them as Taliban sympathizers. Many of these tribesmen were also fighting against Akhundzada and his cronies and in the past had fought against the Taliban.

Butler immediately saw the value of such a deal. His experience from Northern Ireland suggested to him that only once all sides began talking could a sustainable political settlement emerge. It had taken years to reach that point with Northern Irish dissidents, and Butler was aware that engaging with tribal leaders in Musa Qala might open the British to an American charge that they were "talking to the enemy." He was prepared to take the risk with the fighting worsening and the British only hours from ordering a unilateral withdrawal from the town. He agreed to meet the village elders and the local fighters on the outskirts of Musa Qala to seal the cease-fire. In Kabul, Richards supported the deal from its inception, and promised to stave off any US opposition.

The meeting took place beneath a military camouflage net to shade the participants. British soldiers took up position, out of sight, in case the proceedings turned ugly. A cloud of dust rising into the clear sky heralded the approach of a convoy of twelve pickup trucks carrying the elders and fighters. The long shirts of the tribal leaders flapped in the wind. The young fighters, dressed in black, were stony-faced.

After climbing out of the trucks, the Afghan fighters stood silently to one side as Butler began negotiating with the elders. He promised that if the cease-fire held out for one month, the British would withdraw. Thereafter, western armed forces would not conduct an operation within three miles of the town and would not interfere in its governance, provided the Taliban agreed to the same. Some of those fighters had come from neighboring districts expressly to drive the British out of Musa Qala. They were only too happy to return home having accomplished their mission. The elders even offered to provide a convoy of trucks to facilitate the soldiers' departure.

It was becoming clear to some British officers that without a drastic increase in troops, they were in an unwinnable situation in southern Afghanistan. More troops didn't appear to be in the cards. Instead, the British—despite the UK mission's many failings, or perhaps because of them—had hit upon an exit strategy for NATO troops across Helmand. And while it had involved negotiating with Afghans who may or may not have been Taliban, a fact that had been anathema to western military commanders until now, suddenly that seemed like a fair price for a face-saving withdrawal.

The direct and bloody contact with the tribal realities of a town like Musa Qala had revealed an obvious truth: Supporting the government meant little to the locals. As one resident, Abdul Rahman, commented, "Here there are only tribes against tribes, and families against families."[19] In this reality, the soldiers' role, if they had any, was to act as a power broker, bringing sides to-gether—preferably not by blundering into communities and uniting everyone against them.

A few weeks later, one hundred and fifty British soldiers, some of them riding in brightly colored and festive Afghan trucks, threaded their way out of Musa Qala, never to return.

CHAPTER 18

Bad Guests

Pakistan's dictator, Pervez Musharraf, seemed to regard NATO's blunders in Afghanistan with grim satisfaction. For over a year he'd had American diplomats and generals queuing up outside his office, telling him he had to do more to combat Taliban fighters and other militants in Pashtun areas along the Afghanistan border. He had told them he was doing all he could but that sending troops to such places would only stir rebellion. And now here were those same western governments, locked in a desperate fight against an insurgency having gone into similar areas on the Afghan side. Musharraf had some advice for the Americans about how to fix the mess they'd created, and it started with recognizing that the key to peace in Afghanistan lay with him. So in mid-September 2006, he flew to Washington with a proposal for restoring calm.

The years since 9/11 had taken their toll on the Pakistani general. His attempt to consolidate his rule had had only limited success. It was true he had retained the support of the military, as well as the country's powerful business community. The country's economy was booming, partly due to the influx of American aid money. Yet, when it came to sidelining his rivals from the mainstream political parties, one of the strategies he hit upon—to support religious parties in provincial elections—had created its own headaches. In 2002, the Muttahida-Majlis-e-Amal, an alliance of religious parties, was elected to power in two of the provinces bordering Afghanistan. The MMA was dubbed the Mullah-Military Alliance by some, but in reality, the MMA's success reflected a rising sense of Pashtun resentment in tribal areas. Its leaders were vociferously anti-American and critical of Musharraf's support of the "War on Terror," which only raised the stakes in Musharraf's high-wire policy of appeasing both the West and militants within his own country.

Musharraf had bet on America losing interest in the region, and that his support for militants would ultimately pay off, especially when it came to Afghanistan. The Pakistani leadership viewed the Karzai administration as an ally of India, and hostile to their interests in the country. Musharraf wanted militant groups like the Taliban to be primed and ready to stake Pakistan's claims to the country once the Americans left. Pakistan would regain its hegemony over Afghanistan and win the admiration of its own militant groups.[1] In October 2004, Musharraf appointed Lieutenant General Ashfaq Parvez Kayani as the head of the ISI, whom some believed to be an advocate of formal assistance for the Afghan Taliban.[2]

The problem was that the Americans hadn't left as swiftly as all parties had anticipated. Nor had they farmed out the war to Islamabad as they had during the fighting against the Soviet Union. If anything, the US and NATO appeared to be committed to ever more troops, and had conceived of ever greater nation-building designs, both of which were inflaming tribal tensions on either side of the Pakistani-Afghan border. Pakistan's ISI spy agency reported that militant groups and their tribal hosts regarded Musharraf as a puppet of the foreign powers that had invaded Afghanistan.[3] What's more, they were adopting al-Qa'eda's mantle of global jihad.[4]

This was a dangerous development for Musharraf. In 2003, Harkat ul-Mujahideen, a group the ISI set up to defend Pakistan's interest in Kashmir, helped two of the British Pakistani radicals behind the London Tube attacks set up a terrorist training camp to learn how to manufacture bombs. That same year, Musharraf narrowly survived two assassination attempts orchestrated by a Harkat ul-Mujahideen spin-off organization based in the tribal areas along the border with Afghanistan. The dictator was in danger of becoming caught between the militant groups on the one hand and, on the other, a frustrated Bush administration that increasingly blamed Islamabad for providing sanctuary to the Taliban and other militants.

In March 2004, Musharraf sought to tackle his militant problem and appease Washington by ordering the Pakistani military into southern Waziristan, the region along the Afghan border from which the assassination attempts had been hatched. Waziristan's history made it even more intractable than other parts of the region. It was part of the Pashtun heartland, which stretched across both sides of the Afghan-Pakistani border. In the north the Haqqani family had great influence; the south was dominated by Mehsud and Waziri tribes. The region had its own form of tribal administration, a hangover from colonial rule; after decades of trying to control the Pashtun, the British had ultimately settled on a form of indirect rule through community elders.

That spring of 2004, the Pakistani military surrounded a village in southern Waziristan looking for the leaders of the militant group that had attempted to kill Musharraf. Instead a Pakistani Frontier Corps detachment found itself lured into a trap, ambushed, and routed. Sixteen soldiers were killed. Dozens more from the Pakistani Frontier Corps, predominantly made up of Pashtuns, deserted. In response, Pakistan rushed 8,000 regular soldiers to the area while helicopter gunships, bombers, and artillery blasted the region into a brief submission. Eventually 80,000 Pakistani soldiers were dragged into the fighting, yet the operation was a humiliating failure—a demonstration that Pakistan was just as deluded as NATO in thinking that it could subdue the Pashtun tribal areas.

The crucial difference was that Islamabad was prepared to learn from its mistakes and move on. On April 23, 2004, the Pakistani military signed an agreement with the militants' leader, Nek Mohammed, a charismatic twenty-nine-year-old who resembled, according to *New York Times* reporter Mark Mazzetti, a "Pashtun version of Che Guevara."[5] In return for ending the violence, the military would pull out of its garrisons in southern Waziristan, compensate tribesmen who had suffered losses, and hand over prisoners. The Pakistani commander of the operation, Lieutenant General Safdar Hussein, embraced Mohammed live on television before crowds of tribesmen. "When America's World Trade Center was hit by a plane, how many Afghan pilots were involved?" General Hussein asked the crowds in Waziristan. "Since there are no Afghan pilots, why is there this situation in Afghanistan?"[6]

Western and even some Pakistani officials were furious that Musharraf had empowered the fighters who would later call themselves the Pakistani Taliban. "If [Pakistani troops] had carried through with the operation in 2004 . . . the Taliban would not have spread," said Asad Munir, a former senior ISI officer. But from Musharraf's perspective the agreement was pragmatic. Musharraf recognized that Islamabad had limited control over the toxic blend of Islamists, jihadists, and disaffected tribesmen that had been stewing in the area. Instead of risking outright war to quell these dissidents, Musharraf told one associate he was happy to let them find a more "natural outlet" for their anger: the western nation-building project in Afghanistan.[7]

Two weeks before Musharraf flew to Washington, the Pakistani military and the US target Jalaluddin Haqqani struck a deal to end hostilities between Haqqani's network of tribal contacts and the Pakistani military in northern Waziristan. As a result, Haqqani would coordinate the other militant groups in the area and direct their attentions against the Karzai administration.[8] As Musharraf prepared to meet with President Bush, he appeared ready to offer the Americans their own deal to avoid this consortium of terrorism heading their way, one that would dramatically increase Pakistan's power over its neighbor and herald the start of a US exit.

Musharraf arrived in Washington on a crisp autumn day in September 2006. The Bush administration was reeling as the Iraq war spiraled out of control and violence soared in Afghanistan. Yet even then, Musharraf had to be careful how he framed his proposals. He didn't want to directly antagonize the superpower. Instead he presented the deal with Haqqani to President Bush as a chance for peace in Pakistan's tribal region. At a meeting in the Oval Office, which Waziristan governor Ali Jan Aurakzai also attended, Musharraf outlined how Pakistan could assist the US in replicating a similar deal with southern Afghanistan tribes, allowing American and NATO troops to withdraw sooner than expected. In effect, Musharraf was offering to take over management of the war in southern Afghanistan.

Bush was immediately skeptical. He still held Musharraf in high regard for his decision to risk his presidency to side with the Americans after 9/11. Combating militants was a "shared concern," they all agreed.[9] Bush's loyalty toward Musharraf had done much to shape American attitudes toward Pakistan even as evidence mounted that the ISI was complicit in militant attacks on coalition forces in Afghanistan. At one stage in 2006, the Bush administration approved the "hot pursuit" of fighters who attempted to escape into Pakistan, but this tactic was not carried out for fear of damaging relations with Islamabad. Instead both sides approved a Predator drone program, provided the unmanned aircraft stayed away from sites the Pakistanis deemed sensitive and Washington alerted Islamabad before any strikes.[10] Bush also signed off on a $750 million aid package to tribal areas, although the Pakistani military subsequently siphoned off much of this money.

Bush was prepared to bend to Pakistan's wishes only so far, however. Many in his administration already considered Musharraf's peace deal with Haqqani to be little more than a handover of the region to militants. Afghan President Karzai also strongly opposed the Musharraf-Haqqani deal and had accused the Pakistani leader of sheltering the Taliban's leadership. The plan Musharraf was suggesting sounded as though it would give control of southern Afghanistan to the likes of Haqqani and the Taliban, and wouldn't fly in either Washington or Kabul, Bush believed. He told Musharraf as much and reminded him that the two of them were due to meet Karzai at the White House in a few days. The trilateral meeting would be a Bush-style attempt to break the ice between the Afghan and Pakistani leaders in the hope they would work together to solve the Taliban problem. It would be a challenge even for Bush's charming brand of personal diplomacy. The bad blood between the men extended back to early meetings, when Karzai had first raised the issue of Pakistan's relationship with the Taliban. Musharraf had been openly contemptuous of his Afghan counterpart. When Karzai said he had Mullah Omar's address and phone number in Quetta, the Pakistani president dismissed with a wave of his hand the notion that he was sheltering the Taliban leader.[11] The claim was less far-fetched than it seemed, given that many Taliban members were living quite openly in the city at the time, although Mullah Omar remained well hidden.[12]

Since then the men's rivalry had festered, with Karzai coming off the worse for it. He couldn't understand why Washington continued to support Musharraf, given the mounting evidence that the ISI was supporting the Taliban. Furthermore, the botched NATO expansion into southern Helmand was making the Afghan leader start to wonder whether the US wasn't deliberately trying to sow chaos in order to occupy the country indefinitely, an increasingly popular conspiracy theory in Afghanistan at the time.[13] In recent meetings with American officials, Karzai had started complaining bitterly about civilian casualties. Indeed the number of civilians who had died in the fighting in Afghanistan had increased threefold, up to 4,500 that year, many attributable to botched US air strikes. The US military had made little or no effort to recognize the scale of the problem, and Karzai had become increasingly withdrawn and sullen.

All of this made for an awkward *Iftar* dinner at the White House to celebrate the Muslim holy month of Ramadan. Not even Bush's bonhomie could dispel the tension in the Family Dining Room. The two leaders had traded accusations a few days before the meeting, with Karzai accusing Pakistan of breeding extremism in the country's religious schools, or madrassas. Musharraf had replied by saying the Taliban were an Afghan problem, and likened Karzai to an ostrich with his head in the sand. When they met at the White House, shortly before dinner, the leaders pointedly refused to shake hands. Bush joked to the assembled reporters he'd be watching their body language.

The first course, Jerusalem artichoke soup, had barely been served before the men were again trading barbs, with Karzai accusing Musharraf of harboring the Taliban, and Musharraf responding testily, "Tell me where they are." The sniping continued over spicy sea bass and endive salad until the meal was over, when Musharraf brought up the idea of extending into Afghanistan his peace deal with the tribal areas.[14] Karzai visibly winced and looked at Bush, who neither condemned nor condoned the idea.

And just like that, the plan was dropped. The trip ended with all sides just as deeply entrenched in their positions as before, but this time a militant alliance in Pakistan's tribal regions was primed to attack American forces.

Unbeknownst to the three leaders as they met in Washington, the United Nations had been working on a deal that might have allowed all sides to come to an understanding with the Haqqanis. After meeting with Ibrahim Omari Haqqani in December 2005, Australian diplomat Tom Gregg had believed the UN could turn its limited reconstruction work in Haqqani's home community into a broader settlement in Loya Paktia that was likely to have an impact across the border in Pakistan's tribal areas. The UN leadership in Kabul had been excited about what Gregg had already achieved through initial exchanges with the Haqqanis. He was invited to Kabul to brief both Tom Koenigs, the UN head, and his military counterparts. However, discussions about a wider deal had been sidelined by the escalated fighting over the summer of 2006, as NATO and American forces expanded their presence to the east and encountered resistance. Loya Paktia had escaped the worst violence, in part because of the UN's arrangement. Yet it was all Gregg could do to hold the peace together.

The deployment of NATO forces to Kandahar and Helmand had allowed Ben Freakley's 10th Mountain Division to send additional troops to Gardez. They brought with them an aggressive attitude, leading to "kill or capture lists" being drawn up of local tribal leaders—the very men Gregg was working with. On one occasion, the military called a shura in Gerda Tserai, only to haul away two of its members.

"You just can't do that; it's unbelievably insulting," Gregg later complained down the phone to the commander.

"We showed them respect by asking them to step outside before we arrested them," the officer replied.[15]

Gregg didn't consider the US troops unduly violent; they were merely exhibiting a characteristic mix of ignorance and aggressiveness. "They thought these tribal guys were in contact with the Taliban and Haqqanis, which they were," said Gregg later. "What the military didn't realize was the tribal leaders were caught in the middle."[16]

Gregg sought to temper the military instincts, share his understanding of tribal dynamics, and work the phones to get detainees released before the peace process was damaged irrevocably. "It was different worlds colliding," he recalled.

One of the ironies of Gregg's close relationship with the tribal elders in Gerda Tserai was that when the 10th Mountain Division commander,

Lieutenant Colonel Steve Baker, announced he was going to build a patrol base in the town, Gregg was able to smooth over any of the elders' objections. "They welcomed the US military at first, although it was clearly a direct provocation to the Haqqanis," recalled Gregg.

The elders' attitude rapidly changed, however, as the base began to draw fire, and as the troops stationed there returned it with interest. At one point in 2006, Taliban fighters were reported to have entered the bazaar in Gerda Tserai. They had left by the time the US base had scrambled a patrol. Unfortunately, in the ensuing confusion, a teenage boy was shot and killed and several more injured.

Such incidents made it increasingly difficult for the UN to operate in Gerda Tserai. By the summer of 2006, the situation was so bad that Gregg once again reached out to the Haqqani leadership, this time writing to Sirajuddin Haqqani to ask for help. The letter was delivered by hand through the tribal network. Gregg arrived in Gerda Tserai two days later to hear the reply: The Haqqanis once again extended their protection to the UN—but only the UN. That point was plainly emphasized a few minutes later when Gregg's convoy left the town and passed a convoy of US Humvees going in the opposite direction. A minute later they heard a roadside bomb detonating and a large-scale ambush kicking off. Gregg chose to step back from his local work after that, recognizing that increased tension in the region between the tribes and the US military made his trips across the region increasingly difficult and dangerous. He chose to focus on tribal engagement from the relative safety of Gardez and Khost.

Gregg was sympathetic to the military's position and believed US forces had a role to play in staving off what he saw as increasing interference from Pakistan. After Musharraf's visit to Washington, the US commander Karl Eikenberry noted a threefold increase in Taliban attacks against Coalition forces inside Afghanistan.[17] Pakistani support for militants had also become more overt. US soldiers on the Afghan border watched as Pakistani army trucks delivered fighters right up to infiltration points from which they then entered the country and attacked Afghan border outposts, with Pakistani artillery occasionally giving the Taliban covering fire. Meanwhile, the Pakistanis appeared to have set up medical facilities for treating Taliban who were wounded during their clashes with US forces. "We all knew the Pakistanis were as guilty as hell," said Major General Freakley.[18] He had the disconcerting experience of briefing the Pakistani military on a large-scale operation in Afghanistan, only to watch on a drone feed as Pakistani military trucks delivered Taliban fighters right up to the border to counter his plans.

In May 2007, tensions between American units on the ground and Pakistanis came to a head. The US military had begun constructing border outposts to curb the flow of fighters over the border, a move the Afghan government supported. The new outposts appeared to antagonize the Pakistani military, who sided with militants in launching a number of assaults against Afghan soldiers manning the positions. On May 4, American and Afghan forces fought off a group of twenty-five attackers at one of the new outposts at Gawi in Jaji district territory that the Pakistani's claimed as their own. Over the following days the fighting escalated as both sides traded gunfire, mortar rounds, and artillery fire. Pakistani troops moved up to the Afghanistan border.

The American battalion commander of the 508th Brigade Special Forces Battalion, Lieutenant Colonel Steve Baker, in whose sector the border crossing fell, attempted to defuse the tension by calling a meeting to bring together all sides. On May 14, two Blackhawk helicopters flew Baker, his deputy Major Larry Bauguess, and their Afghan counterparts over the border to Teri Mangal, an outpost on the Pakistani side of the border. There they were met by a Pakistani detachment that ferried them in a convoy of Land Cruisers and pickup trucks to a single-story school building three hundred yards from the landing zone, on the edge of a small town. They drove through the school's gates and into a central courtyard, dismounted, and entered a concrete room on one side of the square. Pakistani soldiers from the Frontier Corps stood guard on the roof and at the building's entrance.

Over the next five hours, the three parties conducted rambling and sometimes tense negotiations. Baker didn't think it was his job to lead the discussions, so he let the Afghans and Pakistanis hash it out, stepping in only occasionally to adjudicate.[19] By the end of the meeting, the two sides had both agreed to abandon their claims to the Gawi outpost and to create an exclusion zone on either side to prevent further conflict. Baker was delighted to have secured what he thought was a significant breakthrough.

The American and Afghan delegation left the building after shaking hands with the Pakistanis. Baker suggested they walk back to the helicopters, which were due to arrive at the landing zone in ten minutes, according to a prearranged pickup time. It was only a short walk. The Pakistanis insisted, however, that Baker and his men get back into the convoy vehicles, claiming a security concern in the nearby town. Baker demurred and along with the Afghan governor got back into the lead Land Cruiser for the short drive. Behind him he glimpsed his men preparing to leave in the other vehicles. Baker's Land Cruiser had just pulled out of the school gates when shots rang out behind him.

For a split second, Baker thought it was some local confrontation. Only when he heard the distinctive staccato burst of American M160 rifles in return did he know the situation had gone horribly wrong. "Stop the vehicle," he bellowed at the Pakistani colonel in the front seat. The man ignored him. Baker's Land Cruiser and a second one behind his drove straight past the turn to the helicopter landing zone and down a short slope. Baker took out his pistol. "Stop the fucking vehicle now," he yelled.

The Pakistani driver slammed on the brakes then, as did the Land Cruiser behind them. Baker and the Afghans who were accompanying him leaped out of the vehicles and began running back toward the landing zone. Baker could hear the thump of rotor blades as a helicopter approached. He was certain they had just avoided a kidnapping. They stumbled toward the landing zone just as the rest of the American delegation from the school house sped into view. The pickup truck they were driving was riddled with bullets and bloodied soldiers were hanging over the side.

Unbeknownst to Baker, as soon as his vehicle had pulled away from the school, one of their Pakistani hosts had pumped Baker's deputy, Major Bauguess, full of bullets at point-blank range, mortally wounding him. A second American soldier was shot in the chest, a third in the groin. The Afghan interpreter was hit in the shoulder and thigh. The detachment's medic, Corporal Don Adams, managed to get his gun up and dispatch the first shooter. He provided covering fire as two of his colleagues who had avoided being shot struggled to get their injured colleagues aboard the pickup truck they were due to travel in. A Pakistani soldier was still behind the wheel. One of the injured soldiers, Specialist Marcus Twine, dragged the driver from the seat, jumped in, and fired the engine.

More Pakistani soldiers now appeared at the school building windows and had begun firing at the Americans. One Pakistani scrambled onto another pickup with a heavy machine gun mounted on the back, but Adams shot him just in time. Twine gunned the pickup, and the vehicle tore out of the compound. The Pakistanis were preparing to pursue in their own pickups, but at that moment, an American Apache helicopter appeared, part of the Blackhawk's escort. By the time they reached the helicopters and safety, it was clear that Major Bauguess, a thirty-six-year-old married father of two girls ages four and six, was dead.

The UN Envoy Tom Gregg met Baker that evening, a few hours after the attack, when the American officer was still in shock, tearful and angry at what he saw as Pakistan's betrayal. Baker was close friends with Bauguess and knew his wife, Wesley, who had been in the army and led the battalion's support group helping families who had lost loved ones. It was a harrowing phone call that night to Wesley. She showed more composure than he did.

The exact motivation behind the attack was not clear to Baker, but his soldier's instinct told him that his Pakistani hosts had been acting according to a prearranged plan, and that there was a possibility that their chain of command was involved. It was impossible for Baker to verify the claim. Was it simply a retaliation for the recent exchange of fire over the border posts, or was a deeper, more sinister plot afoot? Either way, Baker fully expected that his superiors would launch an inquiry into the incident and that Washington would finally wake up to the threat Pakistan posed. To Baker's dismay, however, the Pentagon quickly moved to accept Pakistan's explanation of the incident. The Pakistani soldier who killed Bauguess had been a deranged and lone gunman, Islamabad claimed. Both countries' senior military appeared determined to put the matter to rest.[20]

For Gregg, the incident had deeper ramifications: The US failure to recognize reality on the frontier, and Pakistan's inability to moderate its aggressive self-interest, doomed any hope of advancing his peace plan with the Haqqanis. Talks had the potential to bring together Pashtun clans on both sides of the border, but getting to that point required all parties to lay their agendas on the table. "You can't talk about peace if both sides are pretending they're not in a state of war," Gregg reflected later.

At the very least, Bauguess's death should have convinced the US of Pakistan's active support of the insurgency. Instead, the US military returned to business as usual, and Gregg went back to trying to prevent an all-out war between the US military and Zadran tribes. But as the violence flared, his job was getting harder.

In May 2007, US forces searched the house of one of the UN's principal allies in Gerda Tserai. The man was already under considerable pressure from the Taliban, having received a number of death threats that same week. He promptly stopped talking to Gregg. When the UN tried to host a shura in Gerda Tserai to affirm the tribal leaders' commitment to the peace accord, most elders did not show up. The tribal militias and local police force had also largely faded away.

Over the summer of 2007, attacks by Haqqani fighters surged, prompting the US military to plan a large sweep of the area using armored vehicles and close air support. The UN issued a worried pre-operation assessment: "Despite the willingness of [NATO] and the [Afghan National Army] to embrace this operational model, there was broad agreement that this *style* of military operation, . . . will displace insurgents, but in order to kill or capture, a different style of operation with ambush tactics and local engagement is required."

As it turned out, the operation failed to find any Taliban, so the US military decided to host its own "super shura" in Gerda Tserai. They invited none other than Pacha Khan Zadran, the troublesome warlord and relative of Haqqani (and erstwhile US target) who had once again worked his way into American affections. He was not a popular figure in Haqqani's hometown. As Apache gunships circled overhead, the elders sat glumly through the meeting, which was interrupted by incoming missile fire, followed by a suicide car-bomb attack. US soldiers later arrested a group of teenagers for behaving suspiciously.

Gregg, whom the military had choppered into the meeting briefly and who left before the attacks, was due to leave for a job in Kabul the following day. He spent his last few hours in Gardez trying to secure the teenagers' release. The teenagers later complained that they had been roughed up during their detention.

CHAPTER 19

All the Way

When he arrived in Kabul in February 2007, US General Dan McNeill, the incoming NATO commander, was struck by how badly the mission in Afghanistan had deteriorated. He had commanded US forces during the war's first months and left in 2002 believing that combat operations were over. The country he returned to was descending into chaos. Snipers and suicide bombers attacked western forces a dozen times a day.

McNeill's answer to these problems was simple and decisive: more troops. He had long criticized Donald Rumsfeld's "light footprint" strategy and indeed had supported creating Provincial Reconstruction Teams in part to expand the US military's role in the country. In 2002, when Rumsfeld had been preeminent, the defense secretary had resisted escalating the war. But four years later Rumsfeld was on his way out for his disastrous handling of the "War on Terror." The most damning assessment of the man was given by his former Centcom commander, General John Abizaid: Rumsfeld had lost all credibility. The US military was in need of salvation.

The situation was particularly critical in Iraq, where American forces were on the verge of defeat, and the US's strategy of handing over security to Iraqis clearly failing.[1] Soldiers were clearing towns of insurgents and withdrawing to their bases in the hope that Iraqi security forces would hold the ground, only for their allies to be rapidly overwhelmed. At the same time, the country was slipping into civil war between the Sunnis and Shi'ites, the two major branches of Islam.

In November 2006, President Bush accepted Rumsfeld's resignation and prepared to launch a new strategy in Iraq that drew on the counterinsurgency approach being promoted by Lieutenant General David Petraeus.[2] A former divisional commander in Mosul, northern Iraq, Petraeus had spent the past year drafting a game-changing field manual on counterinsurgency warfare while at the US Army Command and Staff College at Fort Leavenworth, Kansas. His doctrine upended current military thinking on Iraq. Instead of withdrawing, Petraeus believed that US forces needed to stay behind, live among the community, and provide the security necessary to facilitate the country's political development.

Petraeus's take on counterinsurgency drew on strategies that the French in Algeria, the British in Malaysia, and most painfully the Americans in Vietnam had employed with notably mixed results. Petraeus was, of course, aware of this record. What suggested this approach would work in Iraq was that it aligned the US military with a deeper trend among Iraqis. At the war's outset in 2003, Sunni tribes had sided with al-Qa'eda spin-off groups to battle the Americans but they had grown weary of the war and the extremists' dogma. The tribes were prepared to back the Americans.

In early 2007 Petraeus was arriving in Baghdad at the same time that McNeill was taking up his post in Kabul. McNeill also wanted to expand counterinsurgency tactics across the country. But where Petraeus was getting a "surge" of troops—25,000 more, on top of the 130,000 already in the country—McNeill would be lucky if he got more than a couple of thousand. He had inherited 25,000 American soldiers in Afghanistan, mostly stationed in the east. He also commanded a 12,000-strong international contingent of British, Canadian, and Dutch soldiers in the south. Some 60,000 Afghan soldiers were also being trained.[3]

General Dan McNeill commanded American forces in Afghanistan twice. On his second tour, he urged his NATO allies to confront the Taliban. (Photo by Staff Sergeant Michael Andriacco)

When he suggested to the Pentagon that the US also needed to surge in Afghanistan, he was informed that the war remained an "economy of force" effort, that is, he would get no more troops. That meant he would have to employ counterinsurgency where he could, and do more with the forces he currently had. In eastern Afghanistan, Colonel John Nicholson was already experimenting with counterinsurgency and placing his men into small patrol bases along the Pakistani border. At the same time, McNeill intended to aggressively pursue the Taliban's leadership across the country, tripling the number of both US special force raids and air strikes over the course of 2007.[4]

The American troops under his command would rise to the challenge, McNeill knew. He was less confident in getting a response from the 12,000 international soldiers he would be leading. The American and NATO commands had merged in October 2006, so the soldiers from two dozen nations were to do what he told them. In practice, though, any decision was usually related via the military hierarchy of each contributing nation, which made for fractured command. On a wall in his office in Kabul, he had plastered a list of each nation's rules and caveats, which he liked to point out to visiting dignitaries.[5]

The problem was particularly acute in southern Afghanistan, where British, Canadian, and Dutch troops had deployed and some of the heaviest fighting of 2006 had taken place. McNeill didn't entirely blame this state of affairs on NATO, although he—like most other American commanders at this point—agreed the organization had botched its deployment in 2006. He questioned the wisdom of getting rid of the province's governor, Sher Mohammed Akhundzada, in the first place. "Sometimes you got to deal with the agents of Beelzebub to get things done," he later reflected.[6] The UK's performance in Helmand left him "particularly dismayed." The British had subsequently "made a mess of things in Helmand, their tactics were wrong, and the deal that London cut on Musa Qala had failed," he told a US State Department official.[7]

McNeill made correcting the situation in Helmand one of his priorities. But he soon discovered that the British were more circumspect than they had been a few months before.

Indeed the British were confronting their own moment of existential doubt. Lieutenant General Robert Fry's scheme to switch Iraq for Afghanistan had fallen apart. Surging violence in Basra had prevented the British from handing over the southern Iraqi city to local security forces and withdrawing. At the same time, the reconstruction mission to Helmand had turned into a full-blooded counterinsurgency campaign. The result was that the British contingents in both countries wanted more troops, but none were available until one or the other of the conflicts died down. The strain on the military's resources led the head of the British army to liken the organization to an engine that was "running red hot."

Unlike the Americans, the British lacked the readily available manpower or the political will for a surge with which to rally support at home. Indeed, in September 2006 Tony Blair had announced he would step down as prime minister, having lost the support of the Labour Party, partly as a result of Britain's travails in Iraq. His likely successor the following year, Gordon Brown, was not expected to bail out the British military by approving more troops for both wars. Brown had never been an active proponent of the Iraq invasion, and he believed the military had taken advantage of Blair's interventionist creed. He had a straightforward solution to the challenges the military faced: Start planning British troops' withdrawal from Iraq—no matter what state they left Basra in or the damage it might do to US relations.

The prospect of leaving Basra in tatters divided military officers between those who considered it a betrayal of their soldiers' sacrifices and those who were only too happy to say good riddance to an unpopular war. Fry, for one, believed the British had done all they could in Iraq, and it was time to leave. If anything, the situation in Iraq had the unintended consequence of boosting British resolve over Helmand. "We needed to prove that we remained a crucial strategic partner," said Fry. "We needed to find salvation."[8] That meant more troops to wrest the province back from the Taliban's hands and show the value of British arms.

Not every officer agreed that renewed aggression in Helmand made sense. The incoming commander in the province, Brigadier Jerry Thomas, a no-nonsense British marine, considered such mixing of strategic objectives with tactical reality to be a profound mistake. The evidence so far suggested that the UK had only pushed the province into armed revolt, and that far from rebuilding the province, the British had devastated much of it. An aerial survey of northern Helmand upon Thomas's arrival in October 2006 attested to that. Sangin's once-thriving bazaar near the district center was now a pile of rubble, with shopkeepers staying away after the fighting.[9] Musa Qala had also taken a pounding, with refugees living in tents in the craters where their homes once had stood. In the northwest, the entire town of Now Zad had been entirely abandoned. British fortifications in each town had also grown, with outposts surrounded by heaped sacks of earth fifteen high and topped with barbed wire.

As much as Thomas wanted to clear up the mess, he was pragmatic enough to realize that further intervention by the British, however well intentioned, was likely to lead only to more fighting. The Afghans Thomas was speaking to were telling him the same. "We were trying to push for something the Afghans didn't want. The message was pretty clear: We [the Brits] weren't wanted in Helmand," said Thomas.[10] It was time to draw back.

He wanted to replicate the peace deal in Musa Qala and pull out of Sangin. He had maintained a company there over the winter of 2006 but he saw little strategic value in holding the town. He had arrived in Helmand with almost double the troops of his predecessor, yet even with 5,000 men he didn't see how he could maintain security around Lashkar Gah and hold outlying towns like Sangin. The idea of building anything was even further from his thoughts. "We could have left right then," said Thomas of that Christmas period. "I sometimes wonder if we could have spared more lives if we had."

Yet withdrawing appeared almost as difficult as staying. Tribal interlocutors capable of helping the British find equilibrium between tribal networks were hard to access. Then there was the question of managing the relationship with the US and the need to demonstrate British strength of arms, which put pressure on Thomas to defend the local deal he did have in Musa Qala.

Before taking command, General McNeill had made it perfectly clear that he considered talking to the Taliban as tantamount to defeat and the deal in Musa Qala as jeopardizing everything NATO was trying to achieve. Under such pressure, the NATO headquarters had authorized an air strike against one of the tribal leaders who had brokered the deal with the British the previous year.[11] The strike in early February 2007 missed its intended target, prompting the Taliban to drive into Musa Qala at the head of a two hundred–strong militia and raise their black flag over the district center a few hours later.

The Helmand commander Jerry Thomas was not informed about the strike and was furious when he learned what happened. He feared the British were about to be sucked back into northern Helmand—just as the US military wanted. His staff hastily prepared a military estimate to show that he did not have enough troops to clear Musa Qala. McNeill agreed to postpone an assault on Musa Qala—"for now."[12]

McNeill had expected some pushback from his allies as he sought to reenergize the campaign. However, he was not prepared for a public fallout with President Karzai on the inevitable consequences of more military action: civilian casualties. When McNeill had been the commander in 2002, US air strikes had mistakenly targeted a wedding party in Oruzgun province, which led to forty-seven deaths.[13] Karzai had accepted his expression of regret back then, and McNeill had expected that he could smooth over similar mistakes during his second tour.

Instead he received worried calls from Karzai almost every day about some errant air strike or raid. Every strike, it seemed, was hitting civilians. At first Karzai was courteous, as McNeill had come to expect, but he became increasingly shrill over the spring of 2007 as the casualties mounted.

On March 4, 2007, nine civilians—five women, three children, and an elderly man—were killed when their mud house in Kapisa province, just north of Kabul, was hit by a pair of 2,000-pound bombs. A seven-year-old girl, Mujib, emerged from the wreckage to discover the bodies of her family scattered around the rubble.[14] On April 29, 2007, Afghan officials said forty-two were killed during air strikes in Shindand, Herat province. The bombs rained down: In 2007, at least 1,633 Afghan civilians were killed in fighting related to the armed conflict. At least 321 were killed by US or NATO air strikes, a tripling from the year before.[15]

McNeill tried to mollify Karzai, but he wasn't getting through. Karzai felt that the air strikes were undermining support for his government and creating more Taliban than they were killing. The mounting death toll also appeared to be taking a deeper toll on the president. In the 1980s he had heard similar stories of Afghans being caught in the crossfire and was horrified at the thought that he was overseeing renewed suffering. On several occasions he had been moved to tears by images of dead Afghan children being pulled from the rubble of their homes after a missile strike.[16]

He had never stood up to the Americans, but when it came to the issue of civilian casualties he told McNeill in May that the air offensive must end. He was supported in his stand by the UN Special Envoy Tom Koenigs. Since early 2006, Koenigs, a German diplomat, had instructed his field offices to start conducting interviews and filing reports on all such incidents. In December 2006, he had presented a report on civilian casualties to the United Nations General Assembly, in which he'd pointed out the record numbers of Afghan civilians killed in the preceding six months, and that the US military and NATO were responsible for many of the deaths.[17]

McNeill confronted Koenigs over the report when the two men met in Kabul in early 2007, with the American accusing the UN man of discrediting the military. There was an added frisson to the exchange: Koenigs had given away part of his family inheritance to the Vietcong whom McNeill had spent his early career fighting in the jungles of Vietnam. McNeill didn't have a brass ear when it came to the subject. He recognized that airpower was being used too indiscriminately, not least among America's NATO partners. On one occasion, the British had called in an air strike in Helmand, four hours after the initial ambush, long after the attackers had withdrawn, killing three civilians.[18] McNeill

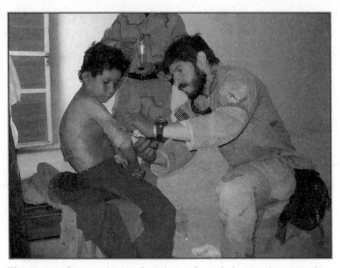

The issue of air strikes and night raids and the resulting civilian
casualties drove a wedge between Afghan President Hamid Karzai
and the US military. Here a boy receives medical attention from
US special forces after being caught in an attack. (Photo courtesy
of Jim Hogberg)

sent out a memo to all commanders instructing them to take better care. But he
wasn't going to lessen the intensity of the campaign.

As the civilian casualties mounted that spring, Karzai decided to take to the
media to express his growing sense of outrage and had a number of increasingly
vitriolic exchanges with McNeill at the palace as a result. McNeill was incensed
by the fact that Karzai was talking to the press before the facts of the case were
established. Some of the figures Karzai was citing were clearly exaggerated.
Yet when McNeill confronted the president with the details, sometimes ascertained by personal fact-finding missions to speak to survivors, Karzai continued to insist his figures were right, or he'd simply say that his overall point
still stood. The US military was killing civilians and making matters worse.[19]

On several occasions the two men's rows became so heated and protracted
that the US and British ambassadors had to be summoned to try to defuse the
situation.[20] They succeeded each time in patching up their relations, but there
was no disguising the fundamental breach between Karzai and the Americans.
"He recognized that his interests were not the same as the Americans', and
began to think differently," said Hanif Atmar, one of Karzai's advisers at the
time.

Brigadier Jerry Thomas sought to withdraw British forces from northern Helmand but was opposed by his chain of command. (Photo courtesy of Jerry Thomas)

McNeill had agreed to delay an assault on Musa Qala in part because of planning for another large-scale offensive to "re-occupy" Sangin. This was being pushed in the spring of 2007 by, of all nations, Holland, which had recently taken over the rotating leadership of NATO operation in Kandahar—an effort to gain some hollow military plaudits, in the opinion of the British Brigadier Jerry Thomas.[21]

McNeill was naturally in favor of the Dutch plan to take back Sangin, and US Ambassador Ronald Neumann joined him in exerting pressure on the British to approve the mission.[22] Sangin was a crucial hub for power lines coming from the hydroelectric turbines at the Kajaki dam. Although USAID had spent over $100 million on a contract to install a new turbine at the dam and refurbish the existing ones, so far they had little to show for it. The deteriorating security situation in Helmand meant that US contractors could not repair existing power lines or deliver new parts. Britain's failure to pacify the area had taken on a strategic significance in Neumann's eyes.

Thomas, who was in the final weeks of his tour, considered the Kajaki dam project to be "barking [mad]." "It was something that might have made sense a few years before," he explained. "By the spring of 2007, we no longer had a permissive environment." Three of Thomas's marines manning the district center in Sangin had been killed in March, as the war of attrition once again resumed. The marines hung up a sign reading WELCOME TO SANGINGRAD at the entrance to the base. He resisted the Sangin plan, just as he had the Musa Qala, only to be told by London to toe the line.

The resulting plan called for Royal Marines to mount sweeping operations around Kajaki dam. The next step was to reoccupy Sangin. Two companies of British soldiers were to drive down from the north, along the route of the electric pylons that carried power from Kajaki through Sangin and on to Kandahar. US troops from 1st Battalion, 508th Parachute Infantry Regiment, 82nd Airborne, would simultaneously launch a helicopter assault at locations a few miles to the south of the town.

Thomas still had his doubts about the operation. But he recognized that more than just Sangin's fate was wrapped up in the operation, not least the seemingly endless task of maintaining the British military's reputation. And so that April 2007, Thomas and his men played their role in the assault on Sangin, which involved tank maneuvers in the desert, airborne assaults, and extensive air strikes. NATO had regained control over Sangin, but the peace lasted only a few weeks.

As soon as the bulk of the forces withdrew, the Taliban returned and British outposts in the city were besieged once again. A correspondent for the Qatari television station al-Jazeera, James Bays, got a battlefield tour of Taliban positions around Sangin and visited a gathering of four hundred fighters in the desert. "Out of 100 per cent, the British don't even control one per cent of Helmand," boasted the local commander.[23]

A major oversight of the latest NATO operation to pacify Sangin was that one of the town's major tribes, the Alakozai, were seeking a peace deal the same month of the NATO assault. The tribe's territory stretched from the northerly reaches of the Helmand River valley all the way to the Arghandab River in the east. It was one of the largest and most prosperous clans in the country, and several prominent sub-tribes had supported the government. If the NATO leadership had been attuned to this, they might have had second thoughts about embarking on an operation that risked alienating a tribe that had long opposed the Taliban.

However, British forces and the Afghan government had largely ignored the Alakozai. In villages like Nasozai, local tribesmen felt neglected. When Mullah Dadullah and his small band of Taliban had arrived in the village in the spring of 2006, they had found ready support for his cause if not his ideology. The Taliban commander subscribed to global jihad and brought a particularly uncompromising brand of terrorism to his operations. As Dadullah and his acolytes established themselves in northern Helmand, senior members of the sub-tribe in Nasozai village began voicing their irritation with the Taliban.[24]

The elders' ire focused on the local subcommander, Wali Mohammed. That he was from the tribe and an upstart made his tyranny harder to bear. By the spring of 2007, a steady stream of Taliban fighters from outside the area used his house as a base, set up checkpoints, and intimidated farmers. Finally, they approached Mohammed Yusef, a local schoolteacher and head of an Alakozai sub-tribe, to confront the Taliban.

The Alakozai's plans to launch an uprising were delayed by the major Co-alition operation around Sangin that April. Having hunkered down during the operation, the Alakozai emerged in May ready to take on the Taliban. Yusef gathered a group of five hundred villagers in the town's main mosque. They marched over to the town's other, smaller mosque, which the Taliban frequented.[25] Wali Mohammed and his deputy, a Waziri from over the border in Pakistan, nervously met the group of Alakozai outside. So Wali had good reason to be anxious about this confrontation. His Waziri deputy certainly was. "I have just come to fight the foreigners," pleaded the Waziri.

It's not clear who fired first, but after an exchange of gunfire, Wali lay dead and the Waziri was last seen running up the street chased by a pack of locals.

Yusef moved quickly to inform the local government head in Sangin that they had kicked out the Taliban and that other area villages were prepared to follow suit if they received guns and ammunition. By then, the British had a new commander in charge of their forces in Helmand, Brigadier John Lorimer, who disagreed with Thomas's assessment that the British should pull out of contested areas of northern Helmand. Lorimer believed he needed to do the exact opposite and assert the Afghan government's presence as well as their own in the Green Zone of the Helmand River valley. Nonetheless, Lorimer was prepared to entertain Yusef's request, which NATO chain of command rather quaintly referred to as a "levee en masse."

At the end of May, Brigadier Lorimer met with the latest provincial governor, Asadullah Wafa, to discuss the uprising against the Taliban. Wafa was a cantankerous sixty-eight-year-old, with no power base in Helmand yet with far-ranging and obscure gripes against many of the region's tribes, including the Alakozai.[26] Wafa rarely traveled outside Lashkar Gah and appeared to have little interest in helping the Brits. Indeed a few British officers increasingly came to regard Wafa's appointment to the provincial governorship as payback from Karzai for removing Akhundzada.

An awkward meeting ensued between Lorimer and Wafa under a pomegranate tree in the small enclosure of the governor's palace in Lashkar Gah. Lorimer was the great-grandson of a former political officer in Waziristan who had written a definitive guide to the local dialect, a document that is still in use today. Some of his ancestor's fortitude was on display as Lorimer listened to Wafa's rambling for half an hour, before he finally asked him directly about events in Sangin, and whether this was an opportunity to support the community against the Taliban. Wafa claimed he had raised the issue with Karzai, and the answer was no.[27]

Lorimer had considered views about Afghan tribes, but he was not in a position to countermand Wafa, and neither did he have political officers at his disposal to explore the option independently. As it was, he was struggling to hold the territory his troops cleared. Afghan National Army and police units were meant to backfill these areas, but they were in short supply. The result was that Lorimer spent much of his time "mowing the lawn," as he put it, returning to areas they previously pacified only to discover a new growth of insurgents (the "mowing the lawn" analogy also played to the image of what the Brits ironically dubbed "Helmandshire").

No further action was taken to assist the Alakozai. The Taliban's leadership in Quetta proved much more proactive. On learning of the revolt in Nasozai and surrounding villages, the Taliban were intent on exacting revenge. They were rapidly closing in on Mohammed Yusef. "As soon as they saw there was no support for him, they came back," said Mohammed Daoud, his brother.

If anything, the Coalition had recently strengthened the Taliban's hand by killing more civilians. On May 10, an American air strike on the nearby village of Sarwan Qala killed at least twenty-one people, mostly women and children. Haji Mahmud, a shopkeeper in the area, helped carry out the bodies from the rubble. He claimed fifty-six were killed. "Three houses were completely destroyed," he told *New York Times* reporter Carlotta Gall. "One of the houses belonged to Faizullah. The family of seven is dead, the whole family."[28] The bodies were brought to the district center in Sangin, where the district governor, before a large crowd of angry onlookers, was forced to defend the action.

Shortly after this incident, Yusef learned that the Taliban were about to attack him and his family. He tried to flee the village but was caught and then roped to the back of a pickup truck and dragged up and down the road. His bloody remains were left by the roadside for several days. "We were caught on all sides. It was a very difficult time," said Mohammed Daoud. The Taliban had sent other would-be tribal opponents a dramatic message. Yet the group's leadership back in Quetta had also learned an important lesson: Dadullah's brand of terrorism was a liability, and they would need to temper some of their excesses.

As it was, Dadullah was killed by US special forces in May. His replacement, Mullah Abdul Qayyum Zakir, was less extreme in his interpretation of the

Quran and meted out fewer punishments. He was also far more dangerous. Zakir had spent six years in Guantánamo Bay but had been released in December 2007 after convincing the Administrative Review Board that he was "very happy" with the western rebuilding effort. He was handed over to the Afghan government, which set him free after only six months—according to one British intelligence officer, at the request of Sher Mohammed Akhundzada, the ousted governor of Helmand. Zakir told his friends, "I have a strong feeling of revenge in my heart. Until this fire of revenge is quenched, the jihad will continue."

Zakir was to turn roadside-bomb manufacturing from an occasional threat into the Taliban's weapon of choice, one that would isolate the British at their bases and thereby undermine their relationship with the locals. At the same time, he would encourage the Taliban's own shadow administration, rooting out unpopular commanders, convening shuras, dispensing justice, and delivering aid to Afghans.[29] In places like Sangin, the organization moved from an insurgency to something that resembled a government, and was often seen as being less corrupt and predatory than the US-backed Karzai administration.

CHAPTER 20

Salam

The British had skirted around the idea of local accommodation with the Taliban, but it wasn't until the arrival in Kabul of the latest British ambassador, Sherard Cowper-Coles, that the idea received the high-level support it needed. Cowper-Coles was erudite, flamboyant, and ambitious and believed he had a mandate to fashion a political strategy for the country. As he saw it, the Bush administration and his own government were hopelessly distracted by Iraq, and it was his job to bring some focus to the war in both nations' capitals.

He'd read up on Britain's colonial experience in the region. Admittedly, it was a mixed bag, but two truths shined through: The war could be concluded only through diplomacy, and success depended on staying power and deep cultural awareness. As he surveyed the current western effort in Afghanistan, there was little to suggest much of either. Soldiers and diplomats rotated in and out of the country in a few short months, taking with them whatever knowledge they had.

An exception to that rule was the UN work in its regional offices, where diplomats like the Australian Tom Gregg were spending years at their posts. Cowper-Coles quickly seized on tribal outreach in Loya Paktia as an example of what the West needed to start doing more of if American and British troops were to take a step back. He wanted community defense volunteers across the south, based on the old British model of tribal levies used in Pashtun regions known as Arbakai. Every Afghan had a gun, he reasoned, so why not enlist them in the effort to protect their village?[1]

To his military colleagues, Cowper-Coles was keen to stress he wasn't proposing that they start raising militias, with all of its loaded connotations. "We were proposing something which went with the grain of tribal society in the areas where we [were] trying, with very limited conventional forces, to protect the population," he explained later.[2]

Some of Cowper-Coles's other ideas reflected his quirky personality, which mixed intellectual rigor with a certain private-school flair. In addition to his village militia scheme, he suggested creating regional regiments of Afghan soldiers, following the British colonial (and subsequently Indian) army system of drawing recruits to units from individual counties or provinces, thereby ensuring strong community bonds. Cowper-Coles went so far as to sketch out the uniforms of the "1st Battalion the Helmandi Rangers," complete with ceremonial turbans.

US General Dan McNeill questioned whether Cowper-Coles's proposals would work. His own research of the use of levies in Afghanistan was that they had only ever been effective in areas with high levels of tribal cohesion. In this he found a rare moment of accord with the increasingly disillusioned Hamid Karzai. The Afghan president had not yet forgiven the British for removing his favored warlord, Sher Mohammed Akhundzada, from power in Helmand and, as he saw it, plunging the province into chaos. Like many Afghans, he saw British actions in light of their past imperial meddling and saw Cowper-Coles's plans to engage with tribal leaders behind his back as a British attempt to weaken his grip on power.

Yet Cowper-Coles was not put off by his colleagues' opposition. If anything, they helped spur more ambitious thoughts. It wasn't enough to simply reach out to a few tribal groups, he realized. Such engagement made sense only if it formed part of a broader strategy that included reconciliation with the Taliban. The very idea of talking to the Taliban was anathema to the Bush administration, and by extension his own government, but Cowper-Coles pursued the idea all the same.

His thinking took shape under the tutelage of Michael Semple, the Irish diplomat and self-appointed peace envoy to all sides and one of the great characters of the war. The Irishman informed Cowper-Coles about the Afghan government's own low-grade and largely useless efforts to reintegrate Taliban fighters into local Afghan communities. The government had set up the program in 2003, along with a peace council that would provide a forum for reconciliation. Semple quickly realized that the reintegration process was a sham. Fighters who pledged support for Karzai were meant to receive a sum of cash and immunity from prosecution.

In reality, they were ignored and, worse, local officials were reported to be locking up reconciled fighters and extorting money from their families.

The Taliban killed off others. Some 5,000 fighters swore allegiance to the government, but they were mostly foot soldiers; commanders of any standing wisely stayed away. Still, the fact that so many switched sides was a minor miracle and testimony to the deep-seated desire for peace within Afghan communities.

Semple informed the British ambassador when they met that Karzai's failure to genuinely share power with disaffected tribes was leading whole regions of the country to side against the government. These tribes needed to be dealt with at every level, and that would require the Americans and the British to develop a far greater understanding of the complex relationship between the Taliban and tribal unrest.

The US military typically saw the Taliban as a monolithic entity, and the Brits weren't much better. American and British forces developed a whole lexicon to establish distinctions within their ranks: There were the "$10 a day" or "village" Taliban who were paid to fight, the "have a go" Taliban who struck opportunistically, the "commuter" Taliban who traveled to other areas to fight, and the "foreign" or "Tier 1" Taliban who came from Pakistan. Such labels provided only the most simplistic analysis of Taliban fighters' motivations and did little to reveal the tribal and religious dynamics of the insurgency that was spreading across the country.

Semple told Cowper-Coles that the Taliban had a potent brand, and the group's leadership maintained a powerful ideological cohesion. But they had no special claim to represent the south; they were simply far "better manipulators of local politics than the Americans or British."

Cowper-Coles would have done well to heed that warning. As it was, he embraced Semple's view of the country, and encouraged the Irishman to apply his insights to Helmand, where the American General McNeill was pushing hard for further operations. Semple needed no encouragement. Technically, as the European Union's deputy envoy, Semple had the clout to do so; he was already conducting multiple discussions. His office in downtown Kabul resembled a tribal dignitary's, as a succession of locals came and went, seeking his advice, suggesting possible contacts, or merely stopping in to gossip over tea and sugared almonds.

Indeed, some in Kabul's international community considered Semple an idealist who'd gone hopelessly native; he had a bushy red beard and a penchant for local garb that extended to a cockily tilted Afghan cap, and he exhibited a willful disregard of diplomatic convention (holding hands with and kissing his Afghan interlocutors were among his many eccentricities).

Semple's connection to the Afghan community allowed him to piece together some of the relationships that linked the Taliban in Helmand. He told the British ambassador that not only had the Taliban appointed a shadow governor, but they had also constructed an entire alternative administration that extended down to the district level and included a brutal but effective justice system, along with what amounted to a micro-credit loan scheme and even a program of limited reconstruction work in areas damaged by air strikes. By comparison, the British Provincial Reconstruction Team had produced very little besides considerable documentation about its "rule of law" and development programs.

Semple reckoned he had been in touch with most of the Taliban's network in Helmand in 2007. His efforts bore modest success. Six Taliban leaders had deserted the Taliban and pledged their allegiance to the Afghan government, along with around 150 fighters, most of whom the British military had hired as a form of tribal levy near Gereshk, similar to Tom Gregg's program in Loya Paktia. Semple also envisioned creating a training camp in Helmand, run by the Afghan government, to offer training and possible jobs down the line.

"The idea was simple," said Semple. "You needed somewhere to invite people to. An assurance of love and goodwill from them was not enough. But simply recruiting them into a fighting force wasn't a good idea or something that NATO could accept."[3] Cowper-Coles called it the "boy scout plan." Semple had considered raising the scheme with Karzai, but the Afghan president had already shown his lack of interest in it; indeed he viewed with outright distrust any suggestions that he expand his base of support in the south. Instead, Semple worked with a couple of deputy ministers to create centers to house former Taliban fighters as they transitioned from armed rebellion in the hills back into their communities.

In the meantime, Karzai made a mockery of reintegrating the Taliban by suggesting a new offensive against the tribal consortium that had ruled in Musa Qala since the British withdrawal the previous year. He informed Cowper-Coles that an influential Taliban commander outside Musa Qala, Mullah Salam, was ready to come over to the government and liberate the northern Helmand town, but only if NATO forces launched a large-scale operation to help Salam.

That was, of course, music to General McNeill's ears. But Cowper-Coles was immediately skeptical. If this Mullah Salam was so powerful, why did he need NATO backing? The last thing Britain needed was to get involved in another ill-conceived foray, least of all to Musa Qala, a town of limited strategic importance. As it turned out, Cowper-Coles was right to have his doubts.

Mullah Salam was *not* the influential Taliban commander Karzai claimed he was. He was another man altogether, one with little clout in the area. The impostor was also called Mullah Salam, hence the confusion. This man's main virtue—at least for Karzai—was that he was a close associate of Sher Moham-med Akhundzada, whom the ousted governor wanted to put in charge as a prelude to his own return to power.[4]

British sources on the ground soon alerted the British and Americans that they had the wrong man. Instead of confronting Karzai, Cowper-Coles opted for pragmatism. The Afghan president was becoming increasingly reclusive as the violence escalated over 2007, and the ambassador hardly wanted to dissuade him from asserting his leadership, even if his aims were not entirely altruistic. Then there were the Americans, and their constant criticism over Musa Qala. Here was an opportunity to satisfy all sides, it seemed to the British ambassador. Still, Cowper-Coles was determined that if the operation were to go ahead, the Afghans would have to lead the way. He told Karzai and McNeill that he was happy for Musa Qala to "come to us," that is, for this Mullah Salam to stake his claim to leadership and oust the Taliban.[5] Then NATO could back him up. The British ambassador was not prepared for NATO forces to preempt Afghan initiative. He hoped that Karzai might even engineer a resolution through local diplomacy.

Cowper-Coles left for a break in England in early December 2007, only to find upon his return that Mullah Salam had not lifted a finger, but that Karzai had persuaded General McNeill to launch an operation. Even the sensible British Brigadier Andrew McKay in Helmand—who had written, "the more force is used the less effective it is and counterintuitively the more we engage in force protection the less secure we may be"—had signed up.[6] The message for Cowper-Coles was clear that military prerogatives had once again taken precedence over the political.

The reporter Stephen Grey has brilliantly chronicled the operation in Musa Qala that winter of 2007. A total of 4,500 American, NATO, and Afghan troops advanced on the town from multiple directions. After three days of fighting, western forces claimed they had killed 300 insurgents (the Taliban said 2,000 civilians died) for the cost of only one British and one American killed in action. By the third day of the operation, the resistance disappeared.

The mission appeared to be an overwhelming success. NATO had re-moved the town's administration of tribes affiliated with the Taliban, and installed the representative of the Afghan government in its place. After a year of squabbling, the Karzai administration, the Americans, and the British looked to have patched up their differences. Yet these appearances soon proved deceptive.

Mullah Salam turned out to be corrupt and despotic, and was rapidly under attack from the local tribesmen. The British, having so carefully disentangled themselves from the town, were forced to step back and defend the mullah, and were soon losing soldiers in defense of a dishonest local official once again. "He was loathed by pretty much everyone," said James Connolly, a British diplomat who served as his adviser during this period.[7]

As for the future direction of the West's strategy, Cowper-Coles's worst fears were soon realized. The new British prime minister, Gordon Brown, visited Afghanistan after the operation and made clear that his country would support similar military operations to force the Taliban to concede. Political accommodation, such as the earlier peace deal in Musa Qala, was out of the question. Upon returning to London, Brown informed Parliament that NATO would "defeat the insurgency by isolating and eliminating their leadership. I make it clear that we will not enter into any negotiations with these people."

Another blow to the British effort occurred at the end of December when Helmand governor Asadullah Wafa arrested Michael Semple—visiting the province to brief the governor on the training camp plan—on suspicion of aiding and abetting the enemy. Semple was unceremoniously ejected from the country, along with another talented and knowledgeable diplomat, Mervyn Patterson.

What triggered the expulsion is not entirely clear. It appears that although Semple had discussed the training camp with two deputy ministers in the Afghan government, Karzai's inner circle had not been informed. Instead the Afghan president got a garbled message from Wafa saying that the British were creating some sort of Taliban militia. Even when Cowper-Coles confronted Karzai with the truth, he didn't back down. That would have entailed a loss of face at a delicate moment for the Afghan president.

Another explanation for Semple's expulsion from Afghanistan was simply that, as the journalist Stephen Grey speculates, the man "knew too much about the country," and his presence made it harder for Karzai to run rings around the international community. Either way, his departure represented the loss of one of the few western diplomats capable of talking to all sides in the conflict. In his absence, British efforts at reconciliation ground to a halt while the pendulum swung back to war.

"Musa Qala turned into a major setback. But we didn't realize it because we kept insisting what a great success it had been," said Cowper-Coles.

The British Ambassador Sherard Cowper-Coles argued for tribal engagement and negotiations with the Taliban but was opposed by the US. (Photo courtesy of Sherard Cowper-Coles)

In June 2007, shortly after becoming British ambassador to Afghanistan, Cowper-Coles had explained to the BBC network that building a viable, truly national government in the country would take thirty years.[8] This should have been a statement of the obvious as the war intensified in its sixth year and more troops arrived. Yet it was taken as an unacceptable admission of failure in London and Washington, where both governments were permanently preparing to declare victory and withdraw. Their optimism had made some sense in the early going as the initial hostilities had abated quickly. Yet as the war carried on, many British and American officials remained convinced that victory was imminent, even as the war intensified and more troops arrived.

After Musa Qala, Cowper-Coles came to believe this false optimism was due to a western war apparatus built to reinforce the *impression* of success and to discount the reality of failure. This was particularly true in Britain, where the military system of six-month combat tours seemed intentionally designed to compel officials to produce overly positive assessments. The pattern was always the same. At the beginning of each tour the newly arrived commander would declare the situation grave. He would then implement a new short-term plan, which he would declare a success. "Each Brigadier did what he could only be expected to do," he later reflected, "as he enjoyed what had to be the highlight of his professional career as a soldier: commanding a brigade in war."[9]

Cowper-Coles wrote to London to argue for longer tours. He had in mind a system modeled on the deployment of British officers to the North-West Frontier during the colonial era, when soldiers spent much of their careers focused on one region. The military records of the time were voluminous and showed a detailed understanding of village life in the Pashtun heartlands. He suggested creating a standing "Helmand brigade" for the army with multi-year tours for the headquarters staff, similar to their civilian counterparts. The idea would be for the troops to develop a deep knowledge of Helmand, learn the language, foster bonds with local leaders, and above all, break out of the six-month mind-set. Even the modern US military, Cowper-Coles pointed out to London, required soldiers to deploy for at least a year.

The chief of the general staff, Richard Dannatt, dismissed the proposal out of hand and took umbrage that a *civilian* would suggest how the military should conduct its business. (Cowper-Coles readily admitted he had been "rather cheeky" to raise the idea in the first place.)[10] Dannatt's reasoning was revealing of the British military's mind-set: The British army fought in brigades, he contended, and they trained for months to prepare for deployment. Altering the length of a brigade tour would "interfere" with their timetable. Put more plainly, the military was unwilling to adapt to conditions on the ground in Afghanistan if it meant disrupting their training schedule.

Cowper-Coles's frustration extended beyond the military to the western reconstruction effort. The mission, from the agricultural programs of USAID to the quick-impact projects of the Provincial Reconstruction Teams, also assumed a short-term war and as a result was prone to the same irrational optimism. The ambassador felt that if western governments could only bring themselves to commit to Afghanistan for the long term, it would open up a new way of thinking about the conflict that would perhaps yield more sustainable security and development.

Cowper-Coles had yet to resolve whether his vision for a longer-term commitment required a more muscular western mission. He was assisted in his thinking in this regard by the former diplomat-turned-aid worker Rory Stewart, who had helped Britain's Prince Charles set up the Turquoise Mountain Foundation, a cleverly conceived NGO designed to foster and share some of the dying handicrafts of Afghanistan. The resulting finely carved wood products and porcelain were just the sort of artistic goods that would please the royal patron, and allowed two dozen artisans to make a living. The thirty-five-year-old Stewart was a genial host in the foundation's headquarters in an old fort on the outskirts of Kabul. Just as Michael Semple had pushed

Cowper-Coles to rethink the Taliban, so too did Stewart challenge him to rethink the direction of the western mission.

Was sending tens of thousands more troops to Afghanistan sustainable in the long term? No, of course not, argued Stewart, so why do it?[11] Was pumping millions into western-administered "alternative livelihood schemes" creating a healthy economy? Again the answer was no. For all its effort, the West wasn't creating a viable Afghanistan; it was creating a bubble nation that would collapse when the West withdrew.

In January 2008, Cowper-Coles and Stewart publicly debated the best approach in *Prospect* magazine, under the title, "Are We Failing in Afghanistan?" Stewart argued that the sooner the military pulled out and the toxic billions were slashed from the aid budget, the sooner the Afghans could reach a sustainable political settlement between the country's factions. That's not to say the West wouldn't have a role in Afghanistan's future, but it should focus on areas where it could be successful: denying al-Qa'eda sanctuary, for instance, or engaging in limited reconstruction in areas where the Afghans could take rapid ownership of the projects. Only the Afghans, he contended, could succeed at rebuilding Afghanistan. "We do not have a moral obligation to do what we cannot do," Stewart noted.[12]

Cowper-Coles agreed with much of what Stewart had to say, and both saw eye to eye on the need for the West to maintain a long relationship with Afghanistan. But Cowper-Coles couldn't publicly endorse Stewart's position. The problem wasn't merely that he would be contradicting London—he would be confronting the Americans. The Bush administration had recently approved a further 5,000 troops for Afghanistan and was debating sending more following the first signs that the surge in Iraq was working. Meanwhile, Cowper-Coles's American counterpart, Ambassador Bill Wood, was looking to double USAID's budget, with a special focus on reinvigorating Afghan agriculture by encouraging exports. To this end, USAID had committed $150 million to building refrigerated warehouses.[13]

To Cowper-Coles it was all more of the same: more new plans, more false optimism, a bigger bubble, and no long-term strategy or enduring vision for Afghanistan. He wasn't immune from the desire to pitch in with quixotic aid projects: He had himself persuaded Eton College, the elite British private school, to donate six rowing skiffs to Afghanistan in the hope of encouraging water sports in the country. The skiffs had been lost for months in some aid warehouse in Kabul, and when they were finally uncovered, they had been damaged and had holes in them, a sad symbol of western efforts.[14]

PART III

THE BLOOD PRICE

2009–2014

CHAPTER 21
An Education

What would a sustainable strategy for Afghanistan have looked like? The solutions were manifold, but the path to an answer was simple: Listen to Afghan leaders, such as Hanif Atmar, who had launched a pioneering reconstruction program and had recently been appointed as education minister. He had been wrestling with development issues as both a leader and a citizen for most of his adult life. Education had been one of the few success stories of the western effort. Under the Taliban, roughly 1.2 million children were enrolled in schools and fewer than 50,000 were girls. Five years later, over 4 million were attending primary school, over 1 million of them girls.[1] The numbers dropped off at the secondary school level, but for students who graduated, an internationally funded higher education program offered excellent options. USAID had built an American University of Afghanistan in Kabul, and other nations had chipped in to refurbish universities in Kandahar, Nangarhar, Herat, Balkh, and Khost. Belatedly, the US had also funded a National Institute for Management and Administration to train a new generation of civil servants. According to Atmar, this provision of education was "the greatest achievement in the history of the country."[2]

Yet Atmar estimated that half of the country's children still were not attending school and, despite an effort to construct or renovate 5,000 school buildings, 60 percent of those in education were being taught in tents or dilapidated structures. The lack of security in these makeshift schools made parents reluctant to send their daughters. Then there was the question of teachers: 80 percent of Afghanistan's 143,000 teachers lacked teaching qualifications, and only a quarter were women, another reason parents kept girls at home.[3]

These shortfalls did not mean simply that a generation of children would miss out on schooling. They also meant that thousands of children would seek their education in a rival system of over 15,000 religious schools—or madrassas—just over the border in Pakistan. Some madrassas were venerable centers of religious education. But many had been built with Saudi money in the 1980s to train a cadre of radicals to fight the Soviet occupation of Afghanistan. Students might emerge from these schools able to recite the Quran in Arabic from memory, an impressive feat given that most Afghans did not speak Arabic. But they were also likely to espouse a radical interpretation of Islam and a burning hatred of America. One of the great failures of both America and Pakistan since 9/11 had been the low priority both countries had given to the subject of religious education.

The Pakistani madrassas were widely popular with Afghans because they satisfied the desire for teaching grounded in Islamic values. Atmar estimated that some 1.5 million Afghan schoolchildren attended these schools, and it was customary for families to send at least their eldest son to a madrassa. Atmar came up with an elegant and simple alternative. He believed his government should embrace its citizens' desire for religious education and build a system of state-run madrassas, where 40 percent of the curriculum would be focused on the Quran. The rest would be devoted to English, math, and computer studies. Atmar wanted $250 million to build a network of 350 madrassas as well as a teacher training center.[4]

Atmar knew that even if the plan was approved, his schools would still face competition from Pakistani madrassas. The Taliban had also announced their own program of madrassa construction in southern Afghanistan. At the same time, they were attacking western-built schools: 180 had been burned down and 396 closed through intimidation. "How can the Taliban talk about education, when they are attacking schools?" asked Atmar. He urged donors to embrace his own plan for a regulated madrassa system. "Let's train our next generation to have a balanced view of Islam and the skills they need to get jobs," he told them.[5]

Atmar was aware his proposals were likely to prove controversial, especially to the Americans, since Congress prohibits government agencies from funding religious programs overseas. A deeper problem was that the US had a blind spot when it came to Islam's role in Afghanistan. For all the work of Provincial Reconstruction Teams on rule of law, social services, and government legitimacy, the US carefully avoided mentioning, let alone addressing, radical Islam, at least directly.[6] This partially reflected a desire to stay away from Afghan religious affairs but ignored the fundamental way in which religion dominated Afghans' lives and defined how many viewed the West's efforts. By standing back from religion, the US was ceding the argument to the mullahs, who routinely painted the Karzai administration as godless and under the control of infidels.

Atmar was not prepared to accept such defeatism. Western-backed reconstruction needed to be aligned with Afghan values and that meant supporting the many moderate Muslims, for whom progress and modernity were consistent with their faith. The problem was that the Bush administration was as reactive to Islam as most village mullahs were to the sight of US troops. Atmar tried to rebrand the madrassas as "centers of excellence." However, the American Ambassador Bill Wood, who began his appointment in April 2007, saw through that name change immediately.

"We're not going to win the war on terror by building madrassas," Wood told Atmar.[7]

"On the contrary," Atmar said. "I can't think of a better way to take on the Taliban." Western-funded madrassas could reduce the numbers of many *already* radicalized youth, he pointed out, as well as disprove a persistent Taliban accusation that the Afghan government was against Islam and intent on sidelining young people seeking a religious education.

Wood held firm. The only country willing to provide funds was Canada, to the tune of $25 million, but that was unlikely to go far. As it was, the education ministry was struggling for funds. Atmar had a budget shortfall in his existing budget for maintaining the schools he already had. "There was a sense that the international community had 'done' education. That was unfortunate," said Atmar.

The Education Minister Hanif Atmar sought to build government-run madrassas across Afghanistan to offset Islamic militancy in the region, but he struggled to get funding. (Photo courtesy of Sergeant Brandon Aird)

The idea of building madrassas might have ended there, but Atmar was not entirely isolated in his line of thinking. At an aid conference in Kabul that spring of 2007, Atmar had lobbied a group of US military officers, which included Commander Dave Adams, the head of the PRT in Khost province, southeastern Afghanistan. The province had been a troubled one for US forces. Miranshah, headquarters of the Haqqani family, was less than twenty-five miles away, over the border in Pakistan. Taliban attacks were frequent with heavy-handed American tactics contributing to the province's violence. In December 2006, US special forces had conducted a night raid in Bari Khel that ended up killing two sixteen-year-old students at a girls' school, inflaming local sentiment. The PRT head Dave Adams and the US commander in Khost, Lieutenant Colonel Scott Custer, had put an end to night raids, which they adjudged to be one of the single most damaging practices of the military.

Adams, a garrulous naval officer, was keen to make amends. He told Atmar he had his own money—the so-called Commander's Emergency Relief Program—that was not as closely tracked as bilateral aid or the USAID budget and could thus circumvent congressional restrictions. In 2006, the CERP budget for the whole country had been just $20 million. In 2007, that amount was increased to $250 million, and Adams was to receive over $50 million of it. He was looking for projects to spend money on, and had already started bidding out contracts to build a dozen schools, health clinics, and 150 miles of asphalt, all under the shadow of the mountains along the Pakistan border. The US military had embraced the nation-building credo, and Adams just hoped he was spending his money wisely. He told Atmar he'd be happy to fund madrassas in Khost.

As the diggers started breaking earth on the first US-funded madrassa in Khost that summer of 2007, Adams was about to be joined in the province by an American diplomat who would deepen the initiative. In September 2007, Kael Weston, a thirty-five-year-old American diplomat, arrived in the southeastern province of Khost as its political officer. He had served as the State Department's lone representative in al-Anbar province of western Iraq for three years from 2004, when the US Marine Corps had conducted two disastrous campaigns into the insurgent stronghold of Fallujah, killing several thousand people, turning half the town's 250,000 inhabitants into refugees, and leaving homes and businesses in ruins.

Weston's job in Fallujah had been to bring together the different sides of the conflict, including the marines, to find a lasting political settlement. He understood that religious leaders were the heart of Iraqi communities. So he met them in the town's mosques and meeting halls, where he cut an unlikely figure with his blond surfer looks, untucked shirts, and jeans. The religious leaders were the only men, Weston believed, who could credibly persuade the townsfolk to turn their backs on al-Qa'eda. Weston figured he had won their trust when they started trying to convert him to Islam.

Weston was already thinking about religion's role in Afghan education when he arrived in Khost. Like Hanif Atmar, he recognized that Afghanistan was an intensely religious country and that the West needed to help the Karzai administration assure towns and communities that American forces were not a threat to Islam. He worried that the international community was clearly losing this battle of perception.

In one of his first meetings with the provincial governor, Arsala Jamal, Weston asked to meet some of the students from the local madrassa.

"Are you sure?" the governor asked, concerned that the students would receive the American with hostility.[8]

He wasn't far off.

A black-turbaned mullah from a nearby school brought his class to meet Weston in a clean and spacious room in Khost's recently constructed university. The mullah sat next to Weston with a sour face that cast a pall over the proceedings. The students were unresponsive. Weston left frustrated, though determined.

The next day he asked Governor Jamal if he could go again, this time without the mullah present. This meeting was more encouraging. The students opened up, albeit to angrily accuse the Americans of destroying mosques, killing Afghan women and children, and seeking to subjugate the country. It was clear what had contributed to such news. Violence had tapered since Adams had pushed for an end to night raids in Khost, but they had continued elsewhere. In June 2007, a US special forces operation in a neighboring province to kill or capture an al-Qa'eda commander in the village of Nangar Khel ended up destroying the local madrassa, killing six children and mortally wounding a seventh.[9]

Weston felt the blowback from the students in the class. They wanted to know why the Americans were against Islam and kept attacking madrassas and mosques. Weston struggled to convince them the US military wasn't targeting their religion.

He mollified some and after a few visits with the students, Weston started to notice that the madrassa students were divided into rough groups. About a third of the class sat close to him: These young men confessed to wanting careers as engineers and doctors. Another third sat in the middle of the room listening, rarely commenting. At the back sat the final, angry third. They avoided looking at him, and if they were forced to shake hands, they covered their own with their shirts to avoid skin-to-skin contact, signalling that they considered him to be unclean.

Most meetings began with Weston as the center of attention, as the different groups pressed him with questions about American intentions, the Karzai government's agenda, and his own views on Islam. But over the course of several weeks, Weston found himself playing a smaller role in the debate. He listened, rapt, as they argued over what the Americans offered, religion's role in education, and their own visions for the country. Gradually Weston understood that the most important battles weren't being fought in the hills but inside schools and madrassas. It was a battle that could only be won through talking, and one in which America's main role was to bring all sides together.

Weston realized his critical task was to keep the conversation going. He started paying taxi fares for the dozens of students who came from outlying villages to visit the university and join in the debate, costing less than $5,000. "Probably the best money I spent," he noted. "Just showing these guys that they could get an education and what that might mean."[10]

Weston wholeheartedly supported Atmar's proposal to build madrassas, and set to work with Adams planning where they could build more religious schools. The American diplomat was frustrated that Washington had not recognized the virtue of national support for the program. But he knew that before he could start pressing the State Department to change its policy against religious schools, he could strengthen his position by building a few model madrassas and showing how they could weaken the hold of extremism.

Money at least was not an issue. Adams was well aware of the country's culture of corruption, exacerbated by free-spending Americans, that had so far stymied reconstruction. To ensure money wasn't siphoned off in the bidding process, he invited local contractors to the US military base at FOB Chapman, and had the Afghans bid right then and there. This had both the advantage and disadvantage of cutting Jamal out of the process, about which he complained bitterly (Khost Governor Jamal's outlay was $55,000 in 2007, compared to Adams's budget of $52 million). The upside was that Adams could build schools for half the price of other PRT commanders at the time—$100,000.

Adams wanted to build a further four religious schools. Weston suggested building one alongside Khost University, which would provide a powerful symbol, he thought. Together the two men began the intense negotiations around the town that were needed to secure permission to build the schools while ensuring that they were distributed in a way that did not favor one of the area's tribal groups over another. Early on his tour Adams had discovered one negotiating tool: An aging mullah kept asking him for "magic power," which eventually he understood to be Viagra. The CIA had been liberally distributing the pill to tribal leaders since the war's outset.[11]

At the same time, Weston used his pull at the embassy to bat aside political pressures. In the fall of 2007 Johnny Isakson, a US senator from Georgia who served on the Foreign Relations Committee, got wind of the madrassa plan and fumed about American money being spent on Islamic education. Weston told a worried embassy in Kabul that they should simply refer the good senator to the Pentagon and see how far he got; although Weston would have been happy to openly debate the program's merits with Isakson, he knew the PRT's involvement meant the US military establishment would back the program.

In December 2007, Weston sent a cable to the embassy reflecting his insights after six months on the job and laying out what he hoped to achieve.

"We need to have a map showing every university and madrassa in the country. That's the strategic terrain where this war will be won or lost," he told Kabul.

At the start of 2008, Ambassador Wood himself came to visit Khost University to hear the students debating. The only mildly mollified radicals laid

The US diplomat Kael Weston pioneered education outreach work in the eastern province of Khost and urged policy makers to adopt a long-term approach to Afghanistan. Here he is pictured with children in a village outside Khost. (Photo courtesy of Kael Weston)

into Wood over civilian casualties and the corruption of the Afghan government. "It was probably the first time he got the unfiltered truth about what Afghans thought," Weston told his military colleagues afterward. Wood handled
the occasion as sensitively as he could—it was a "spirited conversation," he
later noted in a cable. He agreed to support building a madrassa next to Khost
University, although the chance of funds for further schools was limited.[12]

During this period Weston met with former midlevel Taliban commanders,
some of whom had only recently returned to civilian life. The first meeting
was nerve-wracking. He walked into a room of armed men who had recently
been inducted into the local police force. The members of this security detail
asked Weston if he wanted them to accompany him, but Weston didn't think
a couple of guards would make much difference if he was attacked by a roomful of Afghan fighters, and his faith was swiftly rewarded. He picked out two
leaders among the group and delved into a discussion of life in Waziristan.
He carefully evaded the question of when they had killed any Americans.
Specifically he wanted to know why the two men, Habib and Zairullah, had
returned, given that the Taliban was known to behead deserters.

Habib and Zairullah told him they were drawn to the promise of jobs
American reconstruction projects were creating. Both men were in their thirties, tired of the constant fighting, and ready to settle down. What they had
seen in the madrassas of Miranshah also made them nervous: The younger
generation of jihadis was more extreme and radical than they had been, constantly pushing for more suicide operations. Weston himself had been caught
in a suicide car-bomb attack while accompanying Governor Jamal on a routine trip; it was the fourth such attack on Jamal.

The meeting with the Taliban left Weston asking himself provocative questions: What good could a single government-funded madrassa do against a
growing tide of radical would-be suicide bombers? Had they started work too
late? Or was this jihadi anger inevitable, the result of decades of neglect, with
the only solution being to ride it out until a new generation could emerge?
And what about the hundreds of unregulated madrassas in Pakistan? Even if
he succeeded in Afghanistan, he realized, it would all be for naught without
a matching reform effort over the border.

A new generation of young radical jihadists was indeed emerging from the
madrassas in Pakistan. These men had come of age during the western
intervention and had seen or heard enough about the war, and the demonic
foreigners behind it, to seek retribution, even if it meant killing themselves
and innocents to bring the fight to their enemies.

One of the members of this generation of madrassa graduates was Moham-med Qari Ramazan, who had been sixteen when the US arrived in Afghani-stan. His journey from a small mudbrick village in the Waziristan mountains to his subsequent radicalization in one of Pakistan's madrassas was to have particularly devastating results for western forces and Afghans alike.

Ramazan had grown up in a strikingly isolated community. The nearest town of Miranshah, which housed a large refugee camp for displaced Afghans during the Soviet invasion, was over six hours' journey away by rough trails that are frequently impassable during the winter months. Peshawar, the near-est city, was a day's journey. There was no electricity in the village other than that produced by a handful of diesel-powered generators, and no running water. Ramazan's only access to the outside world came via his father and older brother, who both worked as long-haul truck drivers, moving vegetables and other commodities between Pakistan and Afghanistan. Both were absent for most of the year, leaving Ramazan to "look after" his mother, which boiled down to selling cigarettes to local shepherds as they returned with their flocks from the mountains above.

Ramazan's isolation, though, did not make his radicalization inevitable. His father held few political views, and the village's local mullah was a dod-dering old man who had no teeth and dribbled soup down his chin when he ate. Ramazan's trajectory changed when his family sent him to Peshawar to attend a private madrassa funded and run by the Haqqani network, in the hopes of giving him the best possible education.

Ramazan was still a boy as he sat in the back of a pickup truck, bouncing down the mountain paths. At first he was intimidated by Peshawar, a bus-tling, gritty frontier city of tribesmen from the hills, petty heroin smugglers, dissident Arabs, Chinese businessmen, and Pakistani intelligence officers. Ra-mazan joined a class of one hundred students at a madrassa—which, in a later interview, he would not name—that offered free room and board.

Ramazan grew to be a quiet, introverted young man and did not get on well with his fellow students in their cramped concrete quarters. Where he did excel was in study. For four hours his *mualim*, or teacher, led the class in discussing individual *suras* from an Urdu translation of the Quran, focusing on the core tenets of justice and community cohesion, along with rudimen-tary reading skills. The students spent the next four hours memorizing the Arabic version.

After two years of diligent study, Ramazan could recite the Quran in its entirety, making him a star of the class. "I was very proud of my abil-ity," Ramazan later said.[13] His talents might have afforded him a career as a professional Quran reciter. Throughout the Islamic world there are national and international Quran reciting competitions, and several countries had their own popular television programs based on the format whereby scholars were tested on their knowledge of the holy book and on the beauty of their recitation, opening a path to moderate fame and fortune. Afghanistan had its own version called *Quran Star.* Ramazan's skills, however, brought him a different kind of attention.

Ramazan was one of a handful of students the school's imam invited to attend extracurricular courses focusing on the evils of American imperialism. A favored teaching tool was to show short videos of Muslim prisoners at Guantánamo Bay, Cuba, and images of US soldiers abusing prisoners at Abu Ghraib in Iraq. Ramazan was riveted—and radicalized. When he saw what the Americans were doing to his Muslim brothers and sisters, he vowed revenge.[14]

In early 2007, Ramazan was introduced to a veteran Pakistani member of the Taliban named Hamid. Ramazan was vague about the details of the meeting, but at some point Hamid took him to a training camp in the mountains near Miranshah, where he was drilled in basic guerrilla techniques, which included bomb making and AK-47 shooting practice.

At the end of the course, Ramazan saw a map of central Kabul that Hamid had drawn by hand. Hamid's operatives had been observing the Serena Hotel in downtown Kabul for months.[15] It was the city's only five-star establishment and a fulcrum of the capital's expat community, which by the following year, 2008, would grow to 10,000 people. The *Guardian* writer Simon Jenkins compared Kabul to "Klondike before the goldrush," with the mass of foreigners "driving up rents, cruising around in armoured jeeps and spending stupefying sums of other people's money, essentially on themselves."[16]

In addition to the Serena, other popular night spots included a French restaurant called L'Atmosphere, the Gandamack Lodge, and the British embassy's bar. The latter was constructed from bombproof temporary housing on the embassy grounds. A competition led to the bar's defiant name: Inn Fidel. The atmosphere was raucous, drunken, and testosterone driven. Expat security guards, with swarthy beards, sunglasses, and combat attire, awkwardly rubbed shoulders with pasty-looking diplomats. The odd female NGO worker or Department for International Development staffer fluttered around the bar, drawing slack-jawed gazes and frequent advances. UK embassy accommodations—a portable-building village called Podistan—was conveniently close by.

Some in the international community recognized the dangerous potential of this western-style recreation. "In an environment like Kabul drinking could be a problem. . . . Too many Embassy staff spent too many evenings drinking late in the bar: we never achieved a completely satisfactory balance," reflected the British Ambassador Cowper-Coles later.[17] Cowper-Coles himself was forced to intervene at one point when DFID's conflict prevention adviser got involved in a brawl. The ambassador had to ban the man from the bar for three months, "feeling more than ever like the headmaster of a bizarre boarding school."[18]

For the Taliban, Kabul's nightlife was corrupting the country's morals, with the Serena Hotel the most visible symbol of the divide between the simpering elite and the grueling poverty outside the Serena's walls. They regaled their young recruit with lurid tales to stoke his anger. "I was told that this hotel was where Americans were torturing and abusing Muslims like I had seen in the videos of Guantánamo," said Ramazan. He also saw a detailed layout of the hotel.

After he signaled his willingness to attack the hotel, the Taliban sent Ramazan back to the madrassa and told him to wait. Two months later, in early January 2008, the Pakistani Taliban veteran Hamid returned and packed Ramazan in a minivan bound for Kabul. Ramazan had barely a day to recover from the two-day journey across Afghanistan's frozen wastelands before being dressed in an Afghan army uniform, strapped with explosives, handed an AK-47, and told that his life's mission would soon be complete. He was twenty-three years old.

The young Afghan set about his task with deadly determination. On January 22, the Norwegian Foreign Minister Jonas Gahr Støre was hosting a reception at the Serena Hotel. Every embassy had received an invitation, and a sizeable crowd had gathered in the hotel's reception room, drawn by the promise of a warm crowd and canapés. Despite repeated warnings about an imminent attack, including the arrest of two Taliban operatives a few months before with hand-drawn maps of the premises, security was light. Just five guards were standing around a makeshift sentry post of sandbags outside the gates, chain-smoking in the biting -13 degrees Fahrenheit as Ramazan and his partner Mohammed—a local Afghan he had not met until the day before—approached the entrance to the hotel.

Ramazan and Mohammed ran forward, guns blazing. Killing or disabling the guards, the two men forced their way into the hotel's inner courtyard. They had not even reached the foyer when Mohammed reached for the detonation cable of his explosive jacket. Ramazan ducked inside the lobby as the blast shook the building.

Ramazan's next moves, caught on the Serena's security camera, show him marching on, his gun held at hip level as he sprayed the room with bullets and the Norwegian foreign minister's guests ran for cover. One journalist was hit in the arm, leg, and stomach and died two hours later. Turning right at the foyer, Ramazan headed down a passageway to the Serena's spa and gym. As he entered the spa's reception, a Filipino hotel worker dashed across the room. He gunned her down before spotting a young American aid worker named Lisa Gans who was crouching behind the gym's front desk. Gans's thin, pale arms were wrapped around her head. The firing stopped and she looked up to see Ramazan standing over her, his AK-47 temporarily silent.[19]

For some reason, he didn't shoot but instead entered the men's locker room, walking past the steam room and massage parlor before entering the gym and dispatching an American contractor who was cowering beside a treadmill. He exited the building and fired at fleeing staff and guests as they ducked behind ceremonial urns in the hotel garden. At that point Ramazan took off his suicide jacket, set down his gun, and tried to escape the hotel along with the other fleeing guests, when he was spotted by the police. His three-inch beard and short hair, the classic jihadi look, gave him away.[20]

Cowper-Coles was horrified when he heard of the attacks and, as details began to emerge, of just how much the attackers had known about the comings and goings of western diplomats. He issued an immediate ban on travel for all members of his staff, for anything that wasn't strictly embassy business. Other embassies and aid agencies followed suit. Overnight, Kabul's party scene ground to a halt. It was a shock to many internationals to have the war brutally intrude on their lives in Kabul.

Yet even after this attack, few western officials linked the attack's origins in Pakistan's madrassas and the absence of an educational policy that met Afghans' desires for a religious education. Cowper-Coles did, and knew this suicide attack wasn't a one-off but the shape of things to come.

The West had failed to tackle the issue of madrassas, but the new generation of insurgents was not to be ignored. On April 27, 2008, a Sunday, the diplomatic corps turned out en masse for a military parade in Kabul to celebrate, of all things, the fall of Mohammed Najibullah's communist government in 1992. Najibullah had been installed in the presidential palace by the Russians and was widely loathed by all sides of Afghan society, who blamed him for Soviet excesses during the war. His defeat was seen as a final victory over the Russians, although they had left two years before, and in reality his departure heralded the country's complete collapse into anarchy.

Karzai often dwelled on the fate of Afghanistan's past rulers—most of them bloody—but showed no signs of trepidation that day.[21] He appeared at the

parade ground standing up in the back of an American Humvee, looking restrained, as he inspected a line of soldiers. His friends knew he rarely enjoyed
these public affairs, preferring the intimacy of a tribal gathering. Eventually
his entourage stopped at the reviewing platform where the diplomats were
gathered. Karzai joined them to listen to a military band playing the Afghan
national anthem.

The band had barely finished playing when gunfire overwhelmed the
sound of clashing cymbals. Decorum evaporated as Karzai's guards suddenly
leaped from the stand to return fire. The Afghan army broke ranks and ran, as
did the defense minister, his uniform clinking with medals; others dropped to
the floor and assumed fetal positions. British Defense Attaché Simon Newton
led some in the audience to safety beneath the reviewing platform, where they
cowered as the bullets flew. Cowper-Coles's security team dragged the ambassador to the rear of the mêlée, where his American counterpart Bill Wood
was already in an armored Land Cruiser, about to speed away. Cowper-Coles
dived into the backseat to safety.

A total of six attackers were later identified; they had been hiding in an
old hotel to the south of the parade ground for weeks and had thus avoided
security checks. The attack was as audacious as the one launched against the
Serena Hotel, except this time there were no suicide bombers among the assailants—only marksmen who picked off members of the crowd before making a hasty getaway. One Afghan member of parliament and a tribal chief
were shot dead, and a ten-year-old boy was caught in the crossfire. Three of
the attackers were killed, but the other three escaped.

The television footage of the event—showing the Afghan leadership and
its western backers fleeing a surprise attack in the nation's capital—provided
an unfortunate commentary on the state of the war. The message conveyed
seemed to be that Afghanistan elite were unable to defend themselves against a
handful of committed fighters, or to stand together when under pressure. The
attacks on the Serena Hotel and the parade also revealed how the Taliban were
growing ever more ambitious. Their members had been probing the West's
weaknesses and now they had found the soft center.

CHAPTER 22

The Switch

A s the insurgency intensified over the spring of 2008 the US military was coming to believe that the only sure path to victory in Afghanistan lay in replicating the Iraqi surge and employing counterinsurgency measures. In Iraq, General David Petraeus was on the verge of quelling the country's most dangerous province after pushing his men into small patrol bases and partnering them with local tribes. The surge would not have been a success without American support for the tribes, but by the same token, neither would the military have made any inroads without the readiness of Iraqis to take on hard-core insurgents.

Kabul seized upon the stirring example of US success as the answer to the country's own problems. General Dan McNeill, approaching the end of his tour in 2008, argued for an Afghan surge and nationwide adoption of counterinsurgency doctrine. Yet while the evidence from Iraq was positive, the same could not be said for America's own experiments with these tactics in Afghanistan, which various commanders had tried since 2004. In some areas, the presence of US troops living among the people had been welcomed or tolerated, mostly in and around the big cities. However, American efforts in the remoter valleys of eastern Afghanistan, where the push into smaller bases had led to the heaviest fighting of the war so far, resulted in some questions being raised about the direction the military leadership wanted to take the war.

At some point in 2007, Lieutenant Colonel Chris Cavoli, commander of the 1st Battalion, 32nd Infantry Regiment, came to the uncomfortable realization that counterinsurgency doctrine wasn't working in the Korengal valley of Kunar province. It wasn't from lack of effort on his part, or that of his men, who had been stationed in the narrow valleys of eastern Afghanistan since May 2006 in the hope of winning over the local tribesmen and driving out the Taliban. The conditions had been atrocious. They'd sweated in the claustrophobic heat of summer and shivered in the winter snows. And the Taliban attacked, day and night. In the Korengal, Cavoli had encountered a major flaw in the doctrine: The locals didn't want to partner with the Americans. They wanted to fight them.[1]

The past fifteen months had been grueling evidence of that fact. Cavoli's men had arrived in Korengal during Ben Freakley's Mountain Lion operation in 2006. Back then, Cavoli had welcomed expanding the American presence into the remote valleys along the Pakistani border to stop fighters from slipping in and out of the country and to work on protecting the people, as good counterinsurgency doctrine demanded. The plan conceived by his commander, Colonel John Nicholson, required Cavoli and his 1,200 men to establish a dozen outposts over an area covering thirty square miles that would be cut off from immediate reinforcements. American troops would establish a secure perimeter around the villages and then seek to gain the locals' trust with reconstruction projects.

This ambitious enterprise paralleled Petraeus's own thinking that appeared in his transformative field manual the same year, and heralded a shift in both wars from large-scale military sweeps to a more sustained engagement with communities. Most of these outposts in Afghanistan were little more than a patch of earth scraped out of the hillside, with earth-filled gabions, creating small enclosures that could be traversed in a few bounds. The bases often overlooked the heavy vegetation of the river valley below while in the shadow of the towering hillsides.

When Cavoli visited B Company in the Korengal valley that summer of 2006, he recognized how exposed his men were. The company had set up a base in an abandoned sawmill on a mountain slope covered with vegetation and rocks that provided ideal cover for any ambushes. Avoiding attacks would depend on their relations with the hill tribes in the valley. But that would be a challenge, Cavoli learned. The largest Safi sub-tribe in Korengal had migrated there from Nuristan province and had not embraced their neighbors for a century. They weren't going to roll over for the Americans.[2] In the first shuras Cavoli attended in the small village nearby, he offered the elders roads, schools, and medical supplies. They were unimpressed. "Most people respond positively to kind intentions backed by money," Cavoli mused later. "But that failed."[3]

As for his offer to provide the villagers with protection, Cavoli was startled by the elders' response. There were no security issues in the village, he was told, but there would be one "if US soldiers stuck around." Gazing into the elders' impassive, creased faces, with their rheumy eyes, toothless gums, and beards dyed red with henna to hide the gray, he was struck by their sheer otherness.

It didn't take long for B Company to outstay what little welcome they had been granted. Some attacks on their outpost came from the greenery below, others from the ridgelines above, the enemy unseen except when a muzzle flash or a puff of smoke from a mortar betrayed the position. Soldiers found themselves ambushed as they left meetings with the local elders where they had just discussed attacks. Fighters would flit between the low stone houses on the outskirts of the village, shooting as they ran, daring the soldiers to pursue them.

On their handheld radios, the jihadis in the Korengal and elsewhere called the Americans "monkeys," "infidels," "bastards," and "the kids," knowing they were listening in on the open frequencies.[4] When the US translators passed on the insults, the soldiers usually yelled out a few of their own. Not all the radio intercepts were filled with such bravado. Once, when an Apache helicopter swooped in on a group of fighters in a neighboring valley, US translators relayed a much more somber message. "The end is near. Tell my wife I love her," an Afghan voice said. There was no whooping from the Americans after that.[5]

When Cavoli confronted the elders, they said the attacks were the work of foreigners. Senior US commanders told him the same. Yet the radio traffic clearly revealed most of the young men were from the valley. The better Cavoli's men got to know the Korengalis, the more murderous they seemed. American tactics subtly evolved to reflect the hostile reception they were getting. Instead of charging their ambushers, US soldiers increasingly pinned them down while they waited for air support to arrive: The AC-130 gunship with an artillery piece slung beneath was called "Slasher," and the Apache attack helicopter, plain old "Gunmetal." By the end of their tour, in May 2007, the brigade had fired 30,000 rounds of mortar and artillery and was responsible for 75 percent of all the missiles expended that year in Afghanistan. There were 973 insurgent attacks in Kunar province during this period, most of them in the Korengal, which was rapidly becoming one of the most dangerous parts of the country.[6] New pilots coming in were directed simply to "fly north until they saw the smoke columns marking the Korengal."[7]

Collateral damage was unavoidable. If a patrol approached a village and the feed from surveillance drones showed a young man rushing into a house that might contain women and children, would any commander risk his men's lives potentially to save a couple of civilians? Afghan villagers frequently found themselves caught between the warring parties. It's not clear how many Afghan civilians were killed during this period. Cavoli believed the number was half a dozen.[8] The figure is likely to be higher. The US military was not required to record civilian deaths at that time, and the dead were often buried quickly, as Muslim custom demanded.[9] In one six-month period in 2007, the Coalition estimated it killed 350 civilians in Afghanistan, compared with 438 by the insurgents.

After the strikes, US soldiers would sometimes visit the stricken communities to hand out blankets and medical supplies—not as compensation, as Cavoli stressed after one of a handful of visits, but rather as relief and an example of what the government does for its people when imposing peace. The Americans were at once promising security and killing civilians in their battles with insurgents. They were trying to have it both ways, but blankets were no consolation for grieving families. To them, the Americans were a hostile force.

The fighting in the Korengal took its toll on the soldiers, many of whom had seen their tours extended from one year to fifteen months over the course of 2007. Several soldiers had been "stop-lossed," meaning that even though their army contracts were up, they were forced to stay on. All that time switching between channeled rage on patrol and the hollow comforts of base had a profound effect on them. Many took sleeping pills and the antidepressant Prozac to calm their nerves. Most were desperate to get out.

Cavoli tried to follow good counterinsurgency doctrine throughout 2006 and into 2007, even as Petraeus was rolling out the surge in Iraq. He expanded the number of outposts up the Korengal and Waigal valleys from twenty to forty-three, and encouraged his men to patrol more and greet the people. During this period, an Australian counterterrorism expert, David Kilcullen, visited the region on behalf of the US State Department. As an adviser to the new US Secretary of State Condoleezza Rice, Kilcullen had persuaded her to advocate a "clear, hold, build," strategy in 2005. He also helped Petraeus draft the counterinsurgency manual the following year.

Kilcullen was encouraged by what he saw in eastern Afghanistan, assuring his superiors that their efforts were paying dividends. He went on to report that: "The case of Kunar shows that the Taliban are not invincible and that their weaknesses can be successfully exploited. . . . This area has seen significant improvement in security, largely as the result of a consistent US strategy of partnering with local communities to separate the insurgents from the people, and bring development to the population."[10]

Kilcullen was right that in areas of Kunar, near the major towns along the Pech valley, locals had allowed reconstruction efforts to begin. Cavoli supported a road-building program to replace Kunar's dirt track with asphalt that would connect the province together. Yet that level of tolerance was clearly not shared in remote valleys like the Korengal. Cavoli had come to a nuanced understanding of counterinsurgency doctrine. It worked in some places but needed to be employed sensitively and welcomed by the local community.[11] "Clear, hold, build," the mantra of counterinsurgency, didn't make much sense in remote mountain valleys where a more effective strategy was to try and separate areas infiltrated by the Taliban from nearby communities. Such views went against the tide of opinion in the military hierarchy that counterinsurgency was the answer for the entire country.[12]

The counterinsurgency campaign in Kunar continued to struggle with the arrival of Cavoli's successors in the valley, the 2nd Battalion, 503rd Regiment, in the summer of 2007. Lieutenant Colonel William Ostlund also took a circumspect view of the situation. The fighting in the Korengal was intense, but as he saw it the American outpost there was a crucial breakwater protecting the Pech valley from infiltration. He mounted a major operation called Rock Avalanche that went some way to reducing Taliban activity.

However, Ostlund was less convinced of the need to man bases along another remote valley that crossed into Nuristan called Waigal. There were far fewer attacks in Waigal than in the Korengal, but the situation was worsening. In August 2007, the US military had sacked the leader of a local tribal militia Cavoli had installed in an effort at community outreach in Waigal. This provoked a sustained Taliban assault on an outpost called Ranch House that month. The position was almost overrun and left eleven Americans wounded in the attack, which was so close that troops were lobbing grenades from the entrance of the base and calling in aircraft to strafe parts of it.[13]

After two months of fighting, McNeill abandoned the outpost. Ranch House could only be reached by helicopter or a grueling two-hour hike along a mountain track. Cavoli had wanted to extend a road all the way up the Waigal, but Ostlund didn't see that happening during his tour, and it didn't make sense to keep part of a company in such an exposed position in the meantime. The Taliban released YouTube videos showing jubilant fighters sacking the deserted base.

The following year, the Taliban began attacking a second US outpost in the valley called Bella, which also had no road leading to it. In June, the Taliban hit a civilian resupply helicopter as it was taking off from the outpost's landing zone. Until the disabled bird could be lifted away, the reinforced platoon stationed at Bella would have to rely on a smaller site outside the base. Intercepted cell phone chatter suggested that as many as two hundred insurgents were preparing to attack. "I consider it a miracle they didn't hit us when we were exposed like that," said Ostlund, who was already preparing to withdraw from Bella.[14]

To stem the retreat, Ostlund decided to build a base in Wanat, the largest town in Waigal with a population of several hundred. It was five miles from a much larger US base called Blessing, and although there was no paved road to Wanat, the track was wide enough for vehicles and could be reached in forty-five minutes. The military had built a school and health clinic, and relations with the locals appeared to be good, although negotiations with the tribal elders to lease land for the new outpost had gone on for months with little progress. On July 3, the townsfolk were outraged after Apache helicopters fired at two pickup trucks that were suspected of ferrying mortar tubes, killing seventeen people. Some of the survivors were subsequently treated at Blessing and were found to have gunpowder residue on their hands—a routine check on Afghans treated by US forces—suggesting they may have been involved in recent attacks on US positions.[15]

Despite the increased tensions, Ostlund decided to go ahead with the occupation of the outpost at Wanat anyway, which was intended to coincide with the withdrawal from Bella. In the early hours of July 4, 2008, a platoon from Chosen company arrived at Wanat from Blessing only to find an empty patch of ground on the town's outskirts where the base was supposed to be. They soon learned that the Afghan contractor hired to build it had failed to show up, and the locals refused to help. The company commander, Captain Matthew Myer, ordered his men to form a circle of Humvees and to start filling gabions with earth and rocks to build their own rudimentary base. The location of the outpost wasn't ideal—at the bottom of a hill, in close proximity to the town, and overlooked by the surrounding hills—but Myer was confident they could create a defensible position given time.[16]

The early hours of the following day promised to bring another backbreaking day fortifying positions in 100-degree heat and a lukewarm water bottle for each man. The night sky was just lightening when the first shots rained down on their position. The Taliban had also been busy, ferrying munitions and rockets to buildings overlooking the base before taking up firing position. Displaying their intimate knowledge of US equipment, they proceeded to target the company's only Humvee carrying a mobile rocket system, the mortar pit, and the main machine gun in Myer's command post.

Myer called for air support only to hear that it would take an hour. Artillery from the battalion headquarters at Camp Blessing was also limited given the proximity of their attackers, who were shooting from rooftops a few hundred meters away and appeared to be working their way closer. At one point,

Afghan fighters were spotted shooting from the base's own recently dug latrine trench. They succeeded in knocking out a radio antenna but luckily not the soldiers' main communications system.

Early on, fighters concentrated their fire on an observation post that was outside the main base's perimeter, a couple of hundred meters from the main town up a rising slope. A barrage of small arms fire and rocket-propelled grenades aimed at the post's raised firing position had left five soldiers dead or dying, and another, Sergeant Ryan Pitts, grievously wounded. Two injured men managed to stagger back to the main camp. Pitt's remaining colleague, Corporal Jason Bogar, tied a tourniquet around one of Pitts' legs before grabbing his weapon and dashing beyond the post's sandbag walls in an attempt to flank the Taliban's position. He was shot through the chest before he'd made it a dozen yards, leaving Pitts to fight off further attacks alone.

A relief effort led by Lieutenant Jonathan Brostrom and two others reached the post twenty minutes later as Pitts held off the Taliban. The newly arrived soldiers were setting up a machine gun position close to where Bogar had fallen, when they too were fired upon and killed. By the time that Myer himself made it up the hill, another relief party had also been hit, and one of the rescuers, Sergeant Israel Garcia, now lay gasping for breath inside the post, mortally wounded by shrapnel from an RPG round. Beyond the sandbags lay six bodies in a tangled heap. Myer rushed over to vainly check for pulses. He was lifting the body of Bogar over his shoulder to carry him away when one of his men pointed out that he was potentially standing in the line of fire and he needed to get under cover.

The Taliban continued to attack for almost two hours until air support and reinforcements from Blessing saved Myer and his men. By the end of the fighting, nine US soldiers were dead and twenty-seven wounded, the second largest loss of life by US forces in a single engagement. Sergeant Pitts grimly held on at the post before he was finally evacuated. He was later awarded a Congressional Medal of Honor.

When Dave Brostrom, the father of the lieutenant who had been killed at Wanat, received a hero's tale of his son's death and the US military's exemplary actions, he feared he was hearing an airbrushed version of events. A former officer himself, he knew the sort of blunders the military was capable of. Brostrom started pulling contacts, asking difficult questions, ultimately prompting the official military historian Douglas Cubbison to write a scathing account of the 173rd Brigade's lack of preparedness before the battle.[17] Over a year after the battle a fresh investigation concluded that the move to Wanat had been "poorly conceived and terribly executed." Two senior officers retired, and

Myer and Ostlund received letters of reprimand, only to have them rescinded a few months later, reflecting the awkward seesawing of blame around the incident, which later became known as the "Battle of Wanat."

In June 2010, General Charles Campbell briefed grieving families on their conclusion, including Brostrom senior, telling them starkly, "[The chain of command] did not kill your sons. The Taliban did."

That prompted Brostrom to respond, "You tell me what the battalion commander did to mitigate those risks! . . . If he was too busy taking care of 13 other outposts, then why in the hell did they go there in the first place?"[18]

It was a poignant question, one that hinted at the real culprit: the doctrine and resulting strategy that put his son in danger. The inquiry focused on small-bore questions of specific orders. No one stood back and examined the counterinsurgency approach or the wisdom of America's almost inevitable march toward an Iraq-style surge in Afghanistan.

When General David McKiernan took command of US forces in May 2008, he was as committed as his predecessors had been to embracing counterinsurgency tactics. He believed the problem with the approach in Kunar, and for most other areas of the country, was the lack of troops. The main question for McKiernan was whether the White House would approve more, and what areas of the country to send them to.

That summer, McKiernan's attention was naturally drawn to eastern Afghanistan, where the US had been focused since the start of the war, at first in counterterrorism operations involving special forces raids, and increasingly in efforts to man isolated outposts in the name of counterinsurgency. Over 2007, attacks against US forces had increased by 50 percent, and the mounting death toll had already led troops to retreat from some areas. The previous year 117 US soldiers died, most of them in the east, leading some in the Pentagon to question the viability of other outposts in Kunar and Nuristan.

McKiernan was hardly a "coinista," as some adherents of counterinsurgency doctrine called themselves, and he distrusted the evangelical fervor that surrounded the concept and its main proponent, David Petraeus, whom he had commanded during the Iraq invasion. That said, he believed that counterinsurgency was the right approach for American forces in Afghanistan; the reason for the strategy's failure to date, in his estimation, was that the US hadn't gone far enough in implementing it. McKiernan wanted more troops to saturate the border region with Pakistan. He also wanted Washington's permission to pursue the enemy into their sanctuaries over the border.[19]

The idea of escalating the war in Afghanistan was beginning to find a receptive audience in Washington. The Bush administration was entering its final months. The relative success of the surge in Iraq allowed the White House to recognize how badly its other war was going. That process had begun with Bush's appointment of Lieutenant General Douglas Lute to the National Security Council the previous year to oversee both Iraq and Afghanistan, becoming, as the press liked to dub him, the "war czar." He had no direct power over the military, but his views would shape White House policy, and thus the war's future direction.

In June 2008, President Bush asked Lute to conduct a review of the Afghan war. The NSC man met McKiernan in Kabul as the general was preparing his own assessment. Both men agreed the war was going badly and that more manpower was needed. McKiernan was putting together a request for 30,000 soldiers, which amounted to a doubling of the war effort. Lute agreed with the number. Where the two men differed was over the details of how to apply any surge in troops.

McKiernan's assessment that Pakistan was at the root of Afghanistan's problems made sense to Lute, but he was wary of using troops to pursue Taliban fighters over the border into Pakistan. Lute felt that would only broaden the conflict, inflame tensions between the two countries, and place at risk other American interests with Pakistan.[20] In May 2008, the increasingly unpopular Pervez Musharraf had stepped down, taking with him what little faith the Bush administration had that the country could be steered away from extremism. What Lute did agree with, and President Bush subsequently signed off on, was a massive increase in the use of drones to infiltrate Pakistan and attack al-Qa'eda and insurgents taking refuge there. The move threatened to replace diplomacy with drone strikes, but it was overdue as far as Lute and the CIA, which managed the program, were concerned.[21]

Lute and McKiernan also saw differently how to deploy any further troop increases. Lute felt that the fighting in eastern Afghanistan played a role in protecting Kabul. However, the decisive battles, he believed, were being fought in Kandahar and Helmand, where he did not think NATO forces were capable of shifting the momentum. The British and Canadian militaries needed more troops, yet were not prepared to escalate the war on their own accord. Even if they dispatched more units to the south, Lute believed that the malfunctioning command structure that rotated every six months and a long list of national caveats made success unlikely. When Lute had seen a map of NATO operations, it looked like each nation was fighting its own private war. Nobody was running the show and there was no common purpose. Lute wanted to deploy US troops in southern Afghanistan and replace the NATO headquarters in Kandahar with a two-star American command, similar to that in the east.[22]

When Lute started airing the preliminary findings of his review a few weeks later, he received pushback from McKiernan and the internationals. As he had no authority to compel anyone to do his bidding, he needed to win them over. The Canadians, who had recently committed to staying in Kandahar for three more years, did not want to share their battle space or their mission with the Americans. The incoming Dutch commander of the south, Major General Mart de Kruif, was equally concerned about having his headquarters taken over. Instead, he directed Lute toward Helmand and suggested the British, whatever their protestations to the contrary, were desperate for more help. In this, he was right.

T he idea that the British military would one day have to be bailed out of the wars in Iraq and Afghanistan would at one time have been greeted by the UK's senior leadership with a chorus of harrumphing. Yet by April 2008, the Americans had already had to bail the British out of Iraq, where UK forces had struck a deal with a Shiite militant group with ties to Iran so that they could withdraw. But American commanders accused the British of "cutting and running."[23] The timing was all the more difficult because Petraeus was surging to victory.

The British had intended that ending their commitment in Iraq would free up additional resources for Helmand, thereby bringing the province back under control. But even though they now had 8,000 troops garrisoned around the province, there had been no letup in the attacks. If anything, the violence had worsened. In 2008 there were 3,276 attacks against NATO forces, just under half of those in Helmand.[24] In addition to the intense fighting, the British were dealing with an increase in roadside bombs, against which their lightly armored Land Rovers were ill-suited to defend.

The British found themselves in a conundrum. After their exit from Basra, they could hardly consider withdrawing from some of their more isolated outposts in Afghanistan such as Sangin and Musa Qala. Yet neither did they have enough troops at their disposal to surge as counterinsurgency doctrine demanded. That left the British with little choice but to embrace the offer of American assistance.

The British had already accepted the principle of American involvement in Helmand earlier in the spring of 2008, when 1,500 US Marines had deployed to the town of Garmsir in southern Helmand. That move had been greeted with trepidation. The Brits needed the Americans there, but at the same time there was a risk that their aggressive tactics might make things worse. It was like inviting family members from the "wrong side of the tracks" to a party, said one British officer.[25] Yet the three-month American deployment that was limited to Garmsir eased pressures on UK forces elsewhere, and led the leadership to consider extending the marines' stay, and even expanding it.

The best illustration of Britain's perilous position in Helmand had transpired that summer when, after much urging from the US embassy, the British military had at last agreed to transport the missing third turbine to the Kajaki dam. The USAID project that Zalmay Khalilzad had initiated in 2003 had already racked up bills of $200 million due to cost overruns, delays, and ineptitude. The turbine parts were now ready, but the security situation was such that the flatbed trucks that would carry the pieces would need a massive military escort. Some on the UK side had been against the idea from the start, pointing out that even if the turbine was installed, there was little chance of building the power cables through the heart of Taliban territory between Kajaki and Sangin.[26] But Brigadier Mark Carlton-Smith, the commander of British forces at the time, felt that the operation was within the UK's mission remit.[27] Other senior officers came to see that the operation might show the locals, themselves, and the Americans that the British deployment to Helmand had a purpose.[28]

On August 27, Canadian troops escorted the turbine parts out of Kandahar airport on a dozen trucks. Just before the border with Helmand, they met up with a larger British force, including the logistics trucks and a contingent of tanks.[29] The convoy headed into the desert, bypassing the dangerous main road that led to Sangin. Three days later, the turbine made it to Kajaki with relatively little fuss. Back at British headquarters in the provincial capital of Helmand, Lashkar Gah, there was a sense of euphoria: A major logistics operation had come off without a hitch. Senior staff at the PRT shared a glass of whiskey; its younger members planned a "Lash Vegas Pimps and Hoes" night. In London, the press lauded the operation. Under the headline "Triumph for British Forces in Boy's Own–style Kajaki Mission," Brigadier Carlton-Smith announced the maneuver as the "end of the beginning."[30]

Such optimism made what happened next all the more disappointing to the British. The Taliban's Helmand governor, Mullah Abdul Rahim, sought to take advantage of what he saw as the UK's focus on the Kajaki operation and moved fighters into the town of Marja, a short distance from the provincial capital. For much of the past five years Marja had been a quiet backwater, but a disastrous DynCorp poppy eradication operation there in April 2008—a campaign backed by US special forces—had driven the locals into Mullah Abdul Rahim's arms.[31]

On October 12, Rahim ordered an attack on Lashkar Gah, which so far had avoided trouble. Two hundred fighters gathered on the outskirts of the town. As they started swarming through the streets, the soldiers guarding the British headquarters spotted the attackers and called in air strikes, but not before fighters had begun skirmishing with local Afghan police and UK forces. Gunfire echoed around the headquarters, the ground shook with the sound of explosions, and the base's air raid siren wailed insistently. Jumpy diplomats from the PRT, at the center of the camp, were asked to stay indoors, some taking shelter in concrete sentry boxes outside the temporary housing. For most this was their first taste of war, and an uncomfortable reminder of their relationship to the country in which they were stationed. They greeted the first air strikes with cheers, an unconscious release of tension.[32]

The British fought off the attack, along with a second attempt three days later. As a military spokesman, Lieutenant Colonel Woody Page, explained, "Lashkar Gah is home to nearly 50,000 people. It is a well-governed city with a strong military force to defend it, and cities like this don't fall into insurgents' hands. That will not be allowed to happen. The insurgents will not gain a foothold here."[33]

Just the possibility that Lashkar Gah could collapse caused jitters in Washington, given what happened in Iraq. By the fall of 2008, McKiernan had accepted Doug Lute's arguments that the south needed to be the focus of any escalation, but he still wasn't convinced that they should be sent to Helmand. McKiernan asked newly promoted US Brigadier John Nicholson, the former commander of US forces in eastern Afghanistan and the current director of operations in Kandahar, and the most senior-ranked American in the south, to assess where to put the additional 30,000 troops he had requested.

Nicholson had pioneered counterinsurgency in the east in 2006, and knew the approach had raised some questions among his officers about the use of such tactics.[34] But Nicholson remained committed to the approach, believing it represented the only way to separate the insurgents from the people and establish government control. Like McKiernan, he had come to the same, difficult conclusion that any new force needed to be put where the majority of the people lived, and that meant Kandahar—even if that meant there would be no relief for American forces in the east.

Nicholson's conclusions were challenged by the Dutch commander in the city, Major General Mart de Kruif, who was adamant that it was the British mission in Helmand that was most in need of support. When de Kruif and

Nicholson discussed the situation in November 2008, the Dutch general told his counterpart that the incoming troops—already flagged as US Marines—would be far more effective tackling insurgent sanctuaries and ratlines there than negotiating the complex political terrain of Kandahar. If the US military could control the outlying regions around Kandahar and create "a pocket of security" for the city, de Kruif argued, then he was confident that local security forces and some arm-twisting of tribal chiefs could keep the peace.[35]

Nicholson was not so sure. His experience of trying to seal the porous border with Pakistan made him question how effective western troops could be trying to do the same in Helmand. He also had his reservations about how a large marine deployment would fit with the already creaky command structure in the south and was aware from his British opposite number, Brigadier David Hook, of UK sensitivities about being bailed out by US forces.[36]

Nicholson agreed to take a look for himself and at the end of November flew to Lashkar Gah. It was a potentially embarrassing moment for UK's top diplomat in Helmand, Hugh Powell, but he sought to turn the moment to his advantage. Powell began the meeting with Nicholson by recognizing that British forces were "overstretched," which appeared to be a polite way of saying that taking on trouble spots like Marja was beyond their current capabilities. Powell explained that public support for the war was flagging, but that the equation was likely to change with an influx of American troops and a clear shift in the war's momentum. If the US could take on some of the outlying towns that had proven so troublesome to the British, then they could focus on central Helmand.[37]

Nicholson was sympathetic to the UK position, especially given how his family history was steeped in British imperial folklore. His namesake had almost single-handedly saved the British Empire during the Indian Mutiny in 1857. Early on in the uprising, he had been tipped off that the Indian cooks of the British officers' mess tent at Jullunder were preparing to poison them with aconite. Nicholson interrupted his colleagues' meal by saying, "I am sorry, gentlemen, to have kept you waiting for your dinner, but I have been hanging your cooks." Nicholson went on to lead a charge to retake New Delhi, and was mortally injured in the assault.[38] By contrast, Powell's great-grandfather, a Welsh vicar, had helped bring about the end of the empire by campaigning for the Labour Party's first leader, Kier Hardie (Powell's family had since moved into considerably more elite circles).

Nicholson repeated his reservations about the difficulty of interdicting fighters, but Powell returned that the landscape of Helmand was more straightforward than the maze of mountain valleys in the east that had made it easy for insurgents to slip past American outposts. Most of the British province was undulating desert that could easily be monitored for activity. The crucial terrain to dominate was the Green Zone on either side of the Helmand River, where the province's main towns lay and the main road ran. The British didn't have enough soldiers to do that, but with the arrival of the US Marines they could lock down the province.

Over the course of a three-day visit, Nicholson was sold on the idea of changing the whole direction of the troop surge from Kandahar to Helmand. "It was a big decision, but once Mick [as Nicholson was nicknamed] recognized the strategic necessity of the switch, he backed it all the way," said Powell.[39] Nicholson was still concerned about the command arrangements in the province. Lieutenant General Jim Conway was looking to deploy a large marine force under a single command with a discrete area of operations, which might end up subsuming the smaller British contingent, but that was a secondary concern.[40]

McKiernan agreed to the campaign shift in early December, and Nicholson, Hook, and de Kruif set out the plans for sending up to 10,000 US Marines to Helmand in anticipation of the White House troop request being approved. As it turned out, that was a decision that the Bush administration appeared only too happy to pass on to its successor. Bush's presidency was winding down and he didn't wish to confront the shortcomings of his policy toward Afghanistan. That burden soon came to be Barack Obama's.[41]

CHAPTER 23

Ghosts

Before he became president in 2009, Barack Obama's foreign policy record was limited to his three years and ten months on the US Senate's Committee for Foreign Relations. The positions he staked out on the committee reflected the liberal orthodoxy of the moment: Iraq was a strategic disaster that had siphoned critical intellectual and military capital from the more serious security threat in Afghanistan. However, as his presidential campaign gathered momentum in 2008, he joined this bandwagon rhetoric with more soaring talk of America's moral responsibility to the Afghan people. Soon he too was referring to the conflict as the "Good War."

The moral patina Obama applied to the Afghan war no doubt reflected the influence of his foreign policy adviser, Samantha Power, the journalist-turned-Harvard professor who had gained international notice for provocatively arguing that the US should use military might to stop genocide and safeguard human rights in the developing world. But Obama's thinking on using American force was more cautious and arguably more nuanced. He counted as an influence the pragmatic realist philosophy of Reinhold Niebuhr, the Christian theologian who advocated for the use of military force to counter such dangers as Nazism but warned against "messianism."[1] The blunders in Iraq were an example of the Bush administration's inflated sense of what American firepower could achieve. Obama also consulted with another noted realist, former national security adviser Zbigniew Brzezinski, who passed along his unadorned view of global affairs.[2]

Obama's self-styled position on foreign policy—at once muscular, moral, and realistic—made him the ideal Democratic candidate. He reassured conservative middle America by sounding tough on national security. He pleased his liberal base by bashing Bush over Iraq. What's more, Obama argued that he was prepared to make the tough calls in Afghanistan. The political reality, though, was that he was painting himself into a corner that would require him to escalate the war, regardless of his own deeper reflections about what the US could achieve there.

The tension between his public position and his doubts became clear in the debate that surfaced once Obama took office in January 2009. He was immediately confronted with the question of whether to green-light General David McKiernan's earlier request for 30,000 more troops. Despite his campaign rhetoric, Obama was not convinced that such a large-scale escalation was the right call when the US lacked a clear strategy. Bush had been so consumed by Iraq that he had delegated much of his Afghan policy to an ad hoc array of Washington subordinates, generals, and ambassadors, who were often at loggerheads with America's allies in Kabul. Some of Obama's advisers felt the president needed to reestablish control over the war by sending more troops.[3] But Vice President Joe Biden strongly disagreed.

Obama dispatched Biden to Afghanistan in January 2009 to assess the situation. The sixty-three-year-old vice president was a long-term member of the US Senate Foreign Relations Committee and a powerful voice in the Democratic establishment. He had opposed the Iraq war and believed that America's nation-building effort in Afghanistan was fundamentally flawed. Top of the list, in Biden's mind, was America's alignment with Hamid Karzai. Western ambassadors reported to Biden that Karzai's increasingly erratic leadership was an obstacle to their plan to rebuild the country. Some went so far as to accuse him of being addicted to painkillers and even opium. Others felt he had withdrawn into the palace while his minions made billions by siphoning off reconstruction funds and through the illegal opium trade. Meanwhile, Karzai blamed the West for the mounting insurgency and the US military specifically for its use of air strikes to target the homes of his countrymen.[4]

Biden made his concerns plain to Karzai at a state reception at the palace in Kabul. He told Karzai that America had given him a free ride for far too long. Biden pressed Karzai over his unwillingness to travel around the country to build political consensus, and his failure to reach out to tribes outside his own nepotistic huddle. He then mentioned the ornate homes of Afghan officials near the palace, and wondered suggestively where US taxpayers' money had gone. According to the US inspector general's office, almost $100 billion had been spent on reconstruction, of which only 15 percent was estimated to have reached its intended recipients.[5]

Karzai appeared taken aback. This wasn't how he was used to being addressed by Americans. In his fortnightly video conferences with Bush he had often bounced his infant son on his knee. Now he felt like *he* was the child in the relationship. The Afghan president told Biden he was not used to being chastised. There was corruption in Afghanistan, he acknowledged, but much of the problem lay with western contractors. In 2009, the annual foreign aid of nearly $16 billion comprised 97 percent of the country's gross domestic product, and yet most of it bypassed the Afghan government and went to contractors. Karzai pointed this out before turning to civilian casualties.[6] "This has gone on for too long," Karzai said of the US military presence, a nervous tick below one eye betraying his anger. "The Afghans will not support it."

"We may have reached that point ourselves, and we'll have to cut our losses," Biden rejoined.[7]

"The Afghan people must be partners, not victims," Karzai said.

"If you don't want us, we're happy to leave; just tell us," Biden retorted. "Instead of sending 30,000 [troops], maybe it'll be 10,000. Or maybe it'll be nothing. Or we could just send you economic assistance. If you don't want us, just tell us."

The conversation's vitriol seemed to blind the two men to the fact that they actually shared similar views on the war, most critically that it was a mistake to send in more troops. Listening, though, was not Biden's style and Karzai was in full self-pitying mode.

"We're just poor Afghans," Karzai simpered at one point.

"This is beneath you," Biden declared, throwing down his napkin and leaving before dessert was served.

The vice president returned to Washington and reported to Obama that Afghanistan was adrift and that he had grave doubts about escalating the conflict. America needed to return to the war's first principle: a counterterrorism operation against al-Qa'eda, which meant taking troops out, not putting them in. But Obama was a prisoner to his campaign promise to support the Good War. What's more, his top military leaders were pushing him publicly to replicate the Iraq surge.

In 2008, David Petraeus had left his command in Iraq as a war hero, having appeared to achieve the impossible by bringing peace to the shattered country. To do so he had bucked the Washington consensus and sent more troops to the war when most of the country wanted the US to withdraw. But he hadn't doubted that American force, judiciously applied, would deliver results, and now he wanted to do the same with Afghanistan.

Since leaving Iraq in 2008, Petraeus had risen to head of Central Command and as such was overseeing both the Afghan and Iraq wars. With the latter campaign finally winding down, the US military had troops to send to Afghanistan. He had surely listened intently to Obama's election promise to escalate the war, and expected it to be at the top of his agenda after his inauguration.

Petraeus prepared for Obama's first National Security Council meeting by touring the war zone himself and asking one of his trusted Iraq advisers, Derek Harvey of the Defense Intelligence Agency, to compile a dossier on the insurgency and the Taliban's motivations. "We know too little about the enemy to craft a winning strategy," Harvey had reported.[8] The military was narrowly focused on targeting insurgent leaders; the CIA, on al-Qa'eda and its drone war in Pakistan.[9]

Harvey set to work trying to get a grip on what was happening on the ground, scouring intelligence, journalistic accounts, engineering reports, and transcripts of Afghan radio shows—anything that would give him insight into the country. Over the past year, the military had launched a program to place anthropologists with field units to better understand local politics.[10] The Human Terrain System had been hit-or-miss, reliant as it was on local commanders' willingness to see a deeper picture. For Harvey, the research papers were invaluable in drawing up a map of Afghanistan, broken down to every sub-tribe and isolated hamlet. The result looked like a sandstorm of competing groups and factions, and far more complex than a similar breakdown for Iraq had been.

Harvey's conclusion matched the earlier British prognosis that the Afghanistan war might be winnable but that success could take thirty years or more. As he saw it, that made the war untenable: The US would have to commit to the war for longer than any president could politically tolerate. Indeed, the American people were already starting to have their doubts about the conflict. Without enduring support, any gains on the battlefield couldn't be sustained. He recommended against sending in more troops.

Petraeus didn't buy it. He'd overcome similar political challenges in Iraq. He told colleagues he believed the perception of the war would improve if he could achieve a tipping point on the battlefield in Afghanistan just as it had in Iraq. But the president was under pressure from Biden, who opposed further escalation. He feared that the vice president's arguments were starting to change Obama's calculations.[11] Petraeus needed to choose his words carefully when the National Security Council met on Afghanistan for the first time under the new administration, both as a gauge of Obama's commitment to escalating the war and as a moment to face down the naysayers like Biden.

The meeting took place on January 23, 2009, in the White House situation room. Present were the president and his national security team and an assortment of generals. Biden and Obama's chief of staff, Rahm Emanuel, also attended. Obama opened the discussion with remarks in which he recognized that he had campaigned on a promise of more troops but hadn't yet made up his mind. He wanted to reposition US foreign policy and its approach to terrorism so that the military was no longer driving it.

Obama's words concerned Petraeus according to one member of his staff. It sounded like the president was already favoring a counterterrorism option.[12] His response was a precise argument for more manpower in Afghanistan, framed in terms he knew everyone in the room would endorse. He understood the objective in Afghanistan was to stop the country from becoming a sanctuary for extremist groups like al-Qa'eda. But drone strikes and raids alone couldn't stop terrorism.

"You need to have troops on the ground to provide the intelligence first. And you need troops on the ground if you're going to stop terrorists coming back," Petraeus argued. The US had to stabilize the country first by separating the people from the Taliban and ensuring their security. That meant more soldiers, starting with McKiernan's request for 30,000 additional men.[13]

What Petraeus didn't say was that he would need a *lot* more troops to implement his counterinsurgency plan. McKiernan's request would be only a first step to reaching the troop densities he believed Afghanistan needed. Exactly how many, Petraeus didn't know yet. But the ideal ratio of one soldier or Afghan policeman per fifty civilians suggested that the US would have to make the same commitment to Afghanistan as it had to Iraq: over 100,000 soldiers and a greatly expanded Afghan military.

Petraeus had barely finished speaking before the vice president blurted out, "We have not thought through our strategic goals."[14]

Rahm Emanuel followed Biden's cue and asked Petraeus directly if this was the beginning of a larger ramp-up. Petraeus ducked the question. Emanuel's suspicions were indeed correct, but Petraeus wasn't about to alarm the White House with a request for even more troops. Emanuel's hostile questioning underscored just what a tough sell his plans for Afghanistan would be.

Obama himself appeared determined to take a circumspect view of the war. Before leaving the meeting he indicated that he wanted another review of the campaign so far. It was a rational approach, and one that would buy time—and wiggle room—as he considered increasing troops. A few days later, Obama announced that Bruce Riedel, a former CIA analyst and election adviser, would lead the review, which the president wanted completed in just sixty days. He planned to decide on McKiernan's request after the review.

The military appeared content to sit through another strategy review. Senior officers believed they could prevail upon Riedel to champion counterinsurgency. The former analyst was an expert on Pakistan with little knowledge of the military or the war in Afghanistan and was unlikely to stand in the way of the US military's proposal. However, Petraeus wanted McKiernan's troop request approved sooner. If they waited until after the review, the time it would take to deploy might mean they'd miss the summer's fighting season altogether. His staff were already in contact with the marines about sending troops to Helmand.[15]

On February 13, President Obama convened the National Security Council again, this time to hear a military proposal to send 17,000 troops immediately. Obama was irritated at having to make a decision before Riedel's review. After a two-week delay, he convened a further meeting on Afghanistan, which his national security team, including Petraeus, Richard Holbrooke, recently appointed as the US special representative to Afghanistan and Pakistan, and Riedel, attended. Petraeus once again laid out the pressing need for more troops. Obama conceded that election security was paramount.

Before the meeting concluded, one of the attendees, the veteran Holbrooke, couldn't resist mentioning that the last time a Democratic president had sought to escalate a war had been Lyndon Johnson in Vietnam. In June 1965, General William Westmoreland had requested 41,000 more soldiers in Vietnam, a year in which troop numbers had increased five times. Johnson's defense secretary, Robert McNamara, later wrote that "of the thousands of cables I received during my seven years in the Defense Department, this one disturbed me most. We were forced to make a decision."[16]

The Vietnam reference sent jitters around the room. "Ghosts," muttered Obama. Yet a few days later, he agreed to send the troops, along with 9,000 more to help train the Afghan military. What Petraeus didn't tell the president then was that the US Marine commander, Major General Larry Nicholson, was already on his way to Helmand to plan the deployment.

For the military, this was only the first step of a bigger surge. The real question for the military was how to boost the number of troops to the levels that a full-fledged counterinsurgency campaign required. Petraeus had worked on the figures for the surge and concluded that he needed 60,000 additional troops to bring the number of foreign troops in Afghanistan to over 100,000.[17] If the US could match that commitment with a massive expansion of the Afghan training program, from 80,000 to over 200,000, the US would begin to approach the numbers it needed. After his early encounters with Obama and his team, it was clear they weren't even close to talking the same numbers. The military had to try a new approach.

It was retired marine General Jack Keane who first suggested firing the commander of US forces in Afghanistan, General David McKiernan, to reboot the war effort.[18] Keane had been an influential figure in the Bush White House, pushing for the surge in Iraq and for Petraeus's appointment as commander. Ever since the summer, when McKiernan had pushed to put troops in the east, Keane and others in the military leadership had questioned the Kabul commander's judgment. When Petraeus had met McKiernan in Afghanistan in January, it was a stiff and slightly awkward affair, with the latter insisting he was already "doing counterinsurgency." Why then had McKiernan asked for only 30,000 troops, Petraeus later put it to his staff, when that clearly wouldn't be enough?

McKiernan's defense was that with 130,000 still in Iraq, he believed Afghanistan to be an "economy of force" effort and that the White House would not release more troops until a drawdown in Iraq began.[19] He might be right, thought Petraeus, but was this the man to push a reluctant president to send more troops? Crucially, replacing McKiernan would allow the incoming commander to make a fresh assessment of troop numbers.

Petraeus already knew whom he wanted to replace McKiernan. The razor-sharp Stanley McChrystal, the former commander of special forces in Iraq. Here was a man who had worked closely with Petraeus and understood counterinsurgency and wouldn't be afraid to kick in a few doors. Keane began briefing his former colleagues on the possibility of replacing McKiernan.

Even as the military pushed ahead uncompromisingly in his negotiations with the White House, Petraeus had private doubts about the direction he was taking the war. He was by no means the sole force pushing through the surge in Afghanistan, but given his experience in Iraq his voice carried unique weight. Petraeus recognized the dangers of reading his Iraq experiences into Afghanistan, or of believing in the hype that surrounded his success. He was too intellectually demanding for that. "I've looked very hard at that," he told some of his staff that spring of 2009. "That is something that can have you spring awake in an early hour of the morning, that you turn over a thousand different ways when you're running."[20]

General David Petraeus turned around American fortunes in the Iraq war and sought to do the same in Afghanistan using counterinsurgency tactics. (Photo by Staff Sergeant Brent Powell)

Petraeus lacked something that no amount of war-gaming or reporting could provide: a *feel* for Afghanistan. He'd been a division commander in Iraq for a year from 2003 to 2004, meeting Iraqis every day and getting a grip on local politics. The insights that turned around the country hadn't come from a four-star general's office but from a dusty headquarters in northern Iraq. He'd spent a further year training the Iraqi security forces, before returning as overall commander for yet another deployment. Every soldier has one good war in them, he said to his fellow Iraq veterans, one where they gave everything.

If the Afghan war left Petraeus feeling cold, he kept coming back to one simple question: What was the alternative in Afghanistan? The status quo seemed to be failing. One option was to withdraw troops and focus on counterterrorism, as Biden appeared to be suggesting, but that ran the risk of ceding control of southern Afghanistan to the Taliban. The option smacked of defeatism to Petraeus, and he didn't think Obama was prepared to sell it to the American people, given the lives already lost and money spent. No, he repeatedly concluded, the better option was to surge. Sending in more troops was a gamble. But Petraeus told colleagues he was more comfortable staying positive in the hope of success than losing faith in what American arms could achieve.[21]

B ruce Riedel fully intended for his strategic review to focus on the question of Pakistan. For too long American strategy had gotten the region the wrong way around. In Riedel's view, Pakistan rather than Afghanistan represented the genuine regional threat to American interests. It was a hotbed of Islamic insurgency, had nuclear capabilities, and appeared to be rapidly deteriorating.[22]

In July 2007, the Pakistani military had stormed an Islamist stronghold, the Red Mosque, located in the heart of Islamabad. In response, militants launched an unprecedented wave of suicide bombings and revenge attacks that left 770 people dead and nearly 1,600 injured. A new organization called the Tehrik-e-Taliban Pakistan—the Pakistani version of the Taliban—sought to "liberate" tribal areas from the intrusion of the country's armed forces and foreign spies. That summer the group seized the Swat valley, just ninety miles from Islamabad, and withstood a series of Pakistani military offensives. Their rise reflected the dangerous foment the Afghan war had created and blowback for ISI's long-standing support for militant groups.[23]

Meanwhile Pervez Musharraf, increasingly unpopular and labeled "Busharraf" by his critics for his alliance with America, was forced from power in 2008, leaving the government in the hands of a politician, Asif Zadari, who had only come to power in the wake of the assassination of his wife, Benazir Bhutto. Musharraf's exit had been a blow to Pakistani-American relations. But it also made it easier for American intelligence analysts to identify Islamabad's agenda and disabuse the Bush White House of the false notion that Pakistan's interests were aligned with America's. The Bush administration responded by stepping up US drone strikes in Pakistan's border region without consulting the host nation.[24]

By the time of President Obama's inauguration, the consensus in Washington was that Pakistan was dangerously unstable. This appraisal reflected a tendency among American intelligence officials to judge Pakistan's stability through the prism of its political class. In fact, the country's tribal networks gave it a naturally stable and conservative bedrock that opposed Islamic extremists. The problem was they were equally disillusioned with the politicians, their corruption, and endemic failure to address issues of poverty and disenfranchisement.[25]

In May 2009, Islamabad was taking the first steps toward confronting militant groups in true Pakistani style. The Pakistani military retook the Swat valley by evacuating over a million inhabitants and then blitzing the fighters. Elsewhere they carried out a succession of punitive raids in tribal areas before withdrawing. It wasn't counterinsurgency, but it worked up to a point in sending an unambiguous message to Islamist and tribal groups in the area that the government was taking a tougher stance after years of turning a blind eye to or actively conniving with the militants.[26]

Riedel saw Islamabad's action against the militants as an opportunity for Pakistan and the US to recalibrate their relationship. After all, they both were seeking to pacify versions of the Taliban. Their tactics might differ, and their attitudes toward Karzai's administration were off-kilter, but when it came to dealing with the Pashtun heartlands on either side of the border, their interests were fundamentally aligned.

Given this immense opportunity, Riedel was frustrated by the way the conversation in Washington kept circling back to the issue of troop numbers and counterinsurgency doctrine. When he did brief the principals at the National Security Council in May 2009 on the preliminary findings of his review, both sides of the debate hijacked the meeting. First Joe Biden lectured the group on his own evolving thoughts about troop numbers—don't send many more was his advice. Then National Security Advisor and former marine commandant Jim Jones proposed dispatching 100,000.

Riedel thought the debate over troop numbers was shallow and foreclosed on the possibility of more nuanced and achievable political solutions that could secure the peace. Even so, he felt that the US needed to do something to counteract the Taliban's rise in Afghanistan, and he was prepared to accept the military's arguments for counterinsurgency. He inserted into his review a call for an "integrated civilian-military counterinsurgency strategy in Afghanistan."[27]

On March 18, 2009, Riedel finally briefed Obama aboard Air Force One as the president made his way to California to appear on *The Tonight Show*.[28] Riedel had correctly gauged that Obama was interested in finding out more about Pakistan and its links to terrorist organizations. The president sat at his desk, sleeves rolled up, eyes rapt, as Riedel explained the continuing threat that al-Qa'eda represented, and the renewed importance of Osama bin Laden within the organization's command structure. Whether bin Laden was issuing orders for attacks was unclear, but his foot soldiers seemed to believe he was directing them. However, Riedel explained, focusing on al-Qa'eda without considering other militant groups in Pakistan would be a mistake. Al-Qa'eda's activities were inextricably linked to these other groups, and thereby to the Pakistani government. That meant that tackling al-Qa'eda also involved addressing Pakistan's fundamental security concerns, and the reasons it had supported a network of militants for so long, namely its rivalry with India and the vexed issue of Kashmir, a region claimed by both Pakistan and India and a subject the Bush administration had ignored for fear of stepping on either country's toes.

Riedel's advice on Pakistan was thoughtful and imaginative. When his presentation shifted from Pakistan to Afghanistan, somewhere over the Rockies, his analysis was much thinner and revealed his limited experience of the war. He told Obama he supported the military in asking for more troops, because, "When an 18-year-old Pashtun warrior has 5,000 Marines in his neighborhood he may say, 'You know, I think I'll sit out the next campaign season. I'll just go home.'"[29]

Recent events, unfortunately, suggested the exact opposite: that Afghan tribesmen would rally to the cause of attacking foreign invaders. Few Afghans had been consulted during Riedel's research, and Karzai's recent behavior called into question whether he would be an active partner in any American surge. There was no meaningful national reconciliation program. The lack of political support from many Afghans undermined the entire premise of a US surge force: to create a lasting peace in the country. Yet the war's politics was not, Riedel told the president, "in my purview."

On March 27, 2009, Obama gave his first speech on the war in Afghanistan, announcing that the US would commit 21,000 more troops to the theater. That number did not commit the US to a full-blown counterinsurgency offensive. Obama wanted to hold open the idea of withdrawing troops after the upcoming Afghan election. But even though he remained of two minds about what approach to ultimately take, the language of his speech seemed to commit him to the same Manichean battle that Bush had waged.

"If the Afghan government falls to the Taliban—or allows al-Qaida to go unchallenged—that country will again be a base for terrorists who want to kill as many of our people as they possibly can," said Obama. "For the Afghan people, the return to Taliban rule would condemn their country to brutal governance, international isolation, a paralyzed economy and the denial of basic human rights to the Afghan people, especially women and girls."

By using such language, Obama was creating a false dichotomy. The opposite of sending troops wasn't a precipitous withdrawal from the country. Yet, the terms Obama used to characterize the conflict appeared to commit the US to a war in which victory would be defined in terms of a defeated enemy and a victorious Afghan state.

The following month, the chairman of the Joint Chiefs of Staff, Mike Mullen, flew to Kabul to ask David McKiernan to resign. McKiernan had made a number of mistakes during his tour, not least approving the Kajaki dam operation that had contributed to Helmand's destabilization. But ultimately his error was failing to anticipate the greatly expanded mission his bosses were envisioning that spring. McKiernan refused to go, forcing Mullen to fire him.

A few weeks later, on May 11, Defense Secretary Robert Gates announced McChrystal's appointment as the top commander in Afghanistan. "Our mission there requires new thinking and new approaches from our military leaders," said Gates. He listed the questions he expected McChrystal to answer as the new commander: "How do we do better? What new ideas do you have? What fresh thinking do you have? Are there different ways of accomplishing our goals?"

When Riedel heard these questions, he realized at once what was going on. The strategy for Afghanistan he had outlined to the president was itself subject to review. The military wasn't going to wait to see how the recently dispatched troops did. They wanted more, now.

CHAPTER 24

A Cruel Summer

I n March 2009, British officers found it increasingly difficult to motivate their men to continue patrolling Helmand as they waited for the Americans to arrive. Taliban fighters were hitting them with a dozen bombs a week, and it sometimes felt as if their only contact with civilization was the medevac helicopters that arrived to remove their injured or dying comrades. Many soldiers privately questioned in their journals why they were there. Yet patrol they did, a testimony to both their courage and that old truism of war that in the end you don't fight for a cause but for the men around you. Most of them took quiet comfort in suffering in the company of their comrades.

British Brigadier Tim Radford was well aware of the trauma his men were going through.[1] The arrival of more than 10,000 US Marines as part of the first batch of troops approved by President Obama promised to relieve some of the pressure the UK was under. Yet at the time, he needed to make it look like the British were not being bailed out and that they remained an autonomous fighting force. Otherwise the British public might judge the mission to have failed. Radford was a subtle, sensitive officer with a wry sense of humor; the US Marines, on the other hand, didn't do understated. When Brigadier Larry Nicholson had visited Camp Bastion in February 2009, his hosts had shown him a parking lot and field within the confines of the British base where he was expected to put his headquarters. It clearly wouldn't do. Scaling a guard tower, he'd gestured to the desert stretching west.

"Who owns that space?" he asked.[2]

"Fucking you do, if you want it," the British colonel showing him around had said.

And so the Americans had started building a vast city in the desert. For the next two months, US Navy and Marine engineers leveled land, built airstrips, and installed thousands of portable housing units that collectively became known as Camp Leatherneck. In the months ahead, this would be the headquarters of the American effort to pacify Helmand.

McKiernan's earlier decision in the fall of 2008 to flip the focus of the surge from east to south had suited the marines just fine. The wide-open spaces of Helmand would play to the marines' mobility and allow them to carve out their own territory. Ever since World War II, when marines felt they had not received enough navy support as they fought across the Pacific islands of Guadalcanal and Tarawa, the Corps had insisted on being supplied with their own convoys and air support. Furthermore, marine commandant James Conway also wanted a three-star marine general and not the US commander in Kabul to have ultimate supervision of the force. The recently appointed US Ambassador Karl Eikenberry, a former army commander in Afghanistan, joked that the forty-one nations making up the international coalition in Afghanistan should consider welcoming the American marines as the forty-second, considering they acted so independently from other US forces.[3]

The arrival of US Marine commander Brigadier Larry Nicholson highlighted the challenge that Radford faced in channeling marine hyperactivity. Nicholson was fresh from Iraq's Anbar province, where the US Marines had fought some of the war's hardest battles, including an assault on Fallujah that had left the city in ruins. A smart, self-aware officer, Nicholson had a penchant for Toyota Land Cruisers from his time working as a UN military observer, and for trawling secondhand bookstores for old history books. He also liked to grow tomato and squash plants from the seeds of vegetables at the chow hall salad bar, and the windowsill of his office usually contained a box of plants. But no one was going to accuse him of too much refinement, with his heavy features and ruddy complexion. He took an impish pleasure in talking rough around his British counterparts, who seemed so ill at ease when he talked about hunting the enemy.

Nicholson's first question upon meeting Radford: "Where's the worst place you've got?"[4] The NATO headquarters in Kandahar had devised an operational plan that would place the marines in the south of the province, but Nicholson wanted to make up his own mind. There were several hellholes to choose from: Sangin remained the bloodiest outpost in the province, although since its fall to the Taliban, Marja was of mounting concern. The British hadn't dared to enter in force. Radford explained this to the American.

"That's easy then," said Nicholson. "We'll go to Marja."

Nicholson's declaration confirmed Radford's fears about the marines' arrival, and how their aggressive posture would be perceived back in the UK.

The American Major General Larry Nicholson and the British Brigadier Tim Radford forged a partnership for tackling Helmand and
easing tensions between their respective chains of command. (Photo
by private contributor)

Having the marines storm Marja, a town just outside the provincial capital,
with Afghan elections approaching, threatened to expose Britain's grip on the
region at the very moment that the world's attention was focused on Afghanistan. The British also believed, in typical fashion, that they were better than
the Americans at negotiating central Helmand's complex politics.[5]

Radford stood his ground over Marja, promising Nicholson that the marines could tackle the town later, after the elections. Instead the Brit directed
Nicholson to southern Helmand, where UK forces were struggling in towns
like Garmsir and Nawa. If the marines took on those towns, Radford could
send whatever troops were freed up for operations in central Helmand, which
the British were determined to hold. Nicholson was happy enough to focus on
the south of the province, which conformed to the NATO plan drawn up the
previous fall. "Provided there's a fight to be had," he said, with a characteristic
twinkle in his eye.

Postponing Marja and redirecting the marines to the south created a new
problem for the British command: They had to secure central Helmand by
themselves. To appear as equal partners to the Americans, both Radford and
Nicholson felt the British needed to conduct their own operation to assert
control of other districts to the north of Lashkar Gah, where a belt of tribal
land around the main road was firmly in the hands of Taliban fighters and
tribal discontents. "We wanted the Taliban to see the marines landing in the
south, the Brits coming from the north, and to have an 'aw shit' moment,"
recalled Nicholson.

The trouble with this plan for Radford was that he and his men had a fraction of the Americans' firepower. "We were forced to bite off a great deal," Radford conceded.[6] Radford privately entertained the idea of simply letting the Americans take on the security of Lashkar Gah and central Helmand. In this scenario, the British might focus on training and mentoring local security forces and managing the Provincial Reconstruction Team, while the Americans fought. But he felt trapped by the weight of expectations coming from London to prove his—the military's—worth. Nicholson had to constantly remind himself about the British preoccupation with their reputation. So he decided to proceed with the mission. "So the British hadn't lived up to their reputation in Iraq," said Nicholson. "They were still in Helmand, they were doing a job; that's what mattered."[7]

Nicholson and Radford quickly struck up a firm and formidable partnership as they and their staffs shuttled back and forth from each other's headquarters with plans for the US Marine insertion into Helmand and a simultaneous British operation around Lashkar Gah. Nicholson's thinking was fresh and unencumbered by past mistakes; the limber Radford offered genteel assuasiveness and a subtle grasp of Coalition politics.

The one area of disagreement was where exactly the Americans would go in Helmand. The first tranche of marines to arrive broke down into four battalions. One would take over from the British in Garmsir, the site of the successful clearance operation the year before. Another battalion would be based at Nawa, a little to the north. Another was scheduled to go to Khanashin in the south. The British would have dearly loved to use the remaining battalion to relieve hard-pressed outposts like Sangin and Musa Qala.

Nicholson, however, had other ideas. He wanted to send the fourth marine battalion to Now Zad in northwestern Helmand. The town had seen heavy fighting in 2007, when it had been dubbed Apocalypse Now Zad, and the local population of 18,000 had fled the rubble-strewn street and not returned. A small reinforced platoon of ninety-five marines had been based there since the spring of 2008 working with a few dozen corrupt Afghan cops. Every night Taliban planted roadside bombs around the Americans' base. Two dozen US soldiers had lost their legs in the past six months.

Nicholson had visited Now Zad on his reconnaissance trip in February. He took one look at the cratered streets, the broken shop hoardings, and the graffiti daubed over the police station—"Welcome to Hell"—and realized that this was Helmand's ground zero. He recognized that Now Zad had no strategic value in terms of its location on the outer fringes of the province, but it was a symbol of everything that had gone wrong over the preceding three years. If the marines were going to prove their value to the people of Helmand, and the value of counterinsurgency doctrine, it would be by turning places like Now Zad back into thriving communities. At the very least, he wasn't going to pull out without avenging the marine blood spilled so far.

Radford and Hugh Powell, the senior foreign office representative and head of the British PRT, who had already been in Lashkar Gah for over a year, tried hard to suggest that US troops could be best used elsewhere: Now Zad, they pointed out, was deserted but for the Taliban. If the central tenet of counterinsurgency theory was to protect the population, then they'd need to look elsewhere; the town simply didn't have any population left.

The British weren't alone in this analysis; equally concerned was Nicholson's political officer, Kael Weston, who had left his work on educational outreach in Khost the year before, only to be headhunted by Nicholson, with whom he had worked in Fallujah. It was a mark of Weston's standing with Nicholson that he not only tolerated dissent from his civilian adviser, but also welcomed the debate.

"I don't believe in the time we've got that Now Zad is where we should focus our attention," Weston told Nicholson that summer of 2009.[8]

"When Now Zad starts to be repopulated it will be one of the biggest stories to come out of Afghanistan," replied Nicholson.

"If the world still cares about Afghanistan," said Weston.

Like some of his British counterparts, Weston had come to believe America needed to see Afghanistan as a thirty-year war and recalibrate its plans accordingly. Indeed he'd taken the job with Nicholson in the hopes that he could convince the marines to make more strategic decisions.

"Does Now Zad matter to the Afghans, or does it just matter to us?" Weston asked Nicholson pointedly.

"I've got the governor calling me twice a week," Nicholson responded. "It matters to him. It fucking matters to him."

"He wants to raise the flag everywhere," said Weston, who also opposed the deployment to Khanashin, a town he also adjudged to be of limited strategic importance.

"Why shouldn't he?" Nicholson retorted. "He wants to govern his province."

Nicholson held firm on Now Zad, and the NATO commander in Kandahar, Mart de Kruif, signed off on it. The operation went ahead, along with the moves to Garmsir, Nawa, and Khanashin in early July 2009. Nicholson was soon celebrating success in his new outposts, as his marine battalions swooped into their new homes with little resistance. "The largest [US] airborne assault since Vietnam," he boasted.[9]

"Fine," thought Weston, "but our real test is going to come in the duration and sustainability of what we establish in Helmand." As he quickly surmised, the province's political fate would be decided in central Helmand, and it would be determined in the near term by the British.[10]

Weston's caution about the marines' early success was matched by the concern of some in the British camp about their own operation, dubbed Panther's Claw, scheduled to begin June 19. The operation was to clear the road leading from Lashkar Gah north to Gereshk, the province's main commercial hub. Before the British had arrived in Helmand in 2006, the drive along the packed-earth road took only an hour. Since then, it had become so laced with mines as to be impassable. The farming communities on either side of the road were believed to have sided with the Taliban, but the British weren't sure as no one had really engaged with the area since an abortive attempt to pay off a local warlord and former Taliban commander in 2007. Following the fuss President Karzai made over the UK outreach to the Taliban and the expulsion of the UN diplomat Michael Semple, the British withdrew their funding for the warlord. The militia leader took this as a grave insult, and his men had sided with the Taliban ever since.

Earlier in 2009, the British had attempted to occupy the nearby town of Nad Ali, which lay several miles to the west of the road, and met fierce resistance. The area still wasn't Taliban-free, and British patrols there were subject to repeated attack. Radford expected a similarly tough fight clearing the road. Indeed, he had received intelligence that the Taliban leadership in the Quetta shura had learned of the marines' arrival in Helmand, and was asking all Afghans to head to the province to repel the foreign invasion.

The brigade's plan for Panther's Claw envisioned two lines of attack. The primary mission would be the advance of the Light Dragoons down eighteen miles of road from Gereshk to Lashkar Gah. At the same time, the Welsh Guards battle group would advance from the south, securing the four-mile length of the Shamalan Canal, which initially ran parallel with the road, before the latter veered to the northeast. The wedge of farmland that opened up between the road and canal was called Babaji, and likely Taliban country. As the Light Dragoons advanced, the enemy in the area would flee, only to run up against the guns of the Welsh Guards. In addition, the Brigade Reconnaissance Force would sit at the northerly junction where the Shamalan dead-ended into a perpendicular canal.

It was textbook stuff, which was one reason it alarmed Lieutenant Colonel Rupert Thorneloe, the Welsh Guards commander. As he looked at the plans for Panther's Claw in early June, he feared the operation was going to be just another slug through Helmand that would stretch his resources. He didn't have the troops necessary to control the areas around Lashkar Gah he was meant to be securing, let alone expand his reach thirty miles to the north. Furthermore, the brigade's limited helicopter and surveillance assets would be focused on the Light Dragoons.

The shortage of helicopters had been a chronic problem since 2006. That summer of 2009 there were just thirty to support 8,000 troops. In Northern Ireland a British patrol of a dozen men could expect to have three helicopters in support. Supplies were regularly flown in to avoid bombs the IRA planted. Helmand insurgents planted more bombs in one month than during a year in Northern Ireland and yet, as Thorneloe angrily noted, his men were having to clear mines by hand just to reach water and battle rations to stock his outposts.[11]

He was deeply concerned about the Taliban's use of these buried mines, or improvised explosive devices. Since the early years of the war, the Taliban had been constructing bombs from cheap fertilizer produced in Pakistan, and rigging the devices to a pressure plate that triggered detonation. The lack of paved roads in Afghanistan meant the IEDs could be quickly planted and used to devastating effect, often as a prelude for an ambush. One of the cruelest ironies of the war for Thorneloe and his fellow officers was that the more troops they sent out on patrol, the more targets they provided for the IED planters. In 2008, there had been 3,276 attacks against NATO forces; the following year there were 9,304. All told, 70 percent to 80 percent of Coalition casualties were caused by IEDs.[12]

To make matters worse, the British military remained ill-equipped to cope with IEDs. The problem wasn't an issue of funding. The British army had plenty of money to spend on vehicles capable of withstanding mine strikes— typically having a V-shaped hull to deflect explosions to either side of the cabin. The Rhodesian government had developed a model in the late 1970s, and several defense manufacturers offered modified versions of the same basic design in 2009 "off the shelf," that is, ready for instant delivery. The trouble was that the British army had squandered its budget on a program of futuristic "networked" vehicles and equipment as part of the so-called Future Rapid Effects System. FRES was meant to use the latest technology to link together vehicles, surveillance equipment, and satellites to give units a panoramic view of the battlefield. It was a bad idea from its inception in 2000, lacking a clear set of requirements and relying on technology that in some cases was still at only a conceptual level. By the start of the deployment to Helmand in 2006, the program clearly was nowhere near ready and costs were skyrocketing, from £6 billion ($10 billion) to £16 billion ($28 billion).[13]

General Richard Dannatt, the new head of the army and an early champion of the FRES program, decided to persevere with the program, despite the fact that mine-resistant vehicles were desperately needed and available at a fraction of the cost. Lieutenant General Robert Fulton, deputy chief of the defense staff for equipment capability, explained that buying such vehicles might "divert much needed funds from FRES or from some other program. . . . It would be a stopgap but it would be a dead end."[14]

The Americans had had similar problems overcoming the inertia and myopia of Donald Rumsfeld's Pentagon. His successor from 2006, Robert Gates, made reequipping the military with mine-resistant ambush protected vehicles—or MRAPs—the "highest-priority Department of Defense acquisition program." As Gates noted, the US military had made the flawed assumption that the Iraq war would be short, and "seemed unwilling to invest substantial dollars to provide the troops everything needed for protection and for success in their mission, and to bring them home safely."[15]

Under Gates's guidance, more than 11,500 MRAPs were shipped to Iraq in just over two years, and a further 8,000 were built for Afghanistan in sixteen months, the largest defense procurement program since World War II. During meetings he cut through the bureaucracy with a simple mantra: "Every delay of a single day costs one or more of our kids his limbs or his life."[16] The US Congress laid aside its partisan issues to agree to an additional $1.5 billion for the initial vehicles. As a result, deaths from IEDs in Iraq fell by 90 percent in 2007.[17] The following year, a lighter, more maneuverable vehicle was designed for the off-road terrain of Afghanistan, and had a similarly dramatic effect saving lives.

The British had not gone nearly as far in solving the IED problem. When Radford's men deployed to Helmand in 2009, two-thirds were still driving in soft-shelled vehicles called Vikings and Snatch Land Rovers that provided no protection from roadside bombs. "Coffins on wheels" was what the soldiers called them. Furthermore, the British also lacked standard operating equipment the Americans used: surveillance systems that allowed Coalition troops to interdict the Taliban before they laid their devices in the first place, route-clearance robots for dangerous routes, and designated mine-sweeping vehicles fitted with ground-penetrating radar. GPR, as it was known, had become an important countermeasure to an emerging threat in Afghanistan: IEDs made with graphite components that avoided conventional metal detectors.[18]

The new IEDs, and the lack of the tools needed to detect them, forced British soldiers to manually clear their patrol routes on foot, with a combination of metal detectors—the Taliban still used some conventional IEDs—and long metal poles to insert into the earth in the hope of locating a bomb. The British had coined their own verb for this hellish job: to "barma." Fear of barma-ing was intense: It left soldiers paralyzed with fear or vomiting by the side of the road; some even had to be airlifted out after falling into a panic. The men drew lots for barma duty, or played Rock Paper Scissors; some solicitous soldiers took the place of others, sometimes to protect the younger men or those about to go on leave. In the end, every patrol got its barma team: four men who walked ahead of the rest, metal detectors sweeping ahead, each man's arc overlapping, eyes scanning the desert for anything suspicious, desert sand a darker shade of gray, or markers like a rubble pile that the Taliban sometimes left to warn locals to stay away.

If the soldiers did detect an IED, standard procedure was to drop to the floor to probe the ground as thoroughly as possible, controlling the panic, before calling in a bomb disposal team. Every moment lost gave the Taliban more time to plant bombs, yet a missed patch of earth could lead to their colleagues' death, the cruelest moment for any barma team. Lieutenant Charles Fraser Sampson noted, "It is just the most awful feeling in the world thinking that every step you take could be your last, or you might miss the device and someone else will be killed. You're almost wishing the Vallon [metal detector] not to detect anything because when it does start beeping you know then you've got to get down and start confirming. The whole time you're thinking: 'I didn't join the army to do this, I'm not an expert, I don't know how to deal with these devices.' And when you see what a device does to somebody all you can think about is, 'Jesus that might be me.'"[19]

Thorneloe, the Welsh Guard commander, took his concerns about the British approach to Radford before the Babaji operation was to begin, in particular an aspect of the plan that would have his men clearing an area west of the canal before advancing north. He told Radford point-blank, "With the resources I have got, I cannot do it." To his credit, Radford altered the plan to limit the Welsh Guards to the canal.[20] The broader issues of the operation's purpose went unaddressed, however.

The advance up the narrow road along the canal's raised banks was meant to be flanked by eight Scimitar tanks on a parallel road, to ward off the Taliban and prevent them from approaching the canal and planting IEDs. However, contrary to expectations, the track that followed the raised side of the canal was too narrow and broken up with irrigation ditches, meaning no vehicles could shadow the Welsh Guards' advance, and obliging the entire force to travel in single file along one raised bank of the waterway. The route on the canal itself was only twelve feet wide, leaving little room for maneuver with a treacherous drop of several feet on either side. Furthermore, the waterway was not ten feet deep, as the brigade believed, but barely half that, destroying the whole notion of trapping the Taliban against its banks—the operation's original concept. Instead the Taliban could flit between opposite banks, taking potshots and planting IEDs as the British convoy lumbered slowly northward. The British troops involved in the operation understood that the terrain gave the advantage to the enemy. "The canal filled us with dread," recalled Major Charlie Burbidge.[21]

The operation began at midnight on June 19. The first stage was to airlift 350 troops of the Brigade Reconnaissance Force drawn from the 3rd Battalion of the Royal Regiment of Scotland, or 3 Scots, to the northern edge of Babaji in preparation for the advances of the Light Dragoons and Welsh Guards from their respective positions to the north and south of Babaji. At first the fighting was modest as 3 Scots arrived, and on June 25, the Welsh Guards' 2nd Company began their movement along the canal in a dozen Land Rovers and armored trucks carrying a hundred men. Progress was slow. Sporadic fire from the compounds and dense foliage on either side of the canal were enough to bring the convoy to a standstill. On June 29, a Viking personnel carrier toppled over the side of the bank and into the canal, almost drowning its seven members. Behind schedule and increasingly jittery, the soldiers of 2nd Company needed a morale-boosting visit from their commander, Thorneloe decided.

The Welsh Guard commander made plans to accompany a resupply convoy of Vikings to the canal—if there had been more helicopters, then supplies would have been distributed by air. Thorneloe wasn't the sort of officer to order others to take a risk he himself would not take. He was acutely aware of his men's horror at barma-ing ahead of a convoy. So he insisted on doing it himself. "You need to be careful, sir," said regimental Sergeant Major Mike Monaghan, reflecting his men's surprise. "At the end of the day, you are the Commanding Officer. I don't think you really need to be doing that."[22]

Thorneloe held firm.

On July 1, shortly after 3:18 p.m., he was riding in the lead vehicle of the supply convoy. He'd chosen to man the light machine gun in the Viking's rear cab, which he accessed through an opening that left his upper body exposed to a lick of wind that was a small relief from the 120-degree heat. Thorneloe spent almost an hour barma-ing a 1,000-foot section of the road without incident. The rest of the route leading to a temporary British outpost just visible ahead had been barma-ed three hours earlier. So they proceeded, confident the rest of the way was clear. Suddenly a giant explosion lifted the rear of Thorneloe's Viking into the air. The vehicle hit the ground; the soldiers shocked into silence. The survivors struggled out of the vehicle and found Thorneloe propped up against the toolbox on the rear cab's roof. Both his legs were missing. He was briefly conscious, tried to speak, and then slipped away. Trooper Josh Hammond, an eighteen-year-old who had volunteered to take another soldier's place in the vehicle that morning, also died in the blast.

The bomb had probably been laid days earlier and gone undetected. Farther down the canal, British soldiers listening in to the Taliban's local radio frequency heard fighters celebrating and congratulating each other. News of Thorneloe's death was at first met with disbelief at Radford's headquarters. Some staff wondered whether there hadn't been a mistake, and that a "Thomas"—a common name in the Welsh Guards—had been killed instead. "There was shock, tears even. I felt every death very keenly," recalled Radford.[23] Thorneloe was the first battalion commander to be killed since the Falklands war, twenty-seven years earlier, and only the second in the Welsh Guards' ninety-four-year history.

Radford did not consider stopping the operation. If anything, he felt greater urgency to ensure that it succeeded. But he knew he had to move quickly to reassure the brigade. The next day insurgents attacked his Sea King helicopter and nearly shot it down en route to visit the Welsh Guard headquarters in Nad Ali. After announcing Thorneloe's replacement, Radford ordered the Light Dragoons battle group to begin their advance down the road from Gereshk through the heart of Babaji.

B Company of 2nd Battalion of the Mercian Regiment—attached to the Light Dragoons—came under fire within 600 feet of leaving their staging post. The Taliban, far from fading away as the brigade headquarters had predicted, appeared intent on repulsing the British from the neighborhood. The company suffered devastating losses over the next several hours. A Spartan personnel carrier was hit by an RPG, killing an eighteen-year-old private and seriously injuring his platoon commander. The Chinook helicopter carrying the two men back to Camp Bastion had barely taken off when an IED claimed the life of another soldier and seriously injured Major Stu Hill when the force from the explosion sent a radio antenna hurtling into his head. As the afternoon shadows lengthened, the company had advanced only a few stones' throws.

They retreated to a compound near where they had started. The next day they advanced again, and again came under attack within minutes. With Apache helicopters flying close support, firing Hellfire missiles and 30mm cannon rounds at the compounds on either side of the road, they managed to advance a quarter of a mile. The convoy paused briefly to allow two guardsmen to barma the route ahead. One of the men, Corporal Dane Elson, stepped on an IED on his way to the front line and was killed outright. Three others were injured, including the forward air controller who arranged air support. All told, thirty British casualties were airlifted to the hospital in just two days. They'd struck fifty-three IEDs in a stretch of road just two miles long.

Radford was shaken by the mounting casualties. The commander of the Light Dragoons, Lieutenant Colonel Gus Fair, told him the company was badly beaten up. Radford choppered in to meet Fair on July 6 and found the officer on edge. Fair, like Thorneloe, had initially questioned the operation. He bore no resentment toward Radford over the decision to go ahead. The brigadier weighed up whether to carry on. Further deaths were inevitable, and the idea of securing Babaji with the forces at his disposal seemed unlikely. Yet what sort of message would withdrawing send? Leaving aside London's concerns about the Americans and the reputation of the British military, wouldn't pulling out mean these men had died in vain? If Gus Fair and his men were flagging now, he suspected a retreat would sap what remained of the brigade's morale.[24] Radford instructed Fair to hold his ground while he arranged for the division's reserve based at Kandahar to helicopter into Babaji. He also rushed in a company from Sangin to bolster this new attack. Radford knew it was a gamble. In the short term it worked. By the end of the week, the British succeeded in clearing a route through Babaji at the cost of four more soldiers.

However, the operation in Babaji stretched thin the British forces elsewhere in Helmand, with deadly consequences. The battalion commander in Sangin, Rob Thomson, had sent one of his more capable companies to support Panther's Claw, forcing him to reinforce a dangerous outpost called Wishtun with a company that he had judged to be not as battle-ready. The operation also limited Sangin's access to helicopter support and British surveillance assets, which were already stretched thin. The Wishtun outpost still had access to a number of different methods for keeping watch over the town, one of which was a helium balloon fitted with cameras for a view of potential IED-laying teams.[25] However, the Taliban had already discovered the flaws in this piece of equipment: The balloon hovered at only three hundred feet, so a few well-placed shots could damage it. It also had to be winched to the ground when helicopters arrived to stop collisions, giving the Taliban a window of opportunity to plant bombs.

On July 10, the balloon had been in position less than twenty-four hours when 9 Platoon left the base on an early morning patrol. Almost at once the metal detectors started whining, indicating the path was strewn with bombs. The platoon tried another route, still within a couple hundred yards of the outpost, only for eighteen-year-old Rifleman James Backhouse to trigger a chain of IEDs that killed him and injured six others in his section, including the platoon commander. As the Taliban began to pepper their position with bullets, the platoon's survivors carried the injured on stretchers into a nearby compound to await a helicopter, only to discover an IED on the landing site, forcing them out onto the street to find another location. Back in the open, another series of explosions ripped through the stretcher bearers, killing Rifleman William Aldridge and Rifleman Joseph Murphy, both eighteen, Rifleman Daniel Simpson, twenty, and Corporal Jonathan Horne, twenty-eight.

Oblivious to the dangers, soldiers in the nearby base sprinted the short distance down the road to help. Only after all the bodies had been brought back to the base did the shock give way to grief—anguished cries of pain for the lost men. At a remembrance service, Thomson ordered the bugle major to sound the advance, a long, lonely note met with his men's sobs. The surveillance balloon had been down at the time, although Thomson said that other assets were still in use and provided adequate cover of the terrain around the base.

"All the guys who were killed died helping each other. They were walking without all the kit and either someone in their arms or on the stretchers. They never thought about themselves," said Jaime Moncho, the 9 Platoon's sergeant.[26] Two years later, long after the soldiers had returned home, Sangin claimed another victim: twenty-year-old Rifleman Allan Arnold, found hanged in woods near his barracks. A note on his body, addressed to his mother, explained that he couldn't cope any longer.

The loss of fifteen soldiers across Helmand in less than a fortnight was front-page news in the UK and drove Downing Street into hysteria. For all his awkwardness before soldiers, Prime Minister Gordon Brown was nonetheless deeply affected by their deaths, often brooding into the early hours after a bad day. He struggled to grasp the war's magnitude; he seemed to view it as a grim symbol, malevolent and impervious to his powers of reasoning. This seemed only to frustrate him the more. At one point, as the death toll mounted that July, Brown ordered his chauffeur-driven convoy to make an unscheduled stop at the British military headquarters at Northwood. He was clearly in a rage, but when he was confronted by a room of senior officers he seemed to lose courage, not knowing what to say or do to stop the carnage. He left after twenty minutes, with the officers unsure about what, if anything, the meeting had been about.

Brown may have agonized over the lives lost in Helmand, but the other, more calculating and tribal side of his character was soon on display once again. The day before Brown was due at the Prime Minister's Questions, his weekly mauling by the opposition leader, the *Daily Telegraph* published excerpts from the diary of Lieutenant Mark Evison, a twenty-six-year-old officer who had been shot through the chest the month before. The extracts revealed his concerns about his battalion's limited resources. The *Telegraph* made clear who was responsible for this state of affairs: Gordon Brown and his decision in 2004 to "cut" the military's budget. In fact, Brown had not cut the military budget, merely asked the defense chiefs to stick to the one he had given them. However, with a general election looming, and with the military keen to find a scapegoat, party politics had trumped the reality of the debate.

Brown wasn't going down without a fight. In preparation for PMQs, he had called up Radford for a brief chat to ascertain whether the British had enough resources for their current operation. Radford said he did.

Before a packed House of Commons, with the press box overflowing, Brown gave one of his infamously turgid performances. When the Conservative opposition leader David Cameron accused Brown of not supplying enough helicopters to Helmand, Brown duly claimed he had "spoken to the brigade commander in Helmand and been assured that resources were adequate." This was stretching the truth of their brief conversation; the evidence from the battlefield was to the contrary, and Brown clearly knew it, as he sat glowering across from Cameron. Panther's Claw was meant to have salvaged the military's reputation and, by extension, his own. Instead, he was taking the blame for the war's mismanagement.

The operation wound to a close at the end of July, having achieved little. As the brigade headquarters candidly recognized, they had opened up the road between Gereshk and Lashkar Gah but failed to clear Babaji, where there were "increasing indications of a residual [Taliban] presence among the population," with Taliban fighters "watching and waiting." In the last week of July, as British soldiers sought to withdraw for further operations, three IEDs exploded inside Babaji by way of a farewell.

Radford was obliged to hail the operation as a success to the media. There was no calculation on his part. After witnessing such harrowing events, Radford had to believe his soldiers' sacrifices had been worth it. But the military leadership in London took a more calculating view. They could have recognized the flaws of the operation and scaled back their ambitions. Yet that would have meant accepting their own culpability. Neither could Brown publicly criticize his own military. It was in everyone's interest to declare the operation a triumph.

Back in Afghanistan Radford and many of his soldiers worried that the politicians, believing victory had been achieved, were in for a nasty shock. Panther's Claw should have served as a warning to the British and their allies of the dangers—if not ultimate futility—of launching more operations in Helmand. Instead, it encouraged the British and American militaries as they geared up to ask for more troops to launch one last desperate gamble.

CHAPTER 25

Elections

The Obama administration had intended for the newly deployed US Marines to provide security for the run-up to Afghanistan's second presidential election in August 2009. Yet almost at once the marines had begun waging an aggressive campaign to occupy the outer reaches of Helmand. They had managed to shore up support in a handful of towns in the province over the summer, but left more important areas of the south, such as Kandahar, under threat of a Taliban attack. For the American military their limited success so far and the continuing instability around Kandahar became evidence for the need to send more troops. Sending additional western forces to Afghanistan only made sense if elections returned a capable government, one that could consolidate the military's gains by administering newly pacified areas and reaching a political settlement among Afghanistan's various factions.

So Washington turned its attention to the elections, and the question of whether Hamid Karzai could deliver this support. If anything, the doubts Joe Biden's awkward visit in January had raised had only grown within the Obama administration in the weeks that followed. Karzai had "plateaued as a leader," according to Doug Lute at the National Security Council.[1] The military viewed his public complaints about civilian casualties as undermining their counterinsurgency efforts. Yet the White House worried that there were no better alternatives. The leading tribal contenders were from the Tajik-dominated Northern Alliance and at a disadvantage when it came to quelling a Pashtun-dominated insurgency. Meanwhile, Pashtun candidates like Ashraf Ghani and Hanif Atmar didn't have critical tribal backing. Ghani in particular seemed to think his most important constituency was Washington and had even hired the veteran election strategist James Carville to boost his image in the West. Faced with these options, Obama's team "grudgingly" retreated to supporting Karzai, with one notable and potentially powerful exception: the US special representative to Afghanistan and Pakistan, Richard Holbrooke.

Given the White House's hands-off approach to the election, Holbrooke had a relatively free hand to shape the direction of American thinking toward the war. His reasons for wanting to get rid of Karzai were deeply entangled with his personal ambitions. He was at the end of an illustrious career in which he had carved out a reputation—which his critics thought bordered on caricature—as a man capable of forging peace in such disparate wars as Vietnam and the Balkans through the sheer force of his personality.

Reflecting on his first assignment as a political officer in Vietnam's Mekong Delta, he wrote, "I had wanted to see war . . . and I had wanted to participate in history, and I was doing both."[2] In a prescient memo to President Lyndon Johnson in 1967, Holbrooke had argued that America was losing the battle where it really mattered, with the public at home. He offered Johnson two choices: Either escalate the war in the hope of destroying the Vietcong once and for all, or seek peace and hand over the fighting to their Vietnamese allies. Holbrooke went on to serve at the 1968 peace talks in Paris.

His greatest success was the 1995 Dayton Peace Agreement, during which he'd personally dragged the Balkan leaders to the negotiating table to forge a landmark agreement to end three and a half years of fighting in the region. He was widely believed to be Hillary Clinton's first choice as secretary of state, had she won the 2008 election. As a consolation prize, Obama gave Holbrooke the Afghan war to salvage and with it an opportunity to further burnish his place in history.

He was sixty-eight when he arrived in Kabul, more tired than he cared to admit, but as determined as ever to impose himself on events. He considered the US military's escalation of the war to be heading for disaster in the absence of a parallel political process. He knew a peace deal involving all the main players in the Afghan war, including the Taliban, was a dim prospect. But he saw little point in aiming for anything less. To that end, he believed that the US suffered from a credibility gap in its support for a corrupt and ineffective Afghan administration that had alarming historical parallels to the fallout from US efforts to prop up the South Vietnamese in the early 1960s. Using that rubric, he believed that delivering a peace deal in Afghanistan was contingent on leveraging the elections to replace Karzai with a partner who could rejuvenate politics and bring on board Afghanistan's fractious stakeholders.[3]

Holbrooke's plan to eliminate Karzai—without overtly bucking Obama's official support for him—was simple.[4] He would encourage more rival candi-

dates to run, thereby signaling to the Afghan people that the US was prepared
to support a new leader. It wasn't a political strategy as such, more a firm stir
of the swamp to see what, if anything, rose to the surface. Holbrooke was
aware that some would perceive his actions as a one-man campaign against
Karzai. But he was prepared to take the gamble that he could oust the Afghan president. That spring of 2009, he told anyone who would listen that
he thought that Karzai's time was up. He even said so to his face (although
he did so by suggesting it was the British who were planning to get rid the
Afghan president).[5]

Holbrooke knew his policy of encouraging as many candidates as he could
to stand for the election was a long shot given Karzai's overwhelming election
in 2004 and the paucity of rival candidates. However, Holbrooke wasn't looking for an outright victory over Karzai. All he had to do was drain support
away from the incumbent. Under Afghan election law, if Karzai failed to gain
50 percent of the vote, he would be forced into a second-round vote against
his strongest opponent. Then it might be possible to unite the opposition.

Over the course of several visits to Afghanistan that spring, Holbrooke
made sure he was photographed with Ghani; Abdullah Abdullah, the former
foreign minister; and dozens of potential candidates, urging them all to run.
By April, two dozen had stepped forward. The first vice president, Ahmed
Zai Massoud bitterly joked, "I must be the only person whom Holbrooke has
not invited to run for the presidency."[6] Holbrooke also asked the recently appointed US ambassador, Karl Eikenberry, to start attending opposition rallies
in the name of "free and fair" elections.

Holbrooke's rigorous approach had worked in the Balkans, where the
macho generals and politicians he was dealing with respected a show of
strength, and gave as good as they got. Afghanistan was an altogether subtler
but no less dangerous culture. Karzai did not respond well to being pushed.
Rather than push back, he was more likely to nod in agreement but secretly
rage and pursue his own agenda anyway. The approaching elections threatened to expose the gap between what Karzai said he was doing and the reality.

Long before Holbrooke had shown up, Karzai had been wary of the upcoming poll. The scale of unrest in the south meant that turnout there was
likely to be low. And yet that was where Karzai drew much of his support. He
had raised his concerns with the British Ambassador Sherard Cowper-Coles,
who agreed with the Afghan president that the elections should be delayed.
"There was no point in holding an election just for the sake of it," Cowper-
Coles later recalled. "Especially one that was going to cost $300 million to
stage."[7]

Yet the Americans insisted on sticking to a summer poll: Any delay threatened to expose the West's tenuous hold on the country. Holbrooke's machinations provided another explanation for forcing a vote Karzai would struggle to win. As Karzai's chief of staff, Umar Daudzai, noted, "If we had any doubts what Holbrooke and Eikenberry thought of him, it was made very clear during the campaign. The American message was, 'We want you out.'"[8]

Given most western diplomats' low opinion of the Karzai administration, there was a dark irony to the scale and efficiency of the scheme the Afghan government hatched that spring to stay in power—carried out under the noses of those same officials. Pulling off election fraud on a national scale amid an insurgency required considerable organizing prowess. Yet a small clique of Afghan officials set about their task with a methodical determination.

The most powerful instrument for doing so was the Independent Election Commission, which had taken over organizing and supervising Afghan elections from the UN. Karzai had appointed all five of its members. Initially the scheme was to center on old-fashioned ballot-box stuffing, according to one election official who wished to remain anonymous. This sort of fraud didn't require much finesse, but it did need to be hidden from eyes of the international community. Afghan officials would not be able to interfere at polling stations in major towns in the south, where the United Nations and other international agencies were likely to have observers. Yet by coordinating with the police, Afghan army, and tribal leaders, polling stations could be opened in dangerous areas where the UN was unlikely to go. In at least one case, the Afghan government prevailed upon American forces to clear districts of Taliban fighters to apparently stage a fraudulent election. Such was the case in Barge Matal, eastern Afghanistan, where four US soldiers died clearing the town, one result of which was to allow the local vote to be rigged, or so the American military unit in the area came to suspect.[9] This was a grueling way to gain votes. "Early on, we realized that this might not get enough votes this way," said the official.[10]

The Independent Election Commission may have come up with a second, easier method to ensure victory. At the UN's behest, the commission had drawn up a roster of polling stations. Many were set deep in Taliban territory and would be impossible to open, except with US military assistance. But what if the station was left on the roster? No one could check whether it actually existed. Ballot boxes could easily be stuffed in Kabul and Kandahar and then fictitiously assigned to these ghost polling stations.

"We wondered why we hadn't thought of it before," said the official.[11] What was even more incredible was how long it took the international community to cotton on to the danger.

The risk of widespread election fraud was first raised at a UN staff meeting in Kabul in May 2009. The UN had no official role in managing the election, but many in the international community would look to the organization to give a verdict on whether the poll had been clean.[12] The UN's local staff who had overseen the 2004 presidential election had witnessed ballot fraud and coercion by all sides. The relative peace back then had allowed them to visit most of Afghanistan's polling stations; the same would not be possible this time, warned the staff. "The implications were clear: There was a real danger of massive fraud," said Minna Jarvenpaa, the Finnish reconstruction expert, who had become the UN's head of strategic planning in Afghanistan.[13] In her view, the election was a foreseeable disaster. But the head of the UN mission, the Norwegian diplomat Kai Eide, insisted on plowing ahead.[14]

Eide's motivations were to prove every bit as complicated as Holbrooke's, and the two inevitably would clash. Holbrooke was the lion at any gathering, Eide the tour guide, puckish, sensitive, and acutely aware of his status. Yet both hungered after the same prize: credit for delivering peace to Afghanistan. They had known each other in the Balkans, where Holbrooke had lorded over proceedings, and Eide, as a UN diplomat, was among the supporting cast. According to several accounts, Eide had been irritated at how the Americans had dominated a UN-mandated peace process. He was clearly concerned that Holbrooke was about to dominate proceedings once again. This personal enmity prevented them channeling their talents to promote a viable political process. Instead their petty battles were about to wreck the western mission.

Holbrooke began the war between the two men with loose talk about the UN, and the apparent "lost opportunity" to appoint his friend, British politician Paddy Ashdown, to Eide's position. Ashdown had been forced to withdraw his candidacy a year before after Karzai had objected, with Eide getting the job instead. Holbrooke's comments on his preferred pick got back to the Norwegian, who saw it as a slight and e-mailed US Defense Secretary Robert Gates and National Security Advisor Jim Jones to complain. This led Secretary of State Hillary Clinton, Holbrooke's main backer in the administration, to quietly reprimand the US envoy. Clinton asked Holbrooke to set up a call with Eide to smooth things over, but it resulted in both men screaming on the phone at each other before hanging up.[15]

The next time Holbrooke and Eide met, at the US embassy in Kabul in February 2009, the breakfast meeting was strained. Holbrooke's flight the night before had been late, and when he showed up, clearly tired and irritable, he was apparently in no mood for pleasantries.

"When does your contract expire?" Holbrooke asked Eide by way of an opener. Eide responded testily that he had just renewed for a year.[16]

Holbrooke next declared that he'd found the perfect deputy for Eide: Peter Galbraith, the former US ambassador to Croatia. Galbraith was an old friend of Eide's; the two had once enjoyed the high life of diplomats, holidaying together on a yacht off the coast of Croatia with their families. Eide had even introduced Galbraith to the woman who would become his wife. Eide, who had already selected a German diplomat as his deputy appeared stoic at Holbrooke's fait accompli, but was privately incensed, viewing the announcement of Galbraith's appointment as more evidence of a US takeover of the country.[17]

Finally at the end of the breakfast the conversation turned to the matters at hand: Karzai's presidency and the upcoming election. Here, at least, there was a substantive difference between the two men. Eide strongly disagreed with Holbrooke's desire to oust Karzai. Certainly Karzai was not the partner the West wanted, Eide recognized, but then again Karzai's perspectives were not those of the West, but rather of an impoverished and war-torn country. The West needed to keep its ambitions in line with Afghan desires; in Eide's eyes, sweeping Karzai aside in the name of an impossible nation-building project amounted to blaming the Afghans for the West's shortcomings.

As Holbrooke launched his campaign to unseat Karzai that spring of 2009, Eide increasingly saw his role as defending the Afghan president from the American envoy's attacks. "He [Holbrooke] is after both of us," Karzai told Eide conspiratorially after one meeting. Eide's relationship with Karzai won him credibility with Afghans and leverage with an international community equally sensitive to American hegemony.[18] Unfortunately, his personal proximity to Karzai appeared to blind Eide to the growing evidence of schemes to rig the election.

The first substantial evidence of ghost polling stations arrived at the end of June when the UN office in Gardez reported that at least 50 of the 175 polling stations in the province could not open because it was too dangerous. Yet local Afghan election officials continued to insist they would be manned. In one of his first meetings, the recently arrived Galbraith learned from UN staff in early July that 40 percent of 7,000 polling stations had yet to be visited by local officials. Galbraith was disturbed by the news, which clearly raised the potential for fraud, but when this matter was raised with Eide, the Norwegian expressed "concern" but took no action.[19] At his next meeting with Karzai, Eide was assured that the Afghans would provide a "security plan" for the country that would ensure most polling stations could open, and thus be subjected to scrutiny. Eide then left for his summer holiday.

In Eide's absence, Peter Galbraith sought to tackle the problem. After learning about the danger of ghost polling stations in Gardez, he immediately conducted a review of the other provinces and concluded that 1,200 sites across the country had no chance of opening. Galbraith called a meeting of election officials to push the Afghans into removing them from the register. Then, in a follow-up meeting with the American and British ambassadors on July 15, Galbraith spelled out the dangers. "Either Karzai loses and says that the elections were unfair—or even suggests that it cannot be held because of the security problem," said Galbraith, "or election officials insist that all polling stations in the South open, which we know to be impossible, and they come back full of Karzai votes."[20] Either way, the election's credibility would be shot, leaving the UN with a devilish choice between condoning the fraud or rejecting the election and plunging the country into chaos. The ambassadors met Galbraith's urgency with resignation. The obvious solution was to delay the election, but it was too late for that, Tim Carney, the American ambassador overseeing the election, told him.

"We'll just have to work to make this as clean an election as possible," said Carney.[21]

Galbraith suspected Carney and others had simply resigned themselves to Karzai winning. What did it matter if he won by 1 percent or 20 percent? Galbraith had equal difficulty rousing the Afghans, whose complacency confirmed his hunch that they were planning to throw the vote. The Independent Election Commission agreed to consolidate some stations to limit the possibility of ghost polling stations, but at best his staff removed a dozen stations from the books. When he urged newly appointed Interior Minister Hanif Atmar to produce a security plan to secure the remaining stations, the Afghans went behind his back and complained to Eide, who immediately took the Afghans' side. Still on holiday, Eide was concerned that Galbraith's questioning was endangering his—and the UN's—standing with the Afghans. He instructed Galbraith over the phone not to raise the matter of ghost polling centers again.[22] In early August, as if to mock Galbraith's efforts, a UN staffer uncovered a roomful of ballot boxes already stuffed with votes at the Independent Election Commission.[23]

Eide returned to Kabul furious at Galbraith, whom he suspected was acting as Holbrooke's pawn in his effort to oust Karzai. "The proposal would have damaged one candidate—Karzai—and benefited others," Eide later wrote, noting that most of the 1,200 sites Galbraith wanted closed were in the south, where Karzai drew his support.[24]

There was an additional calculation for both Eide and Galbraith to make. Against the odds, the past few weeks had seen a rival to Karzai emerge: Abdullah Abdullah, the former Afghan foreign minister. His main proposal was to replace presidential rule with a parliamentarian system, an idea the UN first proposed in 2001. It wasn't the most emotive of campaign topics—that was being waged by former planning minister Ramazan Bashardost, who was living in a tent on the Kabul–Kandahar highway in protest against corruption. Yet Abdullah's rise, and his Tajik base of support, raised the stakes. The perception of a stolen election might draw Abdullah's supporters onto the streets. Even with the looming prospect of unrest, Eide still dismissed Galbraith's initiative to close down questionable polling centers as politically motivated. Indeed, when the two men met on Eide's return, he bluntly told Galbraith, "I know why you're here. You're a little Holbrooke."[25]

There was a certain truth to Eide's accusation. Galbraith was not close to Holbrooke, and had only been championed for the post in Kabul after a chance encounter in Islamabad. Yet he shared with Holbrooke his assessment of Karzai, and was naturally on the lookout to bolster his own credentials in Washington. By the same token, Galbraith considered Eide to have taken his identification with Karzai too far.

United Nation's deputy envoy to Afghanistan, Peter Galbraith, and his boss, the Norwegian diplomat Kai Eide, had a fractious relationship over the fraudulent Afghan elections in 2009. (Photo courtesy of Peter Galbraith)

All of these contentions made for a tragicomic few days in late July at the UN residence in the grounds of the palace. Eide and Galbraith were billeted together, sharing frosty looks on the stairs, or passive-aggressive exchanges in the giant dining room. As Eide lamented, "I no longer had any place to seek rest or a few hours of calm." Galbraith then left for a short break, leaving Eide to push the Karzai administration to submit a final list of polling stations and a security plan. Karzai's ministers told Eide that they would present this material on August 16, four days before the election.

Finally Eide started to get alarmed. There were real logistical issues in bringing material and staff to the polling centers in time. "To believe that the most difficult and inaccessible polling centers could be reached in such a short time was delusional," he said.[26] When Eide presented Karzai with his worries, the Afghan president gave an impression of concern, as if the ability to stage credible polls in Afghanistan's remote valleys would affect the outcome.

G albraith woke on polling day, August 20, with a sense of foreboding. The last few days had seen a flurry of electioneering by the main candidates, with thousands of Afghans attending political rallies. There had even been a televised presidential debate among Karzai, Ashraf Ghani, and the protest candidate, Bashardost. It was all a charade as far as Galbraith was concerned. Even before Galbraith had finished brushing his teeth, his phone rang with news from Kandahar of eight explosions. It was the start of one of the most violent days of the war. How could free, fair elections take place in this environment?

After breakfast, Galbraith visited a women's polling station in Kabul. He saw a short line of women, some in bright blue burkas, others dressed in their finest clothes, clutching their children's hands, all chattering excitedly as they waited. It was galling to think of what was going on behind the scenes.

There were soon reports of what Galbraith called "retail" fraud: officials directing people how to vote, use of "indelible" ink that could be washed off, children voting, and proxy voting. Such tactics, however, were unlikely to change the overall outcome. Galbraith knew that what really mattered was the wholesale fraud—the type possibly being facilitated by the governor in Kandahar, who banned all vehicles from the streets in an order that left UN election monitors locked down in their offices.

By mid-morning, the first rough turnout figures from local UN staff were emerging from the south. There was no single method for collecting the figures. In some areas, UN officials were present at polling stations; elsewhere they relied on phone calls from contacts. All evidence seemed to suggest the count was very low, less than 10 percent in Kandahar and Helmand. Only in Nangarhar was the figure approaching a respectable 50 percent. That didn't stop the British embassy from claiming that 50,000 to 100,000 people had voted in Lashkar Gah in Helmand—which would have meant at least a 100 percent turnout—a sign that many western officials were as keen as the Afghans to pretend all was going well.

When Eide was briefed on the low turnout figures, he gave the first indication of how he intended to approach the disaster. "Don't release the turnout figures," he instructed Galbraith. "We need to wait for the Independent Election Commission."[27]

Galbraith, however, wasn't going to wait for crisis to break. Like any talented diplomat, he had a nose for an opening. Given the low turnout, Karzai was unlikely to have gotten above the 50 percent needed to avoid a second election runoff. Either that, or the fraud was going to be so big that Karzai's position might be untenable. Was this the opportunity that Richard Holbrooke had been waiting for to force the president out and install one of his rivals?

That evening he had dinner with Holbrooke at the US embassy. Holbrooke had been advised by the US embassy to keep a low profile. But that was the sort of warning that all but guaranteed he would make himself visible. What Galbraith told him made it sound like his perseverance was about to be rewarded: Karzai would inevitably be replaced. He simply didn't have the numbers without the fraudulent votes, and if he insisted on using them, the international community would be forced to weigh in against him.

The following morning, Holbrooke had breakfast with Eide, Eikenberry, and a few others and declared, "It's clear that Karzai cannot have won on the first round, and if the results showed he did, they were fraudulent."[28] A second round was inevitable, he added, not least to "clear the air" after all the irregularities. Eide looked uncomfortable but was forced to agree. Holbrooke announced he was on his way to see Karzai for lunch, prompting Eide to warn him about raising the issue of a second-round vote with the Afghan president, who already saw Holbrooke as hostile. "I'm warning you, be very careful; this is very dangerous," Eide told Holbrooke. "You should not tell Karzai that."

"I know how to handle Karzai," Holbrooke asserted.[29]

By the time the American got to the palace, Karzai had already learned what Holbrooke was going to propose, and appeared furious.[30]

He accused the US envoy of "undermining the election process and my presidency." Karzai denied all knowledge of election fraud. Hanif Atmar recalled that afterward, Karzai joked with his inner circle over how he'd run rings around Holbrooke. "Karzai was amused," recalled Atmar later.[31]

It was to be a turning point in Karzai's presidency, and in Holbrooke's own career. Leaving the palace, the American began to doubt his course of action. He had known there was little appetite for change in Washington, but he'd appeared to be hoping that if he pushed hard enough Karzai would fall. He hadn't, and now the risk was that the White House would be left with a fraudulent election, the abiding mistrust of Karzai, and a nation-building effort that looked a shambles. Holbrooke was suddenly having to scramble to save his position, and to avoid becoming the fall guy for the situation he had helped engineer.

Over at the UN, Galbraith hadn't given up hope of rescuing the situation. The next day, on August 22, he visited Abdullah, who had begun to raise the issue of fraud and whose candidacy was backed by the Tajik-dominated Northern Alliance. Galbraith intended to reassure him that the UN was aware of the fraud. There was a certain irony to this, considering Abdullah followers were, in all likelihood, also stuffing ballot boxes. The UN diplomat went on to reiterate his belief that a second round run-off was inevitable, that Karzai's position remained weak. In broad terms, Galbraith raised the idea of him taking on a refashioned prime minister's job, with Karzai moving into a purely ceremonial role.[32] Abdullah was interested but noncommittal. Afterward Galbraith called Tony Blinken, Biden's national security adviser, to tell him about the scheme. Blinken was receptive to the idea, but loathe to get ahead of President Obama or make a move before election fraud was clear.[33]

In working such back-channels, Galbraith was travelling way beyond his mandate. Eide later accused Galbraith of "freelancing," dangerously destabilizing the situation either for his own self-aggrandizement or in pursuit of what he saw as American interests (or a combination of both). Galbraith insisted he was simply keeping all interested parties abreast of events, although few of his staff believed him to have been impartial.[34]

Galbraith's initiative never got going, and failed to slow the swinging of the pendulum towards Karzai. If anything, the intrigues of Holbrooke and then Galbraith were only strengthening his position.

"One of the ironies of the election was that Holbrooke greatly strengthened Karzai's position at the expense of his own," noted Vali Nasr, one of Holbrooke's advisers.[35]

When Karzai met Eide the same day, he announced he had won up to 65 percent of the vote, which even the Norwegian was forced to admit was "unrealistic." Eide then raised the matter of fraud.

"Where do you believe there has been fraud?" Karzai asked. The fraud was too obvious for anyone to accept Karzai's protestations. Yet Eide believed it was important to maintain the election process, no matter how tarnished it had become. And if that meant victory over his enemy Holbrooke, he wouldn't complain. Karzai circled the conversation back to his treatment at the hands of the Americans, a subject on which Eide could only empathize. Eide ended up telling Karzai, "I can't be neutral; when they [Galbraith and Holbrooke] are against you, they are also against me."[36]

As the Norwegian would discover over the next few days, the extent of the fraud was so vast it was hard to identify areas where some form of rigging hadn't taken place. Just as Galbraith had warned, ballot boxes were arriving in Kabul from polling stations that had never been opened. Others contained more votes than the electoral roll suggested were possible, or more than the low turnout projected. In some cases, the ballot papers were still glued together, as they were when they arrived from the printer. The fraudsters hadn't even bothered to separate them into single polling papers. The UN's unofficial figures suggested that as many as 30 percent of Karzai's votes were fraudulent. In several provinces, including Kandahar, four to ten times as many votes were recorded as voters had actually cast.

The operation was, Eide conceded, "impressive," but he resisted calls from within his own team to comment on the scale of the fraud. It wasn't his job to pass judgment on the election; the special Electoral Complaints Commission was meant to evaluate any allegations. The UN had appointed most of its members, and given the growing rumors of fraud, it was more important than ever to follow the constitutional process, Eide believed, and let the commission reach its judgment.

Karzai, though, had no intention of letting the UN rob him of his presidency. On September 2, the Independent Election Commission announced it would not refer suspect ballot boxes to the Electoral Complaints Commission. For many on Minna Jarvenpaa's small UN team in Kabul, that was the final indignity. They had worked for months to deliver a credible election and weren't prepared to rubber-stamp a sham. During a turbulent meeting the team agreed to either go public or resign if Eide continued to ignore the fraud. Galbraith said he would join them in their protest and represent their cause to Eide.

Eide, who was in Norway at the time, realized that his career was on the line. A story about the likely fraud was leaked to the UK *Guardian*, prompting Eide to threaten to fire one of the British diplomats on the team. He rushed back to Kabul and faced down his staff at the UN compound. "We are witnessing the abuse of the UN's reputation. The time for action has come," one of the staffers said. Jarvenpaa and several others suggested that the international community should force Karzai to accept significant concessions, such as creating a prime ministerial role with considerable powers, and UN authority to vet Afghan government appointments.[37]

Eide was flustered and red-faced. He still clung to the idea of adhering to the election process to prevent anarchy, a position that also deflected criticism of his role in letting things come to that pass. Galbraith intervened and suggested that they step outside to talk privately. He had a solution, he told Eide once they were alone in the palace garden. In light of the fraud and the months it would take to conduct a recount, Karzai should be prevailed upon to step aside—technically his term as president had already expired—and allow a new, interim government to be installed, possibly under the leadership of Ashraf Ghani, who had received a paltry 3 percent of the vote, or Ali Ahmad Jalali, a former interior minister, who hadn't run. Galbraith suggested he could fly to Washington at once, and along with Vice President Joe Biden present the proposal to President Obama.

Eide immediately sensed that Galbraith had overplayed his hand. His proposal was as preposterous as Holbrooke's had been, and clearly had not been approved in Washington. The accusation from his own staff that he was ignoring the fraud had shaken him. But Eide felt on surer ground when it came to what he saw as Galbraith's blatant politicking. He wanted to think about it overnight then decide, in part so he could doublecheck with Eikenberry on the official US position, shore up his support in the office, and make sure no more damaging information leaked. Eikenberry confirmed Galbraith was out on a limb.[38]

The next morning, Eide told Galbraith that he thought his idea was terrible, and he rejected it. Galbraith folded and offered to go on an indefinite leave of absence from the office. On October 1, the UN Secretary General Ban Ki-moon went further and sacked Galbraith, despite receiving a letter from the American outlining his concerns. It appeared that Eide had won, but the sense of victory did not last long. A few days after Galbraith's dismissal, the letter he had written to Ban Ki-moon was leaked to the *New York Times*, revealing what insiders had known for weeks: the depth of the fraud and the international community's apparent complicity in covering it up. The accusations were devastating to the war's standing in the West, coming after such a bloody summer for the British and American militaries, and with opinion polls showing declining support for the conflict. "The fraud has handed the Taliban its greatest strategic victory in eight years of fighting the United States and its Afghan partners," Galbraith went on to write in a series of articles.[39]

If anything, Galbraith's charge understated the impact. The election fiasco undermined almost every aspect of the war. Karzai was accused of being the sort of venal, corrupt leader the international community had pledged to relegate to Afghanistan's history with their costly nation-building effort. Meanwhile, the fraud cast western leaders like Obama and Brown, with their rosy pronouncements of Afghanistan's budding democracy, as desperately out of touch. That the deputy head of the UN had apparently been sacked for trying to speak out only added to the impression that the hollow heart of the western project in Afghanistan had been exposed.[40]

Galbraith's career with the UN was finished. But in a sense the fiasco redeemed both him and Holbrooke to the degree that it revealed how profoundly misguided—and ultimately self-corrupting—the West had become in its mission to forcibly remake Afghanistan in its own image. Yet their treatment of Karzai had been high-handed, reckless, and unfair. The only Pashtun-dominated province that had witnessed a sizeable turnout, Nangarhar, gave Karzai a sizeable majority, suggesting that if a free and fair poll had been held in the south he would have comfortably won the election. Karzai's probable victory only underscored the folly of holding an election that could never return a representative vote, and which then risked turmoil when Karzai's supporters sought to fill in the blanks.

Kai Eide did his best to salvage the election—and his own career. He recognized that some form of recount was necessary with the clearly fraudulent votes excluded. That set him on a collision course with Karzai, whose share of the vote would fall below the 50 percent cutoff mark needed to avoid a second round, according to UN estimates. Eide knew that another vote was unavoidable—just as Holbrooke and Galbraith had been urging from the outset.

Karzai was adamant that he had enough votes, leading an exhausted Eide to offer to resign if the Afghan president did not back down. As the diplomat told Karzai, his approach had been based on respecting the democratic process and the constitution. "If you say that you will not respect that, then I have no option other than to resign," Eide said.[41] The impasse was resolved only after a visit by US Senator John Kerry, who suggested including some of the fraudulent boxes in the final tally, which would boost Karzai's vote from 48 percent to 49 percent, a bizarre ruse that appeared to win the Afghan president's support for a second vote, albeit by undermining what remained of the electoral process.

Kerry's solution amounted to a tacit acceptance that the election had been a sham, and Eide came to see that the international community had lost its bearings. "I had serious doubts if we understood [Afghan] society well enough to make the right assessment of what constituted fraud and what did not. What did we know about the life in little Afghan villages of a hundred or so voters, where nobody could read or write. . . . I was afraid that our lack of insight could lead us to serious misjudgment," he later wrote.[42]

The West wanted to put the election debacle to rest, but there was a final, savage twist to come. On October 28, Eide awakened to the sound of gunfire originating a few hundred yards from his bedroom. He did not immediately suspect a Taliban attack—feuds between Afghan militias were regularly resolved with guns. But he grew more concerned when the shooting continued and the first explosions rocked the compound. A few minutes later, the head of his security team texted him that a nearby guest house used by UNDP-Elect, and housing most of the organization's election workers, was under attack.

As Eide was to learn over the course of that same morning, insurgents dressed in police uniforms had quickly overwhelmed security at the walled entrance to the guest house. At least one suicide bomber had detonated his vest within the lower courtyard as insurgents began firing at the main building. Most of the staff on the second floor succeeded in scrambling out of their beds. A US contractor named Chris Turner had grabbed his AK-47 and shepherded them to a first-floor laundry room, where they barricaded themselves inside. Turner, still in his pajamas, provided covering fire. Other UN staffers in the building managed to escape by sneaking out of their balcony windows and onto neighboring rooftops.

Louis Maxwell, a member of the UN's close protection team and a former US Navy contractor who had been staying at the guest house, rushed to the roof with Lawrence Mefful, a colleague from Ghana, and returned fire into the courtyard. This stopped the insurgents from entering the building and killing everyone inside. Instead the attackers fired grenades into the first floor, setting the lobby ablaze. One small group of UN staffers was trapped in a second-floor bathroom, and two more women remained trapped in their rooms. They called their colleagues, as the flames started to consume the upper floors. "They were panicked," Turner recalled. "They were yelling, 'What should we do? I'm going to die.'"[43] One woman tried to make a dash for it and was shot through the head. Another burned to death.

Local police briefly showed up but then mysteriously departed. When they did return to the scene an hour later, the fighting had largely died down. Turner and the bulk of the staff had escaped, leaving just those who remained in the second-floor bathroom and security guards on the roof.

A UN investigation into the incident revealed what happened next. Afghan guards entered the building and dispatched at least two of the survivors, including Mefful. There was no excusable pretext for the killings, the report concluded. "There was no chance of mistaking the UN staff for Taliban attackers," noted one UN worker who had contributed to the investigation.[44]

A third killing took place outside the compound, captured on video by a German diplomat's phone. Louis Maxwell, whose heroics had saved two dozen lives, was standing casually on the street among a group of Afghan guards. He was armed, but there was little mistaking the African American for a Taliban recruit. The video shows him collapsing from a single shot fired from the side; given the narrowness of the street, the shooter likely was standing nearby. As Maxwell collapsed, one of the security guards standing near him grabbed his weapon and ran off. It was a tragic ending to a tragic day. But for Maxwell's intervention, the UN would have lost many more lives that day, which might have ended their mission and made a second-round ballot impossible.

The Taliban quickly claimed responsibility for the attack, but as details emerged over the following days, suspicions mounted that Afghan security forces had connived with them or at the very least knew it was coming. The symbolism of attacking the UN agency that was tasked with potentially overseeing the runoff, was apparent. When pushed on the matter, Afghan Interior Minister Hanif Atmar acknowledged that he had received "warnings" about the attack but did nothing to alert the UN.[45] His motives for not passing on the information are not clear, although UN workers had been subjected to several attacks over the preceding months, and threats were commonplace. Atmar appeared to have fallen a long way since the days of the National Solidarity Program when he was the darling of the aid world.

One clear beneficiary of the attack was Karzai: The same day as the assault, Abdullah agreed to speak with the Afghan president about a possible power-sharing agreement. Abdullah had been holding out for a second-round vote. Yet Karzai offered him nothing when they met. A few days later, on November 1, Abdullah contacted the president to announce his withdrawal from the race. His associates later claimed the Tajik leader withdrew because he feared a second ballot would lead to "increased instability," such as the attack on the UN.

As it turned out, Atmar didn't last much longer either. Early the following year, Karzai sacked him, along with his national security adviser, Amrulleh Saleh, on the pretext they had not provided adequate security for a Loya Jirga. Western diplomats wondered whether Karzai wasn't dispensing with potential rivals now that their uses had expired. Atmar's kudos with the West had been extremely useful in managing the election fraud. But now that the elections were over and the Afghan president had avoided the Americans' push to remove him from office, what use did Karzai have for a West-leaning minister so close to the reins of power?

CHAPTER 26

Political Expediency

The 2009 election was a death knell to international support for the war. This "clumsy and failed putsch," as US Defense Secretary Robert Gates called it, exposed the gulf between the idealized western vision that America and its allies had claimed their soldiers were fighting for in Afghanistan and the corrupt democracy that had taken root there.[1] Of course, Washington had known for some time that President Hamid Karzai wasn't the visionary leader the Bush administration had introduced to the world in the wake of the World Trade Center attacks, and Afghanistan wasn't poised to become the prosperous democracy for the surge. Now that the public was catching up, Obama needed to come up with a new narrative for the war.

The trouble was that the president appeared reticent to stake out a clear position, distracted as he was by the financial crisis and diminishing public support for the conflict. He had deployed 21,000 additional troops, which suggested he favored one final muscular effort to win the war. Yet he had not backed a "fully resourced" counterinsurgency since his earlier endorsement of Bruce Riedel's review in March 2009. Even then, he had made it clear that he saw al-Qa'eda—and not the Taliban—as the principal enemy in the region, which implied he supported a more limited counterterrorism operation. He was aware that to many in the US the conflict was starting to look brutal and senseless, with its connection to the events of 9/11 and America's original enemy—al-Qa'eda—increasingly distant, and the promise of nation-building unfulfilled.

The lack of clarity on where the president stood left his foreign policy and military teams in disarray. Richard Holbrooke had gone so far as to urge the creation of a viable peace process. But he had lost all credibility in the wake of his effort to oust Karzai. Members of Obama's national security team

280

like Joe Biden who had never fully bought in to the war felt the election fraud confirmed their instincts that it was unwinnable and therefore time for the US to extricate itself from the country. However, David Petraeus was determined to turn the war around with a full counterinsurgency campaign. The president's reservations about doing so were clear to some of Petraeus's staff, but they felt that Obama had committed to further increases through the Riedel reviews, as well as through his public declarations that America must defeat the Taliban.

However, as that had not translated into a changed mission statement, the military remained determined to push ahead even though it was becoming increasingly clear over the summer that Obama was not going to accept advice for more troops. Those familiar with Petraeus's thinking said that the general only became aware of a change in the president's thinking later in the year, after the National Security Council issued a directive in August that again affirmed a counterinsurgency approach.

Yet Obama could not have been clearer with Petraeus that the 21,000 troops he had authorized for Afghanistan needed time to settle in before assessing their impact in December at the earliest. That meant no more troops in the short term. From the military's point of view, that sounded like stalling when action was needed, and senior officers weren't to be dissuaded.

The man who would lead the military's drive to escalate the war was Lieutenant General Stanley McChrystal. He was a gaunt, driven fifty-five-year-old, who had made his name in Iraq running the "Death Star," the operational headquarters of the special forces, which was responsible for thousands of Iraqi deaths. While Petraeus lapped up the accolades of victory in Iraq, those in the know credited McChrystal for much of the actual turnaround; he had even kicked down doors on a few raids himself. He slept only five hours a night, often ran eight miles a day, and ate one sit-down meal a day (though this was usually a giant mess-hall affair of burritos and ice cream).[2] Petraeus was thoughtful, sophisticated, as comfortable at a think-tank reception as he was in the back of an MRAP vehicle. McChrystal saw himself as the hard-charging warrior who led men into battle.

McChrystal had taken command in Kabul earlier in June 2009 before the election fiasco broke. His first job was to prepare a review of the war, which Petraeus had already determined would be a means to request more troops from Obama.[3] McChrystal used the opportunity to assemble an influential cast for his assessment team, to add credibility to those findings on Capitol Hill and with the media down the line. His appointees included an aide to Senate Armed Services Committee chairman Carl Levin, the deputy director of the State Department's stabilization and reconstruction office, and think-tank stalwarts like the conservative pundit Frederick Kagan, who'd helped formulate the Iraq surge. Starting in July, McChrystal and his team had criss-crossed the country on their fact-finding mission.

McChrystal asked his advisers to keep an open mind and to judge the war on its merits. The general himself was predisposed to seeing the country as being on the verge of collapse, and hence in need of more troops. Yet he quickly came to realize that large swathes of the country were relatively peaceful.[4] Indeed, the areas where the fighting was heaviest could be boiled down to 60 or so districts out of 398, and most of those were in the east and south of the country. These areas also happened to be those with the heaviest concentrations of western troops.

From these insights McChrystal drew two conclusions about the current disposition of western forces. In the east, he understood, like his predecessor McKiernan, that the American strategy was fundamentally flawed. The US military had employed counterinsurgency tactics in the remote valleys of Kunar and Nuristan provinces for almost three years with limited results. McChrystal didn't regard the situation in the east as a repudiation of counter-insurgency. He felt that US troops were too thinly stretched across the maze of valleys to tip the balance in their favor. But he did question whether sending more troops into places like the Korengal and Waigal valleys made sense given the finite number of troops at his disposal. He made plans to continue the process of withdrawal from some of eastern Afghanistan's remoter valleys the following year.[5]

The rationale of putting soldiers where the Afghan populations were led McChrystal to the obvious conclusion that Kandahar was the place to concentrate forces in the south—the initial instinct of Brigadier John Nicholson the previous year, before the British had persuaded him otherwise. McChrystal's assessment team questioned Nicholson's decision. Andrew Exum, one of McChrystal's advisers, was alarmed by the deteriorating security situation in and around the country's second-largest city. Following Operation Medusa in 2006, Canadian forces had never really gained full control over the troublesome Noorzai tribe in Panjwei to the southwest of the city, and over the past year the Alakozai in the Arghandab—a pro-government tribe at one stage—had also sided with the Taliban.

Just how endangered Kandahar was that summer of 2009 was debatable. At one point in June, the Dutch general in Kandahar, Mart de Kruif, received a worried call from McChrystal telling him he was receiving reports that the city was about to fall. De Kruif, who was visiting local officials inside the city, had to assure him that all was, in fact, peaceful. Nonetheless, Exum dramatically described Kandahar as the "single point of failure in Afghanistan."[6] Any additional surges needed to focus on the city and its environs.[7]

This was where McChrystal's analysis over the summer ran up against the politics of military deployments. A sizeable chunk of any new troops he might get for the surge were likely to be US Marines. The problem was that by the summer of 2009, Camp Leatherneck, the US base in Helmand, was a sprawling city and logistical hub for more than 10,000 soldiers. Two battalions' worth of troops were invested in the southern Helmand towns of Nawa and Garmsir. McChrystal knew the marines would insist on sending additional forces to Helmand to ensure the Corps could be supplied and maintained by their own logistics chain. They would also be reluctant to shift their existing forces to Kandahar, at least not while there were ongoing operations in Helmand.

McChrystal wasn't about to pick a major fight with the marine hierarchy. He wasn't even sure he would have won the argument.[8] Instead McChrystal decided to make a virtue of necessity and "finish off Helmand" with the idea that he could then focus the military on Kandahar. In effect, he was confirming a shift of the war effort from the mountain valleys of eastern Afghanistan to the equally remote communities of Helmand.

McChrystal had no intention of getting bogged down in Helmand. His instinct was to launch an immediate operation into the troubled town of Marja—the same town the British had persuaded the marines to avoid earlier in the year. He once again encountered the UK's objections about picking a major fight before the elections, and the Brits' preference to push the marines into Helmand's outlying districts. McChrystal decided to postpone the operation in Marja until later in 2009.

In the meantime, he was left overseeing the marines' deployment into the remoter corners of Helmand ahead of the elections. It wasn't an ideal situation, but the one thing that could be said about their operation to date was the marines had done a fine job in the Helmand towns they had occupied. Particularly striking was the transformation of Nawa, twenty miles to the south of the provincial capital Lashkar Gah. Where marines had waged pitched gun battles a few weeks before, they now strolled around without helmets, earnestly jotting in their notebooks the local concerns.

McChrystal had taken to calling the town of Nawa "our number one Petri dish."[9] It was an example of what surge troops could achieve, he believed. As he worked on his assessment in July and August, he made sure a steady stream of congressional delegations visited the town and that word was spread in Washington of the marines' miraculous work. The lap from the military base around the town's local market became so well trodden that the marines started calling it the "Nawa 500."

In fact, Nawa's success was less of an emerging trend than a fortuitous blend of factors. Nawa had a single dominant tribe, the Barakzai, which meant that once brought on side, the whole town could be expected to pull together. By contrast, most communities in Helmand had multiple competing groups looking to use the foreigners at their rivals' expense. A further advantage for Nawa was the presence of Lieutenant Colonel William Mc-Cullough, the talented marine officer in charge of the district and a one-man civil administration—"police chief, judge, warrior, school principal, farmer, district governor and counselor," according to one journalist who witnessed him in action.[10] His very ubiquity in Nawa covered gaps in the local government.

Some of McChrystal's assessment team readily discerned the problems hiding under Nawa's calm facade: the fragile social fabric and the lack of Afghan government involvement. The report the team wrote at the end of August acknowledged that so far Karzai's administration had proven itself unable or unwilling to hold the towns that the British or the US Marines had secured in Helmand. However, they believed that American and international forces could provide a "bridging capability" until the Afghans were ready to assume control. But first they needed to wrest the country back from the Taliban.[11]

The assessment that McChrystal sent to the Pentagon on August 31 made the case unequivocally for more troops. The alternative was almost certain defeat, the report claimed, an idea that was raised fourteen times in the sixty-six-page document. No mention was made as to what would make the Karzai government start assuming responsibility for areas pacified by western forces. The election debacle that was gripping Kabul at the time appeared to call into question Karzai's suitability as a partner. Petraeus embraced the findings, and Gates agreed to pass them on to the president.

The one piece of information missing from the analysis was how many troops McChrystal wanted to turn the war around. McChrystal hadn't wanted to pitch hard numbers until he was sure the White House was "primed" by the assessment. All along, however, he and Petraeus had suspected they needed over 100,000 troops in the country, along with a significant increase in the number of Afghan soldiers to reach the troop density that counterinsurgency doctrine required. That required a further 40,000—on top of the 21,000 troops Obama had already agreed to and the 30,000 already in the country before that.[12]

General Stanley McChrystal led the US surge in Afghanistan that sought to defeat the Taliban for good. (Photo by PO1 Mark O'Donald)

The White House appeared to sense the public relations campaign under way in Helmand, and dispatched to Afghanistan National Security Advisor Jim Jones to get a handle on what the military was planning. Jones warned the marine commander in Helmand, Larry Nicholson, that the White House was already feeling "a bit singed" over the earlier troop request, and said that if McChrystal asked for more troops, Obama was likely to have a "Whiskey Tango Foxtrot" (WTF) moment. This last comment ran in the *Washington Post*.

McChrystal had been bracing for such naysaying in Washington. Two weeks after submitting his assessment to the White House in August, he sent his request for more troops, framed as a choice among three options—11,000, 40,000, and 85,000—and made it clear that the middle number was the bare minimum to achieve his objective. At the same time, McChrystal's allies weighed in with their views. General Petraeus gave an interview to Michael Gerson, an opinion writer and former George W. Bush speechwriter, in which he argued that winning required a "fully resourced, comprehensive counter-insurgency campaign."[13] Other commentators accused Obama of betraying the military and throwing away the "progress" in Afghanistan, such as it was. In the White House, it felt like the military was engaged in an aggressive campaign to push Obama into agreeing to more troops.

Most damaging of all for Obama's desire to retain control of the process, McChrystal's assessment was leaked to journalist Bob Woodward within a few weeks of reaching Washington. The general denied any involvement, but there was little doubt that the leak served his argument. Defense Secretary

Robert Gates later blamed McChrystal's staff, but whoever was behind the leak, the damage was done. Obama had asked for the military's advice, and here it was, for the world to see: The president would have to take ownership of the war, either by accepting the assessment's findings or by publicly disagreeing with the military.

For all his efforts to convince Obama, McChrystal appeared strikingly naive when it came to manipulating public perception. He told the television program *60 Minutes* that the president had spoken to him only once since McChrystal took over the war, a comment that came across as a rebuke of the president. Four days later, McChrystal gave a talk at the Institute for Strategic Studies in London in which he was asked about surge alternatives like the one Vice President Joe Biden suggested, for a smaller force increase and a shift of strategy to counterterrorism. That would lead to "Chaosistan," McChrystal suggested, telling a magazine writer that the plan would be like fighting a fire by "letting just half the building burn down." Once again, he appeared to be pressuring Obama and straying into unprecedented—and unconstitutional—political waters.

The White House reacted furiously to McChrystal's comments, which further restricted Obama's freedom to maneuver. The president confronted Gates and Joint Chiefs Chairman Mike Mullen, saying that McChrystal's comments had put him in a box, and he "didn't like being boxed in."[14] He wondered whether there was a scheme by McChrystal, Mullen, and Petraeus to force his hand. "We would never do that intentionally," said Mullen, in carefully couched language.[15]

Indeed, the military was so confident of getting its troops that it began dispatching supplies and equipment to Kandahar before Obama had approved McChrystal's request. It looked like he was being sidelined.

On October 9, Obama finally convened his cabinet to discuss McChrystal's troop requests. That same morning the president had awakened at dawn to news that he was receiving the Nobel Peace Prize. The president was surprised by the news and among the first to admit that despite the high promise of his election, he had yet to deliver concrete results. The cabinet members who convened in the White House situation room that day were, like the president, divided on the merits of pushing the US deeper into Afghanistan.

On the pro side of the debate were the men in uniform, the Joint Chiefs chairman Admiral Mike Mullen, General David Petraeus, and via video link, Stanley McChrystal. Robert Gates and Secretary of State Hillary Clinton were also known to favor additional forces, but hung back at this early stage of the debate. On the other side were Vice President Biden, Richard Holbrooke, Karl Eikenberry, and Doug Lute, the NSC lead on Afghanistan. They advocated for a smaller expansion of troops, largely to help build up Afghan security forces, and a shift of mission back to counterterrorism. Unlike those in the military camp, those opposing the escalation were not working in concert. Lute and Eikenberry shared a frosty relationship and both disliked Holbrooke. That left Biden isolated. Although his views on the war had coalesced and he rambled less than he used to, he was a lone voice against the military's united front.

Obama projected an air of impartiality as his staff argued. That facade appeared to disguise the president's whirling political calculations. He had been able to pass off the last troop increase as his predecessor's decision, not his; this time, though, there would be considerable political cost for sending more troops to Afghanistan. Up until now, managing the war had taken place largely at the cabinet level; Afghanistan had never been Bush's war in the same way that Iraq had. Whether he liked it or not, Obama was going to have to make it his war now.

Neither option Obama's cabinet presented seemed like a good one. If he blindly accepted the military's advice, he ran the risk of escalating the war in Afghanistan and creating another Vietnam. He would also run afoul of his liberal base, who had rallied behind his campaign pledge to wind down the "War on Terror." Yet saying no to the surge request would expose him to the accusation he was weak on national security, the bane of every Democratic president. By refusing the military, he would open himself up to the accusation that he had spurned the chance to win the war.

It's understandable that Obama would want to mull over the decision, in the hope that clarity would emerge, and to give the impression—especially after the military's apparent attempt to box him in—that he was in control of the situation. Yet the debate that October remained weighted entirely in the military's favor: The only options on the table were more troops or defeat, according to McChrystal.[16] Biden had come up with his own plan for 20,000 more troops, half of which would be dedicated to training the Afghan military, the other half to counterterrorism operations. Biden consistently struggled to get the Pentagon to take the scheme seriously.[17]

Instead, the only options under real consideration were McChrystal's. And even then, of the three options the general presented via video link from Kabul—for 85,000, 40,000, or a training mission of 11,000—only one was a genuine option. McChrystal had included the high and low estimations only to give the illusion of choice. It was 40,000, take it or leave it.

McChrystal's angular face appeared on a flat-screen monitor on a wall of the situation room. As he launched into his PowerPoint presentation from Kabul, Obama pressed the general on the issue of al-Qa'eda. Hadn't that been the motivation for the war? If the goal was simply to contain al-Qa'eda, which at that time was believed to number no more than a few dozen militants hiding in the borderlands, why did the military need so many troops? Furthermore, noted Obama, al-Qa'eda's presence—such as it was—lay in the east of the country, and not in the south where the military wanted to dispatch the surge.

McChrystal responded with the Armageddon scenario: If Karzai's government fell to the Taliban, it would "open the door to al-Qa'eda's return." Obama must have recognized the tautological trick; it was the same ploy his speechwriters had used when he announced the first surge in Afghanistan. Without a clearly formulated alternative, however, it was easy enough for McChrystal to paint any option other than a surge as a disaster.

The debate in the White House was trapped by the same terms of the Bush administration. Yet vast areas of inquiry were left unexplored, such as the issue of whether the US was effectively using the troops currently deployed in Afghanistan. At that very moment, marine General Larry Nicholson was preparing to send a US Marine battalion—upward of 1,000 troops—to Now Zad. Few besides Nicholson seemed to think this deployment was of vital importance.

"It was a US Marine–driven operation that had less strategic importance but I knew how it had a strong psychological significance for them," said de Kruif, the Dutch commander in Kandahar.[18]

Had Obama questioned such deployments, he might have turned the tables on the military's leadership and told them that they needed to sort out their command structure and use the existing troops more efficiently before he got any more.

Then there was the matter of what the Afghan government made of a further escalation. Afghans' views were not seriously considered. Karzai had already indicated he was against more troops, and much else of the foreign occupation, prompting US Ambassador Karl Eikenberry to label the Afghan president an "inadequate strategic partner" in a memo that subsequently leaked. Karzai's opposition alone should have called into question the whole premise of the surge. The military's plans didn't contain a strategy for addressing the West's fractured relations with the Karzai administration after the election debacle—and the diplomats didn't offer one either.[19]

In addition, Obama's cabinet spent no time discussing what ordinary Afghans wanted. These were the men and women who would either embrace or kill US soldiers in due course. In Helmand, diplomats like Kael Weston were reporting extensively on public sentiment and had come to the view that many Afghans were ready to embrace a low-key and meaningful relationship with the West, but that more troops would spell trouble.[20]

The October cabinet meeting ended without resolution. Obama wanted more time to consider his options. That autumn, in a fetid atmosphere of leak and counter-leak, the ongoing election crisis in Kabul, and yet more bloodshed in Afghanistan's tribal hinterland, the White House witnessed a dozen more debates, which continued to pick at the issue of the surge without ever achieving clarity. Obama seemed to recognize the insufficient terms of the debate, and to inherently distrust his own military's advice. Nonetheless, he did not seek out alternatives from diplomats and soldiers who had a different view of conditions on the ground. The White House appeared to have lost interest in grand notions of what the western doctrine of intervention could deliver to Afghanistan. Yet it had not reached a more limited and realistic assessment of what could be achieved.

The president announced his compromise solution that December at a speech given to the West Point military academy in New York. He would split the difference. Instead of getting 40,000 troops over a minimum twenty-one-month period, the military would get 30,000 (plus as many as they could drum up from the international community) over nine months. Furthermore, he set a hard deadline of September 2011 for the first troops to start coming home. The speech was roundly condemned by all sides. The president's liberal base complained that the increase, combined with the earlier surge, would triple the war's scope in less than a year. Conservatives, meanwhile, labeled the plan "surge and retreat."

McChrystal told his aides the deadline made the "conditions for success difficult" and lent succor to the Taliban. At the very least it placed massive pressure to deliver a result in eighteen months, a proposition that went against the tenet of counterinsurgency and appeared to cast doubt on the entire western mission in Afghanistan. "It was hard to understand the president's reasoning," admitted one member of McChrystal's staff.[21]

Gates was also dismayed, not just by the deadline itself, but by Obama's entire attitude toward Afghanistan. "When soldiers put their lives on the line, they need to know that the commander in chief who sent them in harm's way believes in their mission," Gates reflected later. "They need him to talk often to them and to the country, not just to express gratitude for their service and sacrifice but also to explain and affirm why that sacrifice is necessary, why their fight is noble, why their cause is just, and they must prevail. President Obama never did that."[22]

Gates had picked up on Obama's fundamental ambivalence toward Afghanistan, as well as the way the president had placed the war's burden back onto the military. Obama might not think they could win the war, but at least he wouldn't be blamed for losing it. That would be for the generals to deal with.

The past few months had seen the military applying an unprecedented amount of pressure on the country's civil leadership. This was Obama's way of fighting back. He wrote a memo to McChrystal shortly after the surge announcement making clear that what he was approving wasn't a fully re-sourced counterinsurgency campaign, and that the military's time was limited. McChrystal's reaction isn't known, but it couldn't have been good. As one senior officer noted, Obama had given the military "just enough rope to hang itself by."[23]

CHAPTER 27

A Reckoning

Obama's announcement at West Point military academy to further escalate the war placed pressure to win the war on US military shoulders.
But it created a different problem for America's allies and particularly the
British in Helmand, where the bulk of the new troops would be going. Yet
they had finally recognized that the situation was so dire that they needed to
give the Americans as much territory as they would accept. Lieutenant General
Nick Parker, the senior British commander in Afghanistan and an officer of
rare insight, understood the stakes all too personally. That summer his son,
Captain Harry Parker, had lost both legs in an explosion while leading a patrol
in Helmand. "The tactical situation . . . was fragile. The reason that it was
fragile was because we were overextended," Parker concluded.[1]

Most urgently the British wanted the Americans to assume control of the
two strategically insignificant but dangerous towns of Musa Qala and Sangin,
which continued to see more British casualties than any other district in Afghanistan. This handover would free them to concentrate their forces in the
center of the province where the British-run Provincial Reconstruction Team
was based and where the UK had enough forces to guarantee security. However, Larry Nicholson, who was commanding the US Marine Corps, would
agree to take on Musa Qala, leaving the British to hold Sangin for at least
six more months and prove once again their commitment to the Americans.

The British Lieutenant Colonel Nick Kitson took over Sangin in October knowing that his men were in for a brutal deployment. The battalion
before his had lost twenty-four men over the summer, and the violence was
increasing. Kitson had 1,500 men in his 3 Rifles battle group, an increase
of several hundred over past tours. Yet like his predecessors, he was missing
crucial resources: A vital unit assigned to the area had been sent to central

Helmand, where UK efforts were increasingly focused. Satellite surveillance was limited, and basic technology, such as remote-controlled cameras to spot insurgents laying roadside bombs, was absent altogether. There was also a lack of mine-resistant vehicles, which the British had belatedly ordered, meaning that Kitson's men were denied a relatively safe means of traveling between bases. If the fighting that summer had begun with a spirit of false optimism, by the fall there was no illusion about what 3 Rifles was about to go through.

"We knew it was going to be a difficult tour, but nothing can prepare you for losing so many of your friends and comrades. It's the soldiers' bravery and determination that got us through," said Kitson, a laconic, levelheaded officer.[2]

Kitson was determined that missing equipment would not hamper his battalion. He wanted to follow counterinsurgency doctrine and push his men out of the larger outposts and into smaller positions around the town. From there they would patrol the alleys of Sangin on foot. The soldiers would be living among the people and providing security. At the same time, to overcome the lack of cameras and armored vehicles, his men would patrol around the clock to keep "eyes on" key routes and mitigate against the IED threat.

It proved a dangerous tactic: Kitson's men were exposed to more attacks, and the smaller bases were difficult to keep supplied. In a fifteen-man patrol base, five soldiers would guard the perimeter, another five would be preparing to set out on patrol, and the other five would already be outside the base. At any moment both the base and the patrol might be under attack, straining to the limits 3 Rifles' ability to respond.

It didn't take long for British casualties in Sangin to start mounting—five dead in 3 Rifles' first month in charge. Although Kitson believed his men were making progress, at Number 10 Downing Street in London, Prime Minister Gordon Brown and his advisers were not so sure. With each death, political pressure mounted for the British military to do less and stop patrolling.

The British General Nick Parker shielded officers like Kitson from much of this, but it only underscored for him the need to consolidate UK forces in central Helmand. At the same time, the American military was exacerbating the political pressure by accusing the British of hunkering down on their bases—demonstrably not the case in Sangin.

The matter came to a head after Obama's West Point address announcing the surge in December. Eight thousand additional marines were bound for Helmand. Parker immediately made the case to London that the UK should hand over Sangin to the US. To Parker's shock, Brown refused. A general election was approaching, and Brown's team feared that handing over the site of the greatest number of British casualties—almost a hundred—might open the government to the charge of cutting and running. With the US preparing to surge in Afghanistan, they couldn't afford to expose the military to another blow to its reputation. These political risks, they apparently calculated, were greater than those resulting from a few more British deaths in Sangin.

In an unprecedented act, Parker approached the leader of the Conservative Party, David Cameron, during a visit to Afghanistan in the hopes that the presumptive future prime minister might raise the matter of Sangin with Larry Nicholson. Cameron met with Nicholson in a cramped briefing room at Camp Bastion in Helmand province. The British brigade commander, James Cowan, made the pitch to Nicholson and his political officer, Kael Weston, that the new troops might be used to best effect in northern Helmand. Cameron nodded along.

Nicholson paused as if to weigh the proposal. In his view, the British had already crossed the line when they had voiced their opposition to the Now Zad deployment and leveraged their control over Helmand's PRT team to block reconstruction money to the town. Their scheme hadn't worked; Nicholson could draw from American funds. But he didn't enjoy being played like that or told what to do. So he looked Cowan in the eye and told him that the British should "stick it out in Sangin" and "get off their bases."[3]

If there was one charge guaranteed to depress and infuriate a British officer, it was that UK forces were shying away from combat. Cowan pointed out that one third of casualties among Western forces were British, although they constituted only one tenth of the international troops in Afghanistan. At the main hospital in Camp Bastion, which treated both nations' soldiers, the Brits received far more pints of blood than their American counterparts because they were doing more of the fighting in Helmand. They were bearing the brunt of the surge.

Weston hastily stepped in to defuse the situation. "There's been a lot of blood shed by all of us here," Weston suggested.[4] Cameron, meanwhile, looked pained. Like Obama, he had proven a conscientious listener to the military's woes, but he also wanted to avoid taking ownership of the war.

A few weeks later on December 15, a similar meeting took place, this time with British Foreign Secretary David Miliband and representatives from the British and American militaries. The question of Sangin was again raised, along with the matter of the US Marine deployment. Weston understood that the British military was not simply criticizing the US Marine deployment but also, he reflected later, "discreetly asking for help." As if to underline the point, Cowan's presentation was interrupted with the news that two more soldiers,

Lance Corporal David Kirkness and Rifleman James Brown, had been killed in Sangin by suicide bombers riding on an explosives-packed motorbike.

Weston drafted a cable to Ambassador Eikenberry; titled "US-UK at a Crossroads," the message argued that the US needed to ease British forces out of the most troubled areas of Helmand. By the same token, he was also starting to wonder why the military was getting sucked into these out of the way places. Weston had opposed the recently announced surge; nothing he saw on the ground in Helmand suggested that more troops were necessary there. If anything, by "going big" the US military was setting itself up to fail spectacularly.

What Afghanistan needed was steady, low-key engagement from America and its NATO allies. There were no easy answers in places like Sangin, but whatever solutions emerged were going to take time, Weston wrote to the US ambassador. He was aware that the British had begun low-level discussions with local tribes to the north of the town—subsets of the same Alakozai clan that had once tried to side with the Brits against the Taliban—but whether these discussions would bring results at this late stage was unclear.

At the very least, the US owed its British allies a hand. "We couldn't have a situation that made Basra look like child's play," Weston told the journalist Rajiv Chandrasekaran later. "Helmand was much more important in terms of British self-respect and the US/UK relationship partnership. We had to help our best friends in the world."[5] Weston persuaded Nicholson to cut the British some slack and agreed to take on Sangin as well.

But once Brown got wind of the British military's overtures toward the US Marines behind his back, he made it clear that the UK would not hand over Sangin anytime soon, leading to a scramble to prepare another battalion to take over from 3 Rifles. The moment was emblematic of the war. The British and American casualties were mounting rapidly, and public support was waning. Yet oddly, the UK deemed the political cost of leaving as too great. That left the soldiers to "crack on," as the British put it, through another brutal fighting season, without much hope but with plenty of bloodshed. It would take another reappraisal of the war's cost, in both Britain and America, before the political calculations would fundamentally change. The issue of honoring the war dead of both countries would play a role in that transformation.

The idea of repatriating the bodies of slain soldiers was a relatively new one in both the US and the UK. Doing so had become the norm only during the Korean War, and up until the Afghanistan war the arrival of the fallen back home turf had been carried out with little fanfare. The military believed this low-key affair was in line with the wishes of the families involved.

The US Department of Defense barred the media from photographing returning caskets. The ban had originally been put in place during the first Gulf War in 1991 and had resurfaced with the invasions of Afghanistan and Iraq. The Bush administration argued that repatriations needed to be treated with the utmost respect and should not be turned into political events by the presence of news cameras. There seemed to be a further consideration: Dead bodies revealed the true cost of war. The sight of coffins being unloaded from the back of transport planes might undermine the war effort.

In the US, bodies arrived at Dover Air Force Base in Delaware without ceremony, before being prepared for transportation to their burial sites.

Unfortunately, the resulting lack of publicity or oversight seems to have allowed for the bodies to be handled in less than respectful ways, as Defense Secretary Robert Gates first discovered in the spring of 2008. In May of that year, his office had received a distressed e-mail from an officer who had witnessed the return of a fallen soldier at the request of the dead man's wife. The transfer of the casket from the plane had "not been particularly dignified," according to Gates.[6] The body had then been driven off-site and stored in a building marked as a pet crematorium. There were separate areas for the storage of animal and human remains, but that was not evident from the exterior of the building. Seventy-five servicemen had been cremated at the site.

Gates was assured that human and pet remains had not been mixed. Still, the situation was clearly unacceptable. He canceled the military's contract with the crematorium and informed the press of his discovery the same day. The story followed on the heels of the revelations of the unsanitary conditions at the Walter Reed military hospital in Washington, DC, and the neglect of recovering veterans.[7] For Gates, the treatment of the country's dead and wounded servicepeople pointed to malaise at the heart of the Pentagon—a failure to recognize the real costs of the wars being fought and to adapt the military to the conflict's demands. One reason for this was the Pentagon's desire to get back to what it knew best: training and equipping soldiers for conventional warfare—not fighting bloody insurgencies in the developing world.

In 2009, in one of his first comments about the war, a newly inaugurated President Obama signaled his readiness to look again at the ban on photographing returning caskets. Gates was also in favor of lifting the blanket ban, provided doing so would be in accordance with the wishes of the grieving families. On April 6, 2009, the remains of air force Staff Sergeant Phillip Myers of Hopewell, Virginia, arrived at Dover. The body was met by eight members of Myers's family and forty journalists, who filmed and photographed as eight soldiers in white gloves carried the flag-draped casket away from the transport plane. Myers's job had been to disarm or detonate roadside bombs in Afghanistan, one of the most dangerous in the military. The thirty-year-old father of two had been caught trying to clear a road ahead of a military convoy.

Myers's was the first US repatriation ceremony to be recorded in the Afghan war. Within a year, just over half the families were allowing media coverage. By then, the air force had constructed a 6,000-square-foot Center for the Families of the Fallen, with a small hotel, meditation facility, and garden nearby. A dedicated mortuary had also been built. In March, Gates went to witness a transfer. There were four caskets in the hold of the plane. The men had been killed by a roadside bomb. Despite Gates's best efforts to re-equip the military with MRAP vehicles, the four troopers had been driving in a lightly armored Humvee.

Gates asked for time alone with the fallen before they were carried out of the plane's hold. It was night, and the rain was falling hard. The plane's side was lit by floodlights, whose cold, harsh glow contrasted with the gloom of the plane's interior and the dark outlines of the caskets. Gates kneeled beside each one, placing his hand on the flags, weeping quietly.

Meanwhile, in the UK, the defense ministry had also found a solution to honor the sacrifices of its soldiers. Up until 2007, the remains of dead servicemen and servicewomen were flown into the Royal Air Force base at Brize Norton, Oxfordshire, where a coroner examined them before releasing the bodies to the families. Renovations at the base, however, meant that they were taken to RAF Lyneham then transferred to the John Radcliffe hospital in Oxford for an autopsy, a route that took the military convoy bearing the caskets through the small Wiltshire town of Wootton Bassett. Local members of the British Royal Legion, a veterans' association, started standing at attention on the main street as the vehicles passed, and it wasn't long before crowds took to lining the road to pay their respects.

The public mourning at Wootton Bassett was uniquely British. For the hundreds who stood waving Union Jacks, there was a quiet solemnity to the occasion, with just a brief outpouring of grief when the hearse stopped in front of the town's war memorial, and wreaths were laid atop the cars. As the local Conservative member of Parliament, James Gray, observed, "There are no politics here: people are not making any comment as to whether this war is good, bad or indifferent. These are solemn, simple little ceremonies and that's all the town wants."[8]

After the procession, members of the British Royal Legion, many of them elderly veterans of World War II, gathered together the cards and other mementos left at the memorial: photos of soldiers holding babies, others in combat fatigues, notes saying, "I'll never forget you, you're my best mate" and "you will truly be missed, you're a braver man than any of us." Ninety-three-year-old World War II veteran Ken Scott was among those gathering up the mementos. "These messages are sacred," he told one reporter. "They shouldn't be blown away on the high street."[9]

CHAPTER 28

The Futility of Force

A fghan President Hamid Karzai greeted Barack Obama's West Point ad-dress with a mix of anger and dread. The election fiasco had proven to Karzai once and for all that the Americans did not have his best interests at heart, or those of his country. He told his inner circle that he viewed the es-calation of the war as counterproductive if not downright dangerous.[1] Yet he was powerless to prevent it, given his diminished status with the Americans. The idea that he was a puppet leader, placed on the throne to cover the dark designs of foreign powers, appeared to gnaw at him.[2] He suspected that the West had no interest in ending the war. How else to explain their blunders except as a plot to destabilize the country and submit him and his people to permanent American rule?

Karzai had started to think about his legacy. Was he prepared to defy the West's commands and prove himself an equal of those canny kings of old, who had taken advantage of foreign largesse without ever bending their knees? Richard Holbrooke's attempt to oust him during the elections had allowed him to valiantly strike that pose by opposing the superpower. That stand had given him a taste of what could be achieved by tapping into his country's rising anti-Americanism.

On November 3, 2009, Karzai gave a speech in which he referred to the West's nation-building effort as a "foreign occupation," and the Taliban as "his brothers." They would be embraced should they return home. The speech was largely rhetoric. The Taliban were well ensconced in Afghan-istan, and Mullah Omar had shown no interest in accepting Karzai's re-peated invitations to negotiate. What Karzai's comments did reveal was the nadir to which US-Afghan relations had sunk—which created a problem for Washington.

The US needed Karzai's support for its military surge to succeed. Yet few in the White House had any appetite—or standing in Afghanistan—to bring Karzai back into the fold. Obama appeared to have washed his hands of the Afghan president. Holbrooke was forever tarnished. And US Ambassador Karl Eikenberry had written a memo that accused Karzai of corruption and taking drugs, which was leaked to the *New York Times*. So the task of trying to win back Karzai fell to the US commander General Stanley McChrystal, who was still struggling to understand the country as he put together the most ambitious military operation of the war.

Over the fall, McChrystal paid court to Karzai in the unlikely hope of establishing a bond and winning support for the surge. The general enjoyed a better relationship with Karzai than almost anyone else in the government. A few months earlier, McChrystal had made a long-overdue offer to the Afghan president: Karzai would be included in future military decisions pertaining to Afghanistan. The offer went only so far; after all, Karzai couldn't veto the surge altogether. Yet it represented a tacit recognition that the US military would be fighting in vain without his support.

McChrystal also made concessions on Karzai's long-running grievance about NATO's indiscriminate use of air strikes and subsequent civilian casualties. The UN estimated that 2,118 civilians had been killed the previous year, a rise of 39 percent from 2007, with roughly half of the deaths caused by NATO and Afghan forces.[3] Karzai wanted air strikes to end altogether; McChrystal was prepared to dramatically rein in the use of airpower by introducing a stringent authorization process. He set new rules of engagement for forces on the ground, asking that they shoot only at Afghans who were armed and presented a clear danger to soldiers' lives. He also insisted that every American patrol be partnered with local security forces.

McChrystal's efforts went some way toward mollifying Karzai, but the election fiasco in September ruined the general's chances of winning over the president ahead of the surge. When it came to the next major operation—slated for the Helmand town of Marja—Karzai did what he had always done: He appeared to give the military his approval, while trying to turn the situation to his advantage. In January, McChrystal sought to fly Karzai to Lashkar Gah to promote the upcoming offensive in Marja and secure the tribal elders' support for the Americans. Karzai insisted on bringing his long-time ally Sher Mohammed Akhundzada, the former governor whose removal by the British the president blamed for provoking the insurgency. The British had accused him of cronyism and worse. Either way it was a rebuke to the western efforts. There was little McChrystal could do to dissuade Karzai.

The result was Karzai had neatly hijacked McChrystal's shura. Sher Mohammed was prominently positioned in front of the actual governor, Gulab Mangal,
raising the question of how much longer Mangal would remain in charge. Karzai regarded the man as a yes-man for the American and British military, and
seemed to resent his reputation for probity among western diplomats.[4] It was a
sign to the locals as to where the province was heading.

On top of that, Karzai stalled on providing officials to staff the local government needed to run Marja once the marines had liberated it. Dozens of
positions needed to be filled, but no local applicants stepped forward. It was
an embarrassing referendum on Afghans' confidence in the coming surge.
When the stipulation of a high school diploma was lifted, four Afghans eventually applied.

The lack of Afghan support for the operation in Marja should have called
into question its validity.[5] McChrystal, however, was not overly concerned. The surge was meant to transform the war's momentum. He believed
that once he started showing success, the doubters—including Karzai and
the White House—would be won over. In the meantime, he would have to
rely on the US State Department to provide stopgap governance in southern
Afghanistan. He wanted teams of US diplomats to deliver basic public services
in areas that were about to be wrested back under Afghan government control.
But here McChrystal was to be similarly disappointed.

The State Department was also finding it difficult to find civilians willing
to spend time in Helmand. The embassy had recently gone through a $500
million expansion to become the second largest such office in the world
(after Baghdad). In preparation for a "civilian surge," it had swelled to over
1,100 staff. But two thirds of those could be found in Kabul at any one
time. What's more, 40 percent did not last six months in the country. As
Marc Chretien, one of the diplomats who was prepared to brave the wilds of
Helmand, noted on the quality of incoming officials, "We're past the B team.
We're at Team C."[6]

There were exceptions, of course, like the deeply knowledgeable Carter
Malkasian, who deployed to the Helmand district of Garmsir and spent more
than three years there. Such dedication, which evoked memories of an ear-
lier generation of political officers (indeed the locals referred to Malkasian as
Carter Sahib, an old colonial title), suggested the quality of recruit the State
Department would need to provide to make headway in Afghanistan.

The embassy was equally poor at managing its cash resources. In 2009,
Richard Holbrooke had made the sensible decision to end DynCorp's

disastrous poppy eradication effort, although ending a multimillion-dollar deal with the Virginia-based contractor required political fortitude. DynCorp and the other large contracting firms hired lobbying firms like the one run by John Podesta to ensure that that money kept flowing—no matter how little was actually being delivered. Holbrooke, though prepared to take a fresh look at some contracts, was not interested in reforming the whole system.

When Clare Lockhart, Ghani's former adviser, pointed out to Holbrooke all the other wasteful US programs in Afghanistan, the American diplomat exploded: "I'm not here to save the taxpayer money—I'm here to do what it takes." In vain, Lockhart and an Afghan official asked for 50 percent of US government aid money to be given to the Afghan government to build up local capacity and cut some of the waste.[7]

Rajiv Shah, the USAID head, appeared to accept these arguments, but in the end the agency's funding for district-level programs was still doubled to $300 million. Like so many other western-designed projects, the program lacked both purpose and accountability and became one of the biggest boondoggles in USAID history. The mechanism for spending this money was called AVIPA—Afghanistan Vouchers for Increased Productive Agriculture—designed to pay day laborers an hourly rate for odd jobs around the district. Without the staff to assess the work or a good grasp of a local community's needs, the only measure of success USAID could come up with was "burn rate," that is, how much money they were able to shovel out of the gates of military bases. A high burn rate equaled success. In towns like Nawa, population 89,000, almost $30 million was spent in one year, $18 million of that through AVIPA and a sister program that handed out tractors and bags of wheat to Afghans the aid workers hoped were farmers.[8]

USAID's skewed metrics profoundly distorted the local economy. Nawa residents soon ran out of cleanup jobs around the town and were left to unclog irrigation canals. Yet because the AVIPA rate of $5 a day represented more than even doctors and teachers could earn on their own accord, Afghans of all professions turned out in droves to toil away at the ditches.[9] Schools and clinics were shuttered, and fields went untended. In fact the only sector the AVIPA program didn't affect was the opium industry, which like any good market merely raised its prices to ensure that enough manpower was available to work the harvest. As for the tractors and sacks of wheat, there were traffic jams at Afghan border crossings as the supplies were driven to Pakistan to be sold or exchanged, in some cases for sacks of fertilizer to make roadside bombs.[10]

Furthermore, AVIPA bypassed the Afghan government, which meant it boosted the Americans' reputation at the expense of the Karzai administration.

As the mayor of Lashkar Gah, Abdul Manaf, repeatedly complained, "The government in Kabul doesn't do anything for us."[11] The Americans, on the other hand, did—at least for the moment. The short-term nature of the American commitment in Helmand, and a sense among Afghans that the cash spigot simply couldn't last forever, only deepened locals' desire to extract what they could before the end. "Because the largesse is fleeting, there is urgency for Afghan government officials and contractors to grasp for as much as possible," wrote Scott Dempsey, a USAID officer who deployed to Nawa in 2009–2010.[12]

Stanley McChrystal often complained about the deficiencies of the US civilian surge that was meant to match his own investment of troops. But in the AVIPA program he had found the perfect counterpoint to the military's intervention: short-term, prone to abuse, and undermining local power structures. It was everything that had gone wrong so far in the war, magnified.

A s the February 2010 start date for the Marja offensive neared, General McChrystal tried to manage the excruciating levels of scrutiny for the operation that the debate had created the previous fall.

Strategically speaking, Marja wasn't the ideal location for such a showdown, but as a symbol of American intentions for Afghanistan it would have to do. McChrystal knew the fighting around Marja was going to be tough: He believed the Taliban were well ensconced within the community, which ran one of the biggest opium businesses in the country, possibly in history. McChrystal insisted this wasn't an operation against the poppy industry but against the Taliban—but that probably wasn't how the locals would see it.

The town itself was modest: a couple of fly-blown streets with steel-shuttered shops. Most of the district's 100,000 inhabitants lived in smaller communities and isolated compounds spread out over a maze of farmland, irrigation canals, and mud tracks. The main roads were heavily mined, meaning that the marines would have to work their way laboriously over canals and ditches to avoid the fate of the British the previous summer. This terrain provided ideal cover for the Taliban to execute its favored hit-and-run attacks.

The plan that McChrystal and his commander in the field, the British Major General Nick Carter, drew up was ambitious. They would avoid a full frontal assault and instead airlift two battalions of marines into the district in scattered pockets. Two Afghan army battalions, or *kandaks,* would be divided among the units to give the impression that the Afghans were active partners (the operation was called Moshtarrak, Dari for "together"). That would prove a hard illusion to maintain, given the woeful performance of Afghan security forces on earlier joint operations.[13]

Major General Nick Carter helped conceive of Provincial Reconstruction Teams in 2002 and played a key role during the US surge. (Photo by Robert Thaler)

As the night of the operation approached, McChrystal hadn't given up on meaningful involvement from Karzai, and updated him regularly on the plans. Karzai remained aloof, except when it came to the subject of reestablishing his old network in Helmand. The new police chief in Marja, he announced, would be Mirwais Norzai, an old buddy of Akhundzada's. A district chief had also been found: a man named Haji Zahir, who had spent three years in a German prison for stabbing his son.

McChrystal still insisted on getting the president's authorization for the operation. On the afternoon of February 12, with the operation due to begin at 11 p.m., the general's staff called the palace. Karzai had a cold and was taking a nap, the general was informed. A few hours later, Karzai was still apparently comatose. Almost 2,000 troops, US Marines and their Afghan counterparts, were readying their gear. Helicopters were fueling up ready to depart. The ninety-minute window for their departure was rapidly approaching. The weather over the next few days was set to be atrocious, meaning that if they missed the window, the operation could be delayed for days if not weeks. Given the hyping of the offensive, such a hiatus might make the surge look like a flop.

McChrystal hurried over to the palace, joined by Afghan Defense Minister Rahim Wardak and a posse of Afghan officials. They waited anxiously until Karzai finally appeared; "fatigue and the effects of his cold streaked his face," according to McChrystal. Karzai still had enough gumption to feign surprise at the general's visit, and ask innocently why he had come.

"Mr. President, the forces are in position and ready to launch the operation tonight, but I won't do so without your approval," said McChrystal.

"General McChrystal, you'll have to forgive me. I've never been asked to approve this kind of operation before," said Karzai.[14]

As McChrystal later reflected, that statement in itself "spoke volumes" about how the war had been conducted as well as Karzai's painful awareness of being treated as a puppet. McChrystal thought he was offering the president an opportunity for leadership. But for Karzai the American was the seventh US commander he had encountered promising to improve the country. Karzai looked skeptical as McChrystal laid out his plans for Marja, along with his intentions to limit civilian casualties and ensure that the Afghan security forces took the lead. "On one level, I think he questioned the genuineness of my request, fearing it was a charade to put a fig leaf, or 'Afghan face' on what was still an entirely Coalition-controlled operation," McChrystal surmised.[15]

Karzai proceeded to go back over the reasoning for the operation in Marja while McChrystal answered as graciously as he could, all the time knowing that the clock was ticking. In fact, Carter had already launched the operation. As the desert sky above Helmand throbbed with the sound of helicopter blades, McChrystal was still patiently explaining the rationale for the operation, and by extension the war itself. Luckily for him, Karzai eventually gave his approval.

As 2,000 marines emptied out of their helicopters and began to wade, stumble, and sprint through the Helmand night, and as the first IEDs ripped through earth and flesh, and gunfire scourged the outlines of buildings, trees, and men, the US was getting ever more enmeshed in a war that for all the discussion of protecting the people looked much like any other. It was bloody and desperate, and only a footfall or a hair trigger separated the living from the dead on either side.

Marja had been divided into three sectors for the assault. Two marine battalions partnered with the Afghan kandaks to occupy northern and central Marja. US special forces would support a third party primarily composed of Afghans that would occupy the south. The aim of each force was to seize key buildings that could be used as staging posts for methodically clearing the rest of the district. The area of operations covered only a few square miles.

As soon as the initial airlift was over in the early hours of February 13, the marines' advance from their sortie points was slow. The terrain of irrigation ditches and mudbrick was perfect for ambushes, and the Taliban appeared to have already sussed out McChrystal's rules of engagement that prevented the marines from shooting at unarmed Afghans. The fighters simply stashed weapons along the route of the marines' advance, took a few potshots, and then dropped their guns and walked away with impunity.

The advance was also hampered by another of McChrystal's stipulations, that every marine unit should partner with the Afghan army. The abilities of the Afghan troops rapidly became a dark running joke with the marines. Despite almost seven years of training and almost 200,000 soldiers under arms, only one Afghan battalion of 1,000 men was capable of carrying out independent counterinsurgency operations. From the marines' perspective, the Afghans were slovenly, often high on marijuana, and generally incapable of the simplest tasks. Most were recruited from the north and spoke no Pashtu. Their main job was to enter buildings first, but they often lacked the wherewithal to kick down doors.[16] During the operation the Afghan army lost more men to self-inflicted injuries than to the Taliban. Occasionally the marines also found weapons pointed at them and then hastily lowered, a sign of the growing tensions between the allies.

"The marines distrusted the Afghan army, and spent most of their time cussing them and shouting orders at them. The Afghans picked up on that and went even slower," recalled Captain Matt Golsteyn, who led a special

During the operation to capture Marja, Captain Matt Golsteyn (right) led Afghan forces into the south of the town, a largely successful operation, but one that won only grudging acceptance from local Afghans. (Photo courtesy of Matt Golsteyn)

forces team attached to an Afghan battalion in southern Marja. Golsteyn had much more success with his Afghan unit because it wasn't broken up and farmed out, and because he made sure the Afghans ran their own operations.

Civilian casualties were inevitable, and in the minds of most marines the dangers for Afghans had only increased because they could no longer directly call in air strikes. The authorization process took so long that most units didn't bother. Instead, the marines turned to using much less accurate shoulder-mounted rockets to hit targets. A few days into the fighting, Charlie Company from 1st Battalion, 6th Regiment, fired at what they thought was a Taliban position on the edge of Marja and hit a house, killing four people and injuring seven.[17] As the bodies were brought out, including a little girl, First Lieutenant Aaron Maclean told the documentary filmmaker Ben Anderson that, "There's just no way to rationalize that this was in any way a good thing or justified. It's just a terrible failing and a terrible sight."[18]

One of the survivors, Abdel Baki, an itinerant farm worker, told the marines that radio addresses had asked families like his to shelter indoors. He seemed lost and still in shock at the sight of his wife and daughters being carried out riddled with shrapnel. He asked the marines to help transport him to the provincial capital. That wouldn't be possible, a marine officer told him. Transport for Afghans on US helicopters was limited. The office brought out bricks of Afghan notes, $2,500 for each of the lives lost. Abdel Baki picked up the money without looking at it. The officer told him, "You know, the US Marines, the citizens of Afghanistan and the government of Afghanistan, together can achieve great things to make Afghanistan a safer and more prosperous place for all."

Abdel Baki had his own forlorn advice for the marines: "The majority of the people in the Taliban are poor helpless Muslims. . . . You have to give them a chance to switch sides."[19]

During the opening days of the operation, the marines frequently heard from the locals that the Taliban were well liked. One resident told them, "When the Taliban governed, there were no robberies. And they ran quick and fair tribunals to settle disputes. If you left them alone, they left you alone."[20] Another claimed that the only problem with the Taliban was that they "smoked too much marijuana and didn't spend enough time with their families."

The Taliban's defenses, while extensive, appeared rudimentary, which seemed to confirm that the fighters were local stock, and not part of some shadowy network of foreign fighters. Considerably more sophisticated was the network of heroin labs and storerooms packed with poppy resin and packets of powdered heroin, a reminder that the locals were more likely fighting to protect their jobs than they were taking up arms in the name of jihad. "To us, it was war. To them, it's business," observed Golsteyn.[21]

By the end of the first week, central Marja had largely been pacified, at the cost of the lives of eight US Marines, six members of the Afghan National Army, and an estimated twenty civilians, as well as an unknown number of insurgents.[22] Now the marines were obliged to run the place. Before the invasion, McChrystal's headquarters had gamely trumpeted the idea of a "government in a box," which gave the unfortunate impression that an assortment of well-meaning Afghan technocrats was waiting to spring out of storage. As McChrystal well knew, the box was largely empty, save for a couple of computers, printers, and office supplies. The British had been promising to deliver some tribal elders but they bolted at the last minute, leaving just the son-stabbing former felon Haji Zahir, living unhappily in a marine tent, to deal with the less than enthusiastic residents of Marja.

Early on, Zahir and the marine commander General Nicholson tried to hold a shura in the town. Zahir spoke no Pashtu and had to use a translator, much to the annoyance of the locals. One elder boldly told them, "We are all Taliban here." Another elder warned, "You represent a corrupt and murderous government. I'll give you a chance. But if you betray me, I'll kill you and your entire family." Nicholson discovered from the elders that the incoming Afghan police units were an object of particular loathing. This confirmed what Nicholson was hearing from his marines: that the locals were imploring them not to leave them alone with the police. The shura broke after gunfire was heard nearby.

President Karzai showed up a few days later with Sher Mohammed Akhundzada and, perhaps more pointedly, Abdul Rahman Jan, the former Helmand police chief who was hated by some for having treated Marja as his private fiefdom. To further show his disregard for American efforts, Karzai gave a speech in which he likened the Americans to invaders.

On May 12, three months into the operation in Marja, President Obama gave a joint press conference in Washington with Hamid Karzai. The relationship between the two men had not improved. Obama had visited Kabul at the start of the year in an effort to soothe relations with the Afghan government. But Karzai remained as erratic as ever. Nonetheless, Obama trumpeted the operation's success. "Not only have we succeeded in driving the Taliban out of Marja," he declared, "but it also is a model of the partnership between US forces and Afghan forces."

McChrystal, who had accompanied Karzai to Washington, began to worry that it had been a mistake to build up such lofty expectations. Nervous senators asked him if, given the success in Marja, it wasn't time to start with-drawing troops. He couldn't exactly tell them that Marja remained troubled. There was a semblance of order around the district center. Haji Zahir had moved into his headquarters. Marines conducted tours without helmets. And locals had started queuing up for handouts from the AVIPA program.

But the actual economy—that is, the opium economy—had ground to a halt. Opinions about the Americans hadn't improved either.[23] At one stage, early on, special forces Captain Golsteyn was approached by a Taliban "en-forcer," who was in touch with the tribal and Taliban shura that controlled Marja and wanted to open talks. Golsteyn raised the offer with his com-manders but knew no one would be interested in accepting. Then the Talib disappeared, and the moment was lost.[24]

Beyond the town center, the Taliban hadn't left. Marine patrols were am-bushed, IEDs laid, and locals routinely murdered. The Taliban taunted the marines daily by driving around the district on motorbikes, brazenly an-nouncing that the US forces would be leaving soon. The marines didn't trust the Afghan army to guard checkpoints, with the result that American forces spent most of their time on framework patrols, raising the probability they would be hit by roadside bombs.

The press had also started to pick up on the problems, and McChrystal knew it wouldn't be long before they started passing unfavorable judgment on the surge. Shortly after returning from Washington, McChrystal traveled to Marja, where he listened to the marine battalion commanders explain why the operation was taking longer than expected to deliver success.

"You've got to be patient," Lieutenant Colonel Brian Christmas told the general. "We've only been here for 90 days."[25]

"How many days do you think we have before we run out of support from the international community?" asked McChrystal.

"I can't tell you, sir," Christmas replied.

"I'm telling you," said McChrystal, "we don't have as many days as we'd like."

Later that day, in Lashkar Gah, McChrystal laid into Nick Carter for not sending in more troops to Marja, which he believed would have pushed out the Taliban more quickly. Carter responded, "The reason that Marja is taking longer to deliver is because we've got to convince the population. And they want to know who is going to be in charge tomorrow. And you don't do that in four weeks." He suggested what McChrystal already knew: The expectation of success was overwhelming their modest progress.

McChrystal finally lost his cool. Carter might not feel it here, but from Washington's perspective, "this is a bleeding ulcer." President Obama had put a deadline on the surge, and although the military hoped to extend it, every day that passed in Marja without marked improvement was a day lost for making the case that the strategy was working.

As it turned out, McChrystal's sense of time running out was prescient. The month before his visit to Marja, he had been interviewed extensively by *Rolling Stone* reporter Michael Hastings. In a series of unguarded moments, including a night of heavy drinking in Paris, his staff confided in Hastings what they really thought about the politicians they blamed for undermining the war effort. One staffer pretended to mis-hear Vice President Joe Biden's name and said "Bite Me" instead. Jim Jones, the national security adviser, was a "clown" who was "stuck in 1985." Richard Holbrooke was a wounded animal, whose e-mails were not deemed worth responding to. McChrystal himself admitted to feeling "betrayed" by an Eikenberry memo criticizing the surge that leaked the previous fall.

The title of Hastings's piece, "The Runaway General," seemed to capture the feeling in Washington, whispered but not openly acknowledged, that the military was running roughshod over Obama's fledgling presidency, and that in the process the war was slipping out of everyone's control. Even McChrystal recognized that the insurgency was "resilient and growing," as he told NATO officials in one of his last meetings.[26] Of equal concern was the article's description of disillusioned troops McChrystal had addressed at an outpost in the Panjwei areas to the southwest of Kandahar, where the US Army had moved to bolster the flagging Canadian presence.[27] The unit had just lost a popular member, Corporal Michael Ingram, blown up by an IED a short distance from their base, the seventeenth member of the twenty-five-man platoon from Charlie Company, 1st Battalion, 12th Infantry Regiment, to be either killed or injured badly enough to be helicoptered out. The remaining members of the unit were seething: at the Afghans, who appeared to want to kill them every time they stepped off the base, and at General McChrystal, whose more limited rules of engagement they blamed for encouraging the Taliban to attack.

"Don't do anything here that you don't want to [*sic*] look at your wife and kid when you get home," McChrystal warned the unit, after they expressed their frustrations.[28]

"That doesn't bother me as much as my soldiers being killed," replied one noncommissioned officer. McChrystal reiterated the principles of counterinsurgency to the sullen group.

The strain the soldiers felt between the war they were being asked to fight and the brutal reality they confronted had already taken its toll on other units. The 5th Stryker Combat Brigade stationed in Kandahar was accused of killing unarmed Afghan men for sport and desecrating their corpses.[29] At one point the unit drove through a village they had raided as a funeral for some of those killed in the attack was taking place. A loudspeaker attached to one of the Humvees blasted out the prerecorded message in Pashtu, "This is what happens when you fight us."[30] Elsewhere, soldiers from the 82nd Airborne took pictures of themselves posing beside the remains of Afghan fighters. One commander, Lieutenant Colonel Frank Jenio, began each morning's battlefield update with a derogatory PowerPoint slide of Afghans and others that often had sexual undertones.[31] In each case, the units were disciplined and commanders were removed. But the mood among the troops, many on their third or fourth tour, was grim.

McChrystal's defenders accused Hastings of betraying the general and his team's trust by publishing what amounted to "locker room" talk. However, from the White House's perspective, insulting the country's civilian leadership could not go unaccounted for. McChrystal's indiscretions formed a pattern and suggested that yet more battles with the military were on the horizon—especially when it came to drawing down troops. The surge was meant to herald the end of America's active commitment. Yet it appeared likely that McChrystal would resist that narrative and insist on fighting on. Within a day of the piece running, Obama summoned the general back to Washington and fired him. General David Petraeus was announced as his successor. Some of Obama's staff saw the posting as a fitting punishment for Petraeus, the man they blamed for really pulling the strings.[32]

McChrystal's firing was one of Obama's more decisive acts when it came to the war. The general's staff had complained about the president's weakness, scarcely anticipating that when he did make a call it would be to ax their leader. But McChrystal's dismissal disguised another missed opportunity, as well. The general had already revealed a greater sensitivity to Afghan views than most of his predecessors. He responded to the political failings of the Marja operation by ensuring that tribal engagement was center stage for the push into Kandahar that summer. He continued to rebuild bridges with the Afghan government and took a fresh look at the Taliban, in the process discovering considerable common ground between their political agenda and the government's. Indeed, McChrystal understood there was much that the Taliban's network of shadow governors did far better than Karzai's administration when it came to providing justice, financial support, and security.

It was clear to McChrystal that some form of accommodation between the two sides was possible, desirable even. But he was sacked before he could pursue the idea. In his place, Petraeus promised to bring a far more brutal approach to the war, as their time started running out.

CHAPTER 29

Endgame

In June 2010 General David Petraeus received a bracing assessment from his trusted intelligence adviser Derek Harvey as he prepared to take charge of US forces in Afghanistan. Harvey ran Centcom's Afghanistan-Pakistan Center of Excellence, the organization Petraeus created to gather data on the war. Harvey's team of eighty-nine analysts had pored over every available source of information on where the country was headed to reach the following conclusions. "Our political and diplomatic strategies are not connected to our military strategy," Harvey told Petraeus. "It's not going to work."[1]

Harvey's assessment was the first time an American official had formally declared that the surge would not produce a victory similar to the one in Iraq. Harvey had been led to this conclusion by a single devastating fact: Over a year since the marines had begun arriving in Helmand, there was no groundswell of support in their favor as there had been in Iraq, even after the Taliban had been sent packing. Afghan communities had responded cautiously to the surge. When a clan came out in favor of the Americans in one village, members of the same clan in the next valley over remained hostile. Neither group appeared to have confidence in the Afghan government or security forces.[2]

The US military had hoped to lure up to 70 percent of the Taliban to the government side with the promise of jobs. That goal was always overly optimistic given the widespread dislike of the Afghan government they were being asked to side with and their distrust of the foreigners. Futhermore, the US undermined their efforts at converting insurgents by targeting and killing several of the more politically minded leaders, who often belonged to the Taliban's shadow administration in the south. As one Talib observed, the US killed most of the insurgents who wanted to maintain a good relationship with the elders, and who might have contemplated discussions with foreigners. In their place, a younger, more radical generation filled the ranks.[3]

Meanwhile, the Taliban's senior leadership was safe in Pakistan. The Americans had hoped that Pakistan would take action against Taliban sanctuaries during the surge. The Pakistanis had indeed launched military operations in tribal areas to deal with their own Taliban problem.[4] But the Pakistani military had stopped short of attacking tribal leaders, such as the Haqqanis, who particularly concerned the Americans.[5] If anything, Islamabad grew increasingly antagonistic toward Washington for its failure to recognize Islamabad's interests in Afghanistan. The Taliban leadership, according to Saudi contacts in Quetta, sensed it was winning and simply had to wait out the surge.[6]

Petraeus was chastened by Harvey's assessment. He had not expected the Taliban to roll over, but believed they needed to be comprehensively defeated on the ground. Only then would the fighters switch sides and the leadership accept American terms. In his discussion with Petraeus in June 2010, Harvey feared that such a scenario was unlikely, and even if the war's momentum shifted, the US would at best carve out a fleeting window of stability. America would not have the political will to extend the mission and nurture any peace deal it might impose.

"We can get to a point of some transient stability and the appearance of success that will not be enduring, that might provide a window for us to withdraw, and to keep things steady for the next three or four years," he told Petraeus. The US strategy called on the Afghan security forces to hold the line after that, yet Harvey had a dim view of their capabilities. The country would once again be prey to "malign actors, disrupted, ineffective, collapsing government in Kabul: a re-emergence of violent extremist groups and safe havens." Afghanistan, in other words, was heading back to its pre-9/11 condition.[7]

Petraeus was trapped. He could not stop the surge at this point, even if he'd wanted to. His only option was to see out the deployment with grim pragmatism. The war might not be won militarily, he conceded. But he could win it in the minds of the western public and perhaps even the White House by ordering US forces to battle their way to a drawdown. The marines would continue to grind their way through Helmand, he decided. The special forces would intensify their "kill or capture" raids against Taliban commanders in Afghanistan. Drone strikes in Pakistan would increase. They would batter the Taliban into submission, hand over to the Afghans, and get out. Ultimately, it would be for the Afghans to hold the country together after that.

Richard Holbrooke saw the flaws of Petraeus's approach more clearly than anyone in the administration. He had regularly urged the US to soften its position and embark on talks with the Taliban. He had in mind a grand bargain, similar to the deal he had forged for the Dayton Peace Accords to end the Balkans conflict. President Karzai had already signaled that he was interested in the approach, but the Obama administration had dawdled early on and unwittingly subverted Karzai's own informal talks. In February 2010, the CIA revealed to the ISI the location of the Afghan president's main interlocutor, Mullah Baradar, and the Pakistanis immediately arrested him and a dozen other high-ranking Talibs. The move by the ISI reflected Pakistan's insistence that any political dealings with the Taliban pass through Islamabad. American involvement at an early juncture might have done a better job of mollifying Pakistan.[8]

As it was, Richard Holbrooke was encouraged to carry on where Karzai had left off (after the election fiasco of the previous year, there was no question of the two men working together). Holbrooke was influenced in his thinking by one of the leading experts on Afghanistan, Barnett Rubin, who had attracted a cadre of young policy makers at New York University's Center for International Cooperation, including the Australian Tom Gregg, who had worked with the Haqqanis in Loya Paktia. Holbrooke seized on a proposal from Rubin and extensive work by German intelligence to bring some members of the Quetta shura to Doha, Qatar, in order to establish a political office. Trust-building measures, such as the exchange of prisoners, would follow, before some form of cease-fire.[9]

Petraeus disagreed with the plan. Unless the Taliban had been all but defeated, he saw no reason to follow through with talks. The 2011 deadline set by Obama had been bad enough in terms of boosting the enemy's morale: Talks would give the Taliban an air of legitimacy without having to give anything in return and bolster their belief that the US was on its way out.[10] When Holbrooke tried to raise the matter of reconciliation with Petraeus during a visit to Kabul in October 2010, the general told him, "Richard, that's a fifteen-second conversation: Yes, eventually, but no, not now."[11]

But Holbrooke was not dissuaded so easily. His bombastic, dogged style had led him to the margins in the Obama administration. Yet those were also the same traits that had brought him success in the past and kept him fixated on peace now. Even when his patron, Hillary Clinton, expressed skepticism about talks, he persisted. Clinton's points against were more subtle than the military's. In her conversations with Holbrooke she wondered just how representative the Taliban were of the Pashtun south. Weren't they in danger of empowering the wrong people again, just as they had the warlords, without addressing the deeper causes of Pashtun discontent? She was particularly concerned about the plight of Afghan women, whose rights she feared would be sacrificed in any deal with the Taliban.[12]

Holbrooke clung to his insight that no military-imposed peace would last without a political process to complement it, and that it was better to have the Taliban's leadership out in the open than lurking in the shadows. A few weeks later, Holbrooke collapsed after a White House meeting with Clinton. He died in surgery of a ruptured aorta a few hours later.

Petraeus's refusal to consider Taliban reconciliation, especially at the district level, also had tragic consequences. In October 2010, US troops were preparing to relieve the beleaguered Brits in Sangin. One hundred and six British soldiers had died, almost a third of the UK's total number of casualties in the war. There were no figures for the numbers of Afghans killed, although the Afghan health ministry estimated "over a thousand." There was still heavy fighting around the town. Ten million dollars was being poured into reconstruction, but the bazaar remained a shadow of its former self with half its shops still shuttered and shoppers scarce. Neither Brits nor Afghans were sorry to see each other's backs.

Yet at this nadir, the British found what they hoped was a path to peace. It wasn't a grand deal as Holbrooke had been envisioning, but when it came to saving lives and de-escalating the conflict, it appeared to have potential. The British had a small group of civilian advisers—called a District Stabilization Team—in Sangin whose job was to spend reconstruction money and advise their military commander on politics. There hadn't been much for the team to do at first, but gradually they pieced together a map of the district's complex tribal structures, which had eluded the British for so long. They learned about the Alakozai's willingness to side with the British against the Taliban fighters in 2007. The UK had ignored that brief uprising, which the Taliban ultimately crushed. The incident might have been labeled as just another missed opportunity, except that the civilian advisers found that some of those same tribal elders—who had reluctantly sided with the Taliban in recent years—still wanted to talk.

Phil Weatherill, the civilian adviser in Sangin since 2009, met with several leaders from the cluster of villages that stretched north up to the Kajaki dam. Initially the elders only wanted to discuss local issues like their failing flood defenses, which Weatherill suggested he had the budget to fix. But by May 2010, the British adviser had gained enough trust to propose a peace deal.

Phil Weatherill was a British adviser in Sangin who came close to striking a peace deal that might have spared the lives of many US Marines. (Photo by Nick Pounds)

The elders promised to stop their attacks against the British and to allow NATO troops freedom of movement through their territory. In return, the British would carry out reconstruction projects and enable the creation of a local militia. The upper Sangin valley peace accord was drafted and ready to be signed by the end of the month.

But Weatherill quickly learned that his superiors weren't interested in a peace deal that would smack of a typical British "deal with the enemy" on the eve of the American takeover. The US Marines also took a dim view of the British adviser's work, which in their minds amounted to giving money to the Taliban and their proxies. They also questioned whether the deal could hold. When one marine commander accompanied Weatherill to meet with Alakozai tribesmen to assess the deal in August 2010, they were warned by locals that the Taliban were about to attack, forcing them to turn back. It was hardly an auspicious sign that a cease-fire would work.[13]

The incoming marines decided that the British approach to Sangin was fundamentally flawed. The British shouldn't be engaging with the Taliban when they were clearly struggling to hold ground. Their policy of manning two dozen small patrol bases around the city had left them too thinly spread. There were whole areas of the city where the British simply did not go. "It seemed they were spending most of their time just defending themselves, and keeping their supply lines open," said Lieutenant Colonel Jason Morris, the commander of the 3rd Battalion, 5th Marine Regiment, which arrived in Sangin that October.[14]

The handover period was particularly tense in Sangin as the Americans arrived and the British withdrew.[15] The two forces cohabited for a number of weeks. While the Brits remained on their bases, the marines went on patrols that lasted days, using new line charges—cords with explosives along their length that would detonate any buried bombs—to blow their way through IED fields and prove there was no part of the town they could not reach. On several occasions US soldiers returned to Forward Operating Base Inkerman, to the north of the town center, only to be refused admittance into the British-operated chow hall because they were "too dirty," according to one US Marine officer.[16]

The British approach was certainly flawed, but they had also grasped some important truths about the nature of the fighting. When they left, much of their hard-won wisdom went with them. The peace initiative was discounted, half of the UK outposts were closed, and a map showing mine-ridden areas of Sangin that the British avoided was redrawn. The marines' rationale was that they needed to reclaim the town first. Morris was not opposed to the idea of a peace accord with the Alakozai, or anyone else, but felt that a deal should only be struck after the Afghan government was in firm control, and that meant taking the fight to the Taliban.

Yet in their desire to do just that, some marine patrols also initially ignored the Brits' most effective techniques, such as dismounting from armored vehicles to conduct mine sweeps in areas likely to be planted with IEDs, marking routes of cleared mines, and not then straying from the line. The result: some of the heaviest losses by US forces since the war began. Twenty-five marines from 3rd Battalion, 5th Regiment, were killed in the first two months, and 140 more were seriously injured.

On October 13, Weapons Company from the battalion was conducting an armored patrol to the east of Sangin through an intersection known to be laced with IEDs. In fact, a mine had struck the unit in the same spot just the day before without casualties. They should have checked the area thoroughly for IEDs before returning—it wasn't just British experience but common sense that suggested doing so. But instead the patrol of MRAPs barreled through the area. The Taliban had learned from their miss the day before. This time the roadside bomb was detonated by a command wire. It split a heavily armored MRAP in half, killing the four marines inside: Lance Corporals Joseph Rodewald, twenty-two, Phillip Vinnedge, nineteen, and Victor Dew, twenty, and Corporal Justin Cain, twenty-two.

Colonel Paul Kennedy, who oversaw the area, was visiting Sangin that day. He and the battalion commander, Jason Morris, spent three hours removing the young men's remains. Their deaths were "unnecessary," reflected Kennedy later. Kennedy also went on a foot patrol with Lima Company and witnessed the soldiers strolling down an IED-laden street with little apparent idea of the danger they faced. When they came under fire, they rushed for cover as they'd been trained only to find that the Taliban had anticipated their moves and laid IEDs in nearby compounds and earth banks. "We knew what the British tactics were. . . . Some of the tactics weren't passed on. We were not using discipline with our patrol techniques," said Kennedy afterward.[17]

Morris subsequently fired the company commander involved. Yet the mine strikes continued to claim lives, because there were simply too many to avoid. Eleven hundred were disarmed or triggered in the first six months in Sangin (compared to the 180 in Nawa over a similar period). Among those killed was First Lieutenant Robert Kelly, the son of a three-star general, who triggered a buried IED as he crawled up the side of an irrigation ditch. The blast ripped off his legs above the knee, killing him almost instantly.[18] He was the sort of officer who gelled a company together, and his loss was keenly felt. Carrying his shattered body back to base should have been a twenty-minute walk, but it took over two agonizing hours as the patrol scoured the ground for further IEDs. Some in the Pentagon suggested pulling the unit out of Sangin altogether, rather than continuing to suffer such excruciating casualties.

Instead, the marines decided to double down. That fall, M1 Abrams tanks were deployed in Helmand for the first time since the war began, each one a sixty-eight-ton beast mounted with a 120mm cannon. Making a menacing appearance in Sangin were Assault Breacher Vehicles, or ABVs, which carried a giant claw, which Morris put to good effect ripping through walls and houses. The ABVs were followed by a convoy of armored bulldozers to flatten the terrain in their wake. Side alleys were cleared with line charges, the larger version of which sounded like a "nuclear device" had gone off, sending a cloud of smoke and debris hundreds of feet into the air.[19]

"When you don't have good situational awareness, you have to compensate for that by using overwhelming force," reflected Colonel Kennedy later.

One of the reasons for their lack of awareness, the marines realized, was that in their zeal to close down British outposts, they had lost control over key sections of the town. So three months after the British left, the unit had to conduct a lengthy operation to reopen many of them, including one in the dangerous Wishtun area of Sangin. The main drag—known as Pharmacy Road—was line-charged, stripped of houses on either side, and given a tarmac surface to prevent more roadside bombs from being laid, all within a few weeks. As one of the officers of the battalion said, "We didn't want to destroy Sangin to save it, but there were places that we had to flatten."[20]

They had to dispense with some of the finer points of counterinsurgency during the clearing operation. "Sangin was a minefield," said Morris, the battalion commander, "and you can't do COIN [counterinsurgency] in a minefield." If they were receiving fire from rifles and machine guns, he wanted his men to respond with rockets. "We needed to make a statement," he said.[21]

As for the peace accord, in the fall of 2010 Phil Weatherill established contact with Abdul Qayoum, the charismatic Taliban shadow administrator for the area. Qayoum was prepared to discuss a cease-fire for all Taliban forces around Sangin, including, for the first time, members of the Noorzai and Ishakzai tribes. Weatherill informed the marines of his outreach work. But they were angry that he had not included them in the talks and refused to participate in any follow-up discussions.

The Taliban leader was killed in an air strike before a broader cease-fire could be concluded. Qayoum's death, and the dramatic increase in the number of civilian casualties since the marines' arrival, led to local protests outside the marine headquarters. Afghan security forces and some marines accused Weatherill of encouraging the demonstrations, a charge he vociferously denied, although he was dismayed by the Americans' hard-hitting approach.[22]

Only by the end of the year did the Americans start working with Weatherill to put a peace deal in place with the Alakozai. It was a bittersweet moment for the British adviser. "We got there in the end, but we wasted a year," he said. He was then reassigned to another town, in a British-controlled area of Helmand. He wasn't told explicitly why he was being removed, although he suspected it was because of his criticism of the US Marines and their increasing belligerency. The deal subsequently fell apart.

The US military gloves-off approach wasn't limited to Sangin. Petraeus loosened the rules of engagement across southern Afghanistan. Aggressive patrolling was encouraged, and soldiers were once again able to call in rapid air support, which had been reduced during McChrystal's tenure to avoid civilian casualties. The number of dropped missiles tripled over the year before. Special forces were also launching a record fifteen raids a night. At the same time, surveillance aircraft flew constant loops over the country, picking up cell phone conversations that were automatically sifted for jihadi talk, and were used to launch drone strikes. As American patrol bases proliferated across the south, so too did a network of blimps—the helium balloons with cameras beneath—providing intimate video coverage of Afghan communities and allowing soldiers to quickly intercept bomb layers.

The results of Petraeus's aggressive tactics were dramatic and in keeping with the history of the war. District after district was wrested back under control at a heavy price. In 2010, 496 US soldiers died, most of them in the final six months of the year as the surge gathered momentum. There were 2,777 Afghan civilian deaths over the same period.[23] Towns and villages had been ravaged, with some deliberately flattened by the US military and others abandoned after being caught in the cross fire.[24] The UN estimated that 600,000 had been forced from their homes, with the number growing all the time.[25] Refugee camps outside Kabul swelled to tens of thousands with many Afghans too poor to return home.[26]

The peace that ensued was uneven and regularly tested by the Taliban. The challenge Petraeus faced was building on the pockets of security and putting the Afghans in charge. One of the surge's biggest successes was achieved in Kandahar with Afghan engagement and little bloodshed. The British Major General Nick Carter, who commanded the NATO headquarters in the south, had observed the intense fighting the surge provoked in Helmand and in the districts surrounding Kandahar. He was convinced that Afghanistan's second-largest city needed a light touch—a view echoed by local dignitaries and Karzai's administration. In the end, extensive negotiations meant that only American military police detachments and a battalion from the Afghan National Army were needed to restore order, a clear case of American and Afghan interests aligning.[27]

Building a sustainable peace beyond major cities like Kandahar was another matter, however. In Helmand each apparent victory only further exposed the problem at the heart of the surge. The Americans could force a temporary peace in the countryside, but the Afghans were neither willing nor able to preserve it.

In Sangin, the marines had tamed the most deadly town in the country only to see the Afghan government fail to take advantage. Sangin's district governor, Mohammed Sharif, was well respected locally, but his administration, which was meant to contain representatives of the major ministries, was always hopelessly undermanned and underfunded. At the height of the fighting, $56.5 million was spent in Sangin, according to budget figures. Much of that money was provided directly by the British government to local contractors for reconstruction, and would ultimately be phased out when the area was delivered to the Afghan government. By contrast, Sharif received a few thousand dollars from Kabul beyond basic salaries. Despite a flurry of school building, four of Sangin's eighteen schools were closed due to a lack of teachers. The local law court was deserted. The district judge had not tried a case in the past three years.

As for the local security forces, they remained corrupt or downright dangerous. Sangin's police chief was forced out of his job for having sex with underage boys, only to regain his position after pulling strings in Kabul. His officers set up as many patrol bases as possible—thirty-six by one count—so they could extort protection money from the locals. US officers sent to mentor them in 2011 tried to consolidate the police bases to allow them to better defend themselves when the inevitable attacks came. But the police weren't prepared to do that. Young officers paid their bosses a premium for the privilege of setting up a base. These senior officers were going to make as much money as they could before the Taliban returned. Outside Sangin, the police were assaulted everywhere they showed up.

"We don't want the police, and we don't want the Taliban," Haji Daoud, the Alakozai tribal leader from the upper Sangin valley, told his American interlocutors.[28]

Petraeus tried to take advantage of these sentiments by instigating a village militia program, drawing on earlier experiments with the concept, and a paper written by US special forces officer Major Jim Gant, who argued that the only way to win the war was "one tribe at a time." When aligned with broader political efforts, militias could be an effective tool for winning over local communities, as the work of the United Nations in Loya Paktia had demonstrated.

However, Petraeus's attempt to scale up the program ran into immediate difficulties. He wanted 30,000 villagers armed by 2015. The Afghan government objected.[29] Karzai feared Petraeus was simply creating a new generation of warlords in the south, and sowing the seeds for the civil war to resume once the Americans left. Tajik and Uzbek groups were clamoring for their own stash of arms from the Americans as well. Karzai folded as usual, but his instincts were shown to be correct. In the upper Sangin valley, the militia program simply empowered one group of Afghans to attack another group nominally aligned with the Taliban.

"We're giving them guns, and they're going fucking crazy, killing each other," said one special forces officer working in the area. Efforts to link the militias to the local government proved impossible.[30]

The only Afghan organization that was responsive to the US military was the Afghan National Army, but here too the results were limited. The Afghan army battalion in Sangin had played at best a minor role following the arrival of the US Marines in 2010. During 2011, they had proven themselves competent enough at patrolling, and when they had been caught alone by the Taliban they had not fled, as some Americans had feared. However, they had little appetite for conducting their own operations into some of the uncleared areas around Sangin, and attrition rates were exceptionally high, with one in seven recruits deserting.[31] On the isolated bases of Sangin, where Afghan soldiers couldn't simply shed their uniforms and walk away, soldiers took to shooting themselves in the feet or hands to be evacuated.[32]

Relations between the Afghan soldiers and the US Marines hadn't exactly improved either. Indeed Afghan soldiers had started killing western troops partnered with them. Five American and British soldiers were killed in 2010, and fifteen the following year. In Sangin, Second Lieutenant Martin Lindig, who ran 3.5 Battalion's training and mentoring team, managed to thwart a number of attempts by the Afghan soldiers he was living alongside to kill his men, including a plot on his own life. On each occasion, Lindig's translator overheard the plotters and the marines intervened before disaster struck, disarmed the Afghan soldiers in question, and ensured that the men were either arrested or disciplined.[33]

No one was killed, but Lindig had just cause to question to what extent the Afghan army had bought in to the war the Americans were fighting—if at all—and time was running out. At one point while on a joint patrol with his Afghan unit, Lindig got into an argument with a Sangin mullah. The mullah was angry about an air strike that had killed a woman and three children. "Whatever you have brought into Afghanistan, your people are here for killing. Your tanks are here for killing. Your cannons are here for killing. Your planes are here for killing. You haven't brought anything that we like. All you have brought are the things for death."[34]

Lindig conveyed his sympathy for the victims and told the mullah that if he and others like him had prevented the Taliban from sheltering among women and children, then such deaths would not occur. Lindig encouraged the mullah to stop complaining and to take action. The marines were already sacrificing a lot for the mullah's security, he told the man. Just a few weeks earlier, the marine company co-located with Lindig's Afghan unit had lost Corporal Derek Wyatt, whose wife was pregnant. All Wyatt's newborn son had left of his father was an iPod of bedtime stories he had recorded before the tour. The marines were putting their lives on the line, but it wasn't being appreciated.[35]

The mullah was incredulous at the suggestion that the marines were providing security. "Do you have binoculars? Look at this area, where are the

Second Lieutenant Martin Lindig (second from left) debated with
a religious leader in Sangin the reasons behind the US Marines'
decision to clear the city of Taliban and tribal militants. (Photo
courtesy of USMC)

inhabitants? They have been killed, imprisoned, or have fled. This revolution
has brought no good for Afghans, it has just caused death." The Taliban would
return to the area "half an hour" after the patrol left, said the mullah.

Lindig suspected that his Afghan army colleagues shared some of the mullah's views. That night, as they did most nights, the radios of the Afghan soldiers
and police were alive with insults from their opposite numbers in the Taliban,
who dialed into the same frequency on their own radio transmitters. There were
the usual threats, and taunts about how the Americans were leaving soon, and
how there would then be no one to protect them. Yet, both sides could also be
playful and reflective, exchanging bawdy jokes and love songs, a reminder of the
intimate nature of a war fought by callow recruits on both sides and the many
ties that link them together.[36]

A few weeks before President Obama was due to decide whether to start
withdrawing troops from Afghanistan, Osama bin Laden—the reason
America had invaded the country in the first place—was killed in Pakistan.
Just after midnight on May 2, 2011, two Blackhawk helicopters approached
a compound on the outskirts of the Pakistani city of Abbottabad. Obama sat
anxiously in the White House's situation room, watching the operation with
his national security team courtesy of a scratchy video feed from a drone.

Within moments of reaching the compound, the carefully laid plan started
to unravel. One of the helicopters was forced to perform a ditch landing after
unexpected air currents had caused the pilot to clip his tail rotor against the

compound wall. There were gasps in the situation room as the helicopter dropped briefly out of sight, before the feed resumed, showing the navy SEAL team sprinting clear of the crash site.

They proceeded to secure the compound, killing a man who poked his head around a door. Three of the SEALs reached a metal gate in the compound wall. Beyond lay a second enclosed area and the darkened outline of what was clearly the main house. Entering the ground floor, the SEALs fired into a first-floor bedroom, killing an unarmed man and woman. At the rear of the house, they found a stairwell with a locked metal gate leading to the second floor. This was destroyed with an explosive charge.

When they got to the top of the stairs, they finally glimpsed their target, a tall man in a tan gown, ducking into a side room. The lead SEAL fired off two shots, before he cautiously approached the room. Two women were standing at the entrance, and behind them a man was lying at the foot of a bed. Seeing the lead SEAL, one of the women, disheveled and hysterical, launched herself at the American, who drove her and the other woman back into the corner. The other two SEALs entered and observed bin Laden on the floor, twitching in his death throes from a bullet wound to the side of his head. The SEALs fired more bullets into his body until they were certain he was dead. After securing the rest of the floor, they returned to the corpse.

"I think this is our boy," said one of the men, leaning over the body.[37]

The killing of bin Laden almost a decade after 9/11 brought to a close one of the longest manhunts in history. In the Obama administration the National Security Council immediately raised questions about Islamabad's role in shielding bin Laden, as evidence came to light of his couriers' links to other Pakistani militant groups and the ISI spy agency.[38] Islamabad reacted angrily to the attack, which had taken place without its knowledge. The Americans had spent a long time wishing the relationship was something other than it was. Now it had fallen apart entirely.[39]

More important, bin Laden's death brought to many Americans a sense of closure to the war that had been waged in Afghanistan in the name of 9/11. The war had grown in complexity and required an entire armory of justifications to keep it going and strategies to win it, whether using Afghan warlords for security and a "light footprint" approach to reconstruction or full-blown nation-building and counterinsurgency. Yet when politicians had needed to explain to their skeptical public what the war was really about, they'd always come back to bin Laden and al-Qa'eda.

Of course, the idea that American troops were fighting al-Qa'eda in Afghanistan had distorted how the West saw the war. It hid the fact that US soldiers were locked in battle with tribesmen, farmers, and religious zealots in southern Afghanistan having taken sides in a civil war and regional dispute. Al-Qa'eda remained an important but limited threat in the tribal hinterlands of Pakistan, one which had been contained by counterterrorism operations for the past ten years. While he was at large, bin Laden had loomed over the war, providing a constant sense of menace, even if his actual ability to carry out attacks was minimal. Once he was dead, however, the rationale for the Afghan war was gone.

The Obama administration went to great lengths to stress that the war itself wasn't over, that al-Qa'eda remained a danger, and that the West had a long-term commitment to Afghanistan. But such comments could not disguise the fact that Obama had never endorsed the interventionist argument that a nation-building program was necessary for removing the threat extremists posed in Afghanistan. Indeed his presidency had taught him that Afghanistan merely needed to be contained.

Six weeks after bin Laden's death, on June 15, 2011, Obama and his national security team met to decide the fate of the surge. Defense Secretary Robert Gates said the US had "basically thrown the Taliban out of their home turf in Kandahar and Helmand provinces."[40] Petraeus wanted to extend the surge beyond its July 2011 deadline. The relative success in the south had shown what could be achieved with more men. Maintaining troop levels would allow him to launch further offensives in the east and north. He proposed a token reduction of around 5,000 troops by the end of the year, warning that drawing down any more than that would jeopardize all they had achieved. Yet an NSC review was skeptical, questioning the progress the military claimed. Another report from the CIA pointed out that squeezing the Taliban in the south had led to an increase in attacks elsewhere in the country. The mounting death toll cast a pall over discussions. By the end of 2011, some 1,234 American soldiers had been killed since the start of the Obama presidency, compared with 630 in the previous seven years of war. For the UK, 257 in the past two years, compared with 137 between 2001 and 2009.

At one point in early 2011, the debate over the drawdown threatened to become as rancorous as the one over the surge two years before, with the same battle lines drawn between the military and civilians. In response to some comments by Petraeus to NATO headquarters that questioned the timetable, Obama began to warn an NSC gathering, "If I believe I am being gamed . . . ," before trailing off.

Gates was left fuming. "The president doesn't trust his commander, can't stand Karzai, doesn't believe in his own strategy, and doesn't consider the war to be his. For him it's all about getting out," he later said. At the time, though, he kept those thoughts to himself.[41]

Obama listened to all points of view, but he had largely made up his mind: America must move on. The country was facing pressing challenges at home and abroad. It was costing the US taxpayers more than $100 billion a year to maintain the current deployment, $1 million for every soldier in Afghanistan. Over $1 trillion had been spent on the war so far. There were surely better ways to spend that money in the middle of a crippling recession. At the same time, the Arab awakenings in Egypt, Tunisia, and Libya were forcing Americans to reevaluate the Muslim world. Here was what looked like a new and authentic voice of protest against the region's US-supported regimes that seemed more relevant than al-Qa'eda and the grim war in Afghanistan.

Indeed Obama wanted to get America out of Afghanistan as quickly as possible. He was determined not to let his decision turn into another messy sideshow. So he decisively told Petraeus that he wanted 15,000 troops out by the end of the year, and the remaining 18,000 by the winter of 2014, at which point US forces would hand over security responsibility to the Afghans. Petraeus, who was about to join the administration as the CIA director, seemed to pick up on the changed tone. But this didn't stop him from bristling to the president that the accelerated withdrawal "invalidates my entire campaign plan."

"David, you shouldn't have assumed I wouldn't do what I told the American people I would," replied Obama.[42]

A few days after his conversation with Petraeus, Obama gave a televised address to the nation. It was simple and somber in tone, and unlike his intellectually incoherent address at West Point two years before to announce the surge, his words seemed like his own. His speech contained the obligatory and vaguely paternal plaudits to the Afghans for "establishing local police forces, opening markets and schools, creating new opportunities for women and girls." But Obama's focus in the address was firmly on American interests. When it came to the sacrifices of US soldiers, he did not gloss over their losses or the challenges many would face upon returning. "America, it is time to focus on nation building here at home," he announced.

Containment

The West's grand experiment in the Good War was effectively lost in 2011 when Obama stuck to his deadline for ending the surge. The US military had shown it could batter its way to a transient peace in Helmand and Kandahar. But the limited accord it achieved after ten years of fighting was not sustainable. The Taliban remained a viable force in most of the country's provinces. Afghans still wanted what the West could offer in terms of reconstruction—but not at the cost of an endless war against the Taliban. Polling of Afghan views on the war was limited, but there was a widespread belief, voiced by President Hamid Karzai and others, that the US military was deliberately provoking the war to prolong its military presence.[1]

By 2012, the White House was concerned strictly with managing the US withdrawal. All combat troops were scheduled to leave the country by the end of 2014, after a progressive handover. A US PowerPoint presentation laid out what the West hoped would be the "Key Tenets of the Afghan Narrative": "2011/12 Notice what is different; 2012/13 Change has begun; 2013/14 Growing confidence; 2015 A new chance, a new beginning."[2]

Predictably, the transition proved messier and more traumatic than anticipated. When the US tried to withdraw from Musa Qala in 2012, militants overwhelmed the local security forces, and the marines had to temporarily move back in. Sher Mohammed Akhundzada stepped into the vacuum, plotted the ouster of the police chief, and seized power through a proxy. Soon even he lost control of parts of the district and the town finally fell to tribal elements, some of them aligned with the Taliban, in 2013. The US military did not intervene this time, signaling that it had decided that Musa Qala—and by extension most of Helmand—weren't that important after all.

Meanwhile, at NATO headquarters the US military began to envision what Afghanistan would look like in the absence of western troops. It was unclear how many soldiers would remain beyond 2014, but their numbers were likely to be greatly reduced, and removed from a front-line combat role. Coming so soon after the military had urged Obama to maintain the surge or risk the country falling into chaos, the drawdown revealed the hollowness of those claims. Senior American officers felt awkward closing down a mission they had argued so vociferously to expand. Yet there was also a certain relief that the country's fate was more firmly in Afghan hands.

In fact, the fading of grand western ambitions had already begun to empower a handful of international and Afghan officials to propose once-unimaginable diplomatic initiatives in some of the country's most troubled regions. For instance, British Major General Nick Carter had taken the initiative back in 2010 to reengage with Ahmed Wali Karzai, the Afghan president's marginalized brother, to help secure Kandahar. The Americans had once considered Ahmed Wali to be an important power broker in the south, given that his offices were regularly packed with hundreds of key tribal leaders and politicians. But as the Americans grew disillusioned with Hamid Karzai, some rebranded Ahmed Wali as an exemplar of the corrupt, money-grubbing, drug-dealing warlord they were fighting against (though they kept him on the CIA payroll). When Carter recognized that the West needed a political process in Kandahar, he sought out Ahmed Wali as a regional partner. Together they created a tribal council that reached out to tribes across the region, reintegrated Taliban commanders into the political process, and demanded more resources from Kabul. Although Ahmed Wali was assassinated in 2011, the council survived as a model for creating an effective Afghan institution that was aligned with Afghan society.

Given the likelihood that large parts of Helmand would not be under the control of central government once Americans and British departed, western officials could have used the success of Carter and Wali's experimental council as the basis for a larger program to reintegrate tribal leaders and the Taliban into district government—and perhaps even grant them some local control. Yet this was rarely discussed as serious policy, with most policy makers preferring instead to hand over towns like Musa Qala and Sangin to the Afghan military and hope for the best.

Where the US did seek to re-envision its role was through broader peace talks with the Taliban—yet this effort was equally flawed. After Holbrooke's death, the White House decided to take up his plan. According to one state department official, Hillary Clinton was won over by the promise of a development fund for Afghan women to help protect their rights.[3] Yet when the Obama administration acted, it did so naively. First of all, there was a side-show created by the British in 2010, when their intelligence agency unearthed a man they claimed was a member of Mullah Omar's inner circle. Despite warnings from their US counterparts that he might be an ISI or Taliban double agent, the British insisted on paying him handsomely and whisking him to and from Kabul, meeting with Karzai and senior military officials. It turned out the man was a shopkeeper from Quetta.[4] "It was a severe embarrassment," said one British official, "but our intentions were in the right place."

The following year, Washington did track down the right Taliban interlocutors but the results were an even bigger disaster. The US excluded Pakistan and the Taliban insisted on keeping out the Karzai administration. Washington began talks with Tayib Agha, a top aide to Mullah Omar, in the neutral venue of Qatar without preconditions. In a show of good faith, the US arranged to release some prisoners held in Afghan jails.[5] The negotiations produced an agreement to let the Taliban establish a political office in Qatar.

That's when the trouble began. In June 2013, the Taliban opened the new offices with a flag-raising ceremony for the Islamic Emirate of Afghanistan—the name of Afghanistan when the Taliban ruled the country. It looked like the Taliban had just inaugurated a government-in-waiting. Karzai reacted furiously, breaking off bilateral talks with the Americans and threatening to boycott any peace process altogether. The office closed shortly thereafter.

Such negotiations were always going to be a long shot, given that the Taliban had never been the coherent entity the West had imagined.[6] Even had senior military commanders like Mullah Zakir agreed to a cease-fire, a truce would stretch only so far without a national reconciliation process. No power-sharing arrangement between Karzai and the Taliban would address the country's deep ethnic tensions or the reasons why many groups took up arms in the first place: the persecution of some tribes and groups by predatory and corrupt government officials.[7]

The failure of the Taliban experiment in Qatar appeared to drain what little energy the Obama administration had left for Afghanistan. "Afghanistan has slipped down the list of priorities," said one State Department official, echoing the mood in London.[8] Washington and Karzai spent much of 2013 in a spat over whether US forces would remain in Afghanistan after 2014. Karzai requested that Obama write a letter apologizing for a litany of American mistakes over the past thirteen years.[9] Obama, naturally, refused.

As for the British, in December 2013 Prime Minister David Cameron declared that UK forces could come home because the war was a case of "mission accomplished." Cameron's declaration of victory amounted to an instruction to the British public to forget about Afghanistan. The war rapidly slipped down the political and media agendas. The fall of Musa Qala, once the epicenter of the British military's anxiety about their standing in the world, barely registered in the national consciousness, and a desperate battle over Sangin in 2013, the site of so many British and American deaths, garnered little attention.[10]

As the West prepared to withdraw most of their combat troops as of the end of 2014, Washington had dispensed with the notion of good wars. This did not mean President Obama had ruled out the possibility of intervention in foreign conflict—as the US support for NATO's bombing campaign in Libya demonstrated. But after the American experience in Afghanistan and Iraq, such involvement was likely to be limited. The armed forces had also retreated to a Colin Powell–esque doctrine of caution. "In my opinion, any future defense secretary who advises the president to again send a big American land army into Asia or into the Middle East or Africa should 'have his head examined,'" said the outgoing Robert Gates.

In place of the Good War, Washington began to embrace a doctrine of containment reminiscent of the Cold War policies that produced the covert wars after the end stages of Vietnam, and which led to the funding of extremist groups in Afghanistan to fight against the Soviets. The Obama administration's approach to Pakistan's tribal regions indicated both how this doctrine promised to shape the region and America's likely approach to failing states going forward. America's operations in Pakistan have been entirely covert and its diplomacy limited, with US drone strikes the favored tool of engagement.

The steady increase in the number of drone strikes in Pakistan has prompted some debate in Washington about whether these operations were effective at preventing terrorist attacks in the West. But there was ample evidence that they fueled tensions across the entire region.[11] One New America Foundation poll of the tribal areas in Pakistan found that almost half of respondents thought the drone strikes largely killed civilians, and the vast majority thought this was because the US was waging a war against the Muslim world.[12] It was easy to see how they might come to this conclusion. Between 2004 and 2012 an estimated 1,562 to 2,377 people were killed by drones, 16 percent of whom were conservatively estimated to have been civilians.

The reasons for these high civilian casualty rates were rooted in the US military's methods for identifying drone targets. The military primarily relied on cell phone and WiFi intercepts, swept up by drones and surveillance aircraft, to locate militants. Cell phones belonging to suspected militants were then tracked ahead of a strike, an approach that fighters learned to thwart by using multiple phones, switching devices with other fighters, or even planting phones on their rivals. According to one former drone operator, strikes sometimes occurred with no way of verifying who was holding the phone.[13] "In the early days—for our consciences—we wanted to know who we were killing before anyone pulled the trigger," said Richard Blee in 2013, one of the heads of Alec Station, the CIA task force that tried to kill Osama bin Laden before 9/11. "Now we're lighting up people all over the place."[14]

Criticism of the drone program came from many quarters. In 2013, Stanley McChrystal was one of several prominent American officials who warned that the military's overreliance on drones was inflaming tensions between America and the rest of the world.[15] Malala Yousafzai, the sixteen-year-old activist infamously shot by the Taliban for her work promoting girls' education, offered a civilian perspective. When Yousafzai met President Obama in October 2013, she warned him that drone attacks were creating more terrorism. She described lying on her rooftop in Waziristan at night and listening with dread to the ominous buzz of the drones overhead. One popular love song in the tribal areas of Pakistan went, "my gaze is as fatal as a drone attack."[16] The people were angry and confused, she told Obama.

Meanwhile, the Pakistani government complained that the drone policy set back its own efforts at reform. In November 2013, a drone strike killed the leader of the Pakistani Taliban, Hakimullah Mehsud, who had been in peace talks with Islamabad. Pakistani Interior Minister Chaudhry Nisar condemned the strike as a "drone attack on the peace process."

Over the course of 2013, the Obama administration appeared to respond to the criticisms by reining back the program and introducing stiffer targeting rules, which reduced the number of civilian casualties and improved accuracy.[17] For a five-month period at the start of 2014, there were no strikes in Pakistan's tribal areas, although during this period, they continued in Yemen and Somalia.[18] The Pakistani military also launched its own, far less accurate air strikes during operations in Waziristan. In June 2014, US drone strikes resumed in Pakistan.

The figures for the number of drone strikes in Afghanistan has been less clear. According to one estimate, there were 1,160 US drone strikes in Afghanistan between 2009 and 2012.[19] That number has gone down as US troops have withdrawn, but drones appear to be an enduring tool of US foreign policy to accompany Obama's more pragmatic and limited definition of American vital interests overseas. At a West Point address in 2014, the same venue in which he had announced the largest troop surge in Afghanistan, Obama described America's uneasy relationship with an unstable world. America would remain engaged, he insisted—and yet his own words were belied by the rapid disengagement from Afghanistan.

The White House's position was no doubt informed by the fact that covert wars were a far more politically viable strategy of engagement than the kind of robust diplomacy and enduring military commitment necessary to achieve a negotiated peace. According to a 2013 CNN poll, only 17 percent of American respondents supported the Afghan war, down from 52 percent in 2008. At the same time, support for assassinations, such as those carried out by drones, was 69 percent, according to a poll conducted by Amy Zegart of Stanford University. Zegart has explained this steady tolerance for targeted killings by observing that covert wars by definition take place beyond public scrutiny.[20]

And therein lie the dangers of covert wars: They never stimulate the level of public debate necessary to push policy makers to *end them*. Provided the West keeps money flowing and leaves behind enough forces to bolster the Afghan army and defend Kabul and Kandahar, the Afghan war may be contained. A limited Afghan government propped up with foreign money: This may be an outcome the West is prepared to accept. Yet the policy containment has allowed the State Department, and by extension the White House, to abnegate its responsibility to bring together the different sides of the Afghan war, and with it the hope for an enduring peace.

"The irresistible illusion" is how Rory Stewart, the former British diplomat–turned–Conservative member of Parliament, has characterized the draw of the Good War. That messianic vision is rooted in the belief that all societies aspire to achieve western-style democracy and that promoting such democracies makes the world at once more secure and just. Western leaders have fallen in and out of love with this approach since at least the Cold War. But it became particularly seductive after 9/11 and led conservatives and liberals to unite in a shared conceit that western military might could be wielded to transform Afghanistan in a western image. The passing of that alliance should not be mourned. Indeed the fundamental lesson of this war is that the idea of the Good War should die with it.

This is not to diminish the war's successes. When US forces left, 85 percent of the country had access to basic medical care, compared to 9 percent under the Taliban. Seven million more children were in school, more than one third of them girls, up from 1 million in 2001. The National Solidarity Program continued on as an important and largely uncorrupted vehicle for delivering small reconstruction projects. Those who knew the war-torn capital Kabul in 2001 can point to several glitzy malls, wedding halls, and a vibrant media culture. The city's population has tripled to over 3 million. Yet these advances have come at a cost of over $1 trillion and 30,000 American and Afghan lives.

Defenders of military intervention cite these victories and often ask: What's the alternative? Afghanistan, they argue, would implode in destabilizing violence without western intervention. This is precisely the kind of circular and self-justifying logic that compelled western leaders to disastrously escalate the war, while ignoring the voices of a small but significant cross section of western and Afghan officials who offered up achievable solutions that served the people. Indeed, after more than a decade of troop buildup, few Afghans equated the presence of NATO soldiers with security.[21]

This is not an indictment of western engagement with struggling states. Rather it is an indictment of the assumption that military force can readily transform societies for the good. There is no great mystery as to why we continually fall for the attractions of this idea. US special forces and the Northern Alliance appeared to effortlessly brush aside the Taliban in 2001; Saddam Hussein's statue came tumbling down in Baghdad eighteen months later. But the painful yet profound lesson of these wars—and particularly Afghanistan—is that the currents that change society move at a considerable pace of their own making. That's why the structure of Iraq's police state, first created by the British in the 1930s, remained in place ninety years later,[22] and why support for the Taliban, with its roots in Pashtun tribalism, was as strong in 2014 as it was on the eve of war in 2001.[23]

The open question is how should policy makers in Washington and other western capitals who remain committed to engaging with the world's dangerous countries proceed? Here the story of Afghanistan offers some hope and direction. The Afghan war taught us that order persists in even the most war-damaged societies and that the most sustainable solutions emerge when the inherent self-interest of these communities is engaged. Those solutions often emerge from the grassroots, especially in a country like Afghanistan that lacks a history of centralized government control. The challenge western leaders face is to seek out those voices that reveal the internal order of these countries, and then listen to their wishes.

Indeed the West—specifically America—is arguably better positioned to make good on this promise in Afghanistan than at any point in its history. American diplomats and their allies have developed an unprecedented knowledge of the country's politics. Military officers and soldiers have proven adept at mentoring the Afghan army and managing tribal relations. USAID has a finer understanding of how to scale its reconstruction work to Afghan needs.

Selling such an agenda will be a challenge for our future leaders. The idea of the Good War is deeply entwined in the western psyche and is what gives voice to the idealistic notion that the developed world can lead less fortunate nations on the road to progress. Perhaps we would be well served to remember that "progress" is a relative idea that history has demonstrated can almost never be imposed. As the former US secretary of defense, Robert McNamara, wrote after the Vietnam War, "We viewed the people and leaders of South Vietnam in terms of our own experience. We do not have the God-given right to shape every nation in our own image or as we choose."

The damage of these misconceptions in Afghanistan has been great. Yet even now it's not too late to chart a different course.

ACKNOWLEDGMENTS

This book would not have been possible without my wonderful agent, Clare Alexander, and my editor Dan Franklin at Jonathan Cape, who recognized the need for a full account of the Afghan war and who has been a brilliant supporter of the book from the outset. Tim Bartlett brought me on at Basic Books after transforming my proposal. My editor Alex Littlefield shepherded the book through its various drafts with his deft and astute edits. Melissa Veronesi, the production manager, was a constant source of calm as she brought together the book's scattered parts. Clare Bullock performed similar feats at Cape. I'd also like to thank Katherine Fry for her exceptional copyediting, and Antoinette Smith, Julie Ford, Peggy Garry, Elizabeth Dana, and Carrie Majer for their help. Jacob Levenson turned a rough manuscript into a book with an unerring sense of what makes a narrative work. Lily Tomson and Karolina Maclachlan provided invaluable research assistance.

Master Sergeant Dean Welch and Lieutenant Colonel Virginia McCabe worked wonders with the US Army, Master Gunnery Sergeant Mark Oliva with the US Marine Corps. Lieutenant Colonel Crispin Lockhart was my Ministry of Defence press minder, and showed impressive fortitude with my constantly changing list of demands.

At Harvard University, I'd like to thank Cemal Kafadar for welcoming me to the Center for Middle Eastern Studies, Roger Owen for his continuing sage advice over many pints, and the fantastic staff at the Monroe C. Gutman library. The *Solutions* team gave me the time and flexibility to tackle the intractable problems of the region. Many thanks to Robert Costanza, Ida Kubiszewski, and Kat Grigg. Hal Straus and Lauren Keane at the *Washington Post* sent me to Afghanistan in the first place.

Rory Stewart kindly lent me his room in Kabul and made the suggestion that made this project possible. I'd also like to thank the rest of the Turquoise Mountain team, Shoshana Clark, Noah Coburn, Zabihullah Majidi, and Jemima Montagu, for their many kindnesses. Rachel Reid, Jon Boone,

Jerome Starkey, Tom Coghlan, Minna Jarvenpaa, Fisnik Abrashi, Khwaga Kakar, Lorenzo Delesgues, and Jeremy Kelly all gave me a brief and memorable introduction to life in Kabul before the surge. Mokdar Amiri followed me across the mountains, repeatedly.

This book would not have been possible without the generosity and openness of those who worked in Afghanistan or contributed from afar. Many spent long hours reliving their experiences. I have not been able to include every story here, but every interview has helped deepen this narrative. Thank you. Others offered additional help, advice, and in many cases gamely went through various versions of the manuscript. My thanks to Clare Lockhart, Jonathan Green, Francis Harris, Michael Scheuer, William Dalrymple, Robert Grenier, Jason Amerine, Peter Krause, Philip Smucker, Michael Semple, John McColl, Said Tayeb Jawad, Roger Lane, Jim Dobbins, Thomas Ruttig, Astri Suhrke, Scott Guggenheim, Hanif Atmar, Samantha Reynolds, Stan Coats, Michael Ryder, Anatol Lieven, Asad Qureshi, Asra Nomani, Nick Carter, George Robertson, Zalmay Khalilzad, Hamdullah Mohib, Ali Jalali, Kay Mac-Gowan, Talatbek Masadykov, Shams Iklas, Sebastian Trives, Tom Praster, Bob Jimenez, Chris Possehl, Rob Fry, Phil Jones, David Richards, Dan McNeill, Ben Freakley, David Fraser, Ian Hope, John Nicholson, Chris Cavoli, Ron Neumann, John Lorimer, Jim Hogberg, Stuart Tootal, Tom Tugendhat, Tom Gregg, Steve Baker, Shahid Malik, Shiv Malik, Josh Meyer, Jerry Thomas, Michael Pattison, Nick Pounds, Jim Dutton, Sherard Cowper-Coles, Gerard Russell, Nick Lockwood, Dave Adams, Mart de Kruif, David Hook, David McKiernan, Tim Radford, Matt Cavanagh, Larry Nicholson, Kael Weston, Grenville Bibby, Peter Galbraith, Scott Smith, James Connolly, Guy Jones, Abdul Ali Shamsi, Carter Malkasian, Rob Thompson, Nick Kitson, Nick Parker, Doug Lute, Graham Lamb, Emma Sky, Matt Golsteyn, Lindy Cameron, Phil Weatherill, Michael Manning, Jason Morris, Martin Lindig, Ben Anderson, Peter Bergen, Theo Farrell, Bill Steuber, Mastin Robeson, and Nikki Dubois.

For their support and love over the years I would also like to thank my parents, Rufus and Cherry, and my wonderful in-laws, Phil and Lynn Asquith.

None of this would have been possible without my wife, Chrissy, whom I fell in love with the day we met, and who told me, whizzing through a dark Baghdad night, that having a partner didn't mean an end to adventures. She was right.

NOTES

PROLOGUE—THE MASK OF ANARCHY

1. Bill Steuber, interview.

2. "Afghanistan: Civilian Deaths From Airstrikes," *Human Rights Watch,* September 9, 2008; www.hrw.org/news/2008/09/07/afghanistan-civilian-deaths-airstrikes.

3. Jessica Donati, "Afghan Civilian Deaths Up in 2013 as War Intensifies: U.N.," Reuters, February 8, 2014; www.reuters.com/article/2014/02/08/us-afghanistan -casualties-idUSBREA1706D20140208.

4. Private interview.

5. Private interview. See also Christina Lamb, interview with Karzai, January 27, 2014; www.bakhtarnews.com.af/eng/politics/item/10808-full-transcript-of-president -karzai%E2%80%99s-interview-with-british-newspaper-the-sunday-times.html.

6. Private interview.

7. Private interview. See also Lamb interview with Karzai.

8. Hanif Atmar, interview.

9. Said Jawad, interview.

10. Atmar, interview.

11. Christina Lamb, interview with Karzai.

12. Ibid.

13. Private interview.

14. William Dalrymple, "How Is Hamid Karzai Still Standing?," *New York Times,* November 20, 2013; www.nytimes.com/2013/11/24/magazine/how-is-hamid-karzai -still-standing.html.

15. Linda J. Bilmes, "The Financial Legacy of Iraq and Afghanistan: How Wartime Spending Decisions Will Constrain Future National Security Budgets," HKS Faculty Research Working Paper Series RWP13-006, March 2013; https://research.hks .harvard.edu/publications/workingpapers/citation.aspx?PubId=8956&type=WPN.

16. "A New Way Forward: Rethinking US Strategy in Afghanistan," Afghanistan Study Group, 2012; www.afghanistanstudygroup.org/2012/05/28/85-billion-of-aghan -aid-wasted.

17. UNHCR Country Profile—Afghanistan; www.unhcr.org/pages/49e486eb6 .html. See also Emma Graham-Harrison, "Afghan Refugees Abandoned by Their Own Government, Report Finds," *The Guardian*, February 23, 2012; www.theguardian .com/world/2012/feb/23/afghan-refugees-amnesty-report.

18. Emma Graham-Harrison, "Prevalence of Malnutrition in Southern Afghanistan 'Shocking,'" *The Guardian,* September 4, 2012; www.theguardian.com/world/2012/sep/04/malnutrition-southern-afghanistan-shocking-levels.

19. "Operation Enduring Freedom," iCasualties.org; icasualties.org/oef.

CHAPTER 1—THE WRONG KIND OF WAR

1. Bob Woodward, *Bush at War* (New York: Simon & Schuster, 2002, Kindle edition).

2. Jane Mayer, *The Dark Side: The Inside Story of How the War on Terror Turned into a War on American Ideals* (New York: Anchor Books, 2009, Kindle edition).

3. Richard Armitage, interview.

4. Condoleezza Rice, interview.

5. Woodward, *Bush at War.*

6. Mayer, *The Dark Side.*

7. Mark Mazzetti, *The Way of the Knife: The CIA, a Secret Army, and a War at the Ends of the Earth* (New York: Penguin, 2013, Kindle edition).

8. Bob Woodward, *Obama's Wars* (New York: Simon & Schuster, 2010, Kindle edition).

9. Michael Scheuer, interview.

10. Richard A. Clarke, *Against All Enemies: Inside America's War on Terror* (New York: Free Press, 2004, Kindle edition).

11. Ibid.

12. Ibid.

13. Mayer, *The Dark Side.*

14. Woodward, *Bush at War.*

15. Ibid.

CHAPTER 2—BLOODY HELL

1. Woodward, *Bush at War.*

2. Winston Churchill, *The Story of the Malakand Field Force: An Episode of Frontier War* (London: Cooper, 1989, Kindle edition). Churchill also went on to say, "Every influence, every motive, that provokes the spirit of murder among men, impels these mountaineers to deeds of treachery and violence. The strong aboriginal propensity to kill, inherent in all human beings, has in these valleys been preserved in unexampled strength and vigour. That religion, which above all others was founded and propagated by the sword—the tenets and principles of which are instinct with incentives to slaughter and which in three continents has produced fighting breeds of men—stimulates a wild and merciless fanaticism. The love of plunder, always a characteristic of hill tribes, is fostered by the spectacle of opulence and luxury which, to their eyes, the cities and plains of the south display. A code of honour not less punctilious than that of old Spain, is supported by vendettas as implacable as those of Corsica."

3. William Dalrymple, *Return of a King: The Battle for Afghanistan, 1839–42* (New York: Random House, 2013, Kindle edition).

4. Ibid.

5. Ibid.

6. Ibid., p. 267.

7. William Dalrymple, "Souter Takes a Call," *Outlook India*, August 30, 2010.

8. Christian Tripodi, *The Edge of Empire: The British Political Officer and Tribal Administration on the North-West Frontier 1877–1947* (London: Ashgate, 2011), p. 60.

9. Sandeman was hardly without his own ideological blinders, which included pet racial theories about the Pashtuns and the inherent superiority of the British. What Sandeman grasped was that tribal warfare and banditry weren't affronts to what the West stood for, but a local blend of gamesmanship and necessity. As one biographer, Alexander Lauzun Pendock Tucker, noted of Sandeman, "He was Scotch himself and clannishness appealed to him."

10. The irrigation from the Kajaki dam was intended to provide enough fertile land to settle 18,000 to 20,000 families on fifteen-acre farms over almost a quarter million acres of former desert. Entire communities were constructed for former nomads downstream from the dam in places like Marja and Nad Ali. Resettled families received a pair of oxen, 2,000 Afghani in currency, and enough wheat seed for the first year. Swiss experts were flown in to teach the Pashtuns how to use long-handled scythes. Nick Cullather, *The Hungry World* (Cambridge, MA, and London: Harvard University Press, 2010).

11. Paul Jones, "Afghanistan Venture," in Cullather, *The Hungry World*.

12. Nick Cullather, "From New Deal to New Frontier in Afghanistan: Modernization in a Buffer State," Working Paper No. 6, Indiana University, 2002.

13. Rodric Braithwaite, *Afghantsy: The Russians in Afghanistan, 1979–89* (New York: Oxford University Press, 2011), p. 75.

14. Ibid., p. 48.

15. Ibid.

16. Alfred W. McCoy, "Can Anyone Pacify the World's Number One Narco-State? The Opium Wars in Afghanistan," *TomDispatch*, March 30, 2010; www.tomdispatch.com/archive/175225. The Beat poet Allen Ginsberg admired McCoy's controversial research.

17. Woodward, *Bush at War*.

CHAPTER 3—GOOD TALIBAN

1. Peter Bergen, *Manhunt: The Ten-Year Search for Bin Laden—From 9/11 to Abbottabad* (New York: Crown Publishing, 2012, Kindle edition).

2. Alex Strick van Linschoten and Felix Kuehn, *An Enemy We Created: The Myth of the Taliban / Al-Qaeda Merger in Afghanistan, 1970–2010* (London: Hurst & Company, 2012, Kindle edition), p. 166.

3. The foreign minister Wakim Muttawakil, waiting anxiously for news of Massoud's death, phoned the Alliance's headquarters pretending to be from the Iranian foreign ministry to ask if they should express their condolences, and thus ascertain whether the plot had succeeded. Michael Semple, interview.

4. Bergen, *Manhunt*. Was there more the US could have done to foster relations? Grenier's predecessor in Islamabad, Milt Bearden, believed the Taliban's offers reflected honest attempts to find a face-saving deal for themselves: "We never heard what they

were trying to say. . . . We had no common language. Ours was, 'Give up Bin Laden.' They were saying, 'Do something to help us give him up.'" Bearden added, "I have no doubts they wanted to get rid of him. He was a pain in the neck," but this "never clicked" with US officials. David Ottaway and Joe Stevens, "Diplomats Met with Taliban on Bin Laden," *Washington Post,* October 29, 2001.

5. Wendy Chamberlain, interview.

6. Strick van Linschoten and Kuehn, *An Enemy We Created.*

7. Robert Grenier, message exchanged with author.

8. Gary Schroen, *First In: An Insider's Account of How the CIA Spearheaded the War on Terror in Afghanistan* (New York: Presidio Press, 2007).

9. Ibid.

10. ISI paper, cited in Ahmed Rashid, *Descent into Chaos: The U.S. and the Disaster in Pakistan, Afghanistan, and Central Asia* (New York: Penguin, 2008), p. 77. For example, an offer by Ahmed Gailani, an Afghan exile, and the leader of a Sufi mystic order, to speak for the south was almost risible to Grenier; many conservative Pashtuns viewed Gailani's version of Islam as a religious aberration.

11. James Dobbins, *After the Taliban: Nation-Building in Afghanistan* (Dulles, VA: Potomac Press, 2008), p. 24.

12. Ibid., p. 43.

13. Francesc Vendrell, interview.

14. Lakhdar Brahimi, interview.

15. Michael Semple, interview.

16. In addition, the US military was readying the 82nd Airborne Division to seize the capital in the event that the Northern Alliance advance stalled. Sean Naylor, *Not a Good Day to Die: The Untold Story of Operation Anaconda* (New York: Berkley Publishing Group, 2005), p. 11.

17. James Dobbins, interview.

18. Brahimi, "An Interview with Lakhdar Brahimi," *Journal of International Affairs,* September 22, 2004.

CHAPTER 4—THE MAN WHO WOULD BE KING

1. Dalrymple, "How Is Hamid Karzai Still Standing?"

2. Steve Coll, *Ghost Wars: The Secret History of the CIA, Afghanistan, and bin Laden, from the Soviet Invasion to September 10, 2001* (New York: Penguin Press, 2004, Kindle edition).

3. Rashid, *Descent into Chaos,* p. 63.

4. Eric Blehm, *The Only Thing Worth Dying For: How Eleven Green Berets Fought for a New Afghanistan* (New York: Harper Perennial, 2011, Kindle edition).

5. Ibid.

6. Rashid, *Descent into Chaos,* p. 85.

7. Private interview.

8. Karzai's memories of the incident later proved to be highly selective. In early interviews, he claimed that Pakistani special forces took him to a deserted air base in southern Afghanistan, rather than the Pakistani air base where he eventually spent several days. Karzai presumably realized that his rescue would appear even more

inglorious if it became known he had been a guest of the Pakistani military. The US was also to keep Pakistan in the dark, given their alleged connivance in Haq's death. "Interview with President Hamid Karzai," *PBS Frontline,* May 7, 2002; http://www .pbs.org/wgbh/pages/frontline/shows/campaign/interviews/karzai.html.

9. Jason Amerine, interview.

10. Ibid.

11. Dobbins, *After the Taliban,* p. 19.

12. This entire scene is recounted in Blehm, *The Only Thing Worth Dying For.*

13. Ibid.

14. Ibid.

15. Blehm, *The Only Thing Worth Dying For.*

16. Amerine, interview.

17. Dobbins, interview.

18. Blehm, *The Only Thing Worth Dying For.*

19. Rashid, *Descent into Chaos,* p. 104.

20. Sarah Chayes, *The Punishment of Virtue: Inside Afghanistan After the Taliban* (New York: Penguin, 2006), p. 218.

21. Thomas Ruttig, interview.

22. Ibid.

23. General Ehsen ul Haq, the new ISI chief, sat down with Jalaluddin Haqqani in Islamabad to gauge his loyalties. Haqqani had once been one of the CIA's strongest allies in Afghanistan. Mazzetti, *The Way of the Knife,* p. 35.

24. Private interview. Thomas Ruttig, "The Haqqani Network Blacklisted: From US Asset to Special Foe," *Afghan Analysts Network,* September 20, 2012, accessed April 1, 2014; www.afghanistan-analysts.org/the-haqqani-network-blacklisted-from -us-asset-to-special-foe. A decade later, members of the Furqan group formed the basis of the High Peace Council.

25. Chayes, *The Punishment of Virtue,* p. 27.

26. Abdul Waheed Baghrani, interview.

27. Strick van Linschoten and Kuehn, *An Enemy We Created,* p. 241.

28. Baghrani, interview.

29. Zalmay Khalilzad, interview.

30. Semple, interview.

31. David Fox, "Interview: Lt. Col. David Fox," *PBS Frontline,* July 9, 2002; www .pbs.org/wgbh/pages/frontline/shows/campaign/interviews/fox.html.

32. Private interview.

33. Ibid.

34. There was a meeting between Karzai and Taliban delegates on December 6, although what transpired at the meeting is not known.

35. Donald Wright, *A Different Kind of War: The US Military in Operation Enduring Freedom October 2001–September 2005* (Fort Leavenworth, KS: Combat Studies Institute Press, US Army Combined Arms Center, 2010).

36. Chayes, *The Punishment of Virtue,* p. 60.

37. Wright, *A Different Kind of War.*

38. Chayes, *The Punishment of Virtue,* p. 51.

CHAPTER 5—AT THE GATES

1. Schroen, *First In.*

2. Gary Bernsten and Ralph Pezzullo, *Jawbreaker: The Attack on Bin Laden and Al Qaeda* (New York: Crown, 2005), p. 72.

3. Ibid., p. 90.

4. Philip G. Smucker, *Al Qaeda's Great Escape: The Military and the Media on Terror's Trail* (Lincoln, NE: Potomac Books, 2005, Kindle edition).

5. Dalton Fury, *Kill Bin Laden: A Delta Force Commander's Account of the Hunt for the World's Most Wanted Man* (New York: St. Martin's Press, 2008), p. 188.

6. Ibid., p. 93.

7. Peter Krause, "The Last Good Chance: A Reassessment of U.S. Operations at Tora Bora," *Security Studies* 17 (2008); web.mit.edu/polisci/people/gradstudents /papers/PKrause%20The%20Last%20Good%20Chance.pdf, accessed April 1, 2014.

8. Another argument was that Pakistan was blocking the border area—despite the absence of any such troops.

9. Franks had other considerations as well. In late November, Donald Rumsfeld had told Franks that President Bush "wants us to look for options in Iraq," and that he should "dust off" the Pentagon's blueprint for an invasion. On December 4, Franks presented the plan to Rumsfeld. Both men agreed it needed a lot of work; Rumsfeld gave Franks eight days. In other words, just as the battle at Tora Bora was reaching its climax, Iraq dominated Franks's thinking. As the author Peter Bergen notes, "It is impossible not to wonder if the labor-intensive planning ordered by [Rumsfeld] for another major war was a distraction from the one he was already fighting." Peter Bergen, "The Battle for Tora Bora," *New Republic*, December 22, 2009; www .newrepublic.com/article/the-battle-tora-bora.

10. Michael O'Hanlon of the Brookings Institution calculated that up to 3,000 American troops might be needed to cover each route. Those forces did exist in the theater at the time—the 10th Mountain Division had deployed in Uzbekistan in October and a 1,200-strong marine expeditionary unit had also recently arrived in Camp Rhino, outside Kandahar. In early December its commander, Jim Mattis, had even offered to send marines to Tora Bora, but his request was declined. The Deployment Readiness Brigade (DRB) of the 82nd Airborne Division, based at Fort Bragg, North Carolina, could also have deployed within a week, the MIT researcher Peter Krause notes. Krause, "The Last Good Chance."

11. Private interview.

12. Ron Suskind, *The One Percent Doctrine: Deep Inside America's Pursuit of Its Enemies Since 9/11* (New York: Simon & Schuster, 2006), pp. 58–59, 74.

13. Fury, *Kill Bin Laden*, p. 133.

14. Peter Bergen, *The Longest War: The Enduring Conflict Between America and al-Qaeda* (New York: Free Press, 2011), p. 77.

CHAPTER 6—WARLORDS

1. Jim Dutton, interview.

2. John McColl, interview.

3. Gary Berntsen and Ralph Pezzullo, *Jawbreaker.* The meeting had an added

piquancy because Fahim, a bullying Tajik, had been the intelligence chief who had interrogated Karzai for treason a few years before.

4. McColl, interview. This was an unconscious echo of the time, almost two hundred years earlier, when British officials had first met the Afghan leader Shah Shuja and were similarly impressed by his sartorial style.

5. Said Tayeb Jawad, interview.

6. Jim Dobbins, interview.

7. Dutton, interview.

8. Dobbins, *After the Taliban*.

9. Richard Armitage, interview. When the US defense secretary visited Kabul that spring, McColl, showing typical persistence, tried to pitch Rumsfeld the idea of an expanded peacekeeping force, but Pentagon flaks carefully kept the British general at bay.

10. Private interview.

11. Thomas E. Ricks and Vernon Loeb, "Ground Operation Done, General Says," *Washington Post*, March 19, 2002; articles.sun-sentinel.com/2002-03-19/news/0203 180519_1_al-qaida-fighters-shah-e-kot-valley-operation-anaconda, accessed January 21, 2013.

12. McColl, interview.

13. Jawad, interview.

14. During their covert campaign against the Soviet occupation in the 1980s, one of the fiercest rivalries into which the Americans were unwittingly drawn was between Akhundzada Senior and ISI favorite Gulbeddin Hekmatyar. In 1989, Akhundzada approached the US embassy in Islamabad offering to ban poppy cultivation in exchange for $2 million in development aid. It might have been a smart move: Akhundzada could squeeze Hekmatyar's heroin labs while being paid by the Americans to do it, in the process raising his profile with the superpower at his rival's expense. In the end, though, he made a fatal miscalculation: He still had to drive through Hekmatyar's territory to get to Islamabad.

15. Sher Mohammed Akhundzada, interview.

16. When questioned by the author, Sher Mohammed Akhundzada did not deny his involvement in the opium trade. Others, including the British ambassador to Afghanistan, Rosalind Marsden, have alleged that he was directly linked. Rosalind Marsden, interview.

17. As Farrell and Giustozzi note, a similar process took place in Nad Ali, with Akhundzada's removal of local shuras that sprung up after the Taliban's ouster. Theo Farrell and Antonio Giustozzi, "The Taliban at War: Inside the Helmand Insurgency, 2004–2012," *International Affairs* Vol. 89, Issue 4, July 12, 2013.

CHAPTER 7—NATIONAL SOLIDARITY

1. "Afghanistan Needs $1.3 Billion to Cover Immediate Needs, $10 Billion Over Next Five Years, Secretary-General Tells Tokyo Conference," *United Nations Press Release* (SG/SM/8108); www.un.org/News/Press/docs/2002/sgsm8108.doc.htm.

2. Private interview.

3. Clare Lockhart, interview.

4. Scott Guggenheim, interview.

5. Private interview.

6. Ibid.

7. Samantha Reynolds, e-mail to author.

8. As Samantha Reynolds noted, "Very early on we took Ghani on a field visit to Panjshir to give him a chance to meet community forum members first hand, and it was them (village elders) who convinced him that they wanted their own elected institutions at the village level and not have projects imposed on them from outside or done for them by government or NGOs. People were more worried about all the money parachuting in and feared the disruption it would cause." E-mail with author.

9. Guggenheim, interview.

10. Ibid.

11. Hanif Atmar, interview.

12. Sultan Barakat, interview.

13. Among these supporters was the UN envoy's adviser Barnett Rubin, who had admired Atmar's work in Peshawar.

14. Ibid.

15. Mohammed Lal, interview.

16. United Nations, "National Solidarity Programme Disburses First Grants to 14 Afghan Communities," *Voices* Vol. 1, no. 2 (2003); https://habnet.unhabitat.org/files /602_Voices_3A.pdf.

17. Barakat, interview.

CHAPTER 8—A CONVENIENT DRUG

1. Michael Ryder, interview.

2. Howard Marks, *Mr Nice: An Autobiography* (London: Vintage, 1997, Kindle edition).

3. John Glaze, "Opium and Afghanistan: Reassessing U.S. Counternarcotics Strategy" (Carlisle, PA: Strategic Studies Institute, US Army War College, 2007).

4. United Nations International Drug Control Programme, "Annual Opium Poppy Survey," *Drug Control Monitoring System (AFG/C27)* 2000; www.unodc.org/pdf/publi cations/report_2000-12-31_1.pdf.

5. "Afghanistan Opium Survey 2002," United Nations Office for Drug Control and Crime Prevention, October 2002; www.unodc.org/pdf/publications/afg_opium_survey _2002.pdf.

6. Ryder, interview.

7. Ultimately Blair didn't use the ten-year figure in his address, although once presented to the cabinet office and logged in the Whitehall system, the ten-year plan was adopted by other departments, such as the treasury.

8. Private interview.

9. Private interview.

10. Gretchen Peters, *Seeds of Terror: How Drugs, Thugs, and Crime Are Reshaping the Afghan War* (London: Picador, 2010), p. 192.

11. "Afghanistan Opium Survey 2004," United Nationals Office for Drug Control

and Crime Prevention, November 2004; www.unodc.org/documents/crop-monitoring /Afghanistan/AFGopiumsurvey04_web.pdf.

12. Vanda Felbab-Brown, "The Drug-Conflict Nexus in South Asia: Beyond Taliban Profits and Afghanistan," *Foundation for Defense of Democracies*, May 20, 2010; www.brookings.edu/~/media/research/files/papers/2010/5/regional%20counter narcotics%20felbabbrown/05_regional_counternarcotics_felbabbrown.pdf, accessed April 1, 2014.

13. Prices obviously vary, but a record high was $350 in 2002. Prices are typically 50 percent lower. www.unodc.org/pdf/publications/afg_opium_survey_2002.pdf.

14. US Policy in Afghanistan, Senlis Council; www.icosgroup.net/static/reports/us _policy_recommendations.pdf.

CHAPTER 9—HOMECOMING

1. Abdul Waheed Baghrani, interview. Baghrani said he initially harbored Mullah Omar. Other sources suggest that he may have hidden in Maiwand, near the border between the provinces of Kandahar and Helmand. Carlotta Gall, *The Wrong Enemy: American in Afghanistan, 2001–2014* (New York: Houghton Mifflin Harcourt, 2014), p. 33.

2. Abdul Waheed Baghrani, interview.

3. Sherzai's targeting of his rivals and patronage of friends wasn't simply down tribal lines; there were frequently sub-tribes with an entirely different allegiance to other branches. Broad patterns did emerge, however.

Panjpai Durranis (Noorzais, Ishakzais, Alizais, Khogiyanis, and Mako) make up about 27 percent of the population but account for only 10 percent of the government positions. Carter Malkasian makes the following excellent point: "To be clear, it is a little misleading to pose the conflict in southern Afghanistan as one of marginalized tribes versus empowered tribes. There is no such thing as a coherent tribe in southern Afghanistan. Tribes are fragmented and laid on top of one another across different districts and villages. A large number of elders wielding varying degrees of power exist in every tribe. No one elder controls an entire tribe. Indeed, under Pashtun custom, no Pashtun can give an order to another. So instead of different tribes fighting tribes, different groups (or sometimes family clans) from different tribes were in conflict. Other groups were not. Plenty of Noorzais worked with the pro-government leaders and plenty of Alizais and Achekzais supported the Taliban. For simplicity's sake, though, we will continue to refer to tribes rather than specific sub-groups and clans." Carter Malkasian, Jerry Meyerle, and Megan Katt, "The War in Southern Afghanistan 2001–8," Center for Naval Analysis; https://info.publicintelligence.net /CNA-WarSouthernAfghanistan.pdf.

4. Official figures for the number of Afghans the US has detained and interrogated have not been released. Carlotta Gall writes that "thousands of Afghans passed through the humiliation and pain of Bagram." Gall, *The Wrong Enemy*, p. 211. A rough estimate is provided here: www.detainedbyus.org/detainees/statistics. In terms of the scale of the abuse, CBS News provided this snapshot: www.cbsnews.com/news/report-108 -died-in-us-custody. Dilawer's death received widespread attention due to the brilliant documentary *Taxi to the Dark Side* by Alec Gibney. A subsequent US investigation

into Dilawer's death also revealed that the American interrogators themselves consid-ered Dilawer and his passengers to be innocent, although that didn't stop them from sending two of the passengers on to Guantánamo Bay in Cuba where, of the first batch of 742 sent there, Bush officials later estimated that 90 percent were innocent.

5. Private interview.

6. Muttawakil had also engaged in discussion pre-9/11 to discuss handing over bin Laden, and was regarded as a moderate. Gall, *The Wrong Enemy,* pp. 53, 74.

7. Private interview.

8. Some former Taliban did attend, such as Abdul Hakin Munib, who served as governor of Oruzgun province for about a year from 2006 to 2007. He was not re-moved from a UN sanctions list, which meant that western countries could not offi-cially support him. Thomas Ruttig, "Negotiations with the Taliban," in *Talibanistan: Negotiating the Borders Between Terror, Politics, and Religion,* ed. Peter Bergen and Katherine Tiedemann (New York: Oxford University Press, 2013), p. 440.

Much of the debate over the Loya Jirga's shortcomings has focused on the treatment of the recently returned king, Zahir Shah, and the prominent positions given to war-lords during the meeting. The notion of not giving a central role to the warlords, many of whom were now governors and ministers, was faintly preposterous and had more to do with the delicate sensibilities of westerners than with Afghan politics. The matter of the eighty-seven-year-old king, controversially sidelined against his wishes, held a deeper significance. Decrepit as the old man was, he was a genuinely unifying figure, one many Pashtun attendees were clamoring to embrace. The US missed an opportu-nity to broaden Karzai's support in the south. Some new Pashtun figures were included in Karzai's government. Many were undoubtedly alienated by the humiliating way in which the US envoy Zalmay Khalilzad announced the king's withdrawal from office before the Shah could make his own decision. Yet the real failure of the Loya Jirga didn't concern who said what or sat where: It was the void created by the Taliban's absence.

9. Details of this conversation were passed on to another former ISI officer, who requested anonymity.

10. Carlotta Gall, "Former Pakistani Officer Embodies a Policy Puzzle," *New York Times,* March 3, 2010; www.nytimes.com/2010/03/04/world/asia/04imam.html?r=0.

11. Asad Qureshi, e-mail with author.

12. Kashmir had come to define Pakistan's sense of identity. It is telling that when Musharraf held an emergency meeting of his generals to discuss the US ultimatum, the primary concern was not an American attack per se, or even the destruction of their clients the Taliban; Musharraf was more worried about the implication of the "War on Terror" for Kashmir. Steve Coll observed, "*Every* Pakistani general, liberal or religious, believed in the jihadists by 1999, not from personal Islamic conviction, in most cases, but because the jihadists had proved themselves over many years as the one force able to frighten, flummox, and bog down the Hindu-dominated Indian army. About a dozen Indian divisions had been tied up in Kashmir during the late 1990s to suppress a few thousand well-trained, paradise-seeking guerrillas. What more could Pakistan ask?" Steve Coll, *Ghost Wars*.

13. See Pew among others; http://www.pewglobal.org/2008/12/18/global-public-opinion-in-the-bush-years-2001-2008/.

14. Rashid, *Descent into Chaos,* p. 76.

15. Shortly after the US bombing campaign began, the spy agency concluded in a strategy paper that the Taliban were likely to remain a cogent force in Afghanistan for the foreseeable future. The same paper also predicted that the US would soon leave. Ibid., p. 77.

16. If Musharraf's speech didn't make clear Pakistan's ambivalence toward American policy, his spy chief Ahmed made it explicit a few days later. Leading a delegation to Kandahar ostensibly to persuade Mullah Omar to hand over bin Laden, Ahmed instead encouraged Omar to stand firm. When the CIA learned of the meeting, an incensed Bush administration prevailed upon Musharraf to sack Ahmed. A changing of the guard at ISI, however, was unlikely to make much difference to Islamabad's policy. Steve Coll, "Don't Look Back," *New Yorker,* March 1, 2010; www.newyorker.com/talk /comment/2010/03/01/100301taco_talk_coll.

17. Private interview. See also Gall, *The Wrong Enemy,* p. 20.

18. This scene was described to a UN official by a member of the Taliban present.

19. Antonio Giustozzi, *Decoding the New Taliban: Insights from the Afghan Field* (New York: Columbia/Hurst, 2009), pp. 13–14.

20. "Taliban Names Anti-US Leadership Council," Reuters, June 24, 2003.

21. Thomas Joscelyn, "Gitmo Detainee Implicated in Red Cross Murder Transferred to Afghanistan," *Long War Journal,* December 23, 2009; www.longwarjournal.org/ archives/2009/12/gitmo_detainee_impli.php. See also Gall, *The Wrong Enemy*, p. 69.

CHAPTER 10—IMPERIAL VISION

1. Condoleezza Rice, interview.

2. Rumsfeld subsequently blamed others, including Rice, for this blunder, but it's clear that the Pentagon was considering retaining control in Iraq for weeks before the invasion. Special Inspector General for Iraq Reconstruction, *Hard Lessons* (New York: US Independent Agencies and Commissions, 2009), p. 44.

3. Rice, interview. Looting was apparent within days of the invasion beginning in the third week of March 2003.

4. Paul Bremer, interview.

5. Ibid.

6. Rumsfeld claimed he had not been aware of the direction of Bremer's thinking, although the Pentagon itself had suggested many of the measures before his arrival in Baghdad.

7. Dobbins, *After the Taliban,* p. 166.

8. Jim Dobbins, interview.

9. Dobbins, *After the Taliban,* p. 126, and interview.

10. Martin Strmecki, interview.

11. Zalmay Khalilzad, interview.

12. Joe Stephens and David Ottaway, "A Rebuilding Plan Full of Cracks," *Washington Post,* November 20, 2005; www.washingtonpost.com/wp-dyn/content/article /2005/11/19/AR2005111901248.html.

13. In October 2004, Patrick Fine, USAID's third country director in under a year, issued a sweeping indictment of the program in a confidential memo: "The schools

and clinics program has been marked by a series of missteps and miscalculations that resulted in a flawed business model, inadequate supervision and poor execution." Louis Berger was, according to Fine, a poor choice of a partner, having "no track record for this kind of work." www.washingtonpost.com/wp-srv/world/documents/USAID correspondence.pdf.

14. David Voreacos, "Berger Group Charged with Fraud in Iraq, Afghanistan," *Bloomberg,* November 5, 2010; www.bloomberg.com/news/2010-11-05/louis-berger -group-charged-with-fraud-over-contracts-in-iraq-afghanistan.html.

15. Stephens and Ottaway, "A Rebuilding Plan Full of Cracks."

16. Further embarrassment was to follow on the reconstruction front with the road-building project between Kandahar and Kabul, a $214 million contract also awarded to Louis Berger. The firm had hired an American security company to guard construction workers. This rapidly turned into a protection racket, with the firm, set up by a Texas couple a few months after the war, hiring armies of Afghan guards to the tune of $36 million, many of whom turned out not to exist. At least $17 million was billed in false receipts, according to a government indictment belatedly filed against the couple. Daniel Schulman, "The Cowboys of Kabul," *Mother Jones*, July 27, 2009; www.motherjones.com/politics/2009/07/cowboys-of-kabul.

17. Jim Bever, interview.

18. Ironically, the presidential palace is also called the Arg—Pashtu for citadel.

19. Khalilzad, interview.

20. Scott Guggenheim, interview.

21. A bevy of Afghan American businessmen appeared in government ministries claiming all sorts of privileged connections to the ambassador. The case of one, Seyed Merzad, briefly of Afghanistan's Geological Survey, is illustrative. A distant relative of Khalilzad, and a former employee of the Survey, Merzad returned to Kabul and promptly installed himself as head of the department sent to the ministry of mines. Khalilzad had flagged the country's rich metal and mineral deposits as key to the country's economy, and the Survey had a potentially important role to play identifying where the richest deposits lay. Merzad was annoyed to discover that the UK's aid agency, the Department for International Development, had recently sent out a team of geologists to start the work. Merzad occupied the director's office, but he lacked the authority to drive out the British, who had been invited by Karzai himself at a donor's conference. They maintained access to the ground floor and the library, which happened to contain extensive Russian aerial surveys of the country—the very information needed to start mining. Merzad and his cronies refused to listen to the British team and blocked all efforts to communicate between their respective staffs.

"And that's where we got stuck. Neither side was ready to cooperate with the other," recalled Stan Coats, a member of the British Geological Society. "It was all a bit silly really, but the impasse lasted for a good year." Stan Coats, interview.

22. Two of the turbines had been installed by 1975 but during the country's civil war much of the infrastructure was looted or damaged. The Taliban managed to get one turbine running at reduced capacity, and even contracted a Chinese firm to install a third turbine at a cost of $3.5 million—a staggeringly low sum compared to what USAID would later invest. Noah Arjomand, "Eagle's Summit Revisited: Decision-Making in the Kajaki Dam Refurbishment Project," *Afghan Analysts Network,* January

30, 2013; www.afghanistan-analysts.org/wp-content/uploads/downloads/2013/02/20 130125_Arjomand_Kajaki_Dam_final1.pdf.

23. Private interview.

CHAPTER 11—PRTS

1. Nick Carter, interview.

2. There was an earlier proposal from the United Nations called Provincial Security Teams, but the UN lacked the resources to implement it.

3. Carter, interview.

4. Sally Austin of CARE was more forthright: "Our security is being put at risk . . . their understanding of neutrality and humanitarian principles is pretty weak." "The Provincial Reconstruction Team (PRT) in Afghanistan and Its Role in Reconstruction," Center for Humanitarian Cooperation, May 31, 2003; reliefweb.int/report/afghanistan /provincial-reconstruction-team-prt-afghanistan-and-its-role-reconstruction.

5. Adam Curtis, "Goodies and Baddies," *BBC Blogs*, March 28, 2011; www.bbc.co .uk/blogs/adamcurtis/posts/goodies_and_baddies.

6. Robert Finn, interview.

7. MSF left the country altogether a few months later, after the death of five of its staff, killings it blamed in part on the adverse association of its work with the US military.

8. Mike Parmly, Larry Carnahan, Tim Martin, and another officer also opened PRTs in Kandahar, Mazar-e-Sharif, Herat, and Jalalabad, respectively, during the spring of 2003.

9. Thomas Praster, interview.

10. Ibid.

11. Thomas Ruttig, interview.

12. Craig Pules and Mark Mazzetti, "US Probing Alleged Abuse of Afghans," *LA Times*, September 21, 2004; articles.latimes.com/2004/sep/21/world/fg-detain21/2.

13. Ibid. US military investigators opened a criminal probe into the incident, but no charges were ever brought against the soldiers allegedly involved, despite extensive witness testimony. The military claimed at the time that Nasir died of natural causes. As the *Los Angeles Times* revealed, there was subsequent evidence of a military cover-up and, perhaps more surprisingly, the UN office in Kabul sat on its report for over a year. Craig Pyes and Kevin Sack, "Two Deaths Were a 'Clue That Something's Wrong,'" *Los Angeles Times*, September 25, 2006; articles.latimes.com/2006/sep/25/nation/ na-torture25.

14. Ibid.

15. Ruttig, interview. Former members of ODA 2121 were not available for comment.

16. Barbara J. Stapleton, "A Means to What End? Why PRTs Are Peripheral to the Bigger Political Challenges in Afghanistan," *Journal of Military and Strategic Studies* 10, no. 1 (September 2007); jmss.synergiesprairies.ca/jmss/index.php/jmss/article /view/38/36.

17. The general in question was Lord Hastings Ismay, NATO's first secretary general. For an example of extensive commentary on NATO's decline, see https://www .theatlantic.com/past/politics/foreign/mearsh.htm.

18. George Robertson, interview.

19. Phil Jones, interview.

20. Ibid.

21. Robertson, interview.

22. Ruttig, interview.

23. Sebastian Merz, "Still on the Way to Afghanistan? Germany and Its Forces in the Hindu Kush," *SIPRI*, November 2007; www.sipri.org/research/conflict/publications /merz.

24. Private interview.

25. Konrad Freytag, "Afghanistan—A Report from the Ground," *World Security Network*, May 26, 2004; www.worldsecuritynetwork.com/Broader-Middle-East/Freytag -Konrad/Afghanistan-a-report-from-the-ground.

CHAPTER 12—A SPECIAL RELATIONSHIP

1. Gavin Berman, "The Cost of International Military Operations," House of Commons Library, UK Parliament, October 1, 2012; http://www.parliament.uk /business/publications/research/briefing-papers/SN03139/the-cost-of-international -military-operations.

2. Richard Dannatt, Iraq Inquiry.

3. The bitter reaction to the Iraq war stung the military. "It's immensely hard to fight a war which the country doesn't believe in, because it damages the relationship between the military and the country," reflected Fry later. Rob Fry, interview.

4. Ibid.

5. Thomas Metz, interview.

6. Michael Walker, Iraq Inquiry.

7. Geoff Hoon, Iraq Inquiry.

8. Canada had also rejected a proposed missile defense shield.

9. David Fraser, interview.

10. Private interview.

11. Andrew Kennett, interview.

12. Nigel Sheinwald, interview.

13. Gil Baldwin, interview.

14. Minna Jarvenpaa, interview.

15. Mark Etherington, interview.

16. Robert Fry, interview.

17. Private interview.

18. *Great Britain: Parliament: House of Commons: Defence Committee, Operations in Afghanistan: Fourth report of session 2010–12*, Vol. 1: Report, together with formal minutes, oral and written evidence (London: Stationery Office, 2011), Ev130.

19. Earlier that year, Karzai and the international community had agreed to "the Afghanistan Compact," one of the more deluded documents to emerge from the war, meant to "commit" the Afghan government to sweeping reforms in return for extra cash.

20. Jarvenpaa, interview.

21. Etherington, interview.

22. Mike Jackson, Iraq Inquiry.

23. Mike Jackson, interview.

CHAPTER 13—ERADICATION

1. Private interview.

2. Rosalind Marsden, interview.

3. "Opium in Helmand," www.nps.edu/programs/ccs/Docs/Opium/RCSouth/helmand.pdf.

4. As in the case of Bashir Noorzai, who was ultimately arrested in New York in 2005. Benjamin Weiser, "Afghan Linked to Taliban Sentenced to Life in Drug Trafficking Case," *New York Times*, May 1, 2009; www.nytimes.com/2009/05/01/nyregion/01sentence.html.

5. Greater success was had striking drug labs that had sprung up on the border with Pakistan; Task Force 333 directed air strikes against several in Nangarhar province in 2003. Private interview.

6. Sher Mohammed Akhundzada, interview.

7. Bashir, interview.

8. Nick Lockwood, interview.

9. Over the two years prior to 2005, Helmand's opium production was well on the way to tripling from 2002 levels, amounting to almost half the country's opium production.

10. Taliban did benefit from the opium harvest—to the tune of $50 million in 2006, according to one study. While it was true that the cadre of fighters who had followed Mullah Dadullah into Afghanistan in 2003 did take advantage of the trade, they hardly needed vast sums of money to wage a low-level insurgency.

11. Robert Charles, interview.

12. In fact the Colombia example, often cited, was much less clear-cut, and confused the military's success in driving FARC rebels out of the cities and into the jungles, with the impact of eradication, which proved devastating to the communities involved in production, but only had a limited effect on cutting off supplies to the rebels, who merely started growing operations in a different area of the jungle. By 2010, it appeared the pendulum was swinging the other way: "Paramilitaries' Heirs: The New Face of Violence in Colombia," *Human Rights Watch*, February 3, 2010; www.hrw.org/en/reports/2010/02/03/paramilitaries-heirs.

13. Charles, interview.

14. Doug Wankel, interview.

15. Jon Lee Anderson, "Letter from Afghanistan: The Taliban's Opium War," *New Yorker*, July 9, 2007.

16. Ibid.

17. Ibid.

18. Joel Hafvenstein, interview.

19. A congressional study found that the DEA had requested military air lifts on twenty-six occasions in 2005 and these requests were denied in all but three cases. Josh Meyer, "Pentagon Doing Little in Afghan Drug Fight," *Los Angeles Times*, December 5, 2005; articles.latimes.com/2006/dec/05/world/fg-afghandrugs5.

20. Jim Hogberg, interview.

21. Wankel, interview.

22. Marsden, interview.

23. Christina Lamb, January 27, 2014, interview with Karzai.

24. Private interview.

CHAPTER 14—FRIENDLY ADVICE

1. Ben Freakley, interview.

2. Private interview.

3. Freakley, interview.

4. Ibid.

5. Carter Malkasian, "The War in Southern Afghanistan," Strategic Studies, Center for Naval Analyses, 2009.

6. Anand Gopal, "The Battle for Afghanistan: Militancy and Conflict in Kandahar," *New America Foundation*, November 9, 2010; newamerica.net/sites/newamerica.net/files/policydocs/kandahar_0.pdf.

7. Sher Mohammed Akhundzada, interview.

8. In Herat, Khalilzad intervened after fighting flared between Amanullah Shah, a Pashtun warlord pledged to Karzai, and the long-term power broker in western Afghanistan, Ismail Khan, who had publicly snubbed the president on a number of occasions. At Khalilzad's urging, the Afghan National Army was dispatched. The army might not have achieved much by itself. Rebuilding the Afghan security forces had not been a success story so far: The Germans had been given the job of reconstituting the police, but their limited effort had done little to transform the organization's corrupt practices. The Americans, in charge of the Afghan army, had been slow to get going, with the US military content to rely on warlord militias. More influential was Khalilzad's decision to fly to Herat in person to persuade Khan to resign and accept a post in Kabul.

9. Carlotta Gall called the Disarmament, Demobilization, and Reintegration program that led to the disbanding of militias an "ill-timed mistake," and likened it to the demobilization of the Iraqi army in 2003. Gall, *The Wrong Enemy*, p. 123.

10. Private interview.

11. Michael Semple, interview.

12. Ian Hope, interview.

13. Ibid.

14. The *New York Times* journalist Elizabeth Rubin, visiting the area several weeks later, established who the victims of the fighting were. One poppy farmer told her, "Why do you think people put mines out . . . [why are they] doing eradication when they came here to save us? . . . Thousands of lands [*sic*] ready for harvest were destroyed. How difficult will it be for our people to tolerate that! You are taking the food off my children, cutting my feet and disabling me."

15. John Keegan, "Let the Infighting Begin: British and US Rivalry Resumes," *The Telegraph*, April 17, 2003; www.telegraph.co.uk/news/worldnews/northamerica/usa/1427766/Let-the-infighting-begin-British-and-US-rivalry-resumes.html.

16. David Fraser, interview.

17. Fraser, interview. The decision to move Butler was not Fraser's but resulted from negotiations between the British Chief of the Defense Staff, Michael Walker, and his Canadian counterpart. As the National Contingent Adviser, Butler's role was to ensure British forces integrated well with their NATO counterparts, that national objectives and caveats were met, as well as having overall responsibility for the British mission.

18. Ed Butler, interview.

19. Dan McNeill, interview.

20. Sandy Gall, *War Against the Taliban* (London: Bloomsbury, 2012), p. 236.

21. Freakley, interview.

22. Ibid.

23. Nicholson later died storming Delhi during the Indian Mutiny of 1857 at the age of thirty-four. During his brief but stellar career, he was dubbed Nijal Seyn by the locals in Punjab and held to be an incarnation of the Hindu god Brahma. The sect continued to flourish in the area until the 1980s. O. Tarin, "Tending to the Dead Sahibs," Unpublished Ethnological Research Report/Paper, South Asian Studies Seminar, SASI, University of Punjab, Lahore, Pakistan, 2006.

24. Lewis Sorley, *A Better War: The Unexamined Victories and Final Tragedy of America's Last Years in Vietnam* (New York: Harvest, 2007). He also encouraged his officers to read other classic books, like John A. Nagl and Peter Schoomaker's *Learning to Eat Soup with a Knife: Counterinsurgency Lessons from Malaya and Vietnam.* John Nicholson, interview.

25. Chris Cavoli, interview.

26. Dave Barno, interview.

27. Cavoli, interview. See also Gall, *The Wrong Enemy,* p. 114.

28. At first the locals were bewildered by the presence of soldiers from the 1st Battalion, 32nd Infantry Regiment. "Are you Soviets?" elders asked at one stage. When the Americans explained who they were and that they represented the government of Afghanistan, the locals sounded nonplussed. "What's that?" many asked. Jake Tapper, *The Outpost: An Untold Story of American Valor* (London: Little, Brown and Company, 2012), p. 67.

CHAPTER 15—FLY-FISHING IN THE HINDU KUSH

1. Tom Gregg, interview.

2. Kate Clark, "Plants of Afghanistan 1: Centre of Global Biodiversity," Afghanistan Analysts Network, June 10, 2012. http://www.afghanistan-analysts.org/plants-of -afghanistan-1-centre-of-global-biodiversity. The plant crops domesticated here include wheat, peas, lentils, chickpeas, sesame, hemp, onion, garlic, spinach, carrot, pistachio, pear, almond, grape, and apple.

3. Thomas Ruttig, head of the former UN mission in Afghanistan in Gardez, was instrumental in the grant, and Sebastian Trives in its early implementation.

4. "Afghanistan: A History of Utilization of Tribal Auxiliaries," *Tribal Analysis Centre,* August 2008; www.tribalanalysiscenter.com/PDF-TAC/Afghanistan%20A%20History %20of%20Utilization%20of%20Tribal%20Auxiliaries.pdf, accessed April 1, 2014.

5. Seth Jones, *The Graveyard of Empires: America's War in Afghanistan* (New York: W. W. Norton, 2010), p. 176.

6. Henry Bellew, *Journal of a Political Mission to Afghanistan in 1857 under Major (now Colonel) Lumsden with an account of the politics and people* (London: Smith, Elder, and Company, 1862).

7. Tom Tugendhat, Daoud's adviser, also fished the Helmand River at Lashkar Gah.

8. Gregg, interview.

CHAPTER 16—A NEW WAR

1. Ed Butler, interview.

2. Ibid.

3. Stuart Tootal, interview.

4. Carlotta Gall, *The Wrong Enemy*, p. 134.

5. Tootal, interview.

6. Stuart Tootal, message to author. Butler was also not directly involved in ordering troops to Now Zad and Musa Qala.

7. Butler, interview. See also Edward Butler, message to author.

8. Elizabeth Rubin, "In the Land of the Taliban," *New York Times*, October 22, 2006. The British military had recognized in the planning stages, back in 2005, that Sangin was one of the main centers of violence and lawlessness in Helmand.

9. Ibid.

10. Daoud was initially happy to learn of the attack, which he hoped had killed Khan or at least weakened his rule, but once Karzai swung behind Akhundzada's man, he backed action. Thomas Tugendhat, interview.

11. Butler, interview.

12. Tugendhat, interview.

13. Tootal, interview.

14. Will Pike, interview.

15. Tugendhat, interview.

16. Pike, interview.

17. David Fraser, interview.

18. Ibid.

19. Ben Freakley, interview.

CHAPTER 17—MEDUSA

1. Butler later disputed this criticism and says Richards was fully cognizant of the pressures the British had been under. Edward Butler, message to author.

2. David Richards, interview.

3. Butler says that Richards told him in June 2006 that he would replace Lieutenant Colonel Charlie Knaggs in charge of Task Force Helmand as soon as he took over command of International Security Assistance Force (ISAF) on July 31, 2006. Butler also briefed the Chief of the Defense Staff Jock Stirrup on a number of occasions both before and during the months leading up to the change of ISAF command. They both agreed that Butler should take command of the TFH as soon as Richards was in charge.

4. Richards, interview.

5. Karzai also weakened the Alakozai tribe, appointing Naquib's son as successor rather than allowing the tribe to choose. The Alakozai split, with one side favoring the Taliban, who rapidly overran the area.

6. In May, an ill-conceived US special forces operation there had provoked a night-long firefight, to which the Canadians refused to send a rescue party for fear of being struck by friendly fire. There was still no way for NATO forces to communicate their whereabouts to American pilots, a sensible concern as events would prove.

7. Omar Lavoie, interview.

8. Adam Day, "Operation Medusa: The Battle for Panjwai," *Legion Magazine*, September 1, 2007; legionmagazine.com/en/2007/09/operation-medusa-the-battle-for -panjwai.

9. Lavoie, interview.

10. Gall, *The Wrong Enemy*, p. 138.

11. Patrick Bishop, *3 Para* (London: HarperPress, 2007), p. 200.

12. In Sangin, the landscape around the soldiers' base was rechristened: To the north, a patch of foliage became known as Wombat Wood; to the south a narrow lane of shops became Pharmacy Road, notorious for attacks. Wombat Wood was named after an old British recoilless rifle variant. Stuart Tootal, *Danger Close*, p. 89.

13. Bishop, *3 Para*, p. 197.

14. Stuart Tootal, *Danger Close*, p. 125.

15. Richards, interview.

16. David Fraser, interview.

17. Jock Stirrup, interview. Butler later said that one of the reasons that Stirrup wanted to extract UK forces from Musa Qala was due to the loss of a Nimrod aircraft that had killed fourteen servicemen the week before. Stirrup called Butler on September 5 saying, "You must withdraw from Musa Qala within a week. If we carry on with the District Centre occupation there will be a serious incident and this will significantly impact on political and public opinion." According to Butler, Stirrup judged that the loss of another strategic asset, such as a Chinook being shot down while going in to medevac a wounded soldier, would have dire consequences for the overall campaign. Edward Butler, message to author.

18. Thomas Tugendhat, interview.

19. Abdul Rahman, interview.

CHAPTER 18—BAD GUESTS

1. Hussein Haqqani, interview. The Pakistani General Talat Masood also noted, "It was not that [Musharraf] wholeheartedly supported the Taliban, but because of his [strained] relationship with Karzai, he became indifferent. He would say of the Taliban: 'At least they are our friends.'" Gall, *The Wrong Enemy*, p. 89.

2. Gall, *The Wrong Enemy*, p. 89.

3. Private interview.

4. Mazzetti, *The Way of the Knife*, pp. 1–4.

5. Ibid., p. 104.

6. Ibid., p. 106.

7. Private interview.

8. Anand Gopal, Mansur Khan Mahsud, and Brian Fishman, "The Taliban in North Waziristan," in *Talibanistan: Negotiating the Borders Between Terror, Politics, and Religion,* ed. Peter Bergen and Katherine Tiedemann (New York: Oxford University Press, 2013), p. 140.

9. Private interview.

10. The first victim of the program was neither a member of the Taliban leadership nor an al-Qa'eda operative, but Nek Mohammed.

11. Said Tayeb Jawad, interview.

12. Private interview.

13. Ibid.

14. George W. Bush, *Decision Points* (New York: Crown Publishers, 2010, Kindle edition).

15. Tom Gregg, interview.

16. Ibid.

17. Seth Jones, *The Graveyard of Empires: America's War in Afghanistan* (New York: W. W. Norton, 2010), p. 278.

18. Ben Freakley, interview.

19. Steve Baker, interview.

20. It wasn't until two years later that the US command in Afghanistan launched an investigation, which ended up accepting Pakistan's view of events.

CHAPTER 19—ALL THE WAY

1. Earlier that year, Bush had appointed the seasoned politicians James Baker and Lee Hamilton to conduct a review of Iraq. They weren't tasked with finding victory: All pretense that this was possible had largely disappeared by then. The question was similar to the one the British in Afghanistan faced: how to achieve the least humiliating withdrawal. The very existence of such a commission helped seal Rumsfeld's fate, along with his insistence that they stick to the failing transition plan.

Ultimately the White House ignored the Baker Hamilton Commission's findings in favor of an opposing plan making the rounds at the same time, and which would become the official US policy known as the "surge." This was unfortunate because the Baker Hamilton report contained a number of insights that applied to both wars. The first was that US troop levels would not solve the "fundamental cause of violence in Iraq, which is the absence of national reconciliation."

One senior American general told Hamilton that adding US troops might temporarily help limit violence in one area. However, as soon as US forces moved to another area, the violence would return.

Their other solution was equally prescient: immediate talks with Iraq's neighbors, principally Iran and Syria, in a bid to find a regional solution. The failure to seek the buy-in of Iraq's neighbors during the build-up to war had been one of the Bush administration's major strategic blunders (especially given that Iran was a signature beneficiary of the American decision to topple Saddam Hussein). James A. Baker III, Lee H. Hamilton et al., "Iraq Study Group Report," United States Institute of Peace, December 6, 2006; media.usip.org/reports/iraq_study_group_report.pdf, accessed April 1, 2014.

2. Bob Woodward, *State of Denial* (New York: Simon & Schuster, 2006), p. 446. Rumsfeld cut an increasingly confused figure within the Bush administration. When Kenneth Adelman, a protégé of Rumsfeld's at the Defense Department and a member of the Defense Board, asked Rumsfeld in 2006 to define success in Iraq, Rumsfeld responded it was "so complicated" that he could not provide a list. Adelman was

shocked because Rumsfeld had once told him: "Identify three or four things, then always ask about [them], get measurements . . . or you'll never get progress."

3. Dan McNeill, interview.

4. "Afghanistan: Civilian Deaths from Airstrikes," *Human Rights Watch*, September 9, 2008; www.hrw.org/news/2008/09/07/afghanistan-civilian-deaths-airstrikes, accessed April 1, 2014.

5. McNeill, interview.

6. Ibid.

7. Michel Rose, Mohammed Abbas, and Louise Ireland, eds., "British Afghan Effort Criticized in Wiki Cables," Reuters, December 3, 2010; mobile.reuters.com/article/topNews/idUSTRE6B24N920101203, accessed April 1, 2014.

8. Robert Fry, interview.

9. "I saw 18 people killed here in this bazaar," said Noor Mohammad, a young shopkeeper. "Not even a cat can live here now. Anyone who so much as moved was shot so full of holes he looked like a soup strainer." IWPR Trainees—Afghanistan, "Helmand Residents Question NATO Success Claims," Institute for War and Peace Reporting, *ARR* Issue 257, June 29, 2007; iwpr.net/report-news/helmand-residents -question-nato-success-claims, accessed April 1, 2014.

10. Jerry Thomas, interview.

11. Private interview.

12. Thomas, interview.

13. Gall, *The Wrong Enemy,* p. 100.

14. Carlotta Gall and Abdul Waheed Wafa, "US Strike Kills 9 Family Members, Afghans Say," *New York Times,* March 6, 2007, and *60 Minutes* interview with President Hamid Karzai, "Bombing Afghanistan," broadcast October 28, 2007; www.cbsnews .com/stories/2007/10/25/60minutes/main3411230.shtml. US forces said they were targeting two insurgents seen entering the house after they had fired a rocket at a US military outpost.

15. "Troops in Contact," *Human Rights Watch*, 2008; www.hrw.org/sites/default/files /reports/afghanistan0908web_0.pdf.

16. Hanif Atmar, interview.

17. Tom Koenigs, interview.

18. McNeill, interview.

19. Another issue that further inflamed tension was the issue of paying compensation to victims' families. When the US made payments they were often less than the Afghanistan standard—$2,500 compared to the $5,000 that *tsali*, or blood money, demanded (for a working-age male), a grievous insult to many Afghans. The Taliban, by contrast, offered anyone the ultimate redress of tribal justice: the opportunity to enact bloody revenge.

20. McNeill, interview.

21. Thomas, interview.

22. Neumann had traveled around Afghanistan in the 1960s, when his father had been ambassador there, and he retained an admiration for that earlier, heroic age of US development projects such as the Kajaki dam. Ronald Neumann, interview.

23. James Bays, "Taliban 'In Control' in Helmand," *al-Jazeera*, June 24, 2007; www .aljazeera.com/news/asia/2007/02/200852519013842404.html, accessed April 1, 2014.

24. According to Mohammed Yusef's brother, Haji Daoud, the Alakozai had passed on his location to western intelligence.

25. Haji Daoud, interview.

26. As governor of Kunar province in eastern Afghanistan, he'd attracted the ire of US commanders by undercutting their efforts to organize local militias, which he worried would threaten a lucrative timber-smuggling business in which he had a stake. Bing West, *The Wrong War: Grit, Strategy, and the Way Out of Afghanistan* (New York: Random House, 2011, Kindle edition).

27. John Lorimer, interview.

28. Carlotta Gall, "Afghans Say Civilian Toll in Strikes Is Much Higher Than Reported," *New York Times*, May 11, 2007; www.nytimes.com/2007/05/11/world/asia /11afghan.html, accessed April 1, 2014.

29. By 2009, Mullah Omar was issuing a long list of instructions or *layha* to Taliban commanders, warning against causing civilian casualties; they were also to refrain from using extreme methods of punishment like cutting off noses and lips. General Stanley A. McChrystal, *My Share of the Task* (New York: Penguin, 2013).

CHAPTER 20—SALAM

1. Sherard Cowper-Coles, interview.

2. Sherard Cowper-Coles, *Cables from Kabul: The Inside Story of the West's Afghanistan Campaign* (London: HarperPress, 2011), p. 62.

3. Stephen Grey, *Operation Snakebite: The Explosive Story of an Afghan Desert Siege* (London: Penguin, 2010), p. 292.

4. Tugendhat, interview. The wrong man was also called Mullah Salam, and had briefly been governor of Oruzgun under the Taliban before being kicked out of office for being useless.

5. Cowper-Coles, interview.

6. Mark Urban, "How to Win Helmand," BBC News, June 19, 2008; www.bbc.co .uk/blogs/legacy/newsnight/markurban/2008/06/how_to_win_helmand.html?postId =66291982.

7. James Connolly, interview.

8. Cowper-Coles, interview.

9. Cowper-Coles, *Cables from Kabul*, p. 64.

10. Cowper-Coles, interview.

11. Rory Stewart, interview.

12. Rory Stewart, "How to Save Afghanistan," *Time*, July 17, 2008, p. 6; www.hks .harvard.edu/cchrp/pdf/RoryStewart/HowToSaveAfghanastan.pdf, accessed April 1, 2014.

13. Rajiv Chandrasekaran, *Little America: The War Within the War for Afghanistan* (New York: Knopf, 2012, Kindle edition).

14. Private interview. The Iranians had donated six racing kayaks to Afghanistan's Water Sports Federation with much more success.

CHAPTER 21—AN EDUCATION

1. Antonio Giustozzi, "The Battle for the Schools, the Taliban and State Education," AAN Thematic Report, 08. (Kabul, Afghanistan: Afghanistan Analysts Network).

2. Hanif Atmar, interview.

3. Aunohita Mojumdar, "Afghan Schools' Money Problem," *BBC News*, April 9, 2007; news.bbc.co.uk/2/hi/south_asia/6533379.stm, accessed April 1, 2014.

4. Atmar, interview.

5. Ibid.

6. West, *The Wrong War*.

7. Atmar, interview.

8. Kael Weston, interview.

9. Pratap Chatterjee, "Afghanistan: Task Force 373, the Secret Killers—Part 2," Inter Press Service, August 21, 2010; www.ipsnews.net/2010/08/afghanistan-task-force-373-the-secret-killers-ndash-part-2, accessed April 1, 2014. On October 4, 2007, TF 373 called in an air strike—500-pound Paveway bombs—on a house in the village of Laswanday, just six miles from Nangar Khel in Paktia province (where those seven children had already died). This time, four men, one woman, and a girl—all civilians—as well as a donkey, a dog, and several chickens, would be slaughtered. A dozen US soldiers were injured, but the soldiers reported that not one "enemy" was detained or killed. Nick Davies, "Afghanistan War Logs: Task Force 373—Special Forces Hunting Top Taliban," *The Guardian*, July 25, 2010; www.theguardian.com/world/2010/jul/25/task-force-373-secret-afghanistan-taliban, accessed April 1, 2014.

10. Weston, interview.

11. Dave Adams, interview.

12. "Development, Security Key Themes in Ambassador's Visit to Khost Province," WikiLeaks, November 7, 2007; www.cablegatesearch.net/cable.php?id=07KABUL3772. "Madrassa Students—'The Real Taliban'"—Cite Gap with Government and U.S., Seek More Resources," WikiLeaks, January 31, 2008; www.wikileaks.org/plusd/cables/08KABUL252_a.html.

13. Mohammed Qari Ramazan, interview.

14. "When we saw what the Americans were doing to our Muslim brothers and sisters, then we realized who we should hate, and strive to bring to God's justice," he said later; Ramazan, interview.

15. Afghan officials later said the ringleader for the attack at the Serena, and the attempted assassination of Karzai later, was an Afghan named Homayoun, who was killed in a firefight with police while planning a third attack. Gall, *The Wrong Enemy*, p. 187.

16. Simon Jenkins, "It Takes Inane Optimism to See Victory in Afghanistan," *The Guardian*, August 8, 2007; www.theguardian.com/commentisfree/2007/aug/08/comment.afghanistan, accessed April 1, 2014.

17. Cowper-Coles, *Cables from Kabul*, p. 94.

18. Cowper-Coles also left his own mark on festivities, by initiating a biannual British Embassy Charity Ball to support local NGOs. For the new year of 2008 Christmas special he flew his old private school chum, Kit Hesketh Harvey, to Kabul to perform a camp cabaret show. Several Americans were invited, including the ambassador, Bill Wood. A fan of P. G. Wodehouse, Wood still struggled with the full range of saucy innuendo, although he did recall being immortalized in a bawdy verse as "Chemical Bill," in reference to his desire to spray Afghanistan with pesticide.

Less successful was Hesketh Harvey's performance before 1st Battalion Coldstream Guards, based at Kabul airport. "While the officers appreciated the humour immensely and immediately, some of the soldiers had found it all a bit, well, poncey [affected], and had taken longer to warm up," reflected Cowper-Coles. (By contrast, the US military offered more populist fare to its troops with Paris Hilton, among others, scheduled for entertainment.)

The suggestion of a class divide captured a quintessential British approach to warfare. When the Americans ventured overseas they blithely assumed the world was aligned with their ideals, whilethe British were perfectly content to set up their own little universes, complete with social demarcations, wherever they went.

19. Lisa Gans, e-mail communication.

20. He was sentenced to life in prison.

21. Atmar, interview.

CHAPTER 22—THE SWITCH

1. Chris Cavoli, interview.

2. John Nicholson, interview.

3. West, *The Wrong War*.

4. Cavoli, interview. See also Elizabeth Rubin, "Battle Company Is Out There," *New York Times*, February 24, 2008; www.nytimes.com/2008/02/24/magazine/24 afghanistan-t.html, accessed April 1, 2014.

5. Ibid.

6. Brian Glynn Williams, "Afghanistan's Heart of Darkness," Combatting Terrorism Center, November 15, 2008; https://www.ctc.usma.edu/posts/afghanistan%E2%80 %99s-heart-of-darkness-fighting-the-taliban-in-kunar-province.

7. Cavoli, interview.

8. Ibid.

9. Ibid.

10. Giustozzi, *Decoding the New Taliban,* p. 244. Kilcullen had been hired by Henry Crumpton, former head of the CIA's Counterterrorism Center, who had become the state department's counterterrorism coordinator. George Packer, "Knowing the Enemy: Can Social Scientists Redefine the 'War on Terror?,'" *The New Yorker*, December 18, 2006.

11. Cavoli, interview.

12. The events in Korengal were vividly captured by Sebastian Junger in his book *War*, and his documentary *Restrepo*, which he co-directed with Tom Hetherington. Rubin described the extraordinary pressure the violence placed on US troops. Soldiers sat alone in firebases talking to themselves, reliving past battles, vainly talking to the ghosts of friends lost (twenty men had died on the tour), or screaming "I hate this country" into the quiet of the night; privates disobeyed sergeants; squad leaders refused to step beyond the perimeter of their bases. Sebastian Junger, *War* (London: Fourth Estate, 2011).

13. Sebastian Junger, "Into the Valley of Death," *Vanity Fair*, January 1, 2008; www .vanityfair.com/politics/features/2008/01/afghanistan200801.

14. William Ostlund, interview.

15. Ibid.

16. See also Matthew Myer, interview.

17. Douglas Cubbison, "Wanat: Combat Action in Afghanistan," US Army Combat Studies Institute, 2010.

18. Mark Bowden, "Echoes from a Distant Battlefield," *Vanity Fair*, December 1, 2011; www.vanityfair.com/politics/features/2011/12/battle-of-wanat-201112, accessed April 1, 2014.

19. David McKiernan, interview

20. Lute, message to author.

21. Private interview. One of the key stipulations of the Pakistanis—that Islamabad's permission would no longer be needed before a strike—was also dropped. In mid-2007, the air force had eight Predator caps, each cap consisting of six crews (about eighty people) and three drones. The following year, there were twenty-four caps, with around 2,250 drones divided between Afghanistan and Iraq. Mazzetti, *The Way of the Knife*, p. 132.

22. Mart de Kruif, interview.

23. McKiernan, interview.

24. Tom Vanden Brook, "Afghan Roadside Bombs Hit Record in 2008," *USA Today*, January 25, 2005; usatoday30.usatoday.com/news/military/2009-01-25-roadsidebomb_n.htm.

25. Private interview.

26. Nick Pounds, interview.

27. Mark Carlton-Smith, interview.

28. Private interview.

29. The key to the operation lay in a simultaneous feint north of Sangin to distract the Taliban. This was carried out by a decoy convoy of Danish trucks, which were escorted north by 1 Para, with a US special forces unit staging a raid farther north, near the village of Sarwan Qala. Predictably both operations ran into firefights, with the US special forces calling in an air strike that killed a dozen civilians and destroyed a popular local mosque. There was something slightly tragic about this secondary mission. A year before, this area had seen a remarkable uprising against the Taliban only to be abandoned. In the weeks before the operation, the British military had distributed leaflets to villages explaining that the turbine would be coming, but that failed to stop another firefight.

30. Jeremy Page, "Triumph for British Forces in Boy's Own–Style Kajaki Mission," *The Times*, September 3, 2008; www.thetimes.co.uk/tto/news/world/asia/article 2609050.ece.

31. Mangal blamed the police chief's assassination on the machinations of Sher Mohammed Akhundzada, and the British were only too happy to follow suit in heaping the province's troubles onto their old foe. Gulab Mangal, interview.

32. Private interview.

33. John F. Burns, "Second Taliban Attack Hits Afghan City," *New York Times*, October 15, 2008; www.nytimes.com/2008/10/16/world/asia/16afghan.html, accessed April 1, 2014. Brigadier Carlton-Smith points out that the Taliban who attacked Lashkar Gah were likely to have been driven there as a result of USMC operations displacing them from Garmsir.

34. Cavoli, interview.

35. de Kruif, interview.

36. David Hook, interview.

37. Hugh Powell, interview.

38. Charles Allen, *Soldier Sahibs: The Men Who Made the North West Frontier* (London: John Murray, 2012), p. 288.

39. Powell, interview.

40. Larry Nicholson, interview.

41. Bob Woodward, *Obama's Wars* (New York: Simon & Schuster, 2010).

CHAPTER 23—GHOSTS

1. Arthur Schlesinger Jr., "Forgetting Reinhold Niebuhr," *New York Times*, September 15, 2005; www.nytimes.com/2005/09/18/books/review/18schlesinger.html?page wanted=all&_r=0.

2. Ryan Lizza, "The Consequentialist: How the Arab Spring Remade Obama's Foreign Policy," *The New Yorker*, May 2011.

3. Private interview.

4. Amrulleh Saleh, interview.

5. "A New Way Forward: Rethinking US Strategy in Afghanistan," Afghanistan Study Group, 2012; www.afghanistanstudygroup.org/2012/05/28/85-billion-of-aghan-aid-wasted.

6. Justin Sandefur, "$16 Billion for Afghanistan: Why Less Money Might Be a Good Thing," Center for Global Development, October 7, 2012; www.cgdev.org/blog/16-billion-afghanistan-why-less-money-might-be-good-thing.

7. Woodward, *Obama's Wars*, p. 68.

8. Derek Harvey, interview.

9. The agency was still reeling from a suicide bomb attack in Khost in 2009, when an informant, thought to be a member of al-Qa'eda's inner circle, blew himself up as he met with his handlers, killing seven CIA operators.

10. The program also attracted considerable controversy among the academic community, who did not believe their work should be used to support military operations. Others, including one of the program's founders, Montgomery McNate, argued that anthropology had always been a "handmaiden of colonialism." By 2009, thirty-one teams were deployed in Afghanistan. On November 4, 2008, HTS member Paula Loyd was fatally injured while surveying the village of Chehel Gazi with a US Army platoon, one of several members to be killed on duty.

11. Private interview.

12. Ibid.

13. Woodward, *Obama's Wars*, p. 80.

14. Ibid.

15. Private interview.

16. Woodward, *Obama's Wars*, p. 195.

17. Private interview.

18. Ibid.

19. David McKiernan, interview. The Centcom commander tried war-gaming alternative scenarios with teams of intelligence and operations officers representing

different sides of the Afghan conflict, although that only threw up new problems, such as Pakistan's role in aiding the Taliban. When they went through the scenario of sending in more troops, the officers representing the Taliban simply withdrew to Pakistan. That raised the prospect of having to strong-arm Islamabad into doing more or taking the fight into Taliban sanctuaries over the border. Both options were daunting. Petraeus's thinking circled back to the idea of securing Afghanistan and developing enough capacity among the Afghans to fend off Taliban attacks.

20. Woodward, *Obama's Wars,* p. 111.

21. Ibid.

22. Bruce Riedel, interview.

23. One of Tehrik-e-Taliban Pakistan's allies and the spearhead of the Swat insurgency, the Tehreek-e-Nafaz-e-Shariat-e-Mohammadi (TNSM) had actually emerged in the early 1990s from a mixture of long-standing local grievances and the return of Islamist volunteers from the war against the Soviets. Message to author, Anatol Lieven.

24. In 2007 there were five drone strikes; in 2008 the number increased to thirty-five. See the excellent work of the UK-based Bureau for Investigative Journalism; www.thebureauinvestigates.com/category/projects/drones.

25. Anatol Lieven, *Pakistan: A Hard Country* (New York: PublicAffairs, 2011, Kindle edition).

26. Sameer Lalwani, "Pakistan's Counterinsurgency Strategy," in *Talibanistan: Negotiating the Borders Between Terror, Politics, and Religion,* ed. Peter Bergen and Katherine Tiedemann (New York: Oxford University Press, 2013), pp. 212–214.

27. Riedel, interview. Some in the White House criticized the report for being rushed: compiled in six weeks, without extensive discussion, field trips to Afghanistan, or thorough analysis, except where material was gleaned from Riedel's own extensive writing on Pakistan.

28. Chandrasekaran, *Little America.*

29. Woodward, *Obama's Wars,* p. 107.

CHAPTER 24—A CRUEL SUMMER

1. Tim Radford, interview.

2. Chandrasekaran, *Little America.*

3. Ibid.

4. Larry Nicholson, interview.

5. Chandrasekaran, *Little America;* Abdul Ali Shamsi, interview. The Afghans didn't appear to agree with the British assessment. What's more, the Afghans agreed. Karzai publicly blamed the British for removing Governor Akhundzada and plunging the province into chaos. He liked to regale visitors at the presidential palace with a story about a stricken woman from the province who had implored the Helmand Governor Mangal to "take the British away and give us back the Americans." Meanwhile, Mangal had lobbied Nicholson directly to take over the Coalition effort in Helmand, having concluded that the British were too cautious.

6. Radford also fought a constant battle with Kabul to provide British forces with enough Afghan army and police kandaks to support operations. Radford, interview.

7. Nicholson, interview.

8. This conversation was recorded by Rajiv Chandrasekaran in October, although similar conversations were held earlier between Weston and Nicholson, and between the British and Americans. Chandrasekaran, *Little America.*

9. Nicholson, interview.

10. Kael Weston, interview.

11. Tony Harnden, *Dead Men Risen: The Welsh Guards and the Defining Story of Britain's War in Afghanistan* (London: Quercus, 2011). Radford had spent eight years working in Northern Ireland and he too was well aware of the challenges he had inherited.

12. Patrick Bishop, *Ground Truth: 3 Para Return to Afghanistan* (London: Harper Press, 2009, Kindle edition).

13. Richard North, *Ministry of Defeat* (London: Continuum Publishing Corporation, 2009), p. 234. See also www.telegraph.co.uk/news/uknews/defence/8052782 /16bn-Future-Rapid-Effects-System-faces-axe-in-defence-cuts.html.

14. Lieutenant General Robert Fulton, Iraq Inquiry.

15. Robert M. Gates, *Duty: Memoirs of a Secretary at War* (New York: Knopf, 2014), p. 122. In 2004, Donald Rumsfeld had dismissed the rising American death toll in Iraq caused by using lightly armored Humvees by saying, "You go to war with the army you've got." Desperate field commanders urged the Pentagon to develop better-protected vehicles. By 2006, IEDs in Iraq accounted for up to 80 percent of soldier casualties. Rumsfeld and his bean counters dug their heels in further, arguing that they did not want to fund a program that might only be ready after the war was over and might then be of limited use. As then-Senator Joe Biden commented, "Can you imagine Franklin Roosevelt being told, 'We need X number of landing craft on D-Day, but once we land, we're not going to need them all again. So why build them?'"

16. Gates, *Duty.*

17. Tom Vanden Brook, "Roadside Bombs Decline in Iraq," *USA Today*, June 22, 2008; usatoday30.usatoday.com/news/world/iraq/2008-06-22-ieds_N.htm?loc=inter stitialskip.

18. By 2009, GPR had become standard issue for specialized mine-clearing vehicles that accompanied most American patrols. A Ground Base Operational Surveillance system photographed up to twenty-five areas of threat every two seconds, allowing US air support to hit the Taliban before an IED had even been laid. When IEDs were discovered, they were quickly blown up in place. However, the British were skeptical about the scale of the threat, knowing that if they did kick up a fuss about GPR, they were unlikely to get anything for months, while potentially "jeopardizing our ability to carry out operations," according to one senior officer. At one point, Gates even offered to supply NATO allies with the equipment, but received only a lukewarm response.

19. Harnden, *Dead Men Risen,* p. 220.

20. Radford, interview.

21. Harnden, *Dead Men Risen,* p. 282.

22. Ibid., p. 296.

23. Radford, interview.

24. Ibid.

25. Rob Thomson, interview.

26. Miles Amoore, "Devil's Playground," *Sunday Times*, October 18, 2009.

CHAPTER 25—ELECTIONS

1. Chandrasekaran, *Little America*, p. 90.

2. George Packer, "The Last Mission," *The New Yorker*, September 28, 2009; www .newyorker.com/reporting/2009/09/28/090928fa_fact_packer?currentPage=all.

3. Vali Nasr, interview.

4. Holbrooke had already missed one opportunity to oust Karzai. The Afghan constitution stipulated that a poll should be held in March and April of an election year to allow time for a handover of power before the end of the presidential term in May. Afghan politicians, including Karzai, had tentatively agreed to an August date only for Ahmed Zai Massoud, vice president and a leading figure of the Northern Alliance, to point out in early February the fact that technically Karzai's term would be over, and the election should be managed by an interim government. Karzai contemplated resigning, but clung on.

5. Cowper-Coles, *Cables from Kabul*, p. 210. "David Miliband [the British foreign secretary] and Cowper-Coles want to get rid of you," Holbrooke told Karzai at their first meeting.

6. Kai Eide, *Power Struggle over Afghanistan: An Inside Look at What Went Wrong— and What We Can Do to Repair the Damage* (New York: Skyhorse Publishing, 2013), p. 128.

7. Sherard Cowper-Coles, interview.

8. Chandrasekaran, *Little America*.

9. West, *The Wrong War*.

10. Private interview.

11. Carlotta Gall also spoke to a businessman from Paktia who later admitted stuffing ballot boxes on behalf of Karzai in both the 2004 and 2009 elections. Gall, *The Wrong Enemy*, p. 198.

12. Because the UN, through technical assistance to the IEC from the United Nations Development Programme, was involved in the electoral organization, the UN would not give a formal "verdict" as it would if it had organized an observation mission. According to the UN's doctrine on electoral assistance, because of the potential conflict of interest, it never observes elections to which it is providing assistance. Informally, however, people would look to the UN and pay heed to its statements on the election. Message to author, Scott Smith.

13. Minna Jarvenpaa, interview.

14. Gerard Russell, interview.

15. Eide, *Power Struggle over Afghanistan*, p. 125.

16. Ibid.

17. He told Scott Smith on the ride back from the breakfast that appointing Galbraith would be a "big mistake." Message to author, Scott Smith.

18. Ibid., and private interview.

19. Peter Galbraith, interview.

20. Ibid., and Eide, *Power Struggle over Afghanistan*, p. 303.

21. Ibid.

22. Ibid.

23. Private interview.

24. Eide, *Power Struggle over Afghanistan.*

25. Galbraith, interview.

26. Eide, *Power Struggle over Afghanistan,* p. 163.

27. Galbraith, interview.

28. Eide, *Power Struggle over Afghanistan,* p. 172.

29. Ibid.

30. Peter Galbraith later accused Eide of phoning Karzai to warn him of Holbrooke's impending arrival, a charge Eide refuted.

31. Hanif Atmar, interview.

32. Eide, *Power Struggle over Afghanistan,* p. 191.

33. Galbraith, interview.

34. Private interviews.

35. Nasr, interview.

36. Private interview.

37. Those concessions included reducing the powers for the presidency, creating a chief executive position beneath the president, a ministerial post for Abdullah, and powers to the UN to vet future Afghan government appointments, and the removal of characters like Ahmed Wali Karzai from the scene. Admirable though some of these might have been, they overstated the hold the international community had on Karzai as a result of the elections. Minna Jarvenpaa, e-mail communication, September 8, 2013.

38. Private interview; also message to author, Scott Smith.

39. Ibid.

40. As Afghan expert Michael Semple noted sarcastically, when he called Galbraith after his sacking, "Peter, it gave me joy to hear that you were fired when I read it in the papers . . . Had you embezzled money, it would have taken the UN eighteen months to fire. Had you sexually harassed an employee, it would have taken them a year. But take a stand on principle? The UN fires you overnight." Michael Hastings, *The Operators: The Wild and Terrifying Inside Story of America's War in Afghanistan* (New York: Plume, 2012), p. 120. Peter Galbraith, "Peter W. Galbraith—UN Isn't Addressing Fraud in Afghan Election," *Washington Post,* October 4, 2009. Other members of the UN team tendered their resignation, including Jarvenpaa, who wrote to Eide that "as Gandhi has said, 'Happiness is when what you think, what you say, and what you do are in harmony.'"

41. Message to author, Scott Smith.

42. Eide, *Power Struggle over Afghanistan,* p. 201.

43. Sabrina Tavernise and Sangar Rahimi, "Attack in Afghan Capital Illustrates Taliban's Reach," *New York Times,* October 28, 2009; www.nytimes.com/2009/10/29/world/asia/29afghan.html.

44. Private interview.

45. Atmar, interview.

CHAPTER 26—POLITICAL EXPEDIENCY

1. Gates, *Duty,* p. 359.

2. Chandrasekaran, *Little America,* p. 59.

3. Before arriving in the country, McChrystal had also indicated to the Senate Armed Services Committee during his confirmation hearing in June that the 21,000 troops Obama had approved would not be enough. The suggestion that *another* troop request was coming raised alarms in the White House, but the president left it to his national security adviser to quash talk of more troops. Jones had played into the military's hands by proposing McChrystal conduct a formal two-month assessment.

4. Stanley McChrystal, interview. See also www.hrw.org/sites/default/files/reports /afghanistan0908web_0.pdf. According to Human Rights Watch, civilian casualties caused by the Taliban had actually fallen in 2008.

5. In October 2009, another outpost came close to being overrun, this time in a remote valley in Nuristan. Up to three hundred insurgents stormed the base, called FOB Keating, which housed a company of soldiers and an Afghan army unit. The Afghan guards stationed at the base's main entrance looted the compound and fled as soon as the Taliban started shooting. Their American comrades were left to stave off the attackers as they swarmed through the main gate and over breaches elsewhere in the compound wall. For most of the day, the US soldiers were trapped in two buildings as Afghan fighters set fire to the rest of the base. The insurgents only fully retreated at dusk, by which time eight US soldiers had been killed and twenty-seven wounded. The outpost was evacuated two days later, and bombed on October 6 by a B-1 bomber to stop the Taliban from getting their hands on ammunition that had been left behind in the hasty retreat. In 2010, McChrystal went on to the American presence in Waigal and Korengal with relatively little fuss. "It's almost more painful to realize that leaving those valleys is as meaningless as staying in those valleys," noted one official. US forces swiftly consolidated their positions in the larger towns of the east, where they had lost control during the push into the mountains. Whether even these were holdable in the long term is unclear, but what the retreat did expose was the elaborate fiction underlying the American presence in the east.

6. Chandrasekaran, *Little America,* p. 60.

7. De Kruif, interview.

8. Gates, *Duty,* p. 340. Gates later called the failure to exert full control over the marine hierarchy his biggest mistake in handling the war.

9. Chandrasekaran, *Little America,* p. 73.

10. West, *The Wrong War.*

11. Woodward, *Obama's Wars,* p. 177.

12. McChrystal, interview.

13. Petraeus was responding specifically to an article by *Post* columnist David Ignatius, which questioned whether counterinsurgency strategy could work in Afghanistan. Woodward, *Obama's Wars,* p. 157.

14. Ibid., p. 197.

15. Ibid. Originally Gates favored a steady and long-term US engagement, building up the Afghan army, pushing tribal outreach, and building economic ties between Pashtun communities on both sides of the border between Afghanistan and Pakistan. He credited an article in August 2009 by Fred Kagan, arguing that Afghans would recognize the difference between the Soviets and their abuses and the more sensitive

approach of the US military. Gates, *Duty,* p. 360. For his part, Gates worried about the size of McChrystal's troop request. As deputy director of the CIA in the 1980s, he had watched the Soviet military get sucked into Afghanistan; now he feared the Afghans were starting to see the Americans as occupiers, too. He was won over by McChrystal's and others' arguments that American troops were far less brutal and despotic than Soviet forces. If US forces could limit civilian casualties and deliver reconstruction, they would avoid alienating the country as the Russians had.

16. McChrystal, interview.

17. Even when he found one of the few kindred spirits in the Joint Chiefs of Staff, indeed the whole Pentagon, Marine Corps General James Cartright, who agreed to work out the figures, the chairman of the Joint Chiefs, Mike Mullen, still blocked the detailed plan from reaching the White House until President Obama made a direct request for it.

18. de Kruif, interview.

19. "How much more valuable would their advice have been if they had explicitly tied their troop request to a viable political strategy—if they had argued that without a policy on Pakistan, without a policy on Afghan government corruption, they did not want that troop surge after all because the sacrifice would quite likely be for naught. But that kind of moral courage failed them," wrote Sarah Chayes later. "What Vali Nasr Gets Wrong," *Foreign Policy,* March 12, 2013; http://www.foreignpolicy.com /articles/2013/03/12/what_vali_nasr_gets_wrong_obama_afghanistan.

20. Chandrasekaran, *Little America,* p. 123.

21. Private interview.

22. Gates, *Duty,* p. 299.

23. Private interview.

CHAPTER 27—A RECKONING

1. Nick Parker, interview.

2. Nick Kitson, interview.

3. Larry Nicholson, interview.

4. Chandrasekaran, *Little America,* p. 213.

5. Ibid., p. 214.

6. Gates, *Duty,* p. 249.

7. Moni Basu, "Why Suicide Rate Among Veterans May Be More Than 22 a Day," *CNN,* November 14, 2013; www.cnn.com/2013/09/21/us/22-veteran-suicides-a-day. The hospital's conditions led to a raft of sackings of the generals responsible, and an improvement in outpatient care. Still, veterans—whether physically injured or not—continued to face serious mental health challenges associated with post-traumatic stress disorder.

8. Audrey Gillan, "How Wootton Bassett Became the Town That Cried," *The Guardian,* February 25, 2010; www.theguardian.com/uk/2010/feb/25/wootton -bassett-audrey-gillan, accessed April 1, 2014.

9. Ibid.

CHAPTER 28—THE FUTILITY OF FORCE

1. Private interview.

2. Hanif Atmar, interview.

3. The issue had been thrown into stark relief for McChrystal in June 2010 when the German military in Kunduz, acting on the advice of a single informant, ordered an air strike at the site of a stricken NATO oil tanker believed to be swarming with insurgents. In fact, they had been civilians trying to siphon off a little diesel; as many as 125 people were killed.

4. Private interview, and Hugh Powell, interview.

5. "The surge [in places like Marja] didn't make sense if we didn't have Karzai's buy-in, and we didn't," said Lieutenant General Nick Parker, the deputy NATO commander. Nick Parker, interview.

6. Chandrasekaran, *Little America*, p. 180.

7. Private interview.

8. Chandrasekaran, *Little America*, p. 191, and private interview.

9. As US contractor Chemonics had discovered in Helmand in 2005, the maintenance of irrigation ditches was usually done on a voluntary basis, so AVIPA was in fact destroying a local custom.

10. Private interview.

11. Chandrasekaran, *Little America*, p. 197.

12. Scott Dempsey, "Is Spending the Strategy?" *Small Wars Journal*, May 4, 2011; smallwarsjournal.com/jrnl/art/is-spending-the-strategy, accessed April 1, 2014.

13. A rather undignified scrap with Afghan police had ensued, with the British Prime Minister Gordon Brown at one point threatening to kibosh the operation if five hundred more officers weren't found, and the Australians and Dutch trying to remove Carter from command when he had the temerity to take some of theirs from neighboring Oruzgun. In the end, two further Afghan army kandaks partnered with a US Army battalion and a British battle group in Nad Ali.

14. Stanley A. McChrystal, *My Share of the Task* (New York: Portfolio/Penguin, 2013), p. 364.

15. Ibid., p. 365.

16. In at least one case witnessed by Ben Anderson, a documentary filmmaker embedded with the battalion, a hapless Afghan soldier kept trying to enter a doorway too small for his backpack. "Each time, he dangled halfway through the doorway, half throttling himself, then re-appeared with a confused look on his face," Anderson wrote. Ben Anderson, *No Worse Enemy: The Inside Story of the Chaotic Struggle for Afghanistan* (Oxford: OneWorld Publications, 2013), p. 165.

17. Ben Anderson notes that with the difficulty in calling air strikes, the marines simply switched to using shoulder-fired rockets. Anderson, *No Worse Enemy*, p.122.

18. Aaron Maclean, interview. Maclean now believes that US rocket fire hit the house.

19. Anderson, p.122.

20. Ibid.

21. Matt Golsteyn, interview. See also West, *The Wrong War.*

22. Aziz Ahmad Tassal and Mohammad Elyas Dayee, "Afghan Recovery Report: New Civilian Death Claims in Helmand Sweep," *IWPR*, February 20, 2010; reliefweb.int /report/afghanistan/afghan-recovery-report-new-civilian-death-claims-helmand-sweep.

23. Anderson, *No Worse Enemy*, p. 186.

24. Golsteyn, interview.

25. Chandrasekaran, *Little America,* p. 145.

26. Jonathan Owen and Brian Brady, "The Last Post: McChrystal's Bleak Outlook," *The Independent,* June 27, 2010; www.independent.co.uk/news/world/americas/the-last-post-mcchrystals-bleak-outlook-2011730.html.

27. The district was called Zhare, a separate administrative unit that had been broken off from Panjwei and neighboring Maiwand.

28. Hastings, *The Operators,* p.264.

29. Craig Whitlock, "Brigade Link to Afghan Civilian Deaths Had Aggressive, Divergent War Strategy," *Washington Post,* October 14, 2010; www.washingtonpost.com/wp-dyn/content/article/2010/10/13/AR2010101306280.html.

30. Chandrasekaran, *Little America,* p. 159.

31. Private interview; Joe Gould, "PowerPoint Slide Spurs Ouster of CO, CSM," *Army Times,* May 22, 2011; www.armytimes.com/article/20110522/NEWS/105220310/PowerPoint-slides-spur-ouster-CO-CSM.

32. Private interview.

CHAPTER 29—ENDGAME

1. Woodward, *Obama's Wars,* p. 346.

2. Derek Harvey, interview.

3. Farrell and Giustozzi, "The Taliban at War." In January 2010, a Peace and Reintegration Trust Fund of $140 million was created. During its first three years only 2,700 Afghans availed themselves of the program.

4. Private interview.

5. "We underestimated Pakistan. We thought they would play, but they didn't," admitted retired British General Graeme Lamb, who had worked with McChrystal on reconciliation. Graeme Lamb, interview.

6. Ahmed Rashid, *Pakistan on the Brink: The Future of America, Pakistan, and Afghanistan* (New York: Penguin, 2013), p. 128. The Taliban leadership, at least according to Saudi contacts in Quetta, was prepared to open discussions. In 2009, Mullah Barader, the Taliban's second in command, urged the US to forget about trying to win over low-level commanders and to focus on the leadership. "We remind Obama to avoid wasting your time on ways which are not pragmatic but focus ways, which provide a down-to-earth and realistic solution to this issue [of talks]," he said in an interview with local media.

7. Woodward, *Obama's Wars,* p. 346.

8. Kai Eide made contact with Syed Tayib Agha, a close aide to Mullah Omar, and Ahmed Wali Karzai held a number of talks with former Taliban defense minister Mullah Barader in early 2010.

9. Christoph Reuter, Gregor Peter Schmitz, and Holger Stark, "Talking to the Enemy: How German Diplomat Opened Channel to Taliban," *Der Spiegel,* January 10, 2012.

10. Private interview.

11. Chandrasekaran, *Little America,* p. 235.

12. Private interview.

13. Jason Morris, interview.

14. 3rd Battalion, 7th Marine Regiment, had arrived earlier in the summer and had already begun the transition process.

15. Elements of 3rd Battalion, 7th Marine Regiment, and the 3rd Battalion of the 5th lived alongside the British.

16. Private interview.

17. Paul Kennedy, interview.

18. Miles Amoore, "US Humbled in Bloody Sangin," *Sunday Times,* December 12, 2010; milesamoore.com/2010/12/12/us-humbled-in-bloody-sangin.

19. Paul Kennedy, interview. Kennedy and Morris discussed deploying tanks to Sangin, as had happened elsewhere in Helmand. The heavy armor did not arrive in the town until the end of the tour.

20. Chandrasekaran, *Little America,* p. 274.

21. Ibid., p. 273.

22. Weatherill believes senior officers in the Afghan National Army spread this charge to try to force out a foreigner who knew too much about local politics. Phil Weatherill, interview.

23. "Citing Rising Death Toll, UN Urges Better Protection of Afghan Civilians," UN News Center, March 9, 2011; www.un.org/apps/news/story.asp?NewsID=37715 #.U4QBiq1dURg.

24. See Joshua Faust on the destruction of Khosrow Sofla. A similar incident occurred in Helmand, as described to author in private interviews. registan.net/2011/01 /13/the-unforgivable-horror-of-village-razing.

25. "2014 UNHCR country operations profile—Afghanistan," UNHCR; www .unhcr.org/pages/49e486eb6.html. See also Emma Graham-Harrison, "Afghan Refugees Abandoned by Their Own Government, Report Finds," *The Guardian*, February 23, 2012; www.theguardian.com/world/2012/feb/23/afghan-refugees-amnesty-report.

26. Rod Nordland, "Driven Away by a War, Now Stalked by Winter's Cold," *New York Times,* February 3, 2012; www.nytimes.com/2012/02/04/world/asia/cold -weather-kills-children-in-afghan-refugee-camps.html?pagewanted=all. Carlotta Gall visited Zhare outside Kandahar in 2013 and noted that even after American troops had cleared the area and compensated people for the destruction, villagers were too destitute to move back home. Gall, *The Wrong Enemy,* p. 286.

27. Nick Carter, interview.

28. Haji Daoud, interview.

29. Anne Scott Tyson, *American Spartan: The Promise, the Mission and the Betrayal of Special Forces Major Jim Gant* (New York: William Morrow, 2014) p. 86.

30. Gant himself recognized the impossibility of ever linking the government with the tribes he was dealing with. When Petraeus visited Gant and his militia program in Kunar in 2010, he told the general bluntly, "Sir, I need to tell you that there is no government of Afghanistan here. The district center is seven kilometers away, but it might as well be seven thousand. . . . Any program that relies on the success of the Afghan government will fail. Any program that relies on the success of ANSF will fail." Petraeus told Gant to write another paper, this time examining how to connect his work with the tribes to the Afghan government. He did; it was a single sentence long: "It cannot be done." Tyson, *American Spartan,* p. 210.

31. Josh Partlow, "More Afghan Soldiers Deserting the Army, NATO Statistics Show," *Washington Post,* September 3, 2011; www.washingtonpost.com/world/asia-pacific/more-afghan-soldiers-deserting-the-army/2011/08/31/gIQABxFTvJ_story.html.

32. Martin Lindig, interview.

33. Ibid. In 2012, Afghan security forces would kill sixty-four soldiers, leading to a suspension of the training mission.

34. Anderson, *No Worse Enemy*, p. 211.

35. Tom Bowman, "A Marine's Death and the Family He Left Behind," *NPR*, November 3, 2011; www.npr.org/2011/11/03/141954997/a-marines-death-and-the-family-he-left-behind.

36. By the following year, the US military was reporting that many Taliban fighters had indeed returned, but were keeping a low profile. David S. Cloud and Laura King, "Taliban Fighter Moving Back into Former Afghanistan Stronghold," *Los Angeles Times*, March 9, 2011; http://articles.latimes.com/2011/mar/09/world/la-fg-afghanistan-gates-20110309.

37. Mark Owen and Kevin Maurer, *No Easy Day: The Firsthand Account of the Mission That Killed Osama Bin Laden* (New York: Dutton Penguin, 2012), p. 229. According to other accounts, there was a fourth member of the SEAL team who was second to reach the top of the stairs, and it was he who fired the fatal shot at Osama bin Laden as he ducked back into his room. Mark Bowden, "Trigger Man," *Vanity Fair*, June 3, 2013; http://www.vanityfair.com/culture/2013/06/two-stories-osama-bin-laden-navy-seals.

38. *New York Times* reporter Carlotta Gall has revealed further connections. Soon after the navy SEAL raid on bin Laden's house, a Pakistani official told her that the US had evidence that the ISI chief, Lieutenant General Ahmed Shuja Pasha, knew of bin Laden's presence in Abbottabad. A former senior officer in ISI also confirmed to Gall the existence of a bin Laden desk to manage relations with the terrorist. Carlotta Gall, "What Pakistan Knew About Bin Laden," *New York Times Magazine,* March 19, 2014; http://www.nytimes.com/2014/03/23/magazine/what-pakistan-knew-about-bin-laden.html?_r=0.

39. Military aid was suspended that summer. In November 2011, American warplanes and helicopters killed twenty-two Pakistanis at a border post, after they shot at American soldiers staging an operation nearby. Islamabad blocked US military logistics convoys as a result. Convoys resumed the following year, and by 2013 the US had resumed its aid money. The issue of bin Laden appeared to have been quietly brushed under the carpet.

40. Gates, *Duty*, p. 499.

41. Ibid., p. 560.

42. Chandrasekaran, *Little America*, p. 325.

EPILOGUE—CONTAINMENT

1. The Asia Foundation conducts the widest annual poll on Afghan attitudes but does not include this metric. Its 2013 survey suggests that just over half of the 9,000 correspondents felt the country was moving in the right direction, but that a record number of Afghans—over 80 percent—felt insecure. For Karzai's thinking, see

Christina Lamb, "Hamid Karzai: America Has Left Me with a Mess. I Can't Wait to Go," *Sunday Times,* February 2, 2014; http://www.thesundaytimes.co.uk/sto/news review/features/article1370104.ece. Findings are mirrored in Pakistan. http://www .pewglobal.org/2013/05/07/chapter-3-attitudes-toward-the-united-states-and -american-policies.

2. Ben Anderson, "TIA: This Is Afghanistan," *Port,* August 2013; www.port -magazine.com/commentary/tia-this-is-afghanistan/#&panel1-4.

3. Private interview. See also http://iipdigital.usembassy.gov/st/english/article/2012 /03/201203212566.html#axzz35rXvT9ql.

4. Thomas Ruttig, "Negotiations with the Taliban," in *Talibanistan: Negotiating the Borders Between Terror, Politics, and Religion,* ed. Peter Bergen and Katherine Tiedemann (New York: Oxford University Press, 2013).

5. There had been efforts to release Taliban leaders held in Guantánamo in return for the US soldier Bowe Bergdahl, whom the Taliban captured in 2009.

6. Julian Borger, "Afghan Insurgents Want a Peace Deal, Says Ex-Minister," *The Guardian,* September 20, 2011; www.theguardian.com/world/2013/sep/20/afghan -insurgents-peace-taliban-minister.

7. Ruttig, "Negotiations with the Taliban," in *Talibanistan,* p. 438.

8. Private interview.

9. As Karzai told reporter Christina Lamb in February 2014, "I want it too, I am not against the BSA, I would have not called the Jirga if I were against the BSA [the agreement to allow US forces to stay beyond 2014], no! I want the BSA too, but I want it under the right circumstances for the right purpose, why do we want the Americans to stay here? Do we want them to stay to perpetuate war and conflict and civilians suffering and families in fear or do we want the US bases to stay here to provide our security and what do you call that an anchor, so the peace process will bring us that, or visible and vivid clarity from America on what it is that's stopping it the launch of the peace process?"

10. Matthew Rosenberg and Taimoor Shah, "Coalition Plays Down Afghan Reports of Major Battle in Helmand," *New York Times,* May 21, 2013. According to the Italian NGO Emergency, which helps provide healthcare in Afghanistan, there was a 20 percent increase in the numbers of hospital admissions due to war injuries between 2013 and 2014 in Lashkar Gah—and a 77 percent increase in 2012. Simonetta Gola, e-mail to author.

11. Karin Brulliard, "Pakistani Anti-Taliban Militias Offer Lessons for U.S. in Afghanistan," *Washington Post,* December 7, 2010; www.washingtonpost.com/wp-dyn /content/article/2010/12/06/AR2010120605836.html.

12. Ken Ballen, Peter Bergen, and Patrick Doherty, "Public Opinion in Pakistan's Tribal Regions," in *Talibanistan,* p. 250.

13. Jeremy Scahill and Glenn Greenwald, "The NSA Secret Role in the US Assassination Program," *The Intercept,* February 20, 2014; firstlook.org/theintercept/article/2014/02/10/the-nsas-secret-role/.

14. Mazzetti, *The Way of the Knife,* p. 319.

15. David Alexander, "Retired General Cautions Against Overuse of 'Hated' Drones," *Reuters,* January 7, 2013; www.reuters.com/article/2013/01/07/us-usa-afghanistan -mcchrystal-idUSBRE90608O20130107.

16. Jon Boone, "Pakistan Drone Attack Love Song Racks Up YouTube Hits," *The Guardian*, September 19, 2010; www.theguardian.com/world/2012/sep/19/pakistan -drone-love-song.

17. According to New America Foundation data, the casualty rate in Pakistan for civilians and also for "unknowns"—those who were not identified in news reports definitively as either militants or civilians—was around 40 percent under President George W. Bush when the drone program was in its infancy. It has come down to about 7 percent under Obama. Peter Bergen, "Drones Will Fill the Sky," *CNN*, May 14, 2014; http://edition.cnn.com/2014/05/13/opinion/bergen-armed-drones-key -future-warfare/.

18. A period that appeared to coincide with efforts to free a US soldier detained by the Taliban.19. Noah Shachtman, "Military Stats Reveal Epicenter of US Drone Wars," *Wired*, November 9, 2012.

20. Amy Zegart, "Torture Creep: Why Are More Americans Accepting Bush-Era Policies Than Ever Before?" *Foreign Policy*, September 25, 2012; www.foreignpolicy .com/articles/2012/09/25/torture_creep.

21. It's interesting to note that the Asia Foundation survey in 2013 found that the majority of Afghans thought the country was heading in the right direction, even as western forces prepared to depart.

22. Iraq was ostensibly a constitutional monarchy, but as the historian Charles Trip points out, the British created a parallel shadow state, which they hoped would allow them to pull the strings. Subsequent Iraqi dictators did just that.

23. As the *Guardian* writer Simon Jenkins noted laconically, "Iraq is post-imperialism for fast learners, Afghanistan for slow ones." Simon Jenkins, "It Takes Inane Optimism to See Victory in Afghanistan," *The Guardian*, August 8, 2007.

BIBLIOGRAPHY

BOOKS

Alexander, Chris. *The Long Way Back: Afghanistan's Quest for Peace*. New York: Harper, 2011.

Allen, Charles. *Soldier Sahibs: The Men Who Made the North West Frontier*. London: John Murray, 2012.

Anderson, Ben. *No Worse Enemy: The Inside Story of the Chaotic Struggle for Afghanistan*. Oxford: OneWorld Publications, 2013.

Anderson, Jon Lee. *The Lion's Grave: Dispatches from Afghanistan*. London: Atlantic, 2002.

Bacevich, Andrew J. *New American Militarism: How Americans Are Seduced by War*. Oxford: Oxford University Press, 2006.

Bailey, Jonathan, Richard Iron, and Hew Strachan, eds. *British Generals in Blair's Wars*. Farnham, UK: Ashgate, 2013.

Ballen, Ken. *Terrorists in Love: True Life Stories of Islamic Radicals*. New York: Free Press, 2011.

Bamford, James. *The Shadow Factory: The Ultra-Secret NSA from 9/11 to the Eavesdropping on America*. New York: Anchor Books, 2008.

Barfield, Thomas. *Afghanistan: A Cultural and Political History*. Princeton, NJ: Princeton University Press, 2010.

Barker, Kim. *The Taliban Shuffle: Strange Days in Afghanistan and Pakistan*. New York: Doubleday, 2011.

Bergen, Peter. *Manhunt: The Ten-Year Search for Bin Laden—From 9/11 to Abbottabad*. New York: Crown Publishing, 2012.

———. *The Longest War: The Enduring Conflict Between America and al-Qaeda*. New York: Free Press, 2011.

Bergen, Peter, and Katherine Tiedemann, eds. *Talibanistan: Negotiating the Borders Between Terror, Politics, and Religion*. New York: Oxford University Press, 2013.

Berman, Paul. *Terror and Liberalism*. New York: Norton, 2003.

Bernsten, Gary, and Ralph Pezzullo. *Jawbreaker: The Attack on Bin Laden and Al Qaeda*. New York: Crown, 2005.

Bishop, Patrick. *Ground Truth: 3 Para Return to Afghanistan*. London: HarperPress, 2009.

———. *3 Para*. London: HarperPress, 2007.

Blehm, Eric. *The Only Thing Worth Dying For: How Eleven Green Berets Fought for a New Afghanistan.* New York: HarperPerennial, 2011.

Bowden, Mark. *The Finish: The Killing of Osama Bin Laden.* New York: Atlantic Monthly Press, 2012.

Braithwaite, Rodric. *Afghantsy: The Russians in Afghanistan, 1979–1989.* New York: Oxford University Press, 2011.

Broadwell, Paula. *All In: The Education of General David Petraeus.* New York: Penguin, 2012.

Brown, Vahid, and Don Rassler. *Fountainhead of Jihad: The Haqqani Nexus, 1973–2012.* London: Hurst & Co., 2013.

Burke, Jason. *The 9/11 Wars.* New York: Penguin, 2011.

Bush, George W. *Decision Points.* New York: Crown, 2010.

Chandrasekaran, Rajiv. *Little America: The War Within the War for Afghanistan.* New York: Knopf, 2012.

Chayes, Sarah. *The Punishment of Virtue: Inside Afghanistan After the Taliban.* New York: Penguin, 2006.

Churchill, Winston S. *The Story of the Malakand Field Force: An Episode of Frontier War.* London: Cooper, 1989.

Clarke, Richard A. *Against All Enemies: Inside America's War on Terror.* New York: Free Press, 2004.

Coleman, Isobel. *Paradise Beneath Her Feet: How Women Are Transforming the Middle East.* New York: Random House, 2010.

Coll, Steve. *Ghost Wars: The Secret History of the CIA, Afghanistan, and bin Laden, from the Soviet Invasion to September 10, 2001.* New York: Penguin Press, 2004.

Cowper-Coles, Sherard. *Cables from Kabul: The Inside Story of the West's Afghanistan Campaign.* London: HarperPress, 2011.

Crile, George. *Charlie Wilson's War: The Extraordinary Story of the Largest Covert Operation in History.* New York: Atlantic Monthly Press, 2003.

Crumpton, Henry A. *The Art of Intelligence: Lessons from a Life in the CIA's Clandestine Service.* New York: Penguin Books, 2013.

Cullather, Nick. *The Hungry World: America's Cold War Battle Against Poverty in Asia.* Cambridge, MA: Harvard University Press, 2010.

Dalrymple, William. *Return of a King: The Battle for Afghanistan, 1839–42.* New York: Random House, 2013.

Dobbins, James. *After the Taliban: Nation-Building in Afghanistan.* Dulles, VA: Potomac Press, 2008.

Dupree, Louis. *Afghanistan.* Oxford: Oxford University Press, 1973.

Ferguson, James. *A Million Bullets: The Real Story of the British Army in Afghanistan.* London: Transworld, 2008.

Fury, Dalton. *Kill Bin Laden: A Delta Force Commander's Account of the Hunt for the World's Most Wanted Man.* New York: St. Martin's Press, 2008.

Gall, Carlotta. *The Wrong Enemy: America in Afghanistan, 2001–2014.* New York: Houghton Mifflin Harcourt, 2014.

Gates, Robert M. *Duty: Memoirs of a Secretary at War.* New York: Knopf, 2014.

Gazeri, Vanessa. *The Tender Soldier: A True Story of War and Sacrifice.* New York: Simon & Schuster, 2013.

Giustozzi, Antonio. *Decoding the New Taliban: Insights from the Afghan Field.* New York: Columbia/Hurst, 2009.

———. *Koran, Kalashnikov, and Laptop: The Neo-Taliban Insurgency in Afghanistan 2002–2007.* New York: Columbia University Press, 2007.

Gopal, Anand. *No Good Men Among the Living: America, the Taliban, and the War Through Afghan Eyes.* New York: Metropolitan Books, 2014.

Grey, Stephen. *Operation Snakebite: The Explosive Story of an Afghan Desert Siege.* London: Penguin Books, 2010.

Hafvenstein, Joel. *Opium Season: A Year on the Afghan Frontier.* Guilford, CT: Lyons Press, 2007.

Harnden, Tony. *Dead Men Risen: The Welsh Guards and the Defining Story of Britain's War in Afghanistan.* London: Quercus, 2011.

Hastings, Michael. *The Operators: The Wild and Terrifying Inside Story of America's War in Afghanistan.* New York: Plume, 2012.

Hennessey, Patrick. *KANDAK: Fighting with Afghans.* London: Allen Lane, 2012.

———. *The Junior Officer's Reading Club: Killing Time and Fighting Wars.* London: Penguin, 2010.

Hersh, Seymour M. *Chain of Command: The Road from 9/11 to Abu Ghraib.* London: Allen Lane, 2004.

Johnson, Chris, and Jolyon Leslie. *Afghanistan: The Mirage of Peace.* London: Zed Books, 2004.

Jones, Seth. *The Graveyard of Empires: America's War in Afghanistan.* New York: W. W. Norton, 2010.

Junger, Sebastian. *War.* London: Fourth Estate, 2011.

Kagan, Robert. *Of Paradise and Power.* London: Atlantic, 2003.

Kaplan, Fred. *The Insurgents: David Petraeus and the Plot to Change the American Way of War.* New York: Simon & Schuster, 2013.

Kilcullen, David. *The Accidental Guerrilla: Fighting Small Wars in the Midst of a Big One.* London: Hurst & Co., 2009.

Lamb, Christina. *Sewing Circles of Herat: My Afghan Years.* London: Flamingo, 2003.

Lang, Eugene, and Janice Stein. *The Unexpected War: Canada in Kandahar.* Toronto: Penguin Canada, 2008.

Ledwidge, Frank. *Losing Small Wars: British Military Failure in Iraq and Afghanistan.* New Haven, CT: Yale University Press, 2011.

Loyn, David. *Frontline.* Chichester, UK: Summersdale, 2011.

———. *Butcher and Bolt.* London: Hutchinson, 2008.

Luttrell, Marcus. *Lone Survivor: The Eyewitness Account of Operation Redwing and the Lost Heroes of Seal Team 10.* New York: Little, Brown and Company, 2007.

Malkasian, Carter. *War Comes to Garmser: Thirty Years of Conflict on the Afghan Frontier.* Oxford: Oxford University Press, 2013.

Maloney, Sean. *Fighting for Afghanistan: A Rogue Historian at War.* Annapolis, MD: Naval Institute Press, 2013.

Mayer, Jane. *The Dark Side: The Inside Story of How the War on Terror Turned into a War on American Ideals.* New York: Anchor Books, 2009.

Mazzetti, Mark. *The Way of the Knife: The CIA, a Secret Army, and a War at the Ends of the Earth.* New York: Penguin, 2013.

McChrystal, Stanley A., General. *My Share of the Task: A Memoir.* New York: Portfolio/Penguin, 2013.

McDermott, Terry, and Josh Meyer. *The Hunt for KSM: Inside the Pursuit and Takedown of the Real 9/11 Mastermind, Khalid Sheikh Mohammed.* New York: Little, Brown and Company, 2012.

Michener, James A. *Caravans.* New York: Random House, 1963.

Musharraf, Pervez. *In the Line of Fire.* New York: Free Press, 2008.

Nasr, Vali. *Dispensable Nation: American Foreign Policy in Retreat.* New York: Doubleday, 2013.

Naylor, Sean. *Not a Good Day to Die: The Untold Story of Operation Anaconda.* New York: Berkley Publishing Group, 2005.

Neumann, Ronald E. *The Other War: Winning and Losing in Afghanistan.* Dulles, VA: Potomac Books, 2009.

North, Richard. *Ministry of Defeat.* London: Continuum Publishing Corporation, 2009.

Owen, Mark and Kevin Maurer. *No Easy Day: The Firsthand Account of the Mission That Killed Osama Bin Laden.* New York: Penguin, 2012.

Pearl, Marianne. *A Mighty Heart: The Brave Life and Death of My Husband Danny Pearl.* New York: Scribner, 2003.

Peters, Gretchen. *Seeds of Terror: How Drugs, Thugs, and Crime Are Reshaping the Afghan War.* London: Picador, 2010.

Power, Samantha. *A Problem from Hell: America and the Age of Genocide.* New York: Basic Books, 2002.

Rashid, Ahmed. *Descent into Chaos: The U.S. and the Disaster in Pakistan, Afghanistan, and Central Asia.* New York: Penguin, 2008.

————. *Taliban: Militant Islam, Oil and Fundamentalism in Central Asia.* New Haven, CT: Yale University Press, 2001.

Rhode, David, and Kristen Mulhivill. *A Rope and a Prayer: A Kidnapping from Two Sides.* New York: Penguin Group, 2010.

Riedel, Bruce O. *Deadly Embrace: Pakistan, America, and the Future of Global Jihad.* Washington, DC: Brookings Institution Press, 2011.

Rubin, Barnett. *The Fragmentation of Afghanistan: State Formation and Collapse in the International System.* New Haven, CT: Yale University Press, 2002.

Rumsfeld, Donald. *Known and Unknown: A Memoir.* London: Sentinel, 2011.

Scahill, Jeremy. *Dirty Wars: The World Is a Battlefield.* New York: Nation Books, 2013.

Scheuer, Michael. *Osama bin Laden.* New York: Oxford University Press, 2012.

————. *Through Our Enemies' Eyes: Osama bin Laden, Radical Islam and the Future of America.* Washington, DC: Brassey's, 2002.

Schroen, Gary. *First In: An Insider's Account of How the CIA Spearheaded the War on Terror in Afghanistan.* New York: Presidio Press, 2007.

Scott Tyson, Ann. *American Spartan: The Promise, the Mission, and the Betrayal of Special Forces Major Jim Gant.* New York: William Morrow, 2014.

Seldon, Anthony. *Blair Unbound.* London: Simon & Schuster, 2007.

Seldon, Anthony, and Guy Lodge. *Brown at 10.* London: Biteback, 2010.

Semple, Michael. *Reconciliation in Afghanistan.* Washington, DC: United States Institute of Peace Press, 2009.

Sheers, Owen. *Pink Mist.* London: Faber & Faber, 2013.

Smucker, Philip G. *Al Qaeda's Great Escape: The Military and the Media on Terror's Trail.* Lincoln, NE: Potomac Books, 2005.

Sorley, Lewis. *A Better War: The Unexamined Victories and Final Tragedy of America's Last Years in Vietnam.* New York: Harvest, 2007.

Soufan, Ali, and Daniel Freedman. *The Black Banners: The Inside Story of 9/11 and the War Against al-Qaeda.* New York: W. W. Norton & Company, 2011.

Stafford Smith, Clive. *The Eight O'clock Ferry to the Windward Side: Seeking Justice in Guantánamo Bay.* New York: Nation Books, 2007.

Stanton, Doug. *Horse Soldiers: The Extraordinary Story of a Band of US Soldiers Who Rode to Victory in Afghanistan.* New York: Scribner, 2010.

Stewart, Rory. *The Places in Between.* London: Picador, 2004.

Stewart, Rory, and Gerald Knaus. *Can Intervention Work?* (Norton Global Ethics Series). London: W. W. Norton, 2011.

Strick van Linschoten, Alex, and Felix Kuehn. *An Enemy We Created: The Myth of the Taliban / Al-Qaeda Merger in Afghanistan, 1970–2010.* London: Hurst & Co., 2012.

Suhrke, Astri. *When More Is Less.* London: Hurst & Co., 2011.

Tapper, Jake. *The Outpost: An Untold Story of American Valor.* London: Little, Brown and Company, 2012.

Tootal, Stuart. *Danger Close: Commanding 3 Para in Afghanistan.* London: John Murray, 2010.

Toynbee, Arnold J. *Between Oxus and Jumna: A Journey in India and Afghanistan.* New York: Oxford University Press, 1961.

Urban, Mark. *War in Afghanistan.* London: Macmillan Press, 1988.

West, Bing. *The Wrong War: Grit, Strategy, and the Way out of Afghanistan.* New York: Random House, 2011.

Woodward, Bob. *Obama's Wars.* New York: Simon & Schuster, 2010.

———. *Bush at War.* New York: Simon & Schuster, 2002.

Wright, Laurence. *The Looming Tower: Al Qaeda and the Road to 9/11.* New York: Knopf, 2006.

Zaeef, Abdul Salam. *My Life with the Taliban.* Edited by Alex Strick van Linschoten and Felix Kuehn. New York: Hurst/Columbia University Press, 2010.

INDEX